CHINA'S WAR ON SMUGGLING

STUDIES OF THE WEATHERHEAD
EAST ASIAN INSTITUTE
COLUMBIA UNIVERSITY

STUDIES OF THE WEATHERHEAD EAST ASIAN INSTITUTE, COLUMBIA UNIVERSITY

The Studies of the Weatherhead East Asian Institute of Columbia University were inaugurated in 1962 to bring to a wider public the results of significant new research on modern and contemporary East Asia.

For a list of titles in the series, see page 381.

PHILIP THAI

CHINA'S WAR ON SMUGGLING

Law, Economic Life, and the Making of
the Modern State, 1842–1965

Columbia University Press / New York

Columbia University Press
Publishers Since 1893
New York   Chichester, West Sussex
cup.columbia.edu
Copyright © 2018 Columbia University Press
All rights reserved

Library of Congress Cataloging-in-Publication Data
Names: Thai, Philip, author.
Title: China's war on smuggling : law, economic life, and the making of the
modern state, 1842–1965 / Philip Thai.
Description: New York : Columbia University Press, [2018] | Series: Studies
of the Weatherhead East Asian Institute | Includes bibliographical
references and index.
Identifiers: LCCN 2017044055 | ISBN 9780231185844 (cloth : alk. paper) |
ISBN 9780231546362 (ebook)
Subjects: LCSH: Smuggling—China—History. | Customs administration—
China—History. | China—Commerce—History.
Classification: LCC HJ7071 .T43 2018 | DDC 364.1/336095109041—dc23
LC record available at https://lccn.loc.gov/2017044055

Columbia University Press books are printed on permanent
and durable acid-free paper.

Printed in the United States of America

Cover design: Noah Arlow
Cover image: Jack Birns

Library
University of Texas
at San Antonio

For my parents, who sacrificed everything

An injudicious tax offers a great temptation to smuggling. But the penalties for smuggling must rise in proportion to the temptation. The law, contrary to all the ordinary principles of justice, first creates the temptation, and then punishes those who yield to it; and it commonly enhances the punishment too in proportion to the very circumstance which ought certainly to alleviate it, the temptation to commit the crime.

—ADAM SMITH, *The Wealth of Nations*

No state is forever strong or forever weak. If those who uphold the law are strong, the state will be strong; if they are weak, the state will be weak.

—HAN FEIZI

The more cunning craftsmen there are,
The more pernicious contrivances will be invented.
The more laws are promulgated,
The more thieves and bandits there will be.

—LAOZI

CONTENTS

CONTENTS

MAPS, TABLES, AND FIGURES

MAPS

TABLES

FIGURES

ACKNOWLEDGMENTS

H AVING BEGUN THIS book more than a decade ago, I long looked forward to the day when I can thank in writing everyone who helped me on my journey. My primary debt of gratitude is owed to mentors who shepherded my training as a professional historian. Matthew Sommer fulfilled a pledge he made long ago on what kind of adviser he would be: one who would always provide guidance to his students but ultimately let them find their own way. His unstinting support, enthusiastic encouragement, and good humor made this odyssey possible, at times even enjoyable. Long after his supervisory obligations have formally ceased, he continues to offer warm friendship and wise counsel that are valued to this day. Kären Wigen pushed me outside my intellectual comfort zones by reminding me to think beyond China. Her critical guidance has had a profound impact on my maturity as a scholar, while her advice to always consider the comparative and connective dimensions of history still animates my thinking. Wen-hsin Yeh shared important insights that I was slow to absorb but quick to appreciate. Her high standards frequently kept me on my toes and ultimately made me a better historian.

My other debt of gratitude is owed to the many teachers I had the honor of learning from. Avner Greif, Christian Henriot, Mark E. Lewis, Martin Lewis, Thomas Mullaney, Jean C. Oi, and Jun Uchida rounded out my education as a graduate student at Stanford. The late David Keightley, the late Frederic Wakeman, and Brett Sheehan sparked my original interest in Chinese history as an undergraduate student at the University of California, Berkeley. Steven Meckna and Mary Massich—teachers from long, long ago—instilled a passion for history that suffuses my work to this very day.

Northeastern University and the Department of History provided a nurturing environment for a fledgling professor growing—and still growing—into his role. Tom Havens personified the ideal senior mentor who proffered sage advice on everything from career, to teaching, to writing a book. Somehow, besides responding to my queries at 4:00 a.m., he found time to provide detailed feedback on my entire manuscript. Other senior colleagues—particularly Kate Luongo, Ilham Khuri-Makdisi, Tony Penna, and Louise Walker—took me under their wing and served as models to whom I look up. Above all, I feel incredibly lucky to have joined the department and kicked off my career with a very talented cohort—Victoria Cain, Gretchen Heefner, Chris Parsons, and Ben Schmidt. They made coming to the office an absolute joy, day in and day out. It is no overstatement that I successfully navigated the vicissitudes of life and work in Boston only with their warm camaraderie. The Northeastern Asian Studies Program—led by Gavin Shatkin, and joined by Hua Dong, Doreen Lee, Shuishan Yu, Liza Weinstein, and Margaret Woo—created a supportive community for all Asia-related research. Finally, my students—particularly those who took my courses "Law, Justice, and Society in Modern China" and "History of Capitalism in East Asia"—made teaching a rewarding endeavor and helped clarify my thinking with their provocative questions.

This project was made possible with the support of numerous institutions and foundations, and I hope my book will demonstrate that their investment in meaningful scholarship was put to good use. A Henry Luce Foundation / American Council of Learned Societies (ACLS) China Studies Postdoctoral Fellowship gave me a full year to devote to writing this book. A National Central Library (Taiwan) Center for Chinese Studies (CCS) Research Grant, Northeastern University College of Social Sciences and Humanities (CSSH) Research Development Initiative Award, and Hong Liu Asian Studies Research Award and Curriculum Award funded my follow-up research trips to China, Taiwan, and Hong Kong. The Association for Asian Studies (AAS) First Book Subvention Program and the Northeastern University Richard and Arlene Offenberg History Faculty Fund provided financial support to defray some of this book's production costs. Stanford University Department of History offered enough assistance to help me focus more on my burgeoning research and less on my humble finances as a graduate student. The Fulbright-Hays Program, Social Science Research Council (SSRC), the Ministry of Education (PRC), the Stanford School of Humanities and Sciences, and the UPS Foundation Endowment supported my graduate fieldwork abroad. The Freeman-Spogli Institute (FSI) and the Chiang Ching-kuo Foundation funded my final years in graduate school. The Blakemore Foundation generously supported my advanced Chinese language studies at the Inter-University Program (IUP) at Tsinghua University. The Stanford Center for East Asian Studies (CEAS) funded my intensive Japanese language studies, Cantonese language studies, and short-term research trips.

Friendship makes bearable the travails of academic life, and I am fortunate to have it in abundance around the world. In Boston, the gang of Julia Chuang, Arunabh Ghosh, and Yajun Mo provided a welcome respite from work over many delicious meals with hearty laughs. Xing Hang, Eugenio Menegon, David Mozina, Leslie Wang, Ling Zhang, and Leah Zuo welcomed me to the New England China studies community. At Stanford, I lived the ideal of "running with the swift" and always found myself trying to keep pace with a remarkable cohort of scholars. Andrew Perlstein lent an understanding ear to problems in research and life over countless cups of coffee. Wesley Chaney made graduate school more fun than it really should have been with his frenetic enthusiasm. Yu Zhang inspired me with her dedication to producing good scholarship and never failed to help me see the sunnier side of life. Koji Hirata fielded my random language and research queries, not infrequently inverting our sempai-kohai relationship. Marcelo Aranda, David Fedman, Jon Felt, Christine Ho, Meiyu Hsieh, Ying Hu, Quinn Javers, George Zhijian Qiao, Gina Russo Tam, Sayoko Sakakibara, Eric Vanden Bussche, and Yvon Yiwen Wang all made Stanford a collegial place to call home. At UC Berkeley, the graduate student community counted me as one of their own, despite my dubious affiliation with a cross-bay rival. Margaret Tillman offered kind support that I did not always deserve but nonetheless appreciated. Peiting Li listened to my many tales of woe with her patience, understanding, and gentle humor, serving as a sister I never had but always needed. Cyrus Chen, Ti Ngo, Linh Vu, and Albert Wu provided fresh perspectives on my own work with their sharp insights and jolly camaraderie. Finally, I would be remiss if I did not acknowledge Arthur Chen, Aileen Hsu, and Young Park, friends who were there before this journey began.

Many people devoted considerable time and energy providing valuable feedback on my work. Emily Baum was the first person to read (and suffer through) a draft of this manuscript in its entirety. Her incisive comments sharped my arguments, while her unbounded enthusiasm reinvigorated me at moments when I needed the most encouragement. I am honored to count such a brilliant and generous scholar as a colleague in the field for years to come. Timothy Yang and Shirley Ye—despite being in different parts of the world—checked in with me almost every day, listened to news good or bad, and never failed to give me feedback on anything I showed to each of them. Jenny Gavacs, Weiting Guo, Jason Michael Kelly, Heidi Kong, Seung-Joon Lee, Sophia Lee, Andy Liu, Andrea McElderry, Ghassan Moazzin, Peter Perdue, Steven Pieragastini, and Zhang Wei generously read parts or all of the manuscript. The readers for Columbia University Press—Elisabeth Köll and an anonymous scholar—have my sincere thanks for their conscientious, constructive, and timely reports.

Organizers of numerous institutions and associations have my gratitude for managing the conferences, workshops, and invited lectures where I have presented parts of my projects during the past years: the American Historical Association (AHA); the American Society for Legal History (ASLH); the Association for Asian Studies (AAS); Business History Conference (BHC); Center for Chinese Studies, National Central Library (Taiwan); Columbia University; Council on East Asian Studies (CEAS), Yale University; D'Amore-McKim School of Business, Northeastern University; Early Career Scholar Workshop, Law and Society Association (LSA); Hagley Museum and Library; Fairbank Center for Chinese Studies, Harvard University; Hong Kong Baptist University; Institute of Chinese

Studies, Free University of Berlin; Institute for Chinese Studies, Ohio State University (OSU); Joint Center for History and Economics, Harvard University; Legal History Colloquium, Vanderbilt University; Maurer School of Law, Indiana University; and Pardee School of Global Studies, Boston University. Ritu Birla, Thomas Buoye, Jeffery Chan, Jane Dailey, Gail Hershatter, Clara Wing Chung Ho, Karl Gerth, Lauryn Gouldin, Alan Karras, Man Bun Kwan, Catherine Ladds, Thomas McGinn, Christopher Reed, Elizabeth Remick, Ruth Rogaski, Philip Scranton, Heather Streets-Salter, Karen Tani, Harold Tanner, and Madeleine Zelin provided helpful comments. The Hurst Summer Institute for Legal History at the University of Wisconsin Law School provided an intellectually formative venue to debate stimulating ideas and forge lasting friendships. Barbara Welke, Mitra Sharafi, and Karl Shoemaker have my sincere thanks for their unflagging dedication in running the workshop. The Fairbank Center for Chinese Studies at Harvard under directors Michael Szonyi and Mark Elliott, executive directors Jennifer Rudolph and Lydia Chen, and their staff—Julia Cai, Nick Drake, James Evans, and Caitlin Keliher—provided a hospitable environment for scholars of Chinese Studies in the Boston area and beyond.

I remain grateful to the many individuals who made my fieldwork a rewarding experience. Chen Chunsheng arranged for my affiliation at Zhongshan University. Choi Chi-cheung and Joseph Tse-Hei Lee generously placed me in touch with their vast networks in South China. Li Aili welcomed me into her Modern Chinese History course and graciously shared with me her knowledge of research on the Maritime Customs. Lin Man-houng and Lee Yu-ping warmly hosted me in Taiwan, offering me not only sound research advice but also delicious meals. Huang Ting and Chen Haizhong helped me secure access to archival materials in Shantou and Chaozhou. Lee Yenchen, Kang Bianxia, and Nicole Zhang Surong helped me shake off the occasional ennui with their warm friendship and put me back on the right path many times over during my sojourn abroad. The staff at the Guangdong Provincial Archives, Zhongshan University Library, Zhongshan Provincial Library, Shanghai Municipal Archives, Shanghai Municipal Library, Academia Historica, Academia Sinica, National Central Library (Taiwan), Chinese University of Hong Kong

Universities Service Centre for China Studies (USC), Hong Kong Public Records Office, Shantou Municipal Archives, Xiamen University Chinese Maritime Customs Service Studies Association, Tianjin Municipal Archives, the Second Historical Archives of China, the Hoover Institution Library and Archives, the Stanford Special Collections and University Archives, the School of Oriental and African Studies (SOAS), and the National Archives (United Kingdom) all have my thanks.

Caelyn Cobb, Miriam Grossman, Marisa Lastres, and the rest of the staff at Columbia University Press expertly guided me throughout the entire production process. Anne Routon originally took a chance on my manuscript and secured the readers' reports. Madeleine Zelin, Ross Yelsey, and the Weatherhead East Asian Institute at Columbia University supported this project even when they had no apparent reasons to do so. Glenn Perkins copyedited the manuscript. Philip Schwartzberg created the maps in this book. Cynthia Col produced its index. Susan Bohandy helped improve parts of the introduction.

Portions of chapters 1 and 3 appeared in "Law, Sovereignty, and the War on Smuggling in Coastal China, 1928–1937," *Law and History Review* 34, no. 1 (2016). An earlier version of chapter 7 appeared in "Old Menace in New China: Coastal Smuggling, Illicit Markets, and Symbiotic Economies in the Early People's Republic," *Modern Asian Studies* 51, no. 5 (2017). I am grateful to the editors of both journals for permission to reuse parts of the articles for this book.

My extended family back in Southern California supported me before and during my long sojourns around the world. My late paternal grandparents, maternal grandparents, and numerous aunts and uncles all have my heartfelt gratitude for helping to raise me, serving as watchful guardians and even as surrogate parents throughout my life. My brothers Louis and Michael, along with my sister-in-law Tammy Louie and my adorable nieces Vivi and Maddie, reminded me to take pleasure in the joys of family beyond the walls of the academy. My maternal cousins—Wayne Lam, Hank Lam, Raymond Ma, Jimmy Ma, Jason Lam, and April Lam—and my paternal cousins—David Lam, Calvin Lam, Caroline Wong, and

Nancy Wong—made me the person I am today as we grew up together in Southern California.

My mother King-fei Lam and my father Peter Thai sacrificed everything for their children, forgoing their own dreams so that my brothers and I could realize ours. While I suspect they sometimes wished that their eldest son's dreams led to a more remunerative career—in business, in law, or even in pharmacology—I know they nonetheless take pride in his accomplishments and delight in his happiness. According to the philosopher Mencius, "The greatest thing a dutiful son can do is to honor his parents." My short inscription undoubtedly falls far short of realizing the lofty ideals of filial piety. Yet I hope my parents can still appreciate the sincere sentiments behind the small gesture. I thus dedicate this book to my mother and father, in recognition of all the sacrifices they made and with profound gratitude for all the unconditional love and warm support they have given me.

Finally, Andrea Juncos made an unexpected but utterly delightful appearance as I was putting the finishing touches on this book. Her sly humor and infectious ebullience made our quotidian days in Boston all the sweeter, giving me the joyful impetus to close one chapter of my life and begin another.

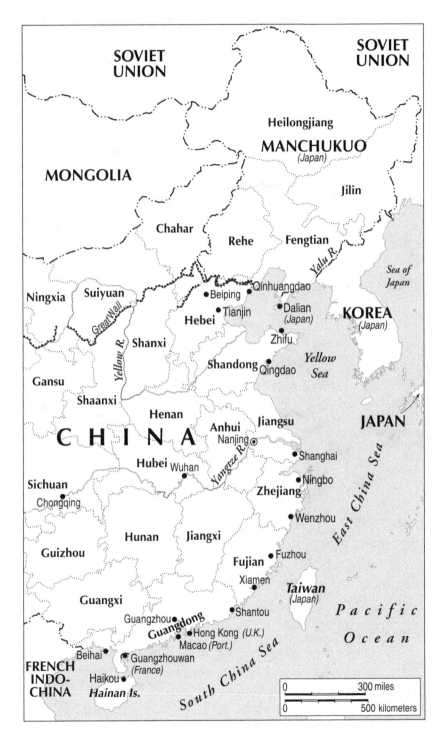

MAP 1

China Coast, mid-1930s

MAP 2

South China Coast, mid-1930s

Rehe

Liaoning

Yalu R.

Great Wall

● Beiping

● Qinhuangdao

Bohai Sea

● Tianjin

● Dalian *(Japan)*

Hebei

● Zhifu

Sea of Japan

KOREA
(Japan)

● Keijo (Seoul)

● Ji'nan

Shandong

● Qingdao

Yellow Sea

CHINA

East China Sea

Jiangsu

Nanjing ◉

Anhui

Yangtze R.

● Shanghai

0			150 miles
0			250 kilometers

MAP 3

North China Coast, mid-1930s

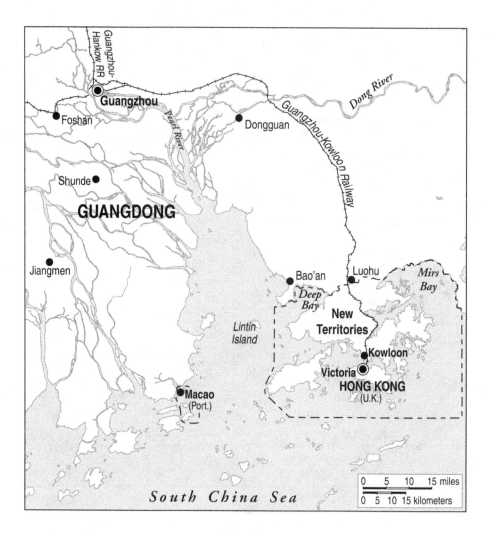

MAP 4

Pearl River Delta, mid-1930s

CHINA'S WAR ON SMUGGLING

INTRODUCTION

O
NE EVENING IN late September 1934, a search party of twelve Chinese customs agents set off from a station near the port of Xiamen. Its mission was to investigate a smuggling ring operating from the village of Beidang, off the Fujian coast. With a nearby harbor offering cover from prying eyes, the village was an active node in a trafficking pipeline between the Chinese mainland and the Japanese colony of Taiwan. Upon arrival, the agents found Beidang quiet, its twenty large warehouses under lock and key. When the few villagers present refused to cooperate, the agents broke into the warehouses and discovered caches of smuggled goods: rayon, matches, and sugar. But as the search unfolded, other villagers ("more than one hundred armed men") arrived and opened fire. A fierce firefight erupted before the search party withdrew, shaken but unhurt. Agents returned several times in the following days to negotiate a surrender of all the illicit goods but found the villagers only willing to hand over a nominal amount. Exasperated by the delays, they finally returned to Beidang in force and burned to the ground all warehouses where traces of the smuggled goods were still found.[1]

The clash at Beidang was more than just a regrettable instance of a routine raid gone awry. It was a small skirmish within a larger, longer contest over the proper role of the state in the economy. Authorities have long campaigned against smuggling on the China coast to secure revenues and manage trade. The Qing dynasty (1644–1911), in particular, maintained and enforced monopolies over select commodities deemed fiscally and strategically important. But starting from the early twentieth century, the fight against smuggling acquired new urgency, becoming implicated in the most important questions of modern statecraft, legal authority, and economic control. Under Nationalist rule (1927–1949), a determined regime sought to modernize the nation with an ambitious agenda undergirded by heavy taxes and strict regulations on foreign trade. New, assertive policies created asymmetrical benefits and unintended consequences. For the government, such policies formed the pillars of a stronger central state and propelled the modernization of the Chinese economy. But for everyone else, new policies dramatically raised prices for everything from luxury goods to daily necessities and restricted the freedom to truck, barter, and exchange. This clash of interests between state and individuals sparked a smuggling epidemic and at the same time invited a counter-smuggling campaign that was as intrusive as it was violent. Up and down the coast, state agents raided homes and businesses, intercepted vessels on land and seas, battled armed gangs, and subjected travelers to invasive searches—all in the name of fighting illicit trade. This intractable conflict proved remarkably durable through war, revolution, and even reform: under Communist rule (1949–present), a new regime waged its own campaigns against smuggling by appropriating the policies and institutions of its predecessor. It faced similar challenges, promulgating and enforcing policies from above that were continually negotiated and resisted from below. If Frederic Wakeman is correct that the rise of the police state is a defining characteristic of modern China, then the fight against smuggling must figure prominently in this history of expanding state power.[2]

Yet how exactly did smuggling, and official efforts to suppress it, progressively amplify state power? Three domains come to the fore. In terms of state capacity, bold economic interventions and coercive measures reshaped the developmental trajectory of the Chinese state by projecting official reach more widely and deeply. In terms of legal authority, fighting smuggling reified the prerogative of the Chinese state to define and enforce "legal" and "illegal" modes of behavior. And in terms of government control over the economy, creeping regulatory encroachment remade everyday life for countless individuals, merchants, and communities by steadily constraining their patterns of consumption and movement. Considering these intertwined issues, this book chronicles the vicissitudes of smuggling and its suppression on the China coast from the last decades of the Qing dynasty through the first years of the People's Republic. In doing so, it argues that the fight against smuggling was not simply a minor law enforcement issue but a transformative agent in expanding state capacity, centralizing legal authority, and increasing government reach over economic life. As successive regimes established and enforced policies in these domains to fight smuggling, state power grew and solidified—even as those policies encountered widespread, vehement resistance.

Exploring the intimate link between coastal smuggling and the amplification of state power brings disparate research agendas into conversation, thereby highlighting an overlooked avenue in understanding the making of the modern Chinese state. Previous accounts examining the growth of the modern Chinese state have generally focused more on traditional paths of state-building, including the development of bureaucracies or the extension of official reach in the countryside.[3] While yielding important insights on the evolution of formal state authority and institutions, such accounts have paid less attention to other forms of state-building that projected state reach in more quotidian but also more fundamental ways. This book thus addresses a scholarly lacuna by focusing on the expanded use of coercive policies and policing to discipline consumption, production, and exchange—the very imperatives that drove the fight against smuggling. Tracing the vicissitudes of smuggling and its suppression enables us to see more clearly the dual agency in the encounter between state and society, revealing the tortuous and negotiated extension of state control. Meanwhile, previous studies of underground economies in modern China have generally focused more on issues of criminality or the trafficking of a handful of commodities like narcotics. They are accordingly less concerned with exploring the broader connections between smuggling and the economy, particularly ways state fiat affected everyday life by continually transforming scores of ordinary commodities into profitable contraband.[4] By contrast, this book embeds smuggling—its practice, its meanings, and its suppression—at the heart of its analysis in charting both the expansion of state power and the conditioning of the modern Chinese political economy. Specifically, it explores the central contradiction embodied by smuggling, which threatened state authority while simultaneously inviting repression that reified and strengthened said authority. Cycles of lawmaking and lawbreaking, this study shows, helped ensure that the central government's imperatives were met, its authority recognized, and its coffers filled. Uneven and fitful though this transformation of state power was, it still produced important, durable consequences for governance and economy that reverberate to this day. Smuggling might well have operated on the margins of the law, but it was far from marginal in the history of modern China.

This study of smuggling on the China coast is thus framed within the dynamic interplay between two developments in modern China: the gradual extension of state authority into the economy and the unceasing resistance to such official intrusions. Its long chronological arc is analyzed not exclusively through the conventional lens of government but also through the perspectives of assorted actors preventing or engaging in smuggling over time. Authorities from the late nineteenth through the late twentieth centuries were especially impelled by geopolitical competition with foreign powers to exercise greater control over coastal trade. But they were also driven by other considerations, particularly fears that trafficking undermined governance by siphoning critical revenues, importing dangerous contraband, and menacing public order. More importantly, they feared the ways uncontrolled trade militated against modern (and later high modern) visions of a unified national economy, where a strong central state could employ policy levers to mediate the impact of unpredictable global currents on the domestic economy. Such concerns over smuggling spanned different regimes. As the Ministry of Finance in Nationalist China complained: "The sale of smuggled goods [leads to] low-priced competition, which cheats legitimate merchants to their detriment. A more flagrant instance of robbing the state and injuring commerce has yet to be found."[5]

An official bulletin from the early years of Communist China echoed such sentiments: "This kind of rampant smuggling activity has already brought about tremendous harm to the country's economy and governance. . . . The consequences of cheap imports flooding the market are not limited to attacking sales for similar domestic goods. It also severely damages the country's trade management, throws markets into disorder, and affects tax receipts."[6] Other nationalistic elites—from late Qing literati, to Republican intellectuals, to Communist cadres—joined the chorus expounding the necessity of suppressing illegal trade. In this official and elite imagination, smuggling was an unambiguous threat to governance, economy, and society in all sorts of ways.

Meanwhile, efforts at fighting smuggling also stirred widespread resentment, if not outright defiance. Individuals and businesses up and down the coast did not uniformly subscribe to official visions of a strong central state disciplining consumption and production for the imagined community of the Chinese nation. Foreigners, not surprisingly, demonstrated little commitment in contributing to the Chinese state-building project, and some flouted official strictures to purchase smuggled goods and even engage in trafficking themselves. But the same held true for many Chinese, whatever the degree of their nationalistic sentiments. Indeed, as the ubiquitous consumption of lower-priced smuggled goods testifies, many Chinese fully participated in an activity ostensibly harmful to their country, their government, and their industries. Forced to bear the brunt of increasingly higher taxes and tighter strictures imposed by a distant, impersonal central government, they proved understandably reluctant to subordinate real self-interest to abstract collective welfare. While some grudgingly complied with new regulations and paid required taxes, many others did not. The ranks of "smugglers" were thus a heterogeneous lot, as diverse as the goods they trafficked. Some sought to make a quick profit: petty runners employing sophisticated "hides" on steamships to conceal smuggled cargos, merchants submitting fraudulent invoices, and organized traffickers attempting to systematically circumvent regulations. Some were inadvertently made smugglers by tightening state strictures that impinged on everyday activities: junkmen sailing along traditional routes suddenly made illegal by faraway authorities and travelers becoming the focus of heightened scrutiny and the target of more invasive searches. Others exploited their legal privileges as shields against state authority: foreign sojourners enjoying the right of extraterritoriality and Overseas Chinese benefiting from their ambiguous national status. But whatever its underlying motivations, smuggling was a blanket category encompassing different types of activities: a deliberate transgression, a reaction to unwanted official intrusion, and a by-product of expansive state policies. Lawmaking and lawbreaking were thus two sides of the same coin, sharing a symbiotic—and ultimately inseparable—relationship that was as complementary as it was antagonistic.

This book explores the broader intersections between commodities smuggling, state power, and the economy. It is less concerned with examining other illicit activities like human trafficking and coastal piracy that are often conflated with smuggling generally but exhibit their own distinctive practices and logic.[7] This book is also less concerned with treating the efficacy of official policies—whether they succeeded or failed—as the sole barometer of historical significance. Indeed, as historians of crime have warned, measuring the efficacy of anti-crime enforcement may be a nearly impossible task.[8] Did the rise in recorded instances of smuggling truly reflect a concomitant rise in illicit activities? Or was it driven by increasing official enforcement and growing public awareness? That is, is the phenomenon under examination driven by *crime* waves or *enforcement* waves? And does more smuggling truly signify state failure or instead reflect how regulations were effective enough to encourage evasion in the first place? Putting aside such epistemological problems with identifying the directions of causality, this book is ultimately concerned with charting more fundamental historical changes: the scope of state power, patterns of enforcement, degrees of compliance, and the extent of resistance over time. All, according to the historian Alan Karras, offer insights into shifting state imperatives as well as "the ways in which those who lived under a particular government, whether individually or collectively, understood that regime's role in their daily lives."[9] How we understand the long campaign against smuggling, then, is also of utmost importance to how we understand the ways official efforts to police commerce and individual responses to those very efforts together came to define the scope of state power in modern China.

THE COAST IN MODERN CHINESE HISTORY

Nowhere was the practice of smuggling more pervasive, the imperative to control trade more urgent, and the challenges to state authority more acute than along the vast Chinese littoral. Stretching nine thousand miles from the Bohai Gulf in the north down to the Tonkin Gulf in the south, the Chinese seaboard steadily emerged as the principal site of modern Chinese statecraft and economic development. This had not always been the case. As an Inner Asian dynasty keenly aware of the military threat posed by nomadic tribesmen, the Qing during its first two centuries was more strategically preoccupied with its continental—rather than maritime—frontier. While the court maintained strict controls over the movement of many commodities and occasionally campaigned against coastal pirates and rebels, it levied light taxes and imposed few regulations on maritime commerce.[10] The China coast was thus an important but not paramount area of imperial concern. Starting with the disastrous defeat of the First Opium War (1839–1842), however, official attention shifted steadily from west to east. The coast became the primary junction of engagement—diplomatic, commercial, and cultural—between China and ascendant Western powers, pockmarked by the most politically compromised but also the most economically developed treaty ports. As private trade under the new treaty system steadily eclipsed managed trade under the centuries-old tributary system, the Qing redoubled efforts to introduce mercantilist policies and exercise control over the Chinese littoral even as it labored under the pressures of foreign imperialism. Meanwhile, coastal trade also became a critical source of state revenues, with tariffs on imports supplanting taxes on land and salt as the most reliable—and eventually the largest—revenue stream to the central government.

The metamorphosis of maritime China from what John Fairbank called a "minor tradition" in Chinese history to the linchpin of Chinese statecraft continued apace even after the collapse of the Qing.[11] Under Nationalist rule, policy makers prioritized asserting sovereignty, fighting smuggling, and modernizing the economy along the Chinese seaboard. During this period, the central government came to rely even more on revenues from foreign trade and demonstrate greater jealousy in enforcing the tariff. Later, under Communist rule, leaders prioritized the "socialist transformation" of the interior and the countryside, but they still had to contend with pervasive coastal trafficking that ostensibly threatened to derail state control over the economy. Waging its own war on smuggling throughout the Maoist era, the People's Republic intensified efforts to stamp out trafficking during the reform era (ca. 1978–present), when tighter links to the global economy reinvigorated coastal cross-border flows both legal and illegal. This study's focus on trafficking and its suppression on the China coast, then, does not deny the significance or prevalence of trafficking on China's continental frontiers. Rather, it mirrors the region's importance to modern Chinese statecraft. It looks to the coast because that is where successive modern Chinese regimes looked too.

Considering the China coast as a whole, as this study does, complements the plethora of research looking at individual treaty ports and coastal regions.[12] It also uncovers the many underground networks, commercial circuits, and official campaigns that crisscrossed and encompassed different localities. To be sure, with the steady decline of central authority and the growing pressures of foreign imperialism, the Chinese littoral from the late nineteenth century onward fragmented politically into an assortment of treaty ports, foreign spheres of influence, and warlord regimes. But at the same time, the China coast also coalesced into a more integrated, more coherent economic entity under the inexorable pull of global capitalism and technological transformations.[13] People, goods, and ideas circulated among different ports and their respective hinterlands. Such circulations—legal and illegal—traversed different political divides and brought many coastal regions into more intimate contact. And with later efforts by Nationalist China to assert sovereignty and official control along the entire coastline, these political divisions were themselves steadily erased. A focus on individual ports or regions might well miss such connections even as it accurately captures local specificities. This book thus seeks to strike a balance. It recognizes ways local actors, local conditions, and local knowledge shaped smuggling and its suppression. Yet it also illustrates how the practice of smuggling exhibited similar dynamics while its suppression confronted similar challenges up and down the coast. A broad geographical perspective thus highlights the tortuous, relentless expansion of state power and the wider consequences of official campaigns against smuggling.

SMUGGLING AND PATHWAYS TO ENHANCED STATE POWER

EXPANSION OF STATE CAPACITY

The war on smuggling was constitutive of the modern Chinese state-building experience, not only suppressing unsanctioned trade but also expanding central state capacity in multiple ways. It helped ensure that tariffs were collected, thereby providing the central government with a reliable, critical fiscal resource. It promoted mercantilist policies to better calibrate imports and exports, thereby achieving a more favorable balance of payments and realizing visions of state-led development. It brought state agents into more intimate contact with individuals, thereby projecting official reach more deeply in everyday life.[14] From the perspective of the state, coercive measures were necessary to overcome the inescapable problem of collective action embedded at the heart of smuggling. The benefits of *unregulated* trade for individuals—lower prices, wider choices, and more freedom of action—were tangible and immediate. By comparison, the benefits of *regulated* trade for society—revenue for the provision of public goods and fair trade for the enhancement of collective welfare—were abstract and indirect. Taxes, after all, had to be paid for an array of governmental services and functions that were not always seen, appreciated, or even wanted. Individuals thus always had an incentive to purchase, sell, and transport smuggled goods instead of complying with state strictures. New institutional economists have argued that the structure of markets and the nature of political institutions are key determinants in the costliness of transactions. Tools of coercion—financial penalties, penal servitude, rigorous enforcement, and even threat of violence—were aimed at ensuring that the transaction costs of unregulated trade always exceeded the transaction costs of regulated trade, thereby lowering the incentives for individuals to smuggle.[15]

Seen in this light, fighting smuggling certainly belongs in the constellation of state-building endeavors such as taxation and conscription that Charles Tilly posits were "difficult, costly, and often unwanted by large parts of the population [but] essential to the creation of strong states."[16] Indeed, the pivotal role of curbing smuggling in modern Chinese state-building mirrored state-building processes scholars have traced for other states around the world. In China and elsewhere, activities like smuggling undermined governance in countless ways. Tightening global connections from the nineteenth century onward lubricated the flow of people and goods like never before, affirming Karl Marx's axiom that capital invariably overcomes any barriers to its circulation.[17] Yet official repression of smuggling helped reinforce state authority and harden national borders. Even as unprecedented mobility and flows made their endeavors more difficult, states and state agents invested considerable effort in enforcing regulations, collecting taxes, mapping boundaries, and policing trade.[18] And besides being impelled by new prerogatives to exercise greater control, these modern regimes also enjoyed distinct advantages over their early modern counterparts by employing new technologies in transportation, communication, and warfare to project their authority across vast distances within shorter times. Modern states harnessed these technologies to translate their despotic powers ("the capacity to make autonomous decisions") into infrastructural power ("the capacity to penetrate and influence society and implement decisions"), thereby bringing stronger regulatory authority to the margins.[19] Admittedly, full and uncontested state control within well-defined territorial boundaries remained elusive, if not impossible. But official efforts at coercion through suppressing smuggling ultimately satisfied aspirations modern states have long sought to realize, however imperfectly—tighter control of borders, greater uniformity in regulations, and better protection of revenues.[20] This study demonstrates that what was true elsewhere was also true for modern China: states certainly made smuggling, but smuggling also remade states.[21]

The fight against smuggling and concomitant efforts at carving out a more intrusive, more coercive role for the state were part and parcel of other late Qing and early Republican state-building initiatives forged in the torturous transition from an agrarian empire to a nation-state. This transition, in turn, was shaped by two countervailing developments. The first was the steady devolution of central authority to both foreign powers and local elites. Beginning with the Treaty of Nanjing (1842), the successive "unequal treaties" ratified after military defeats forced the Qing dynasty to cede treaty ports, grant extraterritorial privileges, and surrender its tariff autonomy to foreign powers. Meanwhile, pressures to quell domestic unrest like the Taiping Rebellion (1850–1864) forced the court to relinquish more authority to local governments. As a result, an increasing number of tax farmers assumed more important revenue collection responsibilities, thereby inadvertently strengthening provincial and local leaders who were permitted to collect and retain taxes on domestic trade to the detriment of the central government. The inability of the central government to raise sufficient revenues persisted well after the end of imperial rule. As R. Bin Wong notes, the late imperial Chinese state had been unitary, but "the collapse of the dynasty brought a halt to central control over finances and personnel decisions."[22] Through the early years of the Republic, regional military leaders across the country—commonly and pejoratively known as "warlords"—retained virtually all revenues collected in their localities and exerted de facto independence from the nominal national government in Beijing. The Nationalists' victory over rival warlords during the Northern Expedition (1926–1928) and their subsequent recovery of China's tariff autonomy, however, halted this deterioration of central authority. In the following decades, the new regime launched its own state-building programs, seeking to translate de jure authority as China's national government into de facto authority beyond its base in the lower Yangzi region. Its efforts partially succeeded until the Communist Revolution of 1949, when a newly inaugurated regime finally eliminated vestigial domestic resistance to central authority.

But during the same period that central authority came under tremendous stress, officials still embarked on successive attempts to refashion the Chinese state to meet foreign and domestic challenges. Qing officials and their Republican successors directed resources to, among other things, creating a modern army along Western lines, promoting strategic industries, and investing in economically vital locales.[23] These efforts—escalated under Nationalist rule and continued under Communist rule—were aimed at centralizing authority, eliminating domestic rivals, asserting Chinese sovereignty on the international stage, and realizing the vision of a unified nation-state. They epitomized what legal historian Nicholas Parrillo terms "alien impositions": directives enforced by a sovereign external to local communities to protect the interests of the former rather than those of the latter.[24] Although alien impositions have always been a key feature of governance everywhere, their proliferation from the late Qing onward marked a decisive break from traditional Chinese statecraft. Motivated by an eclectic mix of Confucian precepts and legalist traditions, the Qing court during its first two hundred years maintained relatively light taxes and refrained from making too many direct market interventions. And constrained by the inherent limits of premodern bureaucratic control, it also relied on assorted local elites—gentry, merchants, and community leaders—to help magistrates assure public order, collect taxes, and carry out the functions of imperial governance.[25] But the drive to secure funds and fend off challenges in an increasingly unforgiving geopolitical environment impelled the late Qing and its successors to arrogate to themselves all sorts of new powers, from levying new taxes to remaking local economies. Such alien impositions sundered the old social order by creating more direct, less mediated links between state and individual. This reconfiguration of central authority proved undoubtedly disruptive but also surprisingly enduring, laying the foundations for a modern state—strict controls over trade and institutions curbing smuggling—that survived the eventual tumult of war and revolution.

CENTRALIZATION OF LEGAL AUTHORITY

At the same time that it dramatically expanded state capacity, the war on smuggling in China also helped centralize domestic legal authority and unbind the legal fetters imposed by foreign imperialism. The proliferation of laws and efforts to enforce them were essentially attempts by successive Chinese regimes to expand their claims to regulate, tax, and police trade within demarcated territorial bounds. If new measures were intended to combat trafficking, they nonetheless reaffirmed the legitimacy of the center and compelled compliance from a wide range of social and political actors. Such efforts also had their parallels elsewhere, mirroring the extension of legal authority and the transition from *personal* jurisdiction to *territorial* jurisdiction that scholars have shown to be intimately connected to projects of state-building—even if this assertion of sovereignty was not uniform and faced continual challenges. Surveying the history of Western European states, James Sheehan notes that law has been intricately bound with the making of sovereign claims.[26] Indeed, the centralization of legal authority was a key feature of modern state formation throughout history, and this imperative to expand and deepen sovereign claims only became more urgent in the era of worldwide imperial competition. "By the late nineteenth century," Charles Maier observes, "states possessed a degree of dedication to governance, of bureaucratic functionality, of at-oneness with fixed territorial space, of belief in their own competitive mission, that was unprecedented."[27] Similar to the monopolization of legitimate authority to wage violence by states that Max Weber traces, the monopolization of legitimate authority to regulate commerce and levy taxes was not "primordial but a product of evolution" enforced by a mix of law and coercion.[28]

This study demonstrates that the dialectical relationship between law, state-building, and smuggling also obtained in modern China. In the course of suppressing illicit trade, successive regimes enhanced their authority, capacity, and reach, thereby steadily departing from the precepts of pre-nineteenth-century imperial statecraft and remaking the modern Chinese state in the mold of its counterparts elsewhere. This transformation was in many ways overdetermined, Philip Kuhn notes, because for China "the main point of making a modern state was to resist foreign domination by using some of the foreigners' own technologies of dominance."[29] But as scholars who warn against universalizing the Western European experience have rightfully noted, this process was also marked by key differences. One was timing: unlike state-building in Western Europe, state-building in modern China proceeded in a "highly compressed chronology" of decades rather than centuries.[30] Replicating certain features of Western states, through conscious imitation or trial and error, required Chinese officials to assume a more active role than they otherwise might have under less urgent conditions.[31] Rather than incubating over longer periods of time to soften resistance or even cultivate assent, state-building efforts were introduced at a more rapid pace, proving more disruptive to the everyday lives of the governed. As Alexander Gerschenkron correctly notes, governments of late industrializing countries intervened more directly and actively than their counterparts in early industrializing countries in fostering economic development. The same could certainly be said of these governments' role in refashioning state authority to meet the challenges of the nineteenth-century world and beyond.[32]

Another distinguishing difference was context: centralization of legal authority in China unfolded within a hostile geopolitical environment and under severe semicolonial constraints. Just as it was the case in other semicolonial polities, nineteenth-century foreign imperialism hindered the development of a twentieth-century nation-state in China. Nothing better embodied the "century of humiliation" than the extraterritorial protections foreign sojourners enjoyed on Chinese soil and foreign concessions, which fragmented domestic sovereignty and created an uneven legal terrain. Initially grafted atop of Qing China's legally pluralistic order—which had long subjected different ethnicities to different legal treatments within the empire—extraterritoriality soon conferred on foreigners in China virtual immunity from domestic laws.[33] The imperial court and Republican governments relied on high-level diplomatic negotiations to unwind the treaty port order, indefatigably pressing their agenda in countless bilateral and multilateral meetings with foreign counterparts. At the same time, they pursued reforms to modernize the Chinese legal system and thereby demonstrate a sufficient level of "civilization" to mollify foreign objections to the perceived "barbarity" of Chinese laws.[34] Unceasing Chinese efforts finally bore fruit only in 1943, when the United States and Great Britain acquiesced to the formal abrogation of extraterritoriality and other vestigial treaty privileges.

While undoubtedly accurate, this narrative of extraterritoriality's rise and demise is also incomplete. Indeed, the rollback of legal imperialism did not unfold exclusively at the diplomatic table or at the highest levels of politics. As this study shows, the fight against smuggling also played an unheralded role in the process. Every time Chinese officials attempted to fine a British businessman for duty evasion, confiscate a Japanese trawler for carrying contraband, or enter a foreign concession to arrest a Chinese smuggler, they confronted fundamental questions of state sovereignty and legal authority. These seemingly inconsequential episodes continuously chipped away at the fundamental constraints of semicolonialism, dismantling the panoply of foreign privilege from the bottom up. Though checked by treaty provisions and buffeted by foreign pressures and domestic turmoil, the Qing consistently sought to exercise its authority overseeing foreign trade vis-à-vis combatting smuggling. The Nationalists later accelerated these efforts by aggressively exercising Chinese sovereignty through policing, including the policing of foreign trade. As they delineated new boundaries of legal trade and sought to exercise exclusive prerogative to prosecute offenders within those boundaries, then, the Nationalists were also untangling the enduring legacies of empire even before the formal abolition of extraterritorial privileges and concessions in 1943. As a result of such efforts, state agents policing trade in Nationalist China after 1945 and Communist China after 1949 were constrained by fewer fetters on their authority even as coastal smuggling continued unabated. The fight against smuggling thus sits squarely at the intersection of projects formerly semicolonial polities like Japan and Turkey have historically undertaken—namely legal modernization and policing reforms—that helped realize greater sovereignty for the Chinese state.[35] It ultimately helped make the ideal of territorialized sovereignty less imagined and more real.

TRANSFORMATION OF ECONOMIC LIFE

With its expanding battery of regulations and enforcement, the fight against smuggling undoubtedly helped the state reconfigure everyday economic life on the China coast. The history of economic life—"human participation in production, exchange, and consumption"—has attracted renewed interest from specialists seeking to make sense of dizzying economic changes since the late twentieth century.[36] Reconstructing the many ways individuals, businesses, and communities adapted to evolving state strictures to trade for survival and profit engages directly with this "economic turn" in history and explores how the expansion of state power reconditioned activities otherwise obscured by the shadow of law. The documentary residues of encounters between state and individuals from which this study draws certainly reveal how taxes were evaded, laws were circumvented, and policing was resisted. But they also reveal the more quotidian ways the coastal economy worked: how goods were exchanged, businesses were financed, partnerships were forged, and deliveries were coordinated. Illegal trade—just like its legal counterpart—implicated many disparate parties, linking producers, distributors, retailers, and consumers in networks crisscrossing borders and operating in the shadow of the law. In their own way, such illegal activities embodied everyday realities just as well as legal activities did, and careful attention to their dynamics thus offers unvarnished, even novel, glimpses into the impact of intrusive state strictures on the economy and the history of economic life in modern China more generally.

The fight against smuggling accorded the state a larger role in economic life by redefining legal and illegal modes of behavior. To paraphrase Eric Tagliacozzo, the category of contraband has no fixed taxonomy; it is whatever the state says it is at any given time.[37] Since no commodity was inherently illicit, official imperatives controlling trade—informed by a complicated mix of financial considerations, policy goals, or wartime exigencies—defined and redefined the crime of smuggling. What constituted smuggling at a given moment was never static but always contextual. Some commodities had long been the focus of official regulatory concern. Weapons and narcotics, in particular, were strictly controlled, heavily taxed, or outright banned from the late Qing through the People's Republic today. Other commodities enjoyed more malleable legal statuses. Like sugar during the 1930s, tungsten during wartime, or wristwatches in the early People's Republic, once innocuous commodities were transformed—seemingly overnight—into profitable articles of trafficking once state policies reworked the dynamic interplay between supply and demand, global flows and local conditions. Expanding Tagliacozzo's insight, this book pays close attention to the ways new laws, regulations, and taxes on trade reflected changing official imperatives and increasing state control over the economy. Such interventions underpinned the financial calculus of smuggling, rendering different commodities more profitable for trafficking at different moments. Understanding how individuals consumed various commodities—and how state interventions transformed this consumption by making it more expensive, more restrictive—sheds light on why they opted time and again for smuggled goods in defiance of state strictures, official enforcement, or nationalistic appeals.

Recognizing that smuggling is simply trade by another name thus reframes activities officially deemed illegal but otherwise widely practiced. Viewed in this light, smuggling is a label affixed by state fiat on exchanges that were once unregulated, unrestricted, and untaxed. Tracing the evolution of mutable categories of criminality is a reminder to avoid unconsciously appropriating state-centered discourse that treats violations of any official strictures or unauthorized movement across borders as illicit in and of itself. Willem van Schendel and Itty Abraham, in particular, have urged researchers of illicit practices to "discard the assumption that there is a clear line between illicitness and the laws of states." In addition, they note, "transnational criminal activities" like smuggling are *forms of social practice* that intersect two or more *regulatory spaces* and violate at least one normative or legal rule."[38] A growing number of scholars have now arrived at the consensus that trafficking bound markets together despite policies created to keep them apart.[39] Smuggling, in other words, was not merely an "aspect" of commercial development—it *was* commerce writ large. This study reveals the many indistinct ways smuggling was woven into the fabric of everyday life, how ordinary people keenly felt the ripple effects of expanding state power in marketplaces and back alleys across the China coast.

The unrivaled opportunity to examine actual business practices provides other opportunities to delineate the many strategies individuals and businesses employed to counter changing regulatory environments.[40] Plumbing the depths of the underground economy, this book identifies ways actors operated inside, outside, and in the shadow of the law. By analyzing smuggling as a business and ways merchants responded to nominally adverse conditions, it builds on recent reevaluations of the resiliency of modern Chinese enterprises, rather than focusing on how they deviated from normative models of economic success.[41] Ultimately, the focus on expanding state power and its transformation of economic life moves beyond two issues that have long dominated research on the Chinese economy: the efficacy of "informal" social networks versus "formal" corporate hierarchies and the extent to which "anti-business" biases by Chinese authorities led to economic failures.[42] Smugglers and their networks proved remarkably adaptable. They nimbly adjusted to the vicissitudes of the market and expertly adopted ever-creative methods of evasion in spite of, or even because of, tightening official controls and more aggressive enforcement. That certain patterns, vectors, and practices of smuggling spanned different divides in modern Chinese history—whether 1911, 1928, 1949, or even 1978—testifies to their durability and tenacity.

Beyond looking at how smuggling operated in defiance of state regulations, we can also consider the ways smuggling interacted *with* state regulations and further reified state authority. Indeed, campaigns against trafficking throw into sharp relief the complex interplay between "laws on the books" and "laws on the ground," offering rich opportunities to explore the varied legal strategies employed by individuals to counter state reconfiguration of economic life. Since smuggling was indeed trade by another name, those who violated growing state strictures often did not accept official criminalization of their actions. This divergence of opinion only widened as an increasingly assertive state introduced more regulations and prosecuted more offenders, thereby creating more expansive definitions of smuggling that often clashed with popular, longtime understandings of legitimate commerce. The friction produced by bottom-up reactions to top-down redefinitions of legal trade mirrored the resistance produced by the clash of two "grids"—existent customary practices and expanding state authority—found in other contexts.[43] Imposing and enforcing new restrictions reaffirmed authority at the top but also provoked challenges from the bottom contesting the state's prerogative to regulate commerce. Such challenges, in turn, dialectically shaped the contours of an evolving legal regime, as authorities were forced to constantly affirm, enforce, or adjust their definitions of permissible trade. The legal conflicts generated by the war on smuggling, therefore, not only offer insights into official imperatives but also into ways litigants conceived popular norms of justice, mobilized the law to seek redress for grievances, and ultimately mediated the enforcement of new regulations. Studying the codification of regulations reveals only half of the story; studying the varied ways they were understood, received, or challenged is critical to revealing the other half. And both halves are part of the primary narrative of how smuggling and its suppression fitfully but progressively expanded state power.

SOURCES OF STUDY

Reconstructing the complex workings of a vast, underground economy and their indistinct connections to governance and everyday life is a daunting task. Historical sources documenting illicit activities are invariably fragmentary and frustratingly elusive. This is especially so for smuggling, whose practitioners did their best to minimize violence and thereby avoid any public exposure. Most often, incidents of smuggling that left their mark in the archives are there because they were incidents of failure. The overrepresentation of foiled attempts in the historical record, combined with the absence of countless other incidents that escaped attention, potentially skew any observer's perspective. Yet by canvassing an array of official and nonofficial materials, this study paints a composite picture of coastal trafficking in modern China that captures as many incidents as possible and reconstructs the perspectives of the government and governed alike.

The empirical core of this study rests on records from the Chinese Maritime Customs Service (1854–1950) and its successor, the China General Customs Administration (1949–present), the two institutions most directly involved with supervising China's foreign trade. Produced by agents on the frontlines of the war on smuggling, these voluminous archives chart changes in the practice of trafficking and efforts to combat it under different regimes. Their rich contents include official directives, commercial regulations, and correspondences with high-level political figures that clearly illustrate evolving strictures over trade from the standpoint of central authorities. Yet they also contain varied materials like a merchant's protest against an unjustified seizure, an officer's patrol report, a village organization's petition for tariff relief, a customs commissioner's musings about local conditions, or a magistrate's response to requests for greater law enforcement cooperation—all of which reveal the variegated experiences of state-building from below. Different Chinese perspectives, then, are captured in these diverse materials even if the Chinese Maritime Customs Service was a foreign-dominated institution during much of its existence. Moreover, such bottom-up, granular accounts are enriched by the agencies' wide-ranging responsibilities and extensive geographical reach across the Chinese seaboard. They neatly complement the top-down, distant perspective from other materials like diplomatic correspondences and government archives that this study also draws on.

Other materials further complicate neat, official narratives. Legal cases adjudicated by various organs—including local courts, the Administrative Court (Xingzheng fayuan), and other specialized courts—highlight the drawn-out interactions between state and individual. According to legal historians Edward Muir and Guido Ruggiero, when a crime is prosecuted, it intersects with complex bureaucratic and legal structures in ways that reveal "the interrelationship between law, institutional structures and procedures, and social values."[44] Chinese legal records from the many campaigns against smuggling are no exception. Testimonies, petitions, and judgments certainly illustrate ways official imperatives were expressed. But by showing how these imperatives were implemented, translated, and challenged in the messy course of adjudication, they also show the intersection of state authority and economic life at its most basic level. Most importantly, the seemingly inconsequential details captured in legal cases often render visible the otherwise invisible aspects of ordinary lives and popular attitudes.

Finally, newspapers, magazines, political cartoons, travel accounts, and even literary fiction capture prevailing public attitudes not always reflected in official sources. Their expansive geographical coverage—drawn from several ports—offers additional snapshots of everyday life on the coast. Their profusion of voices demonstrates to what extent the beliefs of different segments of society accorded with or differed from state-centered discourse on illegality. Even accounts from state-controlled media—particularly those from Communist China—have their value. Such reports sometimes sensationalized individual incidents to drive home didactic messages on smuggling's purported social, economic, and even political harm. But while ideologically tinged, they can nonetheless be read against the grain to uncover smuggling in practice, official anxieties over trafficking, and the degree of state reach in everyday life. In sum, triangulating the perspectives of diverse materials does more than just recover hidden histories. It also highlights ways many different actors shaped—and were in turn shaped by—state efforts at regulating, taxing, and policing coastal commerce.

ORGANIZATION OF THE BOOK

This book is organized chronologically and thematically into seven chapters. Its temporal focus is firmly anchored in Nationalist China, when statebuilding efforts vastly expanded the definition of smuggling to encompass the carriage of ordinary consumables as well as traditional contraband. But to fully understand this transformation—its origins, effects, and legacies—the book also extends its gaze both backward to the late Qing and forward through the early People's Republic. To further underscore this book's contention that smuggling, anti-smuggling, and smugglers were consistently conditioned by evolving state strictures, individual chapters will offer more specific case studies of different commodities trafficked at different times.

The book begins with a survey of the treaty port economy from its mid-nineteenth-century genesis to its early twentieth-century apogee. Chapter 1 looks specifically at ways the unequal treaties compromised central authority over coastal trade by imposing new layers of legal constraints. How was smuggling defined within this legally pluralistic order? And how did its definition shape the incentives for both the practice of smuggling and its suppression? In an era of weak state control and low tariffs, smuggling was narrowly defined and profitable primarily for a handful of commodities like opium, weapons, and salt. Chapter 2 examines the intellectual underpinnings of economic policies later adopted by Nationalist China that inadvertently triggered the smuggling epidemic. How did tariff autonomy, initially a *concern* among an elite circle of literati during the late nineteenth century, transform into a *problem* for the imagined community of the Chinese nation? How did fighting smuggling come to underpin official visions of a more expansive, intrusive state role in the economy?

The next two chapters focus on Nationalist China's war on smuggling and the popular reactions it provoked during the Nanjing Decade (1928–1937). Chapter 3 surveys the consequences of new duties and trade restrictions introduced shortly after the recovery of China's tariff autonomy. Freed from one constraint of the unequal treaties, the new regime erected a new regulatory infrastructure complete with higher tariffs, more restrictive laws, and harsher enforcement. How did new policies create expansive definitions of smuggling and generate more frictions between state and society? Chapter 4 inverts the top-down perspective of lawmaking to uncover the bottom-up logic of lawbreaking by identifying ways entrepreneurs expertly adapted to shifting economic conditions in the face of ramped-up enforcement. Their response is neatly represented in the transformation of illicit markets for rayon, kerosene, and sugar—three of the most frequently and most profitably trafficked articles during this period.

But at the same time that smuggling became more visible and anti-smuggling enforcement became more punitive, a growing number of critics condemned both "treasonous merchants" and overzealous state agents, thereby revealing a discursive dimension of smuggling that intersected with broader social anxieties.

Chapters 5 and 6 focus on efforts by the Nationalist government to maintain economic controls during the turbulent years of war. Chapter 5 examines the pervasive trafficking across frontlines throughout the Second Sino-Japanese War (1937–1945), revealing the varied official responses to widespread smuggling—suppression, toleration, and even encouragement. Using intelligence records and popular press reports, this chapter illustrates how patterns of illicit commerce were reconstituted in the face of "economic blockades" (*jingji fengsuo*) and reconsiders previous interpretations of "trading with the enemy" as strictly an outgrowth of corruption that enervated military discipline and presaged Nationalist collapse. Chapter 6 looks at the continued growth of smuggling and the struggles of Nationalist China in reasserting economic controls during the Chinese Civil War (1946–1950). Moving beyond accounts of Communist victory and Nationalist defeat, this chapter focuses on ways the regime adapted to the collapse of the Japanese empire and the accelerated the tempo of illicit trade.

Chapter 7 continues examining the war on smuggling and the operation of illicit economies through the first decade and a half of Communist rule. Like the Nationalist authorities who preceded them, the new Communist rulers were also beset by coastal trafficking and feared that unbridled foreign commerce maintained the country's dependence on fickle global markets. The new regime thus assumed many of its predecessor's policies, waging its own anti-smuggling campaigns to control transnational connections and to build a new socialist economy insulated from global capitalism. Yet coastal smuggling proved not only stubbornly resilient but also surprisingly integral in smoothing frictions generated by the tumultuous transition to socialism. This chapter explores the ambiguous ways coastal smuggling both challenged and bolstered Communist rule during the regime's formative years, thereby highlighting how the nascent command economy and vibrant illicit economy existed antagonistically as well as symbiotically.

This study concludes with a meditation on the significance of smuggling for contemporary China. Coastal trafficking enjoyed a veritable resurgence after 1978, accentuating anxieties over renewed links to the global economy and threatening to derail the reform agenda. With progressively loosening economic controls during this period, the central government once again confronted an alarming upsurge of economic crimes that eroded public finances and subverted official authority. And once again, it launched various anti-smuggling campaigns, escalating penalties and intensifying enforcement. The conclusion thus connects the reform era to its pre-1978 (and pre-1949) antecedents by demonstrating how smuggling during this time, while undoubtedly a by-product of political corruption and market transition, represented a revival of old commercial connections and a continuation of inherent tensions between unfettered consumption and restrictive policies. Keeping in mind this historical perspective helps us better identify continuities and ruptures across modern Chinese history. More importantly, it also helps us rethink China's engagement with twentieth-century global capitalism and thereby reconsider the efficacy of national regulations mediating international flows.

* * *

Exploring the intertwined relationship between state power and illicit trade throughout modern Chinese history, this book illustrates ways that lawmaking and lawbreaking evolved antagonistically, recursively, and symbiotically. Looking at this dialectical relationship highlights the fractious and still-evolving consolidation of central control over society and economy in modern China. Moreover, surveying the underbelly of the legal economy uncovers a vast illegal economy that was intimately connected to everyday life but has been only sporadically captured or officially denigrated in historical records. This study thus helps illuminate the thin line between legal and illegal commerce drawn more than a century ago and still shifting to this day.

1

COASTAL COMMERCE AND IMPERIAL LEGACIES

Smuggling and Interdiction in
the Treaty Port Legal Order

O N THE NIGHT of February 21, 1878, officers from the Chinese Maritime Customs Service boarded the British steamer *Taiwan* shortly after its arrival in Fuzhou. Notified by an informant that contraband from Hong Kong was hidden on the vessel, the search party scoured the ship's quarters before finally uncovering smuggled opium concealed under pillows and mattresses. Suspicion quickly fell upon a Chinese cook, who was arrested after a failed attempt to flee the scene. The customs commissioner proceeded to fine the vessel's captain 500 taels and called for a hearing to be jointly conducted by himself and the local British consul. When the trial was convened two weeks later, both the consul and the commissioner agreed that the opium was indeed smuggled. Yet the former rejected the latter's contention that the captain should be held liable for the actions of his crew. The consul accepted the captain's claim that he made a "diligent search on two occasions during the trip in question" and the vessel carried no contraband to the best of his knowledge. Since the captain did not willfully engage in smuggling, the consul ruled, he was thus not required to pay the fine. As for the Chinese cook, he was credited for time served and released with his wages forfeited. The commissioner objected to the verdict and forwarded the case to his superiors in Beijing, kicking off protracted negotiations between Qing and British diplomats that concluded only years later.[1]

In the annals of modern Chinese history, the *Taiwan* case was relatively unimportant. It did not implicate anyone of note; it did not change the course of Sino-British relations; and it was not even unique. Yet the case was not altogether insignificant, and it highlights many features common to illicit trade and official interdiction on the China coast in the late nineteenth and early twentieth centuries. Most importantly, it was made possible by the unequal treaties ratified after the First Opium War, which delineated how and where foreign commerce was conducted in China for the next hundred years. This new economy pulled China into the ambit of the emergent global capitalist order and placed complex restrictions on domestic authority. Treaty provisions constrained successive central governments—imperial and, later, Republican—from introducing mercantilist policies or raising import tariffs that would hinder foreign access to Chinese markets. They also formalized durable legal protections for foreign nationals on Chinese soil. Chinese control over foreign trade was primarily mediated through a new, foreign-operated customs service which monitored and policed commerce at the treaty ports dotting the coast. The disintegration of the late imperial order and the instability of the early Republican era further fractured Chinese sovereignty until 1928, when the Nationalists nominally brought the country under central rule and began to reverse the legacies of the unequal treaties. During this era of weak central authority, smuggling in China was widespread, yet it was not particularly profitable because of low tariffs. The range of smuggled goods was thus correspondingly narrow, limited to articles either heavily taxed or prohibited outright like opium, weapons, and salt.

Building on the contention that legality and illegality cannot be understood in isolation, this chapter surveys the workings of the treaty port economy in the decades leading up to 1928. It identifies the geography, practices, and networks that animated coastal commerce—in both its legal and illegal variants. In particular, the chapter looks at a series of smuggling incidents like the *Taiwan* case involving foreign merchants and Chinese authorities. Quotidian though they were, these disputes nonetheless reveal how late Qing and early Republican governments fought smuggling within a rapidly changing economy. They also highlight how the transformation of legal pluralism under the old Qing legal order to legal imperialism under the new treaty system complicated the judicial definition of smuggling in China. Tracing the evolution of the treaty port legal order is key to understanding coastal smuggling. Though riddled with contradictions, loopholes, and inconsistencies, the mélange of domestic laws and foreign treaties ultimately defined the incentives for trafficking, as well as the parameters for enforcement. More importantly, this treaty port legal order served as a prime target of subsequent efforts by the Nationalists to fight smuggling and expand state capacity.

COASTAL COMMERCE: INSTITUTIONS, GEOGRAPHIES, AND VECTORS

Maritime commerce in China flourished in every shade of legality long before the arrival of Western gunboats and the ratification of the unequal treaties. From the Ming dynasty (1368–1644) through the early decades of the Qing dynasty, overseas trade was actively practiced though formally restricted to "tribute trade," commercial exchanges between the Chinese and foreign tribute missions dispatched to the imperial capital in recognition of Chinese suzerainty while earning handsome profits for participants.[2] Starting from 1684, the Kangxi emperor (r. 1662–1723) inaugurated the "open trade policy" that lifted the ban on maritime travel (*haijin*), permitted private trade with overseas locales, and established a Qing tollhouse system on the coast.[3] Although the Qing court in subsequent decades constantly swung between maintaining security and promoting commerce, trade continued apace.[4] Indeed, junks loaded with travelers and goods continued moving up and down along the coast, back and forth on the seas—regardless of the policy that prevailed. During the late eighteenth and early nineteenth centuries, the volume of commerce outstripped the capacity of the state to monitor and tax it. Innumerable ports and bays—many of them not recognized or even recorded by officials—sprung up to handle the burgeoning traffic.[5] Even tribute trade reflected this reality, as tribute missions freely traded with private merchants on the coast.[6] Legal and illegal commerce thus existed side by side and were often indistinguishable.

Trade with the West, meanwhile, was originally permitted at several ports but remained minuscule in volume before the 1750s, when only five to ten ships arrived in China annually. In 1757, Western merchants were officially required to trade only at Guangzhou with licensed Chinese monopolists—collectively known as the Cohong (*gonghang*)—as intermediaries. The creation of this famed Canton System was motivated more by fiscal than security concerns; the Qianlong emperor (1736–1796) acceded to this arrangement on the recommendations of Guangdong provincial officials who promised better collection of taxes.[7] Despite such restrictions, Western trade in Guangzhou rose steadily in the decades before the First Opium War. Moreover, Western merchants frequently and easily circumvented the system to evade paying duties and engage in other forms of smuggling. Opium was the most notorious contraband trafficked, but Western merchants also traded rice, saltpeter, salt, silver, gold, and other commodities controlled or banned by the court. Nor did they restrict their trading to a single port or with the monopoly. Yen-p'ing Hao enumerates the many forms of the "free trade" (i.e., smuggling) that continued to prevail along the Chinese coast after 1757: British and Portuguese merchants moving opium through Macao; Cantonese and British merchants chartering Spanish ships to trade between Xiamen, India, and Manila; and American merchants buying silk from non-Cohong merchants at volumes exceeding export quotas.[8] Despite later complaints by Western merchants of the "arbitrary" fees imposed by Chinese officials, taxation on maritime commerce—interregional or international—was relatively light and varied by locale.

Imposition of the Treaty of Nanjing [Nanking] (1842) and subsequent treaties redefined China's engagement with the global economy in several ways. First, the treaties guaranteed foreign access to Chinese markets by loosening the restrictions of the Canton system. Foreign merchants were permitted to trade at specified treaty ports, which grew from five initially to ninety-two by 1917.[9] Other restrictions such as trading with government monopolies and quotas on imports and exports were lifted. The treaties also forced the Qing to surrender China's tariff autonomy. Duties for almost all imports were fixed at a flat rate of 5 percent ad valorem at all treaty ports. In addition, foreign powers won the right to exercise consular jurisdiction on Chinese soil, putting foreign nationals under the laws of their home country rather than the laws of China. Finally, the treaty system changed imperial China's ambiguous, centuries-long policy toward overseas travel by Chinese subjects. Mass migration was formally legalized in the late nineteenth century but had been already permitted by provincial authorities decades earlier in response to growing Western demand for cheap Chinese labor. The treaties were initially concluded with Great Britain, but their provisions extended to other foreign powers who concluded their own treaties with China due to the "most favored nation" clause.[10] Through force and diplomacy, the international community—led by Britain, France, the United States, and, eventually, Japan—kept Chinese markets opened and Chinese authority constrained.

While historians have debated (and continue to debate) the extent to which the treaty port system transformed the Chinese economy, they have largely agreed that any changes inaugurated by the treaties were not distributed evenly across China. Indeed, international trade played an outsized role in the urban economies of the coast compared with interregional trade for the rural economies of the interior. Tighter connections to imperial markets in Asia and the rest of the world helped incorporate coastal China within networks of Western capitalism. Moreover, this treaty port system with its links to the global economy, limits on Chinese authority, and a panoply of foreign privileges did not emerge de novo after 1842 but actually built on prior practices. The flat 5 percent tariff, for instance, was only slightly higher than the rates charged at the old Qing maritime tollhouses. Extraterritorial concessions were initially viewed as acceptable accommodations by a legally pluralistic Qing empire that had long subjected different ethnic, social, and professional groups to different laws and courts. Practices that were part and parcel of extraterritoriality—including consular jurisdiction and mixed courts—were thus entirely consistent with Qing legal traditions such as personal jurisdiction and joint trials.[11] Nor was the treaty port system consciously engineered by a single architect. Instead, it evolved over decades through continual encounters on the diplomatic table, on the battlefield, and on the ground until foreign powers prevailed in interpreting and enforcing provisions more favorable to their interests. The steady decline and eventual collapse of central authority in the early twentieth century only further weakened China's geopolitical position. The 5 percent tariff remained fixed for decades despite a clause in the Treaty of Tianjin [Tientsin] (1858) permitting adjustments every ten years.[12] Persistent efforts by Qing (and later Republican) authorities to revise the treaties and thereby increase government revenues and protect domestic industries went unrealized. Extraterritoriality, for its part, eventually became so absolute, so pervasive, and so abused that foreign nationals and even Chinese subjects in foreign concessions were practically unconstrained and untouchable by any Chinese authority.

Overseeing China's foreign trade during the treaty port era (and beyond) was a new institution, the Chinese Maritime Customs Service.[13] Established in 1854 by British diplomats to collect duties on foreign trade in Shanghai, the agency emerged during a fortuitous moment when Sino-foreign geopolitical interests converged.[14] For overextended Western powers, the agency assumed many of the responsibilities their consuls were required to—but could not—fulfill as required by the Treaty of Nanjing. For the beleaguered Qing dynasty, it provided reliable and desperately needed revenues during the chaos of the Taiping Rebellion. The Maritime Customs initially possessed a limited mandate: assessing duties on foreign maritime trade at a handful of treaty ports. Yet as its size, responsibilities, and geographical reach steadily expanded, the agency eventually incorporated and supplanted the old Qing maritime tollhouses. It maintained China's coastal and riverine navigation systems along with its network of lighthouses. It collected revenues that hypothecated China's indemnities and bond issues to foreign and domestic investors. By 1930, the Maritime Customs had a presence in almost fifty ports throughout

China, monitoring, regulating, and taxing both international and domestic trade.

The institution itself was headed by an inspector general (*zong shuiwu si*) based in Beijing until 1929, when the Inspectorate General Office was relocated to Shanghai. Each customs district was headed by a commissioner (*shuiwu si*) appointed by and answerable to the inspector general. Each commissioner nominally assisted the local superintendent (*jiandu*) appointed by the Qing court. The post of inspector general was held exclusively by non-Chinese (almost all of whom were Britons) during the entire period of the Maritime Customs' existence.[15] The longest-serving and most influential inspector general was Robert Hart (1835–1911), who carved an indispensable role for the agency within the Qing bureaucracy during its formative years. Commissioners, too, were exclusively non-Chinese until the late 1920s, when the Nationalists pressed to "Sinicize" the agency. Although foreign-staffed at senior levels, the Maritime Customs operated as a bureaucratic arm of successive Chinese regimes on a largely uninterrupted basis from 1854 to 1949.[16] From the Qing dynasty through its Republican successors, the agency maintained its institutional integrity during the almost one-hundred-year span of its existence.[17]

Most importantly, the Maritime Customs was the primary institution operating on the frontlines of the fight against smuggling. Fighting duty evasion was important because of the Qing's growing reliance on import duties to fund its military, infrastructure, and other state-building projects. Despite being capped at 5 percent, tariffs came to make up a significant part of the late Qing court's income. In the decades after the Taiping Rebellion, revenues to the court came primarily from three sources: the land tax, customs duties, and the *lijin* transit tax collected by local government tollhouses on domestic commerce in the interior. By 1870, customs duties and *lijin* taxes made up 16.2 percent and 26.3 percent, respectively, of the Qing court's budget. Almost a quarter of a century later, in 1894, before the disastrous First Sino-Japanese War (1894–1895), these proportions had reversed, standing at 28.3 percent and 17.6 percent, respectively.[18] By the

1890s, customs duties became the second-largest source of revenue for the Qing court, trailing only the land tax.[19]

As with legal trade, the inauguration of the treaty port era did not create illegal trade along the Chinese littoral, but it did shape it. Smuggling always existed in the shadows of commerce, and the geography of illegal trade frequently overlapped with the geography of legal trade. Meanwhile, the channels of smuggling sometimes crisscrossed remote locales away from customhouses and wharves, away from the prying eyes of officialdom and the public. Sparsely inhabited coastal villages and poorly monitored remote islands were ideal conduits for trafficking, especially in bulk. Notorious hubs included Nan'ao Island (Guangdong), Pingtan Island (Fujian), and the Zhoushan archipelago (Zhejiang). Yet the ultimate destinations for smuggled goods were urban centers where consumers were plentiful and markets were active. Indeed, the major zones of coastal smuggling were also the most commercially vibrant locales within some of the macroregions delineated by G. William Skinner: Lingnan (Pearl River Delta, Tonkin Gulf, Hainan Island); the Southeast Coast (Shantou, Xiamen); the Lower Yangzi (Shanghai, Hangzhou Bay); and North China (Tianjin, Bohai Gulf). While scholars have challenged Skinner's representation of individual macroregions operating as self-contained units, they have agreed with Skinner that commercial connections between the macroregions were already extensive by the turn of the nineteenth century, if not earlier.[20] Legal and illegal coastal trade embodied such interregional links that were not confined within formal administrative boundaries but instead traversed them.

Moreover, by the late nineteenth century these macroregions were, in turn, being pulled into a larger, incipient economic order: the littoral zones and shared sites of layered sovereignty in colonial Northeast and Southeast Asia that Catherine Phipps terms "transmarine East Asia."[21] An important entrepôt for all commercial traffic between the macroregions and within transmarine East Asia was Hong Kong. To borrow Adam McKeown's metaphoric description, the British colony could be imagined as a Janus-faced hub through which people, goods, and ideas flowed. In one direction, spokes extended throughout South China to towns and villages.

In the other direction, spokes extended to ports across the Chinese coast and the rest of the Pacific world, branching out from secondary nodes like Singapore, Bangkok, and San Francisco.[22] Hong Kong thus enjoyed favorable geography and extensive connections, but it was politics that truly enhanced its status as a nexus for legal and illegal commerce. Since the colony was founded, local authorities jealously warded off any Chinese encroachment yet adopted a relatively lax attitude toward China-bound trafficking. Aggressive assertions of British sovereignty over lands, waters, and islands abutting Chinese territories frustrated Chinese anti-smuggling efforts. Other nodes of coastal commerce like Shanghai and Tianjin suffered from similarly fractured jurisdictions that made them major smuggling centers in their own right. As "hypercolonies," their urban spaces were relentlessly divided by foreign concessions and competing imperialisms that militated against effective law enforcement. As modern ports, their urban populations expanded with the concomitant growth of maritime trade. These conditions together fostered an ideal environment for traffickers, who found refuge in liminal zones of illegality and profited by meeting the appetites of growing markets.

New modes of transportation like steamships carried an increasingly larger share of this commercial maritime traffic. Already plying the China coast by 1860s, steamships (foreign and eventually Chinese) would transport almost forty million tons of cargo (or nearly 97 percent of all maritime trade volume) entering and clearing treaty ports by 1900.[23] These numbers, of course, do not include all goods illegally carried. Yet just as they did for coastal trade, steamships also quickly became major vectors of coastal smuggling due to their mobility and range. The aggregate volume of this traffic was undeniably large, but individual quantities tended to be small since large cargoes of contraband were difficult to move without detection. Steamship smuggling was thus more prevalent in passenger traffic than in freight traffic, and the growth of the former was stimulated by the abolition of travel restrictions on Chinese subjects. Passengers on board ships plying Chinese and Southeast Asian coasts frequently brought items of all sorts within their luggage. Some personal effects were intended for personal use, others as gifts for family and friends. Still others were intended for commerce, for small profits could be made buying goods at one port and reselling them at another. This petty smuggling—transporting undeclared goods on board steamers—was a common practice. In some cases, it was also an organized business. Especially numerous and active were "runners" (*shuike*), who were frequently cited by popular press reports and official correspondences as the major culprits of petty smuggling. Whether at the behest of a firm or on their own accord, these runners made a precarious living shuttling goods from one port to another while avoiding detection. Since avoiding tariffs was critical to maintaining slim profit margins, they engaged in all kinds of subterfuge to evade detection of their dutiable goods. A common tactic was dividing their dutiable cargo into smaller lots and passing them off as personal luggage, thereby obfuscating detection and making duty assessment difficult. Even more notorious than steamship runners for petty smuggling were steamship crews. Sailors—primarily Chinese but also foreign—frequently exploited their intimacy with the ship and access within its many holds to load unmanifested cargo or to board extra passengers. Such side business, or "pidgin," supplemented the crews' wages and were conducted with the tacit (and sometimes explicit) knowledge of the steamship's managers and captains. The constant mobility of their profession made them ideal carriers of smuggled goods.[24]

Steamships, however, did not complete displace traditional modes of transportation like junks. Besides remaining important carriers of cargo in the treaty port era, these craft also served as active vectors of coastal smuggling. Given their sheer numbers and small size, junks were more difficult to monitor than steamships. Moreover, entire junks could be filled with illicit cargo, thereby achieving better economies of transport and even enjoying comparative advantages in trafficking. The old Qing tollhouses tried to regulate junk traffic by issuing licenses to ship owners and requiring them to provide information on their identity, crew members, commercial plans, and ports of departure and arrival.[25] This system of state surveillance, however, suffered tremendous strain with the explosion of maritime commerce and the decline of Qing power. A commissioner at the Lappa (Gongbei) Customs reported that by the mid-nineteenth century, old regulations had largely become a "dead letter" in the Pearl River Delta. Junks that carried their papers were now the exception rather than the rule. What papers were carried had long expired and lacked the required information on the vessel, crew, and cargo.[26] Moreover, the Maritime Customs did not assume overall responsibility for overseeing junk traffic until the 1930s. Diminishing state legibility and fractured oversight, of course, only enhanced the opportunity for smuggling by junks.

The identity of smugglers was not limited by nationality, profession, or class. Travelers, merchants, sailors, and fishermen alike could exploit their mobility for profit. The identity of smugglers was also not limited by gender. While it was primarily practiced by men, a surprising number of women also engaged in smuggling. Female participation in illicit trading was driven in part by broader social and economic changes beginning in the late nineteenth century that steadily blurred the traditional separation of the sexes, bringing more women into public spaces. It was also facilitated by stereotypes of feminine weakness, natural assumptions of innocence, and social taboos against inspection of the female body—all conferring distinct advantages on women smugglers over their male counterparts.[27] Indeed, women smugglers frequently leveraged such cultural attitudes to their advantage, warding off invasive searches and deflecting official suspicions. During the late nineteenth century, women smugglers were still enough of a novelty to attract outsized attention from the popular press. The newspaper *Shen Bao*, for instance, devoted entire articles to minor incidents of trafficking by women. One article lamented how smuggling was becoming ever more "extraordinary" (*chuqi*) in reporting a case of an old woman caught on board a Guangzhou-bound steamship with opium strapped to her thighs.[28] Another article warned of women traveling with opium hidden in their underwear, shielded by prevailing social conventions despite suspicions by male watchmen.[29] By the early twentieth century, women smugglers were common at every port, running all sorts of commodities for a living and even trafficking dangerous articles like weapons. A 1913 dispatch from the Republican government to the Maritime Customs, for example, called for heightened vigilance against smuggling in forwarding cases of guns being uncovered in the luggage of young women and little girls.[30] Smuggling by women—like smuggling more generally—became an even more severe problem after 1928 as new regulations and tariffs incentivized trafficking as never before.

PROFITABLE TRAFFICKING: OPIUM, WEAPONS, AND SALT

Coastal smuggling remained widespread in the treaty port era, but China's new foreign trade system made some forms of trafficking more profitable than others. The Treaty of Nanjing compelled the Qing court to surrender China's tariff autonomy by maintaining "fair and regular" duties on imports and exports. The tariff schedule issued the following year stipulated that imports be assessed a duty of anywhere from 5 to 10 percent ad valorem and exempted from domestic taxes like the *lijin*. The Treaty of Tianjin lowered duties further still, to a flat 5 percent on virtually all imports. Despite periodic adjustments to account for the decline in the global value of silver, duties remained at roughly 5 percent until 1928. Given the low duties that prevailed, the difference in price between imports that paid duties and imports that did not was 5 percent at most. And with other costs of smuggling taken into account—including transportation, evasion, bribery, and protection—this differential was even less significant. A 1936 article from the *Bank of China Monthly* looking back at this period noted that "the burden on merchants was light, [and] while the risks taken by smugglers were great, the gains were often insufficient to compensate for potential losses."[31] Smuggling for most commodities during much of the treaty port era, in other words, was not particularly profitable because of low tariffs.

To make smuggling truly pay—to make it worthwhile given the risks and costs—traffickers had to move commodities that were either heavily taxed or strictly regulated. One item that satisfied both criteria was opium, whose import was legalized after the First Opium War and exempted from the flat 5 percent tariff. The tariff schedule in the Treaty of Tianjin set the duty for foreign opium at 30 taels per picul. The 1885 amendment to the Chefoo Convention (1876) permitted the Qing court to collect an additional 80 taels per picul as the *lijin*, bringing the total import duty to 110 taels per picul.[32] Such arrangements meant that the opium *lijin* was simultaneously collected with the import duty, effectively diverting revenues on the import of the drug from provincial coffers to the imperial treasury. Revenues from opium were the largest single source of customs duties, which in turn was one of the largest sources of the Qing's overall revenues.[33] For the smuggler, the incentives for opium smuggling were also attractive, since evading high duties on a commodity enjoying inelastic demand was very profitable. Moreover, opium itself was widely available at British imperial outposts like Hong Kong and Singapore, the twin axes of coastal China's intra-Asian trade network.[34] Strong demand, abundant supply, and its status as the most heavily taxed import in China all made opium the most frequently trafficked commodity.

Since the import of opium generated significant revenues for the Qing court, suppressing trafficking thus protected a critical fiscal resource. Moreover, it also helped the center assert its authority by reserving for itself the prerogative to regulate and tax the trade. As early as 1866, for example, provincial leaders in Guangdong permitted opium from Hong Kong to be imported at local stations that charged lower duties than were charged at treaty ports. These measures, intended to clamp down on smuggling and fill provincial coffers, however, effectively created competition to imperial customhouses at treaty ports. Consequently, opium imports at treaty ports—and hence imperial revenues—steadily declined. In 1887 after almost a decade of negotiations with authorities in Hong Kong and Guangdong, the Zongli Yamen (the Qing foreign ministry) approved plans to allow the Maritime Customs to open the Kowloon (Jiulong) and Lappa Customs in the Pearl River Delta to manage junk traffic and opium *lijin* collection between China, Hong Kong, and Macao.[35]

Tighter controls over opium shipments simply encouraged smugglers to shift tactics and geography in their trafficking. Shortly after the establishment of new customs stations in the Pearl River Delta, smugglers in Singapore began removing Indian opium from China-bound steamships, which would be charged the official duty at treaty ports, and transshipped them by junks, where they paid lower duties at provincial stations (or none at all if they landed clandestinely at the many unpatrolled areas around Hainan Island). In response to this "balloon effect"—whereby intensified enforcement in one area simply displaced the targeted activity to another area—the Maritime Customs pushed the line of interdiction southward beyond the Chinese coastline. In 1889, a scheme was devised whereby the Chinese consul in Singapore would telegraph the Maritime Customs of any permits issued by the government of Singapore for the export of opium. Later regulations required all Chinese junks from Southeast Asia to register with the local Chinese consul, call at specified ports in southern China, and carry clearance permits to avoid confiscation of any opium carried.[36] While such efforts helped channel more foreign opium to imperial customhouses, native opium from southwestern China eventually dominated the market by the 1890s and obviated the need for such a far-flung regulatory net.

In the early twentieth century, domestic campaigns and international pressures proliferated to limit consumption, production, and transportation of opium. In 1906, the Guangxu emperor supported a coordinated national campaign in China to control opium that inspired subsequent anti-opium campaigns. In 1907, British and Chinese governments agreed to reduce and eventually end opium imports within a decade. The Hague Convention (1912–1913) and the League of Nations Opium Advisory Committee conventions (1924–1925) sought to regulate the international drug trade through coordination between producer and consumer states.[37] Illegalization at home and abroad certainly made opium smuggling more difficult. After all, "smuggling" opium no longer meant just evading duties on a recreational drug; it now meant trafficking an unambiguous contraband. Yet opium consumption continued despite official campaigns because of inelastic demand among users that still generated sizeable profits for dealers and taxes for governments. The collapse of the Qing and the subsequent instability of the Republic exacerbated the fight over opium revenues. While the weak Beiyang government was (nominally) committed to eliminating opium, local governments and provincial warlords created their own Opium Suppression Bureaus that pursued the simultaneous (if conflicting) goals of decreasing consumption and raising revenues. Dealers who could generate reliable taxes were licensed to effectively serve as official opium monopolies. Their ranks included the leading gangsters of the day, like Du Yuesheng in Shanghai and Ye Qinghe in Fujian, who brokered agreements with a hodgepodge of governments—warlord, foreign, provincial, and even central.[38] Finally, official efforts to suppress opium created other unintended consequences, as new synthetic narcotics like cocaine, morphine, and heroin filtered into China starting in the early twentieth century. Trafficking thus became more consolidated, more profitable, and more dangerous.

Weapons were another smuggled article that commanded substantial premiums on the black market. The ban on the unsanctioned import of guns and other "implements of war" (*wuqi*) was explicitly stated in the Rules of Trade (1858) and reaffirmed in subsequent import tariff rules.[39] Yet controlling the flow of weapons was difficult. During the Taiping Rebellion, foreign arms importers profited from insatiable demand on all sides. Maritime Customs inspector general Robert Hart, relaying complaints from the Zongli Yamen, criticized "certain mercantile firms [that] have made a practice of importing . . . munitions and implements of war, which they have subsequently sold to the highest bidders indiscriminately, thinking it a matter of no consequence whether the purchasers were rebels or imperialists." Besides the growing lethality of foreign technology, weapons continued to be imported because domestic production could not satisfy demand—even after the construction of Western-style arsenals during the Self-Strengthening Movement (ca. 1860–1890). To better monitor imports, the court required all shipments to be accompanied by a permit (*huzhao*) signed by both the customs superintendent and commissioner.[40] Illicit shipments to treaty ports, however, were never fully curtailed, since the lack of coordination among officials compounded the problem of distinguishing between legitimate and illegitimate imports. Provincial leaders, for example, purchased foreign arms in significant volume—sometimes on their own initiative and without the knowledge of the court.[41]

Weapons trafficking also proliferated because of strong domestic demand. The rise of brigandage during the late nineteenth century ignited a spiraling arms race along the coast as local militias snapped up weapons for self-defense. Even junks—already a major vector of smuggling—were permitted to arm themselves to defend against pirates who roamed the coast and preyed on unsuspecting vessels. Junkmasters frequently applied for "arms certificates" (*junhuo qixie danzhao*) at their local customhouse; these specified the cannons, rifles, revolvers, flintlocks, spears, and amount of gunpowder their vessels carried. In theory, junks had to present these certificates and account for any discrepancies whenever they passed a customs station or else risk incurring penalties. But in practice, Maritime Customs oversight of junk traffic was limited to a handful of stations.[42] Regulations distinguishing weapons for legitimate self-defense proved difficult to enforce, creating liminal opportunities for trafficking.[43] Indeed, despite the threat of substantial fines equaling twice the value of any weapons seized, the illicit flow of weapons continued unabated. One customs commissioner report in 1891 neatly summarizes the situation:

> Arms continue to be smuggled in large quantities into the interior by passengers, who pack among their luggage revolvers and Winchester rifles which have been previously taken to pieces to facilitate hiding. It is impossible to search all such travelers, and the handsome profits gained prompt them to run many risks. In this way robbers, pirates, and the unruly generally obtain arms, often of better quality than the Government troops have, with which to intimidate the law-abiding or to resist the authorities in their efforts to maintain order.[44]

Buyers of illegal weapons in government correspondences were frequently labeled as "bandits," but their ranks also included anti-Qing revolutionaries and underground organizations. Chinese sailors, for instance, were notorious for smuggling small arms from far-flung locales like Vancouver and Marseilles to revolutionaries and warlords in China.[45] Politics in some cases thus complemented profit as a motivation for gun-running.

Arms trafficking accelerated in the early Republic, created by mutually reinforcing problems of a deteriorating domestic political scene and a volatile international weapons market. Constant fighting among provincial warlords throughout China and the concomitant rise in banditry drove demand shortly after the fall of the Qing. The Beijing Republican government reaffirmed customs regulations requiring anyone importing armaments to apply for a permit (*zhunyun huzhao*).[46] Foreign powers after World War I sought to contain the internecine warfare that destabilized China and thus threatened foreign concessions and investments. Under the aegis of Great Britain and the United States, several countries concluded the Arms Embargo Agreement (1919) that made the transfer of war materials to China illegal. Yet these restrictions were frequently flouted. China-bound vessels often discharged their cargo to awaiting buyers prior to docking, evading inspection and obviating the need for import permits. Countries like Japan and France who were party to the embargo did not stop their private arms dealers from selling in China. Meanwhile, countries like Czechoslovakia, Germany, and the Soviet Union, not parties to the embargo, continued their shipments. Former foreign military personnel seeking to leverage their expertise and connections also jumped into the China market as freelance dealers.[47] Despite restrictions on their import, weapons were continually trafficked because of legal loopholes that recognized their use for self-defense as well as a fractured international market that supplied warring domestic factions.

The other most commonly smuggled commodity was salt. Just as it was for weapons, the import of salt was prohibited under the 1858 Rules of Trade and import rules.[48] But unlike the smuggling of other commodities during the treaty port era, the smuggling of salt was a longtime problem created by centuries-long domestic regulations. Through much of Chinese history, salt had been a government monopoly.[49] Under the Qing, the empire was divided into ten administrative districts where officially licensed producers were given exclusive markets and sales quotas. "Smuggling" thus occurred when salt was produced or sold outside of sanctioned channels. Coastal trafficking was prevalent, following the same logic and pattern of movement for other commodities. In the mountainous promontory of east Shandong, for example, an estimated three to four million piculs of salt were illicitly produced and exported annually during the early twentieth century to the rest of the province; to overseas locales like Korea; and to the southern reaches of the Chinese littoral, such as the Yangzi River Delta and Hong Kong.[50] Interior trafficking was far more widespread. Salt was primarily produced in the Chinese heartland and commonly channeled through riverine passages like the Yangzi River and the Grand Canal. Cross-district variations in price, supply, and even taste created many opportunities for arbitrage. Easy availability and inelastic demand, meanwhile, magnified the scale of potential profits. Itinerant peasants in Central China, for instance, augmented their incomes by buying salt in one district and selling it in another, making smuggling practically a seasonal occupation. More organized operations were formed by powerful lineage groups, secret societies, and peasant armies of the Nian Rebellion (1851–1868) who could marshal resources and manpower to produce, transport, protect, and sell salt in defiance of state strictures.[51] Since salt was not imported, its trafficking was not as directly affected by subsequent changes in tariff policies after 1928, remaining a serious problem and flashpoint of conflict between state and peasant.[52]

CIRCUMSCRIBED ENFORCEMENT

Meanwhile, the same financial incentives that shaped how smuggling was conducted also shaped how smuggling was combatted. In the decades after the suppression of the Taiping Rebellion, the Qing court kicked off many "self-strengthening" measures, including pacification campaigns targeting coastal smuggling that threatened tax revenues.[53] But smuggling at treaty ports proved more vexing to combat. Petty smuggling on board steamships and junks was especially widespread. But in an era when the flat treaty tariff prevailed, interdiction was rarely worth the effort since the cost of enforcement exceeded the duties theoretically evaded. Hart himself repeatedly expressed ambivalence on striking the right balance between fostering legal commerce while discouraging its illegal counterpart. In 1881, he opined that preventing petty steamship smuggling, while certainly one of the Maritime Customs' primary tasks, was a responsibility that should largely be shouldered by shipping companies themselves which could ultimately better police their own vessels and crews.[54] Almost a decade later in 1890, Hart again noted that the increase in volume of passenger traffic also led to a concomitant increase in petty smuggling. Vigilance was still to be exercised, particularly with regard to contraband, but he directed agents to concentrate more of their attention and resources to handling cargo where duties were primarily collected. Passengers carrying articles for personal use, gifts, or even sale in their luggage were nominally committing "smuggling," but as Hart reminded his commissioners, "however considerable [personal] articles thus carried may appear when 'lumped,' they are in point of fact nothing when compared with the cargoes on which Revenue depends, and were they even allowed to pass unquestioned and untaxed, Revenue would neither be diminished nor endangered."[55]

Hart's views, of course, did not necessarily translate into more relaxed inspection of passengers. In fact, Chinese travelers still complained of overzealous searches by customs agents that bordered on harassment or even extortion. Stories of personal belongings being unjustifiably detained on the suspicion of smuggling frequently surfaced in the popular press.[56] Such complaints reached their crescendo in the 1930s, when the Maritime Customs conducted more invasive searches at the behest of the Nationalist government, which wanted to crack down on the smuggling epidemic then pervasive along the coast. A former customs employee corroborated such stories in his recollection of how searchers often "imperiously and ferociously" (shengshi xiong'e) brandished their authority as a scare tactic to solicit bribes from ordinary passengers and overlook the dutiable goods in their luggage.[57] Yet these small gains from harassment aside, searchers had other incentives to uncover trafficking. The agency's system of rewards gave officers who participated in seizures a share of the confiscated goods' value, and awards were highest for contraband like opium. Different motivations, then, also shaped the scope of enforcement. For officials at the top, the inconvenience to passengers and the costs to officials in prosecuting petty smuggling simply did not justify the 5 percent tariff that theoretically went uncollected. For officials on the ground, the rewards for uncovering the smuggling of ordinary commodities were nowhere near as lucrative as those for uncovering the smuggling of contraband and other high-value products.

Further shaping the Maritime Customs' anti-smuggling efforts was limited jurisdictional reach. The agency did not establish its dedicated Preventive Service until 1931, when the coastal smuggling epidemic necessitated more organized and coordinated interdiction. Until then, its preventive focus was primarily concentrated in its areas of defined bureaucratic control—treaty ports and their immediate vicinities, wharves, and steamships. Limits on the Maritime Customs' geography of interdiction were demarcated early in the agency's existence. In 1867, for instance, a search party dispatched by the Guangzhou customs commissioner to seize smuggled opium reportedly hidden in a Shunde County village was set upon villagers who took the intruders for kidnappers. One searcher died, several were wounded, and—most embarrassingly—the rest of the team was held captive by the villagers. Their eventual release was secured only through the intervention of the governor-general. The fiasco led Hart to later fume "that the expedition ought not to have been undertaken." He further instructed "that such enterprises be refrained from for the future" by reminding customs officials that anti-smuggling efforts were to remain focused on monitoring steamship traffic at treaty ports.[58]

Many search teams were poorly equipped to deal with armed resistance since they were primarily expected to uncover smugglers, not fight them. This widespread problem was especially acute for customs stations in the Pearl River Delta, which were responsible for collecting monitoring trade beyond treaty ports and along the expansive border with Hong Kong while facing a colonial government that was indifferent at best and uncooperative at worst. In a 1917 dispatch to the inspector general, the Kowloon commissioner openly confessed that the resources to fight smuggling within his district were utterly inadequate: the patrol boats were too slow to do anything other than to serve as "deterrence," and the frontier guards along the Hong Kong border had been unarmed and practically defenseless for quite some time.[59] At least twenty-eight raids on customs stations were reported from 1912 to 1928. As public security in China deteriorated, officials accordingly reduced staff at stations to avoid attracting banditry.[60]

The reluctance of customs officials to engage in counter-smuggling operations outside their jurisdictions eventually extended even to cases involving opium and weapons, despite the potentially lucrative seizure rewards. Small-time opium smuggling on board steamships and junks remained pervasive, but trafficking steadily became more organized and militarized after the 1917 prohibition. In the small-arms race between smuggling rings and the Maritime Customs, the latter lagged pitifully behind. Upon the receipt of confidential information that a shipment of opium was headed to his port, for instance, the Shantou commissioner wrote: "I will take the necessary steps, though I have to admit that our efforts to seize opium or contraband are usually of little avail. The smugglers are invariably armed, and object to our interference—their objection taking the form of the sudden pointing of a revolver at one's stomach! My tidewaiters are not cowards; but they are at a disadvantage in such circumstances!"[61]

Smuggling rings also frequently complicated preventive work by operating outside the jurisdictional limits of authorities. In 1908, for instance, Guangdong provincial and customs officials were forced to release the Japanese steamer *Tatsu Maru* despite its cargo of 1,500 rifles and 40,000 cartridges. The weapons were undoubtedly destined for China, but the seizure was made near Macao, beyond Chinese territorial waters.[62] Such forms of trafficking further discouraged officials from being too aggressive in their interdiction efforts. This attitude is neatly captured in a 1928 letter from Frederick Maze, who was serving as Shanghai commissioner prior to his appointment as inspector general, to the Kowloon commissioner regarding information that a Japanese steamer bound for Vladivostok planned to discharge opium off the shores of Shanghai in an area outside the territorial jurisdiction of the Maritime Customs: "I am frequently furnished with such information, but in the circumstances seldom, or never, take any action!. . . [I]n any case the Customs are powerless in so far as effective results are concerned. I have no doubt that the [the Japanese steamer] will tranship [*sic*] the whole, or a part, of the above Opium outside, off Shanghai: is it supposed that I am to dispatch a launch with a few *unarmed* Tidewaiters to seize it?"[63] As if to underscore the pervasiveness of this attitude, the commissioner signaled his own agreement by scribbling the word "True" along the margins. Limited assets combined with restrictions on the scale and scope of operations all served as strong disincentives for customs officials to engage counter-smuggling activities outside certain venues.

DOMESTIC LAWS AND LEGAL MODERNIZATION

Other than the unauthorized carriage of specific commodities, what constituted "smuggling" was difficult to legally define. During the treaty port era, a patchwork of domestic laws and foreign treaties delineated the parameters of legal trade and enumerated punishments for violations. Interdiction efforts were further complicated by the principle of extraterritoriality under the unequal treaties, which accorded foreigners on Chinese soil legal protections and carved out foreign concessions beyond the reach of domestic Chinese authorities. Within this legal context, the crime of smuggling was not defined by any single uniform set of statutes. How individuals in China were punished for evading duties, running contraband, or violating trade regulations was a complex calculus that depended on their identity, the identity of their captors, and the location of their arrest.

Most Chinese subjects within China proper remained formally under the jurisdiction of the Great Qing Code (Da Qing lüli) until the twilight of imperial rule. Regarding illicit trade, the code contained multiple provisions spread across different chapters originally introduced during the Ming dynasty and subsequently revised during the early Qing dynasty. The "taxes" (*kecheng*) chapter stipulated the collection of state revenues, with two statutes requiring merchants to pay duties on cargo to the local magistrate upon arrival at port.[64] Penalties for violators included one hundred strokes of heavy bamboo and confiscation of cargo. Regulations at the old Qing Guangzhou and Fuzhou maritime tollhouses each modified this statute with different gradations of punishments to account for the severity of transgressions.[65] Other stipulations restricted the private trade of commodities in which the court held a monopoly (e.g., tea, alum, and especially salt).[66] The "law of control posts" (*guanjin*) chapter banned the flow of specific commodities deemed essential to internal security. The statute "privately [exporting] by going beyond the land frontiers or by sea in violation of the prohibitions" (*sichu waijing ji weijin xiahai*) reflected the court's fear of communities along continental and maritime frontiers "providing material assistance" (*jieji*) to pirates and other "treasonous bandits" (*jiantu*). Along with its forty-four sub-statutes, it enumerated articles prohibited from export (e.g., rice, timber, saltpeter, copper, iron, and precious metals), as well as articles prohibited from import (e.g., weapons and narcotics).[67] Punishments for "violating the ban on commodities" (*weijin huowu*) ranged from eighty strokes of heavy bamboo for unwitting accomplices to execution by beheading for ringleaders.[68]

The Qing Code was stringent in the activities it restricted and severe in the penalties it levied. For some offenses, Qing officials did indeed mete out harsh punishments, particularly for violent resistance against state authority like piracy. From the late eighteenth through the nineteenth centuries, for example, officials frequently reported capturing and executing pirates marauding the southeast coast.[69] Yet provisions from other parts of the code were rarely enforced as strictly as they were written on the books. Offenses that did not directly challenge state authority were, generally speaking, lightly dealt with. Laws curbing maritime activities had already been relaxed since the Kangxi emperor's 1684 "open trade policy." Overseas emigration had been going on for decades, if not centuries, before being formally legalized in 1893. Provincial governors occasionally launched large-scale campaigns against "salt bandits" (*yan fei*) like the Nian rebels who trafficked the fiscally important commodity, but local magistrates routinely turned a blind eye so long as illicit sales did not reach alarming and visible levels.[70] Chinese travelers caught passing off undeclared items at treaty ports by the Chinese Maritime Customs Service were usually punished with a fine or confiscation. No physical punishments were inflicted. Thus well before the fall of the dynasty, provisions restricting maritime trade in the Qing Code had been effectively rendered defunct by court edicts, policy changes, or nonenforcement. Some had already been repealed, like sub-statutes prohibiting travel to Taiwan from the mainland.[71] Others remained on the books due to the Chinese legal tradition of demonstrating filial deference to dynastic founders by leaving unchanged laws promulgated under their reign.[72] In his extensive commentaries on the code, the late Qing jurist Xue Yunsheng consistently inveighed against the problems created by these lingering, obsolete laws. Maritime regulations did not escape his ire. "These unchanging rules," he scorned, "have all turned into dead letters."[73]

Xue was apparently not alone in his opinion. During its final years, the dynasty initiated two parallel projects aimed at reforming its legal system that also (incidentally) redefined the crime of smuggling. One was drafting new, separate criminal and civil codes patterned after foreign models; the other was revising the old Great Qing Code that had made no formal distinction between criminal and civil matters. The new codes from the first project were completed but not promulgated before the dynasty's fall in 1912. The revised code from the second project was completed in 1909 and promulgated the following year as the Criminal Code of the Great Qing Currently in Use (Da Qing xianxing xinglü). In this revised Qing Code, Shen Jiaben, the jurist and scholar heading the committee overseeing legal reforms, eliminated many of the anachronistic provisions Xue had identified and converted most sanctions from physical punishments to monetary penalties or penal servitude.

Shen and his editors made other changes to the restrictions on maritime commerce that had already been loosened earlier in the dynasty or supplanted by international treaties. In excising the old statute "maritime merchants who hide goods [that are subject to tax]" (boshang nihuo), for instance, Shen noted that tariffs on coastal trade were no longer collected by magistrates and that imported foreign goods now used customs certificates as proof of duty payment. In cases of imports being concealed and not reported, he continued, punishments were applied in accordance with the treaties. With current practices "completely different" (*dayi*) from circumstances of the old code, the statute was hence all the more obsolete.[74] Meanwhile, the statute "concealing [goods to evade] taxes" (*nishui*) was revised to convert fifty strokes of light bamboo to a monetary fine, although it did not apply to duty evasion at treaty ports.[75] Finally, the substatute prohibiting the sale and smuggling of opium was excised. The change was again justified on the basis that treaties now governed the import of opium and any punishments for trafficking.[76] Shen's commentaries thus explicitly recognized another source of legal authority on Chinese soil, namely foreign treaties, and inadvertently affirmed Qing China's legally pluralistic order even in its twilight.

Meanwhile, Shen revised provisions that once regulated the flow of commodities for the sake of maritime security. While he modified restrictions on the trade of commodities like salt and tea and prohibitions on providing material assistance to enemies of the state, Shen removed altogether prohibitions on commodities now regularly traded, including rice, timber, alum, and iron.[77] Sub-statutes under the statute "privately [exporting] by going beyond the land frontiers or by sea in violation of the prohibitions"—which consisted of provisions forbidding emigration and maritime commerce— were either deleted or moved to the statute "interrogating spies" (*panjie jianxi*).[78] Such revisions left the "law of control posts" chapter "changed beyond recognition" in the words of one scholar because they effectively decoupled commerce from security.[79]

Though formulated during the dynasty's final years, these legal reforms survived in another guise for nearly two decades after the 1911 Revolution and continued defining the judicial treatment of smuggling in China. After the fall of the Qing, the Provisional Government of the Republic retained its predecessor's legal codes as a temporary expedient. For the new Republican Criminal Code, it adopted the fully drafted but unpromulgated Qing criminal code as the New Criminal Code Temporarily in Force (Zanxing xin xinglü) by making some minor alterations to the text.

For the new Republican Civil Code, it retained the civil provisions of the revised Qing Code as the Code Currently in Use (Xian xinglü) by stripping the criminal portions and leaving the "civil portions in effect" (*minshi youxiao bufen*).[80] Leaders of the Provisional Government initially planned to replace both codes inherited from the Qing, but political instability delayed the realization of this goal until 1928. Thus, while the Criminal Code of the Great Qing Currently in Use was dropped, many of Shen's other revisions effectively remained in force until the start of Nationalist rule. Neither the pre-1928 Republican Criminal Code nor the Civil Code directly addressed duty evasion, but the former explicitly specified penalties for trafficking certain commodities. Those caught selling or transporting opium, for instance, could be sentenced to two months to five years in prison and fined a maximum of 500 yuan.[81] Those caught selling or transporting weapons—including guns and explosives—could be sentenced to one to three years in prison or fined a maximum of 300 yuan.[82] Finally, those caught trafficking salt could be sentenced anywhere from two months to ten years depending on the amount in accordance with the 1914 Law Governing Punishment for Salt Smuggling (Siyan zhizui fa).[83] The late Qing and early Republican governments ordered Chinese nationals caught by the Maritime Customs for trafficking these articles to be remanded to local officials for prosecution.[84]

Successive legal reforms that began in the final years of the Qing thus effectively wrote out duty evasion from criminal and civil codes. Such revisions expunged laws that the dynasty had long ceased to enforce, such as prohibitions on the transport of certain commodities and on overseas travel. Yet the revisions also redefined smuggling more narrowly to address the carriage of specific contraband like opium, weapons, and salt. More importantly, they acknowledged—implicitly and explicitly—that international treaties had superseded many elements of domestic laws in regulating and policing foreign trade in China. Legal reforms that survived well into the Republic, then, essentially accommodated the prevailing practices of the treaty port system. These legal arrangements made sense to Qing officials in an era when tariffs were low and duty evasion was more of a nuisance against public order. Yet when duty evasion exploded and threatened state finances—as it did after 1928—policy makers, customs officials, and even the public complained that domestic laws and institutions proved inadequate in dealing with offenders and deterring would-be traffickers. A major goal of the Nationalists' legal reforms was redefining— and then expanding—the crime of smuggling, penalties for violations, and parameters for enforcement.

LEGAL PLURALISM TO LEGAL IMPERIALISM

Procedures for prosecuting Chinese subjects for smuggling were governed by Chinese laws that increasingly accommodated foreign treaties. Procedures for prosecuting foreigners for smuggling, by contrast, were governed directly by foreign treaties themselves after 1842. Extraterritoriality, though built atop Qing China's legally pluralistic order, was intended by Qing officials to apply very narrowly to foreigners at treaty ports. Yet as foreign powers asserted more expansive definitions of "foreign interest" from the late nineteenth century onward, foreigners on Chinese soil enjoyed virtual immunity from all Chinese laws. Even more worrisome for Qing officials were the increasing numbers of Chinese subjects in concessions under foreign jurisdiction. On paper, the treaties explicitly recognized the exclusive prerogative of the Qing government to combat smuggling in China. Article 44 of the British Treaty of Tianjin, for instance, noted that "Chinese authorities at each port shall adopt the means they may judge most proper to prevent the revenue suffering from fraud or smuggling." Article 14 permitted British subjects to "hire whatever boats they please for the transport of Goods or Passengers," but "if any smuggling takes place in them the offenders will of course be punished according to Law."[85]

Yet in practice, foreign merchants and consular officials frequently disputed contentions by Qing officials of when "smuggling" occurred and contested the penalties levied. Foreign consuls also believed that punishments levied by Qing officials violated consular jurisdiction and the principles of extraterritoriality. British authorities, in particular, conceded that their Qing counterparts were within their treaty rights to confiscate smuggled goods, but they asserted that British nationals could only be fined—that is, punished—by their own consuls. Qing officials and foreign consuls initially resolved disputes over smuggling in an ad hoc manner through mutual correspondences, but the growing volume of cases made the practice increasingly unwieldy. Moreover, the grumblings of foreign merchants about the arbitrariness and the lack of transparency in how penalties were imposed became increasingly vocal.[86]

To streamline the settlement of disputes, Robert Hart, working with the support of the Zongli Yamen, proposed a set of four rules in 1864 that permitted foreign merchants fined for treaty violations to publicly challenge their penalty. After British and American officials insisted on including four additional provisions covering confiscations, the final set of rules was promulgated in 1868 as the Joint Investigation Rules (Huixun chuanhuo ruguan zhangcheng). Originally applicable only in Shanghai but later in force at all ports, the rules outlined the procedures for adjudicating and penalizing foreign nationals accused of smuggling. Cases involving confiscations were adjudicated at the local customhouse, with a Qing official serving as judge and the foreign consul serving as assessor. Cases involving fines were adjudicated at the defendant's consulate, with the roles of the Qing official and foreign consul reversed. Formally, the customs commissioner attended the hearing to assist the customs superintendent. In practice, the former frequently served as the Qing representative in place of the latter. Both the Qing official and the foreign consul had to agree on the findings before any penalty—fine or confiscation—could be imposed with no possibility for appeal. If either side disagreed, the dispute moved up diplomatic channels to the Zongli Yamen and the diplomatic mission in Beijing for resolution.[87] The division of jurisdiction by penalty remained a central feature of the rules, even after the failed ratification of the Alcock Convention (1869) which would have formally recognized the practice.[88]

The Joint Investigation Rules were adopted at the same time other innovations in the treaty port system like the Mixed Court came into existence. Practices such as consular jurisdiction contained in the Joint Investigation Rules and Mixed Court rules were, as Pär Cassel rightly notes, entirely consistent with Qing legal traditions such as joint trials and personal juris-diction. Foreigners had to abide by domestic laws but could be punished by officials of their own nationality if necessary.[89] Qing officials in their deal-ings with foreign diplomats consistently stressed that this principle also applied to the Joint Investigation Rules. In an 1864 message to the Ameri-can consul Anson Burlingame, Prince Gong conceded that the rules were needed to resolve the "confusion and pertinacious disputing [that] have arisen between foreign merchants and our own officers." Nonetheless, he reaffirmed that "the right and power to punish all cases of smuggling by foreigners, either by fine or otherwise, is undoubtedly in the hands of this government."[90] In an 1878 exchange with the Marquess of Salisbury, Qing ambassador Guo Songtao echoed Gong: "What has been conceded in the Treaties . . . is merely that offenders shall be punished by their own national officials, in accordance with their own national laws."[91] In another exchange a decade later, Qing minister Xu Shoupeng explained his gov-ernment's position to U.S. secretary of state T. F. Bayard: "The jurisdiction to try and punish American citizens in China rests with the consul and the right to confiscate contraband goods under seizure rests with the [Chi-nese] customs authorities. If there be any case wherein some doubt and difficulty exist and which can not be decided without an investigation, then the rules of joint investigation should be appealed to."[92] From the perspective of Qing officials, then, China maintained exclusive preroga-tive to determine when a "smuggling" infraction occurred but outsourced the responsibility of punishment to the offender's consul in accordance with both treaty and tradition.

Qing officials had to constantly issue such reminders because foreign shippers, sometimes with consular support, frequently challenged their interpretations of treaty provisions. As with Mixed Court cases, Qing offi-cials doggedly fought to assert their privileges in joint investigation cases based on their understanding of the treaties. One of the most sensational incidents that tested the prerogative of the Qing government to effect a confiscation involved the British steamship *Carisbrooke*. On June 12, 1875, the ship anchored off the east coast of Hainan Island to discharge passen-gers from Penang and Singapore before continuing its journey to Hong

Kong and Xiamen. Soon after, two Chinese customs cruisers pulled alongside, and their officers boarded the steamship. Since it was anchored 70 miles away from the nearest treaty port of Qiongzhou and its passengers and cargo (which included twelve cases of opium) had not cleared customs, the *Carisbrooke* violated Article 47 of the Treaty of Tianjin, prohibiting foreign ships from "clandestine trade" at non-treaty ports.[93] Customs officials informed the captain of the *Carisbrooke* that the cruisers would escort the steamer back to Guangzhou to settle the matter. Initially obeying instructions to follow customs cruisers north, the captain later sailed for Hong Kong as he neared the British colony until the *Carisbrooke* was fired upon by one of the cruisers after receiving no fewer than three warnings to change course. With its rudder disabled, the steamer—along with the captain—was finally brought to Guangzhou.

During the joint investigation hearing convened the following week, both the customs commissioner and the British consul agreed that the *Carisbrooke* had violated treaty provisions. The customs commissioner invoked Article 48 of the Treaty of Tianjin, which permitted Chinese authorities to confiscate goods from vessels caught smuggling.[94] The British consul, however, urged mitigation of the penalty. Since the *Carisbrooke* regularly allowed passengers to disembark at Hainan for their convenience during its voyages between China and Southeast Asia, the consul argued, it was not willfully engaged in "smuggling." Meanwhile, the treaty port press—Chinese and English—reprinted testimonies from the case and weighed in with their dueling opinions. *Shen Bao* first described the *Carisbrooke* as "hiding smuggled goods" (*cangni sihuo*) and called the ship's discharge of cargo "smuggling" (*zousi*) in subsequent coverage of the case.[95] The *North China Herald* conceded that the *Carisbrooke* should not have anchored at a port not designated in the treaties but agreed with the consul that full confiscation would be disproportionate to the "technical" nature of the violation.[96] The case was resolved in May 1876, after it was forwarded to Beijing for negotiations between the Zongli Yamen and the British mission. Both sides reached an agreement whereby Qing authorities "confiscated" the vessel and cargo but sold them back to their original owners for 5,000 taels.[97]

A key issue in the *Carisbrooke* case centered on whether trading in an unauthorized locale constituted "smuggling." The Joint Investigation Rules, however, were more commonly invoked in other instances of smuggling, especially when a foreign shipper submitted a "false manifest" (*loubao*), where the cargo listed on the shipping manifest did not correspond to the actual cargo on board. Article 37 of the Treaty of Tianjin explicitly noted that such violations were to be penalized with a 500 tael fine. Foreign shippers, however, initially resisted being held liable for smuggling by their crew and passengers, arguing that a manifest could only be "false" if there were deliberate intent to deceive Chinese authorities from the outset. This was the issue at stake in the *Taiwan* case, the incident recounted at the opening of this chapter. The captain had been fined by the customs commissioner for presenting a false manifest when the actual amount of opium on his ship—including smuggled opium—did not accord with the stated amount of opium. His penalty was waived, however, since the original manifest was not willfully false according to the interpretation by the consul. After the case was forwarded to Beijing, both the Zongli Yamen and the British mission held firm to their respective subordinate's findings, and negotiations between the two sides dragged on for another four years. At one point, the Chinese Maritime Customs consulted two London law firms on the merits of the case, and both firms issued opinions supporting the Chinese position.[98] Finally in 1882, the British government agreed to settle the case by levying a reduced fine of 100 taels on the captain and accepting the Qing government's definition of a "false" manifest.[99]

Building on the precedent set by the *Taiwan* case, the Qing government in subsequent joint investigation cases successfully asserted that regardless of the shipper's original intent, any discrepancies uncovered between the cargo listed and cargo on board made a manifest "false." In 1883, the Zhifu customs commissioner secured a favorable verdict penalizing the captain of the steamer *Woosung* for presenting a manifest that did not list assorted uncovered cargo like matches, sapanwood, and shark fins.[100] In 1884, commissioners at three separate ports—Zhifu, Niuzhuang, and Fuzhou—also successfully employed the Joint Investigation Rules to fine British captains for presenting false manifests when they discovered smuggled goods including opium and sugar on their vessels. In each case, the commissioner levied a fine to mark the infraction but, with the superintendent's consent, reduced the amount to anywhere between 25 to 200 taels to demonstrate leniency for what they viewed as the "purely technical nature of the offence(s)."[101]

Other cases were settled even before a joint investigation hearing convened. In two separate incidents in 1884, for instance, a British and a German shipper agreed to pay a nominal fine (50 and 25 taels, respectively) to the Shanghai Customs in lieu of submitting to a joint investigation hearing for submitting false manifests.[102] Such out-of-court settlements, in fact, eventually became the rule rather than the exception. Foreign shippers found that they preferred paying a penalty up front rather than incurring the expense in time and money a formal appeal required. To take one year as a representative sample: of the 2,656 cases of fines and confiscations in 1885, none of the 180 cases involving a foreign national was settled using the Joint Investigation Rules. Individual fines for these cases usually ranged from 5 to 10 taels, though heavier penalties were levied for more egregious instances of smuggling.[103] For their part, customs officials also found that they were still able to hold foreign shippers to account for incidents of smuggling without resorting to formal hearings by threatening to withhold from shippers privileges such as allowing vessels to be cleared before all import duties were paid or loading and unloading cargo outside of business hours.[104] This out-of-court arrangement held true in subsequent decades, serving the interests of both foreign shippers and Chinese authorities.

The Joint Investigation Rules remained in effect until their formal abrogation by the Nationalists in 1934. By then, what was once an acceptable accommodation within the Qing Empire's legal pluralistic order had become an intolerable violation of the Chinese nation-state's sovereignty. Though infrequently invoked during their seventy years of existence, the rules nonetheless formed the legal basis mediating the reach of the central state in policing foreign trade. By splitting jurisdiction over incidents of smuggling, the rules effectively made administrative cases (i.e., disputes between the Chinese state and private parties) operate in a similar fashion as mixed cases. The prospect of foreign intervention in turn made adjudicating smuggling cases as much an act of *international* diplomacy as it was an act of *domestic* law enforcement. Conflicts over joint investigation cases thus embodied repeated efforts by the Qing to assert its treaty rights, as well as demonstrating the limits of those rights.

* * *

Throughout the late imperial and early Republican eras, patterns of illicit commerce on the China coast constantly shifted in response to the complex interplay among regulations, enforcement, and global trade. Each of these features was increasingly conditioned by the emergent international order that prized unfettered commerce over sovereignty for nations like China that ostensibly lagged behind Western standards of "civilization." The unequal treaties were crafted to ensure foreign access to Chinese markets with minimal restrictions and minimal taxes. Constraining domestic Chinese authority to achieve this aim created a host of problems for governance as well as other unintended consequences. Extraterritoriality that conferred legal protections from Chinese authority was easily and frequently exploited. Low tariffs made some forms of smuggling—and interdiction—more profitable than others. Foreign sojourners were not the only beneficiaries. Chinese smugglers proved no less adept at exploiting fractured jurisdictions for profit, essentially piggybacking on treaty privileges intended for foreign powers.

Meanwhile, changes in the legal order had profound consequences for defining smuggling and the parameters for suppression. For domestic laws, late Qing legal reforms whittled down the scope of illegal trade once expansively defined earlier in the dynasty. Such efforts updated laws on the books to match realities in practice, but they also narrowed the scope of smuggling to the trafficking of a handful of commodities. For treaty provisions, innovations like the Joint Investigation Rules were built atop Qing China's legally pluralistic order and thus accorded with Chinese legal tradition. But they further splintered domestic authority already under increasing strain during the dynasty's final years. All these legal changes endured in one form or another after the fall of the Qing until 1928, when a new regime sought to centralize state authority and expel foreign influence from China. Fighting smuggling played a pivotal role in realizing this ambitious agenda.

2

TARIFF AUTONOMY AND ECONOMIC CONTROL

The Intellectual Lineage of the Smuggling Epidemic

T
HE UNEQUAL TREATIES that shaped the contours of the coastal Chinese
economy—in both its legal and illegal variants—were defined by
two key features: the introduction of extraterritoriality and the deprivation of tariff autonomy. The former, officially abolished in 1943, embodied
China's "century of humiliation" and untrammeled foreign privilege on
Chinese soil. The latter, partially recovered beginning in 1928, receded in
historical memory and has attracted comparatively less attention since. Yet
in the decades after 1842, many Chinese viewed the recovery of tariff
autonomy as having equal importance to the abolition of extraterritoriality, if not more. Initially limited to discussions among senior officials in
the late Qing, the problem of tariff autonomy later spilled over into the
public arena and suffused popular discourse in the early Republic. The
topic attracted passionate attention because of the increasing realization
that it implicated many aspects of modern China's economy and sense of
nationhood. Tariffs, in particular, bore a fundamental relationship with
the modern Chinese experience, standing at the nexus of statecraft, sovereignty, and nationalism. In the official (and later public) imagination, the
loss of tariff autonomy had widespread repercussions for China. It limited
its revenues, confirmed its status as a semicolony (*ban zhimindi*), and left
its domestic industries defenseless. Tariffs, moreover, bore a direct, inverse

relationship with smuggling. Higher duties invariably raised the incentives for more trafficking while lower duties invariably lowered them. The absence of tariff autonomy after 1842 left many imports lightly taxed and made smuggling profitable for only a handful of commodities; its recovery after 1928 would transform this financial calculus as the Nationalist government slapped protective duties across the board and thereby incentivized smuggling along the coast. The tariff, Felix Boecking correctly notes, became "an important instrument of Chinese economic nationalism," a tool that would not only fortify government finances but also realize greater official control over the economy.[1] Thus, discussions of the tariff always encompassed more than just the tariff itself.

The explosion of coastal smuggling after 1928 was inextricably tied to growing enthusiasm for economic control among policy makers who assumed that an assertive developmental state could and should employ levers of policy to promote industrialization. The growing enthusiasm for economic control, in turn, was tied to the discursive transformation of tariff autonomy. Previous histories of China's quest to recover tariff autonomy have focused on diplomatic and political negotiations at the highest levels.[2] This chapter goes beyond such accounts by looking more broadly at changing opinions on the tariff among statesmen, intellectuals, and merchants from the late Qing through the early Republic. Discussions of "the tariff problem" (*guanshui wenti*) did not unfold exclusively at international conferences but also within the wider public. Growing interest in the subject reflected an intellectual shift that wove together abstract economic principles with the concept of national well-being. The legacies of these discussions endured well after 1928, and even 1949. Debates over the significance of the tariff consistently emphasized themes that dominated economic thinking throughout twentieth-century China to today: industry over commerce; production over consumption; and state intervention over free markets. Such discursive changes further reified the notion of more state control over the economy and thus animated official imperatives to fight smuggling. While its embryonic traces could be detected during the final years of the Qing dynasty, the ideal of state control over the economy became widely and indisputably accepted during the 1930s, at the nadir of the Great Depression.

How did the once-seemingly technical issue of tariff autonomy transition from a concern of fiscal statecraft among a narrow circle of literati to a symbol of national sovereignty for a wider public? How did a diverse group of policy makers, intellectuals, and industrialists come to subscribe to the ideals of greater economic control by the state? To answer these questions and uncover the intellectual roots of the smuggling epidemic, this chapter offers an overview on the evolution in the thinking and discussions about the tariff as well as attitudes toward the role of the state in the economy from the late Qing through the early Republic. It then explores how Nationalist China made tariff autonomy the cornerstone of its ambitious state-building agenda during the Nanjing Decade and how the ideal of economic control informed the new regime's introduction of higher duties and stricter regulations that together laid the foundations for a developmental state. The tariff thus underwent successive changes in both the official and popular imagination, from a tool of statecraft in the late Qing, to a symbol of national sovereignty in the early Republic, to a prerequisite of economic control under Nationalist rule. Understanding this shift is critical to understanding China's avid pursuit of restrictive economic policies throughout the twentieth century. It ultimately sheds light on why the Nationalists (and later the Communists) opted for an interventionist foreign trade regime, prohibitive tariffs, and harsh enforcement—even as such policies strictly disciplined private consumption and greatly incentivized smuggling as never before. The war on smuggling, in other words, was motivated by a long-standing, overriding desire to exercise official control over foreign trade to satisfy multiple—and competing—imperatives.

LITERATI DISCUSSIONS IN THE LATE QING

By the early twentieth century, many Chinese critics looking back at the unequal treaties bemoaned the seeming carelessness with which Qing diplomats had acquiesced to the demands of their foreign counterparts.

Whether helpless, hapless, or ignorant, Qing officials too easily conceded what later critics believed to be the sine qua non of a modern state—unrestricted, territorialized sovereignty. As one Chinese academic wrote in 1930, "Without knowing what it was doing, the Manchu Dynasty concluded, one after another, these one-sided treaties and signed away China's birthrights without getting any adequate advantage in return."[3] Such criticisms had some merit, for the dynasty initially did not foresee the repercussions of its treaty concessions. Correspondence from negotiations leading to the Treaty of Nanjing reveals how Qing negotiators were indeed unfamiliar with how trade with the West had been conducted under the now-defunct Canton system.[4] By granting extraterritoriality, surrendering tariff autonomy, and accepting the most favored nation provision, Qing officials inadvertently created the legal edifice that constrained Chinese authority well into the twentieth century.

What critics overlooked (or even forgot) was that the dynasty had understandable reasons for making these concessions. Extraterritoriality was consistent with long-prevailing Qing legal traditions. The 5 percent ad valorem tariff had antecedents in existing Qing practices.[5] Hans van de Ven, drawing from findings by Chinese scholars, rightly points out that the new treaty tariffs were in line with the old tariffs Qing maritime toll-houses levied on imports.[6] Moreover, the new tariffs still satisfied two of the Qing negotiators' goals at the time—maximizing revenues on bulk exports by raising duties on tea, rhubarb, and silk and maintaining access to luxury goods by lowering tariffs on ginseng, clocks, and satin.[7] Such thinking reflected the view that customs duties were the property of the *court* rather than the revenues of the *nation*, which the Qing *empire* was decidedly not. Also, whatever confusion or ignorance that did exist was not exclusive to the Chinese side: British negotiators, too, had difficulties ascertaining the duties their own merchants paid. Finally, Qing concessions stemmed not just from ignorance but also from differences in assumptions. In contrast to their British counterparts, Qing officials believed that the new treaty arrangements would not lead to a rise in the overall volume of foreign trade but channel it through five treaty ports instead of one.[8] If the relatively minuscule commercial traffic with the West was to remain confined to specified ports, Qing officials undoubtedly reasoned, why should new tariffs that more or less approximated old tariffs be of any concern?

Even if the dynasty was initially naïve in surrendering China's tariff autonomy, it pressed to renegotiate for recovery at the earliest opportunity. In 1868, the Zongli Yamen announced its intention to exercise Article 27 of the 1858 Treaty of Tianjin, which called for tariff revision every ten years.[9] Tough negotiations between Qing and British diplomats from early 1868 through late 1869 finally yielded the so-called Alcock Convention. The agreement would not have restored full tariff autonomy to China but would have, among other things, increased export duties on silk and import duties on a handful of commodities including opium. It would have permitted the appointment of a Chinese consul in Hong Kong, who would presumably help coordinate anti-smuggling efforts in the Pearl River Delta. Finally, it would have also formally recognized the Joint Investigation Rules, which had just been introduced at all treaty ports. In China, the Zongli Yamen accepted the convention and hailed its ratification as a diplomatic victory. In Great Britain, however, merchants resisted the convention and, to the dismay of Chinese officials, scuttled it.[10] While several provisions of the aborted Alcock Convention were realized piecemeal through subsequent diplomatic negotiations, the tariff itself remained unchanged until the turn of the twentieth century, when China's deteriorating fiscal position finally forced the issue. Foreign powers did not consent to tariff revision when the Qing sought to pay the 250 million tael indemnity from the First Sino-Japanese War (1894–1895), but they did finally agree to a modest adjustment for the Qing to fund the 450 million tael indemnity after the Boxer Uprising (1899–1901). Other adjustments followed in 1918 and 1922, but they were made only to account for fluctuations in exchange rates and bring rates back to the 5 percent ad valorem treaty tariff.

Meanwhile, China's changing relationship with the global economy brought a concomitant shift in fundamental notions of state-economy relations that laid the first intellectual foundations for more assertive economic statecraft. In the century after the First Opium War, according to

Wen-hsin Yeh, Chinese society experienced a "material turn" whereby issues of economy came to occupy a central concern in governance and everyday life. This shift in economic sentiment represented a marked departure from the past, when longtime Confucian precepts advocated a limited role for the state and emphasized the importance of social relations over commercial activities. Both the Ming and early Qing dynasties levied many taxes and operated monopolies on strategic commodities. Yet neither significantly interfered with market freedom. Nor did they strictly enforce existing regulations on commerce, often preferring to delegate such responsibilities to mercantile organizations and other local elites. If some eighteenth-century officials like Chen Hongmou already believed that the government *should* take a more active role for the sake of promoting the people's "livelihood" (*minsheng*), then their nineteenth-century counterparts believed that the government *must* do so for the sake of ensuring China's survival within an unforgiving world of competing empires.[11] Indeed, an important tenet of post–Opium War statecraft held that regulating and promoting commerce was simply another avenue for the empire (and later nation) to resist foreign imperialism as part of a broader "war of commerce" (*shangzhan*).[12] Originally coined by the eminent official Zeng Guofan in an 1869 memorial, the slogan from the mid-1880s onward "became fashionable and popularly accepted, regarded almost as a magic wand that might tide the country over a period of national crisis."[13]

It was within this new intellectual milieu that late Qing thinkers began to recognize the critical role of tariffs in protecting the economy as they took a hard look at the dynasty's condition and interrogated the economic foundations of Western power. In the imagination of these literati, China was poorly equipped to wage the war of commerce without an adequate tariff. Many recognized that tariff *revenues*—even if they were fixed by the treaties—were still sizable enough to fund an array of government expenditures, including big, expensive projects of the Self-Strengthening Movement like shipyards and arsenals. Yet there were growing concerns that tariff *rates* themselves were too low. Maritime Customs statistics began widely circulating among court officials and gentry alike after 1875, revealing persistent and growing trade deficits that made China's predicament legible and quantifiable. For an elite that was already uncomfortable with the growing foreign presence on Chinese soil, the numbers offered the first tangible and irrefutable evidence of Chinese wealth "leakage" (*louzhi*) into Western hands. In their memorials, correspondences, and diaries, officials and writers alike fretted about the unfavorable trade balance driven by the rise of imports like opium and cotton and the decline of exports like tea and silk.[14] This growing emphasis by statesmen on the centrality of commerce in statecraft also manifested itself in writings like *New Collected Writings on Statecraft* (*Huangchao jingshiwen xinbian*). The 1902 edition of this standard Qing guide to statecraft—unlike previous editions from earlier in the nineteenth century—was updated to include essays on foreign trade, tariff autonomy, and translations on political economy. As Susan Mann observes, such intellectual shifts represented yet another marked departure from past notions of state-economy relations.[15] Late Qing thinkers, in sum, no longer viewed the tariff as merely another tax to generate funds for the court but as a critical tool of statecraft that could promote, protect, and shape the broader economy.

A chorus of late Qing voices thus stressed the importance of tariff autonomy and expressed concerns over the repercussions of its absence for Chinese economic statecraft. Yet no one spoke more loudly than Zheng Guanying, merchant-comprador to the British firms Dent and Company (Baoshun yanghang) and China Navigation Company (Taigu lunchuan gongsi). A Guangdong native intimately familiar with the treaty port world and Western business practices, Zheng popularized the term "war of commerce" in his voluminous writings. He leveraged his extensive experience to become the most influential disseminator of economic concepts from the 1870s through the 1890s. The final edition of Zheng's most celebrated work, *Cautionary Words for a Prosperous Age* (*Shengshi weiyan*), was published in 1892, but his essays had already appeared in the decade before in *Words of Change* (*Yiyan*).[16] His thinking best embodied the material turn then sweeping the Qing literati.

Zheng in his many writings argued for prioritizing commercial wealth over military might as the key to escaping China's predicament. China's loss of tariff autonomy and control over the Maritime Customs alarmed Zheng, for they created the conditions under which Chinese merchants competed at a disadvantage compared to foreign counterparts. Besides calling for more Chinese staffing in the Maritime Customs, Zheng also called for more flexible tariffs that could better discriminate among different types of commodities for import based on their utility to the economy. Imports that were necessary should be taxed lightly or not at all; imports like luxury products should be taxed more heavily to protect domestic competitors; imports that were "without benefit" (*wuyi*) should be taxed more heavily still to discourage consumption by the people; and imports, like opium, that "harmed the people's livelihood" (*hai yu minsheng*) should be prohibited altogether.[17] Zheng thus advocated a policy of import-substitution whereby individual consumption was disciplined and subordinated to collective welfare: "Recovering our privileges, enriching our merchants, pouring surpluses into empty [coffers]—nothing is more important."[18] The pernicious effects of the flat treaty tariff and the treaty system, in Zheng's view, went beyond restraining the court from raising additional funds; they also prevented the court from adopting mercantilist policies to adequately defend Chinese commerce from foreign competition. More specifically, they militated against actualizing what later was a key tenet of economic control: leveraging international trade for domestic benefit.

The new shift in economic thinking was also prompted by ongoing efforts to look at economies beyond China and thereby contextualize the country's predicament. Zheng, for instance, highlighted Chinese weakness and Western strength by juxtaposing divergent economic policies. Extending his metaphor of commerce as warfare by another means, he invoked the Chinese classic *Art of War* in urging his readers to pay greater attention to the West: "Know thy enemy, know thy self. A hundred battles, a hundred victories."[19] Other late Qing writers quickly followed such calls. From surveying the late nineteenth-century international order, they became acutely aware of China's anomalous position as only one of a handful of countries still subjected to an externally imposed treaty tariff. As Chen Chi, another prominent Qing official whose thinking was profoundly shaped by the material turn, argued: "Tariffs are determined by countries themselves;

whether to tax or not tax, whether to tax lightly or tax heavily—they are all determined by the country's monarch."[20] Critics also argued that Chinese tariffs were at a disadvantage compared with those of foreign powers, implying, of course, that China invited competition with its low treaty tariffs while the West warded off competition with high self-determined tariffs. Such assertions were not entirely off the mark. In the forty years from 1870 to 1909, on the eve of the Qing collapse, China did indeed enjoy much lower duties on imports than those of major industrialized economies in the West (table 2.1). Even such figures, however, understate China's foreign trade dilemma. Since Chinese duties were assessed on a silver basis, the steady rise in the value of gold drove effective rates further below the nominal treaty tariff of 5 percent ad valorem. Moreover, such data show *overall* tariff rates; *individual* rates for specific commodities might be much higher. Zheng, for example, noted from his investigation of Western tariffs on certain commodities that "most reached 20 percent, others reached 40 percent; the highest reached 100 percent."[21]

China's perilous situation became even more unflattering when juxtaposed with that of Japan. Like China, Japan had ratified its own unequal treaties with the West that accorded foreign extraterritoriality and surrendered tariff autonomy.[22] Even after the Meiji Restoration (1868) brought to power a new regime firmly committed to a modernizing agenda, the treaties remained in effect until Japan could demonstrate a level of

TABLE 2.1 AVERAGE TARIFFS BY COUNTRY, 1870–1909 (%)

YEAR	CHINA	FRANCE	GERMANY	UK	U.S.
1870–1879	3.7	4.4	3.8	5.7	34.7
1880–1889	3.2	7.0	7.1	5.0	29.6
1890–1899	2.8	10.1	9.1	4.7	23.6
1900–1909	3.4	8.6	8.0	5.6	25.4

Source: Data from database provided by Michael A. Clemens and Jeffrey G. Williamson, "Why Did the Tariff-Growth Correlation Change After 1950?" *Journal of Economic Growth* 9, no. 1 (2004): 5–46.

"civilization" to the satisfaction of Western powers. Treaty revision quickly became an overriding foreign policy objective for Meiji Japan, impelling its leaders to refashion the country's legal codes and other institutions along Western lines.[23] Indefatigable efforts finally bore fruit decades later, after Japan's spectacular victory in the First Sino-Japanese War in 1895 and successful abrogation of the unequal treaties in 1899.[24]

Japanese success placed Chinese failure in stark relief and made a distinct impression on many late Qing thinkers. He Ruzhang, the first Qing resident minister to Japan, from 1876 to 1880, was among a handful of Qing officials who fully appreciated the ramifications of Japanese efforts at treaty revision and quickly diagnosed that the two countries suffered "fundamentally from the same illness" (*benshu tongbing*) under the treaty system. Yet He also shared his contemporaries' view that the persistence of extraterritoriality and the absence of tariff autonomy were not equally problematic. The former was certainly a growing irritant in diplomatic relations, yet the latter was already a crippling fetter to imperial finances. "Tariff autonomy," He noted, "is bound with the entire kingdom's life and death; one cannot be too cautious [with respect to this matter]."[25] Liang Qichao, the reformer-turned-writer, echoed He's emphasis on the importance of the tariff for Chinese finances. More critically for Liang, the continued deprivation of tariff autonomy condemned China to the status of a "small country" (*xiaoguo*).[26] China's lingering semicolonialism, once considered a marker of difference between East and West, was now confirmed as a condition exclusive to weak countries. The lack of control over its own tariffs, in the eyes of late Qing critics like Liang, was but one of many symbols of Chinese inferiority on the international stage.

Other disasters compounded China's humiliation during the Qing dynasty's waning days. To fund the crushing indemnity stipulated by the Boxer Protocol (1901), the hapless court transferred management of customhouses outside treaty ports to the Maritime Customs Service. The unequal treaties handcuffed China's fiscal options by precluding raising import duties for revenues. Further surrender of Chinese sovereignty and wealth only highlighted the intractable problems stemming from the inflexible tariff. As Benjamin Schwartz argues, late Qing intellectuals were obsessed with uncovering Western foundations of "wealth and power." This quest assumed new urgency at the turn of the twentieth century, when it appeared that China would be overwhelmed and dismembered in the relentless social Darwinist struggle for survival.[27] China, it was clear to many observers, would not be long for this world without weapons like the tariff.

Decades before the fall of the Qing dynasty, then, many intellectuals already recognized the necessity of a more active state role in managing foreign trade as they grappled with repercussions stemming from China's loss of tariff autonomy. Keeping in mind the examples of the West (and later Japan), they discerned the treaty tariff's pernicious effects beyond court finances to include domestic industries and even Chinese sovereignty. Despite prescient warnings, late Qing intellectuals could not fully translate their calls for change into concrete policy. The continuation of the treaty system, the deterioration of China's geopolitical position, and the conservatism of the Qing court all made the recovery of tariff autonomy difficult, if not impossible. Nor did these writers speak in a unified voice on the subject or come to a consensus on possible solutions. Yet their observations were not entirely made in vain. Indeed, late Qing critiques of China's tariff anticipated those of early Republican statesmen and dovetailed with popular expressions of nationalism in the early twentieth century. Discussions over the tariff soon moved into the mainstream.

PUBLIC DEBATES IN THE EARLY REPUBLIC

Late Qing intellectuals viewed tariff autonomy as an essential weapon absent from China's arsenal. Their early Republican counterparts took this sentiment one step further, arguing that tariff autonomy was an inalienable attribute of the nation-state. The financial fallout from the disastrous First Sino-Japanese War and the Boxer Uprising remained fresh in the minds of many Chinese. Yet it was in the aftermath of World War I (1914–1918) that the issue of tariff autonomy was dramatically thrust to the forefront of public consciousness. At the Paris Peace Conference (1919) to determine the fate of Europe and its colonies worldwide, Chinese diplomats pressed for abrogation of the unequal treaties in recognition of their country's contribution to the Allied Powers' war effort. Spirits and expectations were initially high. Yet in a bitter blow to both the Chinese delegation and the Chinese public who closely followed the talks, the Allies opted instead to transfer German colonial possessions in China to Japan and retain key provisions of the unequal treaties.[28]

The Allies, however, did agree to a minor tariff adjustment (the first since 1902) and to initiate discussions on abrogating the treaties. At the Washington Naval Conference (1921–1922), foreign powers consented to another minor tariff adjustment and outlined steps for restoring China's tariff autonomy. At the Beijing Special Tariff Conference (1925–1926), they assented to a 2.5 percent surtax on foreign goods. Most importantly, they also agreed to an increase in duties starting on January 1, 1929, once China abolished the *lijin* (i.e., domestic transit tax).[29] Republican Chinese diplomats, who represented China's de jure central government, had no de facto authority beyond Beijing and were thus unable to effect changes to satisfy foreign demands for treaty revision. Moreover, the Beijing government under the control of the warlord Feng Yuxiang, who hosted the conference, was soon ousted by a rival warlord, thereby creating a leadership vacuum at the top. The conference adjourned inconclusively on June 10, 1926, without any agreement. It marked the last attempt by China to revise the unequal treaties through multilateral diplomacy.[30]

While tariff autonomy was negotiated on the diplomatic table, it was also hotly debated in the public arena. Discussions surrounding the unequal treaties were integral to the formation of Chinese nationalism in the early twentieth century, and the issue of tariff autonomy—a pillar of the treaty port order—was soon linked to the welfare of the nation in the popular imagination.[31] On the streets, demonstrations like the May Fourth Movement (1919) and the May Thirtieth Movement (1925) targeted foreign imperialism as well as its many manifestations, including the continued deprivation of China's tariff autonomy. In print, neologisms such as China's "tariff problem" and "tariff autonomy" (*guanshui zizhu*) soon became frequently discussed topics. Newspapers filed a steady stream of dispatches on negotiations in Paris, Washington, and Beijing. Magazines, from middlebrow weeklies like *Eastern Miscellany* (*Dongfang zazhi*) to trade journals like *Bankers Weekly* (*Yinhang zhoubao*), subjected Chinese tariffs to detailed analyses and proffered endless opinions on ways tariff autonomy could be recovered. While the abolition of extraterritoriality attracted intense public passions because of its everyday visibility, the recovery of tariff autonomy seemed tantalizingly more realizable. The former required China to revamp its laws and institute a "modern" (or Western) legal system, which required time and resources. The latter, by contrast, simply required the consent of the international community, an ostensibly easier goal that could be immediately achieved through diplomacy.

Widespread coverage of the tariff problem in the popular press varied in tone. Some writings, channeling the rising passion of Chinese nationalism, denounced the vestigial fetters of the treaty tariff and its broader consequences for national development. The inaugural article of the magazine titled simply *The Tariff Problem*, for instance, angrily raised rhetorical questions that tied China's woes to the specter of foreign imperialism and the absence of tariff autonomy: "The decline of our country's foreign trade; the depression of our domestic industry and commerce; the difficulty of our people's livelihood; the poverty of our national economy . . . are they not due to our lack of autonomy over tariffs?"[32] Other writings, meanwhile, echoed the arguments put forth by late Qing writers and implicitly endorsed their logic from a generation earlier. But now in the age of popular media, such arguments were amplified for a much wider, more appreciative public. The article "Tariff Autonomy" by Li Pei'en [Baen E. Lee], for instance, was part of a 1925 special issue of *Eastern Miscellany* devoted to covering ongoing negotiations at the Beijing Conference and one of many writings by public intellectuals who identified the indisputable link between tariff autonomy and national welfare.[33] The article bemoaned the treaty tariff's lack of reciprocity and flexibility that left Chinese tariffs much lower compared to those of other nations—the very same flaws late Qing literati singled out. It then conceded that the recovery of tariff autonomy might lead to more smuggling, especially by foreigners exploiting their privileged status to remain beyond the jurisdiction of Chinese law. But such a scenario, Li argued, would simply mark a continuation of a chronic but manageable problem.[34] Although Li was one of the few writers who actually addressed the potential for more illegal trade, his article—and many others like it—illustrated how aspirations for Chinese tariff autonomy were integral to expressions of Chinese nationalism. Tariff autonomy was simply too important for the imagined community and the economic health of the Chinese nation. Its recovery was a worthy goal to pursue, even in the face of unwanted consequences like more smuggling.

Along with newspapers and magazines, books on the tariff problem also reached a broad readership. Blending concepts from Western economics, attention to Chinese history, and notions of international sovereignty, these books buttressed calls for China's recovery of tariff autonomy with raw data exposing the many ways low tariffs harmed the nation's finances and industries. Trade statistics that once alerted the late Qing literati to China's precarious position were now presented to—and consumed by—a wider public able to appreciate the significance behind the numbers. During the opening rounds of the Beijing Conference in the fall of 1925, for instance, the Commercial Press took out full-page advertisements promoting its lineup of titles, highlighting widespread attention over the negotiations, and urging readers to keep themselves informed (figure 2.1).[35] As it turned out, publishers had little trouble catering to public demand for more information on an ostensibly technical subject. From the disappointment at the Paris Peace Conference in 1919 to the outbreak of the Second Sino-Japanese War in 1937, no fewer than twenty-five books were published in China containing the word "tariff" (*guanshui*) in their titles.[36] Perhaps the most popular version of *The Tariff Problem in China* was the 1923 edition by the economist Ma Yinchu. During the early 1920s, Ma was already a leading academic and adviser to the Bank of China.[37] Later, he played an important role formulating economic policy for Nationalist and Communist China. As an influential public intellectual, Ma was actively engaged in the tariff debate, penning articles in widely read publications and giving speeches around the country. His book argued for the centrality of the tariff in China's economy. As he declared in the book,

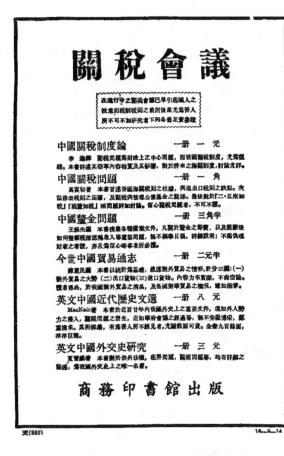

"The Tariff Conference

The ongoing Tariff Conference has already attracted the interest of fellow countrymen. Yet the origins and consequences of the tariff system is something we must study further.

On the Tariff System in China, Li Da (translator), Takayanagi Shōichirō

The Tariff Problem in China, Ma Yinchu

The Lijin *Problem in China*, Wang Zhenxian

Gazetteer of Foreign Trade in Contemporary China, Chen Zhongmin

Modern Chinese History: Selected Readings [English], Harley Farnsworth MacNair

Studies in Chinese Diplomatic History [English], Ching-Lin Hsia (Xia Jinlin)"

FIGURE 2.1

"Tariff Conference" Advertisement

This advertisement from the Commercial Press appeared in the middlebrow weekly *Eastern Miscellany* during the Beijing Tariff Conference (1925–1926). It urges readers to keep themselves informed on the tariff problem with six titles. The inclusion of a translated Japanese title and two English-language titles suggests that the advertisement is aimed at a cosmopolitan audience. It also suggests that the tariff issue, domestic taxation, and foreign relations were closely linked subjects in the minds of advertiser and readers alike.

Source: DZ, 22.20 (1925)

China's biggest problem after the Great War was economic. The most important economic issue, in turn, was public finance. And as for the most important public finance issue, Ma asked rhetorically: "How can it be anything but the tariff problem?"[38] While seemingly similar to Zhu's and Li's works in content, Ma's study was not aimed at foreign diplomats or domestic policy makers. Rather, it was marketed as a title indispensable for a republican citizen's education, aimed at informing the Chinese public on a technical subject with important but unseen links to the health of the nation. Reprinted and updated in at least two subsequent editions—in 1930 and 1933—the book exemplified the subject's enduring interest among the public.[39]

At the same time it was hotly debated in public, "the tariff problem" also became embedded within Republican political discourse. Indeed, politicians, diplomats, and warlords across China all paid lip service to the necessity of recovering China's tariff autonomy—regardless of their differences or allegiances. Abrogation of the unequal treaties was the one goal the many bickering factions could agree on. But perhaps no political figure in the debate proved more prominent or more consequential than Sun Yatsen. Ejected from government shortly after helping to establish the Chinese Republic, Sun became a peripatetic revolutionary, bouncing between China and abroad before leading a separatist military regime in Guangzhou in 1919. While his formal authority was limited during his lifetime, his influence proved immense after his death. As "father of the Chinese Republic" and founder of the Nationalist Party, Sun laid out the economic principles that later guided both Nationalist and Communist policies. Sun, according to William Kirby, bequeathed to his successors a vision of a state-run economy and "a commitment to the rapid and contemporaneous development of heavy industry."[40] Foreign investment was critical to realizing this vision. Sun saw foreign capital, properly supervised by a sovereign, developmental state, as offering what one writer later called "a quick fix, a means to overcome the shortage of technology and wherewithal on the road to a modern yet economically just society."[41]

Also critical to realizing this vision of an industrial China governed by a developmental state was the recovery of tariff autonomy, which defined both Sun's political career and political thinking. Sun, for instance, sparked an international crisis in 1923 when he and his followers threatened to seize the Guangzhou Customs and claim Guangdong's pro rata share of customs revenues. Although the crisis was eventually defused without any meaningful gains to Sun, his confrontation with foreign powers won him widespread plaudits and laid the foundations for the Nationalists' eventual rejuvenation.[42] Sun then elaborated on the importance of tariff autonomy in his famous 1924 lectures "Three Principles of the People" (San min zhuyi). In Sun's view, China by the early 1920s was threatened by "economic oppression" (*jingji de yapo*; i.e., foreign penetration in Chinese economic life), which was pervasive and "even more pernicious because it was more difficult to identify."[43] Economic oppression made China a "hypercolony" (*cizhimindi*), a term Sun coined to describe how the country was "not the colony of one country but all" (*zuo geguo de zhimindi*) and its people were "not the slaves of one country but all" (*zuo geguo de nuli*).[44] Besides domination of key economic sectors and Chinese institutions—namely industry, finance, banking, transportation, and the Maritime Customs—foreign economic oppression was also exercised through continued enforcement of the low treaty tariff that undercut Chinese goods and devastated domestic industries.[45]

But while dire, China's dilemma did have one remedy that was confirmed by the historical experience of other industrialized nations. "Now how do other countries meet foreign economic oppression," Sun asks, "and check the invasion of economic forces from abroad?" The answer, of course, was the tariff. The United States, which Sun offered as an example, moved quickly from an agricultural to an industrialized nation by warding off European competition with a protective tariff. Viewed in this light, the tariff was an indispensable tool of industrialization. As Sun concluded: "Just as forts are built at the entrances of harbors for protection against foreign military invasion, so a tariff against foreign goods protects a nation's revenue and gives native industries a chance to develop."[46] Sun not coincidentally employed a martial metaphor consonant with the "war of commerce" slogan. Although certainly informed by Western ideas as well as changing circumstances in China and the world during the early twentieth century, his own thinking had antecedents in the late nineteenth century. His economic program—which called for employing mercantilist policies to nurture modern industry and was almost treated as gospel by successors—thus bore the indelible mark of ideas from a previous generation of late Qing thinkers.[47] More importantly, Sun's influence proved long-lived in Nationalist ideology, with his calls for more protective tariffs and reassertion of Chinese control over the Maritime Customs forming the core of the Nationalists' policy agenda.[48] And years after Sun died and the unequal treaties were abolished, Nationalist leader Chiang Kai-shek in his memoir still pointed to the deprivation of tariff autonomy as the root of modern China's economic woes.[49]

Finally, another important party in the "tariff problem" debate was Chinese merchants. Unlike politicians and intellectuals, whose interest in the tariff was intensely passionate but still abstract, merchants had a direct, tangible stake in the issue. Late nineteenth-century businessmen like Zheng Guanying had already voiced support for tariff revision. Their early twentieth-century heirs continued this campaign by organizing to influence public policy. A notable example of such elite activism was the formation of the Society for Promotion of Tariff Reciprocity (Zhuzhang shuifa pingdeng hui) in 1918. Initially founded to press China's claims at the Paris Peace Conference, the society boasted leaders such as Zhang Jian, the prominent industrialist who assumed Zheng's role as China's philosopher-businessman, calling public attention to the clear and present danger of wealth "leakage," and Zhu Baosan, chairman of the Shanghai Chamber of Commerce. Other chambers of commerce in Shanghai, Beijing, Tianjin, Hankou, and cities across China soon voiced their support for the society. "Fearful of letting this opportunity forever lost" in the heady atmosphere leading to the conference, representatives prepared a telegram urging President Woodrow Wilson to "uphold justice" by lending American support for Chinese grievances.[50] Such efforts, of course, ultimately ended in disappointment, but they reflected the breadth and depth of mercantile interest in the tariff problem. Moreover, mercantile interest remained undiminished in the next decade and followed a developmental trajectory mirroring that of broader conversations about the tariff: what was once a topic of discussion within a small, educated circle was now transformed into a hotly debated issue among businessmen throughout the country.

Mercantile support for tariff revision was certainly widespread. But it was far from monolithic, for the degree of enthusiasm varied according to the impact of higher duties on the bottom line. Domestic producers welcomed the protective tariff as a relief from foreign competition. So did bankers, who believed higher customs revenues would bolster government finances and thereby stabilize the banking system as a whole. But importers such as trading companies and retailers—together with foreign companies— naturally dreaded the fallout from higher tariffs. Moreover, business support was far from wholehearted. In the mercantile imagination, tariff autonomy would not just end national humiliation and protect domestic industries but ultimately shift the tax burden away from Chinese businesses and toward foreign businesses. The latter would be required to pay more than the 5 percent ad valorem treaty tariff and surrender other tax-exempt privileges that offered them an unfair competitive advantage. Higher duties were also expected to offset domestic taxation. Since the late Qing, Chinese merchants complained of the hodgepodge of domestic taxes—local, provincial, or national—and how this proliferation not only impeded commerce but also fostered predatory tax farming that verged on confiscatory levels. Mercantile support for tariff autonomy, then, was conditional on the relaxation of domestic taxes, particularly the hated *lijin*. By the early Republican era, tax evasion and tax resistance was already widespread. When Nationalist China after regaining tariff autonomy proved tardy in abolishing the *lijin*—and even introduced new domestic taxes— higher tariffs only encouraged more mercantile evasion and resistance.

Taxation and nationhood are inextricably linked because the former "enmeshes [citizens] in the web of generalized reciprocity that constitutes modern society" and its benefits are shared and its obligations are borne by the imagined community of the modern nation-state.[51] As the exhaustive coverage in the popular press testifies, the problem of the tariff and the health of the nation became closely linked in the minds of many in early Republican China. Critics—writers, politicians, or merchants—did not view tariff autonomy as a mere fiscal problem for the government. The relative silence of such critics on the potential for more smuggling after the recovery of tariff autonomy was certainly a reflection of how the problem was well outside the scope of popular consciousness. Instead, they pointed again and again to the unjust deprivation of tariff autonomy as retarding the economic development of the nation. Diverse in tone and coverage, such voices expanded and popularized the critiques of late Qing thinkers. They both reflected and shaped the consensus that the tariff was the inalienable right of the Chinese nation unfairly taken away by a rapacious international community. But in contrast to their late Qing counterparts, early Republican critics saw their vision of a sovereign China in control of its tariffs move closer to reality with the rise of a new, assertive regime.

ECONOMIC CONTROLS IN NATIONALIST CHINA

China finally recovered its tariff autonomy beginning from 1928, although it occurred less through the implementation of conscious policies and more through the convergence of fortuitous events. The conclusion of the Beijing Conference in 1926 left in place an agreement to partially restore China's tariff autonomy and introduce slightly higher duties on a limited range of imports starting January 1, 1929—but there was no central government willing or able to implement it. Indeed, internecine strife among warlord factions only further fragmented this fragile order and exacerbated political paralysis. Meanwhile, the Nationalists under Sun Yat-sen, exiled in Guangdong and staving off collapse in the early 1920s, stepped into this power vacuum and rejuvenated their prospects by securing assistance from the Soviet Union, forging an alliance with the Chinese Communist Party and building a formidable army. Even Sun's death in 1925 and growing dissention between militarist and civil factions did not halt this remarkable turnaround. Now led by Chiang Kai-shek, the Nationalists embarked on the Northern Expedition (1926–1928) to unify the country by military force. Rolling through central and North China, they swept away rival regimes such as the moribund Beijing government before establishing a

new government in the wealthy Lower Yangzi region. As the party consolidated its gains in the last stages of the campaign, it also lurched right-
ward politically, turning on its erstwhile Communist allies, accepting the
nominal submission of most remaining warlords, and cultivating the support of urban capitalists and rural landlords.[52]

Nationalist victory nominally united China under a central government
for the first time since the collapse of the Qing dynasty in 1912. From its
new capital in Nanjing, the regime charted a very ambitious agenda to
continue late Qing and early Republican "Self-Strengthening" policies by
enhancing state capacity, modernizing the economy, and building a nation
capable of resisting foreign pressures. Yet this new government had to
operate in an unforgiving environment, meeting resistance from domestic
rivals still exercising de facto control in other parts of China as well as
foreign powers jealously guarding their vestigial spheres of influence.
The Great Depression, meanwhile, compounded China's economic woes
by weakening global demand for Chinese exports. Fortunately for the
Nationalists, they were able to expertly parlay their internationally recognized status as China's legitimate government. After years of making clear
their intentions to unilaterally abrogate the unequal treaties, they pulled
back their revolutionary rhetoric and launched a round of "revolutionary
diplomacy"—striking bilateral agreements instead of multilateral agreements which in the past often united foreign powers against China.[53] The
first breakthrough occurred in July 1928, when the Nationalists and the
United States concluded the Sino-American Tariff Treaty. The United
States henceforth recognized that "the principle of complete national tariff
autonomy shall apply" in China and assented to the introduction of the
Beijing Conference tariff schedule in 1929.[54] Riding the momentum from
this diplomatic coup, the Nationalists soon concluded similar treaties with
every foreign power save Japan, which consented to Chinese tariff autonomy only in 1930. But despite Japanese intransigence, China still steadily
raised import duties over several rounds between 1929 and 1934. One pillar long supporting the treaty port order thus finally crumbled under the
weight of shifting international conditions and the rise of an assertive
regime.

Higher tariffs proved an unequivocal boon to Nationalist finances. Successive tariff revisions raised average duties from 3.8 percent in 1928 (the last full year before tariff autonomy) to 27.3 percent in 1937, thereby yielding substantial revenues. Total duties jumped threefold from CN\$128 million in 1928 to CN\$385 million in 1931 before settling down to CN\$343 million in 1937. Import duties grew even more rapidly, rising fourfold during the same period from CN\$72 million to CN\$315 million before settling down to CN\$261 million in 1937.[55] Tariffs soon represented the largest and most dependable source of central government income, averaging roughly half of annual revenues throughout the Nanjing Decade. While much of the extra income was used to service foreign loans and remaining indemnities, greater stability in finances nonetheless enabled the Nationalist government to become a more modern fiscal state by tapping capital markets and funding its operations. In reviewing Nationalist China's tariff policy, Kubo Toru concludes, "It would certainly be no exaggeration to say that the Nationalist government's finances critically depended on the customs revenue."[56]

From one perspective, new policies better served the Nationalist Party's—rather than the Chinese nation's—interests by prioritizing government finances over the needs of many consumers and merchants who would invariably shoulder the burden of higher duties. Indeed, the new regime essentially appropriated for its own purposes the recovery of tariff autonomy, which by the late 1920s was deeply embedded within expressions of Chinese nationalism and visions of Chinese modernity. Yet the distinction between the good of the state and the good of the nation blurred in the minds of policy makers, many of whom believed that asserting economic controls, promoting national welfare, and creating a strong central state were entirely consistent, if not identical. Economic control, in particular, accorded perfectly with a core tenet of Nationalist ideology, namely Sun Yat-sen's vision of state-led development and distrust of private capital. So potent was its appeal that it represented one rare point of agreement in a party riven by political rivalries and policy differences. Despite their growing enmity, both the right-wing military faction of Chiang Kai-shek and the left-wing civil faction of Wang Jingwei wholeheartedly embraced economic control as the key to China's salvation.[57] The fractured party thus held a unified belief that industrialization should be guided by a central state "scientifically" coordinating capital, expertise, and resources. The creation of new state-managed enterprises and ministries like the National Economic Council (NEC, Quanguo jingji weiyuanhui) and the National Resources Commission (NRC, Ziyuan weiyuanhui) all embodied this abiding faith in the efficacy of technocratic governance. As William Kirby summarizes, "Nanjing was consumed with the industrial metamorphosis of national life, planned by a central—and centralizing—government. China would be industrialized and internationalized (for the two went hand in hand) through the mediation of the state."[58] So driven were the Nationalists by this imperative that they did not simply seek to guide the development of heavy industry or strategic industries like mining; they also sought to extend control over other facets of the economy like commerce. The new state, Wen-hsin Yeh notes, "assumed new functions, expanded its power, and established an increasing presence in the everyday lives of the people," thereby making China one of the most heavily regulated and tightly planned countries in the world even before 1949.[59]

Nationalist China thus opportunistically leveraged the recovery of tariff autonomy to meet its immediate financial needs and take its first step toward realizing Sun Yat-sen's dream of creating a robust developmental state. But while aspirations for a stronger official role in the economy could be traced back to discussions in the late Qing, inspiration for the ideal mode of economic organization undoubtedly came from ideas gaining popularity around the industrialized world during the 1930s. As the Great Depression discredited liberal capitalism and shattered dreams of restoring the quasi-laissez-faire order that prevailed before World War I, countries worldwide adopted variants of their own controlled economic systems (*tongzhi jingji*) by embracing a bevy of state controls as panaceas for economic ills: raising trade barriers, adjusting supply and demand, regulating labor and capital, and providing more government services.[60] Economists in later decades looking at this global turn toward protectionism concluded that the proliferation of "beggar-thy-neighbor" policies ultimately exacerbated the fallout from the depression.[61] But from the perspective of Chinese policy makers and thinkers, the controlled economy heralded the wave of the future, adopted by nearly every industrialized country from the Soviet Union to fascist states like Germany to even liberal democracies like the United States.

Nationalist China was no less fervently committed to constructing its own controlled economy than its global counterparts. But before the state could successfully guide the industrial development of the country, critics argued, it first had to secure strategic imports, find markets for exports, and amass precious foreign exchange. The recovery of tariff autonomy boosted government finances and prestige but did not immediately pull the Chinese economy from the nadir of the Great Depression. Critics offered numerous solutions for the ongoing crisis, and the diversity of policy prescriptions mirrored the diversity of contending voices. But the most influential voices came from "trade-balancers" (*maoyi lunzhe*), whose ranks included the economist Ma Yinchu, industry and commerce minister Chen Gongbo, and the industrialist Liu Hongsheng. Inheriting the late Qing effort to staunch China's wealth "leakage," trade-balancers linked China's myriad economic woes to its chronic trade imbalance.[62] Reviewing China's foreign trade since the dawn of the treaty port era, the prominent economist Fang Xianting (H. D. Fong) noted that goods responsible for the country's chronic trade deficit were "composed, not of capital goods indispensable to a country's industrialization, but of raw materials and manufactured goods for consumption needs, as well as of smuggled goods such as opium."[63] But beyond merely calling for a higher tariff to rectify this problem—as late Qing thinkers might have advocated—thinkers like Fang argued for state guidance through comprehensive control of foreign trade to encourage productive imports and discourage consumer imports. Indeed, in a world moving inexorably toward "control-ism" (*tongzhi zhuyi*) that had rendered obsolete the traditional policies of mercantilism and laissez-faire, trade-balancers believed higher tariffs were *necessary* but *insufficient* for China to redress its balance of payments and protect its domestic industries. China, in the eyes of such critics, needed a broader policy arsenal that extended beyond the tariff.

Trade-balancers accordingly envisioned an even more active role for the state in managing foreign trade by exercising "trade control" (*maoyi tong-zhi*), another economic program attracting worldwide popularity in the wake of the Great Depression. Although they did not widely use the term itself until the mid-1930s, trade-balancers had already advocated many of its prescriptions, including quotas, licensing, prohibitions, and exchange rate management. Technical expertise could thus be applied to more finely and effectively calibrate imports and exports. Other critics identified trade control as a subset of a controlled economic system but also contended that the former was the "prerequisite" for the latter. Making the case for more comprehensive state intervention in foreign trade, the academic and government official Li Lixia explained: "If we say that tariff policy is a form of protectionism and economic control is also a form of protectionism, then the former is indirect and limited, the latter is direct and unlimited. The difference between the two seems small but in reality is big."[64] The author of one newspaper editorial expressed his concerns over the ongoing national economic crisis and fully agreed that "*laissez-faire* policies were already unsuited to meet the needs of our current environment. . . . But the implementation of economic control begins with trade control."[65] Luo Dunwei, another prominent economist, echoed such sentiments, arguing that rigorously implementing trade controls and high tariffs was crucial "for the national economy to implement a protective policy" fostering heavy and light industries.[66] The notion that the state must first exercise control over international trade before it could exercise control over the domestic economy and thereby realize Sun Yat-sen's vision of an industrialized China was thus a consensus widely shared and frequently articulated.

Taking the first step to exercising control over foreign trade, the Nationalists sought to exercise control over the institution long responsible for regulating China's foreign trade, the Chinese Maritime Customs Service. On the eve of Nationalist victory in 1928, the agency remained one of the few Chinese institutions operating efficiently with true nationwide reach. It not only survived intact the collapse of the Qing but also enjoyed unparalleled political independence in the early Republic. The Maritime Customs formally remained an arm of the central Chinese state, collecting duties and enforcing trade regulations, yet it was still dominated by foreigners and served as China's de facto debt collector, ensuring that the country's tariff revenues repaid foreign and domestic loans promptly and efficiently. The rise of the Nationalists and the collapse of the Beijing government, however, marked the beginning of the end for this period of *imperium in imperio*. Riding the wave of its military victory in 1928, exploiting a leadership struggle within the Maritime Customs, and securing diplomatic support, the Nationalist government brought the agency more firmly under the fold of the central Chinese state through several reforms. First, it remade the agency's leadership by appointing Frederick Maze, nephew of Robert Hart, as the new inspector general, due in part to the cooperation he offered as Shanghai commissioner during the chaos of the Northern Expedition and the sympathies he professed to the Nationalists' cause. Second, it opted to retain foreign staffing at the agency's senior levels but pressed for new hiring policies—"based on principle[s] of equality"—that called for greater equalization of pay among the staff, quick promotion of more Chinese nationals into senior ranks, and an end to the recruitment of foreign nationals into the agency "except under special circumstances."[67] Third, Nationalist China granted the agency some degree of independence from domestic political interference but placed it under the jurisdiction of the Ministry of Finance's newly created Guan-wu Shu [Kuan-wu Shu] (Office of Customs Administration). Most importantly, the Nationalists expected the agency to directly serve the interests of the central state by considerably expanding the agency's mission. Starting in 1930, the Maritime Customs was authorized to police China's entire coastline, assume control of various tax bureaus, assert maritime borders, and effect seizures and arrests. The agency thus came to have an increasingly pervasive presence in everyday life during the Nanjing Decade, and it was no coincidence that the projection of central-level authority into Chinese society and economy occurred as the institution enlarged its jurisdictional reach and expanded its responsibilities.

Opinions on Nationalist China's efforts to subordinate the Maritime Customs were mixed. Some Chinese critics expressed dissatisfaction that reforms did not go far enough. Economist C. Y. W. Meng, echoing a common sentiment at the time, called for greater acceleration in the Sinification of the agency en route to a "'purely' Chinese Customs Administration."[68] Assessing the reforms decades later, the historian Chen Shiqi criticized them as "incomplete" and pointed to Maze's continuing links to the British government as a sign of the agency's divided loyalties.[69] Foreign critics were equally dissatisfied but for an altogether different reason—namely, they considered the agency already *too* "Sinicized." The treaty port press blasted Maze for demonstrating subservience to the new regime. Other observers made more sober assessments of the new relationship between the Nationalists and the Maritime Customs. In a 1933 confidential report, the British consul reported to the Foreign Ministry that while Maze was still successful "in preserving . . . the prestige and authority of the foreign element in the service and in maintaining its traditional efficiency," he admitted that the inspector general was now "first and last the servant of the Chinese Government."[70] Chang Fu-yun [Zhang Fuyun] the first director general of the Guan-wu Shu, who oversaw the Maritime Customs' transition from the Beiyang to the Nationalist regimes, echoed such sentiments, later recalling how the Maritime Customs under Maze largely furthered the goals of the Nationalists despite continuing to exercise some independence: "Sir Frederick Maze had loyally cooperated with me and supported all my measures for the reform of the Customs service."[71] Even would-be detractors noted how closely the government and the agency worked together. In his two-volume study *The History of Taxation in China* (*Zhongguo shuizhi shi*), the academic Wu Zhaoshen conceded: "Although the Customs is managed by foreigners and has an international character, according to Chinese law it may be considered as an administrative unit of the central government."[72]

Putting aside questions of where the Maritime Customs' "true" loyalties lay, the Nationalists were undoubtedly able to harness the agency's organizational cohesion, geographical reach, and operational efficiency for their benefit precisely because of its independence. With some notable exceptions, de facto foreign protection helped shield customs operations from domestic interference. Collecting duties and enforcing regulations certainly helped service foreign loans and indemnities while facilitating foreign access to Chinese markets, but they also ultimately helped extend and reinforce the authority of the Nationalists as China's central government. Drawing from the findings of Charles Tilly, Hans van de Ven observes that the Nationalists' appropriation of semicolonial institutions like the Maritime Customs was not unique; it foreshadowed postcolonial polities' appropriation of colonial institutions "to further their own self-interest and entrench their hold on power."[73] State-building for both the Nationalists and other postcolonial polities, in other words, did not occur de novo but used existing colonial institutions as a foundation.

From the top-down perspective of the Nationalist government, the benefits of its more assertive trade policies were clear, if still imperfectly realized. Higher tariffs created an unprecedented windfall, not only funding civil and military operations but giving Nanjing a significant financial advantage over its warlord rivals. Stricter regulations moved China closer to realizing economic control, then viewed as the epitome of economic modernity. Tighter management over the Maritime Customs helped China recover another piece of national sovereignty it ostensibly surrendered under the unequal treaties. It also ensured that an important institution now worked more closely for national (or at least Nationalist) benefit. The regime continued struggling mightily to contain successive foreign and domestic crises buffeting its rule, but new policies expanded its capacities and fortified its fiscal base enough to ensure its survival as China's central government through the Nanjing Decade and beyond.

From the bottom-up perspective of everyone else, however, the benefits of new policies were more ambiguous. For consumers, higher tariffs raised prices for scores of imported goods from luxury products to daily necessities. Such increases were not trivial. While *average* tariffs never rose above 30 percent during the Nanjing Decade, *individual* tariffs for imports rose much higher. Commodities including rayon, sugar, kerosene, and matches—all of which enjoyed strong, inelastic demand—were slapped with high double-digit and even triple-digit tariffs. Small-time merchants such as retailers and traders, meanwhile, bore the brunt of higher tariffs and economic controls, which were intended primarily to favor large-scale, capital-intensive domestic producers. The persistence of old taxes like the *lijin* and the introduction of new domestic taxes only compounded this burden. With their freedom to truck, barter, and exchange restricted in the midst of a global economic downturn, many businesses soon realized that they stood to reap handsome profits if they could avoid paying crushing duties and circumvent state strictures to undercut competitors.

New policies thus suddenly transformed the financial calculus that had underpinned smuggling since the introduction of the 5 percent ad valorem treaty tariff. Through much of the treaty port era, the handful of commodities that could be most profitably smuggled included narcotics, armaments, and salt. But as new duties were raised across the board, this range expanded to include many consumer and producer goods. Not surprisingly, the most heavily taxed commodities quickly became the most frequently smuggled, and their trafficking soon eclipsed the trafficking of traditional contraband. As quickly as smuggling spread across the coast, it also quickly overwhelmed Nationalist China's existing law enforcement capacity and represented multiple threats to the regime. At the same time that it deprived the state of critical revenues and menaced public order, the illicit flow of goods fundamentally undermined attempts to realize trade control and, by implication, economic control. New tariffs and regulations—introduced with the goal of strengthening the central state—ironically transformed smuggling from a limited, if chronic, problem into a serious threat that undermined the Nationalists' authority, finances, and vision of a self-sufficient China.

* * *

The smuggling crisis that engulfed the China coast and redefined the role of the state in economic life had a long, complex genealogy. Its most immediate catalyst was the twin introduction of higher duties and stricter regulations by Nationalist China after 1928. Yet the motivations behind these policies did not emerge entirely de novo but traced their roots to discussions in the late Qing. Since the unequal treaties were ratified in 1842, the tariff problem slowly but steadily eclipsed other concerns in statecraft. Once realized, tariff autonomy became a tool for a high modernist regime to generate critical revenues, discipline wasteful consumption, and subordinate institutions like the Maritime Customs Service—all to enhance central state authority. Nationalist China's assertive program of economic controls, then, represented both a departure and a culmination. On the one hand, it envisioned a strong central state using policies and institutions to guide an imagined community toward maximizing national welfare—an unthinkable goal before the late Qing. On the other hand, it sought to build up the economy to bolster national strength and resist foreign pressures—key goals of the late Qing's "war of commerce" and Self-Strengthening Movement.

Meanwhile, the links among the tariff, statecraft, sovereignty, and nationhood—so self-evident in the Chinese imagination by the early Republic—did not develop in a vacuum but occurred within broader domestic debates and changing international circumstances. What was once a topic confined to elite discussions steadily spilled out into the public arena and popular media. As the tariff question was continually debated by intellectuals, consumed by readers, and appropriated by political actors for different purposes, it ceased to be merely an esoteric fiscal tool and became a symbol of the Chinese nation's sovereignty. Yet while support for recovering tariff autonomy was almost universal, support for bearing the cost of higher tariffs proved far less so. As the persistence of coastal smuggling testified, not everyone was willing to shoulder the price of building a stronger central state by paying higher taxes or suffering more restrictions on commerce. High modernist visions of economic control, as subsequent chapters show, had to be achieved by state coercion through a battery of new laws, rigorous enforcement, and even violence.

3

STATE INTERVENTIONS AND LEGAL TRANSFORMATIONS

Asserting Sovereignty in the War on Smuggling

I N OCTOBER 1934, the Zhifu Customs received a hot tip. The otherwise unremarkable village of Zhugao off the coast of Shandong was purportedly hiding valuable smuggled goods. A search party dispatched to investigate quickly verified the claim after raiding several homes and uncovering the contraband in question: sixty-nine bags of sugar. Seeking to add to this already sizable haul, agents then scaled the walls of another home and discovered ten more bags hidden in the backyard. This time, however, they were met by incensed homeowner Yu Guangbo, who charged at the intruders with a pitchfork and seriously injured an officer when he tried to seize a handgun. Yu's resistance was undoubtedly fierce but ultimately futile. Outnumbered, he was quickly subdued, beaten, and bound. Left alone in the village temple, Yu untied himself the next day before reporting his harsh treatment to a local court and inaugurating a lawsuit that would not conclude for almost a decade.[1]

The raid on the Shandong village was violent but far from unique. During the Nanjing Decade, the Nationalist government kicked off a militarized campaign to counter the upsurge in coastal smuggling sparked by its own policies that transformed innocuous commodities like sugar into valuable contraband. Impelled by the urgency to protect tariff revenues, assert central authority, and realize economic control, the Nationalists turned to the institution long responsible for managing China's foreign trade and recently subordinated to better serve Nanjing's agenda. The Chinese Maritime Customs Service was given a new mandate to aggressively and proactively combat illicit trade along the Chinese seaboard. It took the fight to far-flung locales well beyond its traditional arena of operation at treaty ports, deploying faster ships, better weapons, and more intrusive technologies of surveillance. As this campaign unfolded and affected countless individuals, it did more than bring the central state and local communities into greater conflict; it also ultimately extended state control, both horizontally across the vast Chinese littoral and vertically into the everyday lives of people like Yu Guangbo.

This war on smuggling, however, required Nationalist China to employ more than just brute violence to ensure compliance. It also required Nationalist China to define and enforce its sovereign claims to regulate, tax, and police trade, thereby reifying its primacy as the country's central government. At the heart of this effort were new laws and regulations, which proliferated in tandem with stricter enforcement and growing smuggling. Customs agents—once tasked with limited powers to counter illicit trade—were empowered by new legal reforms that dramatically enhanced their policing responsibilities and permitted them to conduct ever-more intrusive searches on homes, businesses, and individuals. Meanwhile, the fight against smuggling had other second-order effects. As it delineated new boundaries of legal trade and sought to exercise exclusive prerogative to prosecute offenders within those boundaries, Nationalist China also challenged the legacies of nineteenth-century legal imperialism that continued to fragment domestic jurisdiction over foreign nationals and enclaves. Such efforts helped bring semicolonial China closer to becoming a modern nation-state and realizing greater territorialized sovereignty, even before the formal abolition of extraterritorial privileges and foreign concessions in 1943.

Drawing from legal records, customs archives, and popular press reports, this chapter traces the changing legal context that redefined the crime of smuggling and the treatment of smugglers, merchants, and other individuals during the Nanjing Decade. In particular, it examines three mutually reinforcing initiatives of Nationalist China's anti-smuggling campaign: expanding enforcement, contesting extraterritoriality, and policing maritime borders. It demonstrates how such efforts facilitated the expansion of central authority and Chinese sovereignty across the coastal frontier—even as they encountered widespread, intense resistance on the ground. Besides safeguarding government revenues, fighting smuggling also helped Nationalist China untangle the vestiges of legal imperialism by asserting jurisdiction over more smugglers and projecting policing authority into semicolonial enclaves. The findings of this chapter thus accord with those of recent writings that recognize the tangible, enduring accomplishments of the Nanjing Decade even in the face of foreign pressures and ineffectual administration that hobbled Nationalist rule. Indeed, legal transformations produced by the war on smuggling enhanced state power and produced a host of consequences—intended and unintended—for everyday economic life.

EXPANDING ENFORCEMENT

Almost immediately after the introduction of higher tariffs, officials and media across China reported an alarming upsurge in illicit trade. The dynamics of such widespread trafficking varied by geography. At major urban ports, smuggling on board steamships and railroads had long been common. Now officials uncovered an exploding number of passengers, sailors, and peddlers engaged in petty smuggling by employing all sorts of sophisticated "hides" and ways to misrepresent cargoes. Along the coast, foreign suppliers and domestic distributors forged elaborate and clandestine networks. Traffickers shuttled back and forth between China, foreign concessions, and foreign colonies trying to evade detection and ultimately taxation. Some used motorboats—known colloquially as "snake boats" or "puff-puffs"—which easily outran and outmaneuvered government patrols along the coast even as they were "laden with cargoes of sugar, kerosene oil, alcohol, matches, piece goods, and sundries."[2] Others continued using old-fashioned junks, which were slower by comparison but often evaded detection by hiding themselves within the sheer volume of commercial traffic plying the coast. Whatever the vessel of choice, smugglers were invariably—and formidably—armed. A report from the Kowloon commissioner filed just months after the introduction of new tariffs on an encounter between a customs patrol and smuggling junks underscores the ever-present dangers of interdiction:

> The revenue launch *Yuengshing* [*Yangcheng*] recently approached within hailing distance of three suspicious looking junks, when suddenly, without any warning, the junks opened fire at point blank range. The *Yuengshing* was struck at least 13 times by small cannon balls, rivet heads, and rifle bullets, the iron railing round the searchlight being carried away, life-buoy torn open, gig holed, funnel hit, door to engine room holed by cannon ball, and other minor damage done. Fortunately, there were no actual casualties among the crew—one sailor received a bullet through his cap. Next time, however, we may not be so lucky.[3]

Land frontiers, meanwhile, presented challenges of their own. Already poorly armed and poorly equipped, patrol teams faced uncooperative—or even hostile—local governments and communities that did not acknowledge the legitimacy of the Nationalists as China's central government. Problems with porous borders were exacerbated—or even abetted—by the indifference of authorities on the other side. On the Sino-Korean border, for example, a commissioner sent alarming reports detailing countless cases of aggressive Korean smugglers forcing their way past Chinese checkpoints and emboldened by the disinterest of Japanese border guards. Matters were even worse along the Hong Kong border, where smuggling had long been active but was now even more so. One typical report read: "Piece goods, kerosene, sugar, etc., continue to be smuggled by night practically all along these frontiers. The carrying is done by women under the protection of armed villagers who do not hesitate to fire on our unarmed staff. The individual amounts smuggled are generally small, but in the aggregate the loss of revenue must be considerable . . . With an unarmed and insufficient staff, it is impossible to take energetic measures."[4]

Whether transported by land or by sea, the illicit cargoes were unloaded, transported, distributed, and eventually sold in urban and rural markets. Smuggled goods were accordingly laundered and became virtually indistinguishable from legally imported and hence higher-priced goods. A customs commissioner in the Pearl River Delta later noted that while the various routes and methods of smuggling in the region had remained essentially unchanged over forty years, all had become "more openly used now since the tariffs are higher."[5] Although referring to his locale specifically, the commissioner's observation applied across coastal China generally.

In the face of this widespread smuggling, another customs official issued an ominous warning: "[I]t is no longer possible to check the tendency of this illicit trade to grow, and it shows every sign of swelling eventually to very serious proportions."[6] The surge in coastal smuggling quickly exposed the limited reach and efficacy of the Maritime Customs. In the face of traffickers more incentivized than ever to evade paying punitive tariffs, the agency was effectively outmanned, outgunned, and outmaneuvered. Within months after the promulgation of the new tariff in February 1929, Inspector General Frederick Maze submitted a memorandum to the Guan-wu Shu outlining measures to check the illegal traffic. Since higher duties had created "an impetus to the systematic evasion of fiscal obligations," he warned, the agency "should develop [its] Preventive Service to stop or check the serious organized smuggling now observable."[7] Shortly thereafter, Maze won the Guan-wu Shu's consent and dispatched an investigative team on what turned out to be a sixteen-month fact-finding mission into smuggling conditions on the China coast. Partly informed by team's recommendations, the agency quickly and completely transformed its preventive capabilities throughout the Nanjing Decade. Customs patrols updated their weapons to better defend against armed smugglers, trading old Winchester rifles (which were difficult to maintain and reload) for modern Lee-Enfield rifles (then the standard issue of the British army).[8] New stations were opened well beyond the immediate vicinities of treaty ports, forming virtual cordons along smuggling hot spots like the Pearl River Delta and the French concession of Guangzhouwan on the coast and the China-Burma border, the China-Korea border, and the Great Wall in the interior. A dedicated Preventive Service headed by a high-ranking preventive secretary was inaugurated in February 1931 to oversee anti-smuggling operations on land and sea, thereby addressing a common complaint that past interdiction efforts had lacked coordination.[9] The new department also created new channels of communication, collecting, analyzing, and disseminating the latest intelligence on "ingenious methods of smuggling" from every customs district across China.[10] While they never fully stamped out illicit trade, such efforts undoubtedly expanded central state capacity by projecting official reach and enhancing surveillance.

"The Customs Service," Hans van de Ven rightly notes, "embraced its new responsibility for the prevention of smuggling with great energy."[11] But this ambitious spirit was initially frustrated by existing laws on the books, all of which maintained a very narrow definition of smuggling. The legal framework defining smuggling at the dawn of the Nanjing Decade could be traced back to the Qing dynasty's twin efforts at legal reforms during its final years (see chapter 1). The revised and promulgated Criminal Code of the Great Qing Currently in Use had excised broad but anachronistic restrictions on maritime commerce from the old Great Qing Code. The fully drafted but ultimately unpromulgated Qing criminal code, which stipulated prohibitions on a limited number of articles, was adopted by the new Republican government as the New Criminal Code Temporarily in Force and remained in effect through the early Republic. It was finally replaced by the Nationalists in March 1928, shortly before the Northern Expedition concluded. The 1928 Republican Criminal Code updated the article on opium offences to include prohibitions of newer synthetic narcotics like morphine, heroin, and cocaine. The maximum prison term for individuals caught manufacturing, selling, or transporting opium remained at five years, although the maximum fine was doubled to 1,000 yuan.[12] Many of these provisions, with minor modifications, also carried over into the 1935 Republican Criminal Code.[13] At the end of 1928, the Nationalists also promulgated new regulations restricting the use of weapons to military purposes. Individuals caught manufacturing, selling, transporting, or buying weapons could be sentenced anywhere from six months to five years and fined a maximum of 500 yuan.[14] Finally, the Nationalists permitted to remain in force the 1914 law prohibiting salt smuggling promulgated by the old Republican government.[15]

At the dawn of the Nanjing Decade, Nationalist laws and regulations maintained late Qing and early Republican legal reforms that streamlined outdated restrictions from the late Ming and early Qing on maritime commerce and private trade outside official monopolies. They also left in place the late Qing reforms by the jurist Shen Jiaben that had eliminated domestic laws supplanted by international treaties, including the old statute prohibiting duty evasion. The 1928 Republican Criminal Code and other new regulations thus retained their predecessors' narrow definition of smuggling, which applied primarily to the trafficking of traditional contraband like narcotics, weapons, and salt. And just like their predecessors, they contained no prohibitions on general customs duty evasion or the smuggling of non-contraband. Although they were likely ignorant of this complex legal genealogy, customs officials in their final recommendations to the inspector general on the formation of the Preventive Service nonetheless confirmed this dilemma, noting that the trafficking of contraband was explicitly prohibited whereas the evasion of duties was not.[16]

In an era when the low treaty tariff prevailed and outsized profits could only be made from trafficking a handful of goods, the narrow legal definition of smuggling was not a particularly urgent concern for the state. But when higher duties across the board expanded the scope of profitable smuggling, this legal ambiguity created confusion among officials everywhere. Trafficking narcotics and weapons was clearly illegal—and remained so, even as the Nationalist government operated its own opium monopolies with criminal organizations like the Green Gang.[17] But what about trafficking otherwise innocuous, ordinary consumer products like sugar or rayon? A typical seizure off the Shanghai coast in June 1934 highlighted the crux of this legal dilemma. When customs agents intercepted two trawlers for trafficking, they confiscated and auctioned the illicit 500 bales of rayon but had to release the crew, as a newspaper reported, "in the view of the fact that it [was not a] criminal offense to engage in smuggling of this nature."[18] Prior to tariff autonomy, individuals caught transporting contraband like narcotics or weapons were often handed to local officials for prosecution, but duty evasion was usually punished with a simple fine or confiscation at the local customhouse. After tariff autonomy, customs officials throughout China who sought to hand over smugglers trafficking consumer goods to local officials for prosecution encountered many obstacles. When one customs commissioner in the southeast, for instance, sought to remand two arrested smugglers to local officials, the prosecutor balked, stating that "there were no laws by which he could deal with these so-called offenders." They were then transferred to another local official who accepted—but would not prosecute—them. Local officials left many such suspected smugglers languishing behind bars, "clearly at a loss as to how to deal with the offenders."[19] In the northeast, an official reported that the local police released a smuggler shortly after arrest on the pretext that they had no authority to inflict penalties, since no special regulations punishing smuggling existed.[20] Absent explicit laws, questions of how to deal with duty evasion—or whether it even constituted a crime—remained difficult to answer and created widespread confusion.

Existing laws proved increasingly inadequate to cope with the dramatic upsurge in smuggling. In response, the Nationalists introduced new regulations empowering customs agents to conduct more expansive, more invasive searches as well as restricting and monitoring the movement of vessels. As early as 1931, the Ministry of Finance ordered the Maritime Customs to prepare a uniform set of anti-smuggling regulations for implementation across China. Two years later, the government passed a resolution calling for more authority—"as soon as possible"—to be invested in the agency to effect confiscations, levy fines, and fight duty evasion by "treasonous merchants" (*jianshang*).[21] Officials often stressed the importance of an effective legal framework, declaring that adequate resources for interdiction and clear laws defining punishments "go together" (*xiangfu erxing*) in the fight against smuggling.[22] The need for stronger laws to adequately deter would-be offenders was another widely shared opinion. New regulations punishing smuggling would, a newspaper reported, "remedy the defects of ordinary laws and protect national revenue."[23]

An important product of these legal reform efforts was the Customs Preventive Law (Haiguan jisi tiaoli). Promulgated by the National Assembly in 1934, the new administrative law focused on enforcement by escalating the financial penalties for smuggling and clarifying the authority of the Maritime Customs to operate in areas beyond its traditional jurisdiction at treaty ports. To punish would-be smugglers, customs officials could now levy a "double penalty"—fines to mark infractions and confiscations of illicit cargo or even the vessel of transport itself. More importantly, the law introduced new procedural changes by expanding the timeframe and geography of enforcement. Customs agents were no longer limited to on-the-spot interventions at ports and their immediate vicinities. Instead, they were now authorized to search homes and businesses suspected of harboring smuggled goods, investigate records for evidence of past duty evasion, and levy penalties well after the initial incidence of smuggling. Agents were also authorized to interrogate suspects, witnesses, and other persons of interest in the course of investigations and building cases for prosecution.[24] Empowered by new legal sanctions, customs search teams fanned out across the Chinese seaboard to raid villages, effect seizures, and monitor riverine chokepoints. Extending the reach of customs agents had been a longstanding goal of both the Nationalist government and the Maritime Customs. Since the late 1920s, officials debated employing coastal raids as a tactic in fighting smuggling, going so far as conducting a search and seizure demonstration in early 1930 with the cooperation of the Chinese navy and local troops. The operation yielded sundries confiscated from homes and warehouses and led to the capture of motorboats and junks used in smuggling. Its success led senior officials in the Maritime Customs and the Ministry of Finance to laud the operation, with the former asking the latter to plan for more operations in the future.[25] Although strictly targeting smuggling, the new law helped the central state broaden its reach over many more individuals and communities and ultimately become a more intrusive presence in everyday life.

Promulgation of the Preventive Law dovetailed with ongoing legal reforms by the Nationalists, who sought to renew late Qing and early Republican efforts to expand the coverage of national laws and ensure that interpretation and execution were consistent with central prerogatives.[26] New anti-smuggling measures contributed to legal centralization by reinforcing the primacy of central authority. They also helped the regime extend its reach into areas where Nationalist control was weak or nonexistent by piggybacking on the Maritime Customs' extensive presence throughout China. The Preventive Law, for instance, explicitly stipulated that local authorities—magistrates, policemen, and soldiers—had to assist customs agents in any search and seizure operation. Such requirements, as instructions to customs officials explained, marked a change in operational principle: "The Customs can now quote the Law and demand the presence of the representatives of the local police and other officials, whereas formerly we were entirely dependent on the goodwill and whim of local authorities for such cooperation as they might care to extend."[27] The new law thus clarified the chain of command by subordinating local state agents to central state agents. More generally, it formalized and affirmed the principle that the center held the legal prerogative to demand compliance from the local.

Nanjing intended the Preventive Law to facilitate and legitimate anti-smuggling operations led by central state agents. While some local officials did evince greater willingness to cooperate shortly after the law's passage, many others remained ambivalent.[28] Indeed, the invasive and aggressive crackdown on smuggling faced significant bottom-up resistance. Whole communities persisted in their refusal to recognize the authority of the Nationalist regime as China's central government. Some local magistrates hesitated or even declined to help interdict smuggled goods. A raid on one rural town, for instance, was foiled when the local magistrate failed to cooperate, even though the Preventive Law obligated him to do so. Hostile villagers threatened and pelted the search party with stones before the magistrate finally relented hours later and offered some assistance. By then it was too late; the smuggled goods in question had disappeared.[29] Meanwhile, securing cooperation from local officials proved difficult in remote areas where formal state presence was virtually nonexistent. A commissioner of one frontier station, for instance, reported that law enforcement authorities were rarely available in his locale and that he often had to approach village leaders for assistance.[30] Yet because these leaders were nominated by the villagers themselves, another official noted, "they desire to maintain good relations . . . [and] it is natural that they do not wish to do anything detrimental to the interest of the villagers."[31] Not surprisingly, when village leaders declined to cooperate, heated—and sometimes violent—resistance often ensued. One report describes an operation conducted without the participation of a village leader: "The search commenced with three houses, quantities of smuggled goods were discovered, but the attempt to seize the goods failed, as a mob of the villagers attacked the searching party with poles and pelted our men with tins of pineapple. The party had to retreat in haste with only a few small packages taken as evidence."[32]

That resistance persisted despite new regulations clarifying lines of authority and mandating cooperation should not be surprising. The loyalties of local officials to the communities in which they were embedded were stronger than their loyalties to a distant national government. While many individuals, communities, and organizations willfully flouted the prerogative of the central government, new efforts by the state to collect taxes and enforce restrictions on movement also criminalized existing patterns of commerce and other behaviors. Also, by regulating and policing trade, the central state was effectively expanding and enforcing its regulatory spaces. In some instances, these spaces encroached upon the regulatory spaces of local governments, thus creating conflicts over jurisdictions. This was especially the case for rival warlords who remained outside of the Nationalists' base of the Lower Yangzi, acceding to Nanjing's de jure authority but still exercising considerable de facto independence. With much justification, they feared that the war on smuggling was a Trojan horse that would strengthen and extend central authority into their own localities. Shandong warlord Han Fuju reflected this attitude in a response to a 1936 request from Nanjing to help fight Japanese smuggling in his province: "Past experience shows that foreign aggression has been made use of [by the central government] as the means for crushing political rivals. With such experience fresh in memory, [we] cannot but view the present request for assistance of the local military and police in the suppression of smugglers with grave suspicion." Nanjing eventually overcame Han's reluctance only when it assured the general that the central government would protect his province from Japanese pressures. Han subsequently pledged his support and coordinated his army with customs agents on interdicting smuggling in Shandong.[33] The Nationalists reached similar accords with other recalcitrant local officials through tough negotiations and frequent invocation of the new Preventive Law.[34] These instances of conflict, therefore, did not necessarily signify the failure of the new regulations but represented byproducts of a more assertive central state projecting its authority in new ways and venues.

CONTESTING EXTRATERRITORIALITY

Fighting smuggling also helped the Nationalists better realize territorialized sovereignty, an essential feature of modern nation-states denied to China by extraterritoriality. Introduced through the many unequal treaties from the nineteenth century, extraterritoriality continued to constrain the jurisdictional reach of the Nationalists by preventing their agents from entering foreign concessions and prosecuting foreign nationals. Reversing this legacy of legal imperialism had been a long-standing goal of Republican officials and remained central to the emergence of Chinese nationalism during the early twentieth century.[35] Writing in the American journal *Foreign Affairs*, diplomat C. C. Wu argued that China being a "mistress in her own house is substantially the same policy that every independent and sovereign state has adopted."[36] The vision of civilized nations as sovereign equals on the world stage, scholars have noted, was partly a construction of nineteenth-century legal positivism, international law, and colonial encounters.[37] Wu's invocation of this vision highlights how thinkers in China (and elsewhere) have implicitly accepted the ideal of territorialized sovereignty despite the contingency of its origins. For the Nationalist regime, realizing unrestricted authority within national boundaries moved China closer to becoming a "normal" nation and thereby extirpated another shameful vestige of foreign imperialism.

Eliminating extraterritoriality held another important practical value beyond restoring national honor. Effecting a shift from jurisdiction over *persons* to jurisdiction over *territory* was urgent because ever-growing numbers of smugglers were exploiting China's fragmented sovereignty by evading arrest and punishment. Extraterritoriality by the 1930s had been abolished in other semicolonial polities but not in China. Legal protections for foreign nationals on Chinese soil, in fact, remained formidable. The most sensational cases of smuggling involved Japanese nationals and colonial subjects—Koreans and Taiwanese *sekimin* (registered people)—whose consuls frequently and aggressively intervened to protect them from prosecution.[38] Many Japanese colonial citizens, one historian notes, "were engaging in illicit activities under the umbrella of extraterritoriality."[39] Others employed their privileged status as a legal shield to ward off official Chinese interest in their operations.[40] Yet as many press reports and governmental correspondences attested, extraterritorial privileges were exploited by would-be smugglers of all nationalities, foreign and Chinese. Not surprisingly, Chinese officials often complained that Chinese authorities enforcing domestic anti-smuggling regulations were being prevented from operating within foreign concessions.[41]

Fighting smuggling, then, meant also fighting extraterritoriality. Even though extraterritoriality itself was not fully abolished in China until 1943, the war on smuggling helped the Nationalists chip away at the panoply of foreign privileges in the meantime. The Nationalists dispatched their agents into foreign concessions in an effort to assert exclusive jurisdiction over smuggling-related cases in China regardless of the participants' nationality. More importantly, the government reformed its laws dealing with smugglers with an eye toward winning foreign acceptance. In this sense, Nationalist China was not unique in assuming such efforts, as other semicolonial polities seeking to reverse extraterritorial arrangements often sought to reform their own legal institutions in response to "inherently contradictory" claims by powerful outsiders that "militated for legal immunity and jurisdictional protections for their subjects while at the same time basing their claims on a critique of the failings of local justice and the weaknesses of local state sovereignty."[42] In the case of China, foreigners have indeed justified the necessity of extraterritoriality on the perceived "barbarity" of its legal system or "instability" of its government.[43] To counter this discourse of deficiency, the Nationalists thus followed the lead of other semicolonial polities by pursuing a dual strategy of formalizing and monopolizing domestic channels of legal authority.

At one intersection in the fight against smuggling and the fight against extraterritorially were the Joint Investigation Rules, which at the start of the Nanjing Decade still governed how foreign nationals accused of smuggling were to be adjudicated and penalized. Upon their introduction in 1864, the rules were perfectly consonant with the Qing empire's legally pluralistic practice of dividing adjudication between Chinese and foreign officials based on the type of penalty. They had been infrequently invoked in subsequent decades since it was often cheaper and easier for merchants to pay a nominal fine in lieu of initiating a legal protest. But by the early twentieth century, the rules were an anachronistic relic for the Chinese nation-state, an unacceptable product of the treaty port order that continued to compromise Chinese sovereignty. With the recovery of tariff autonomy in 1928, the Nationalist government moved to roll back such legacies of legal imperialism by asserting its exclusive claim not only to police China's foreign trade but also to adjudicate potential infractions. In August 1931, the Maritime Customs notified its officials that "practically speaking, the Joint Investigation procedure may be said to be now in the discard."[44] In July 1932, the Nationalist government formally and unilaterally renounced the rules after fielding a query from the American legation.[45] Justifications for such actions were based on an expansive interpretation of the Sino-American Tariff Treaty, which restored Chinese autonomy over tariffs and "any related matters."[46] As Chinese foreign minister Wang Jingwei later explained, his government's interpretation of "complete autonomy" encompassed not just the right to fix tariffs and collective revenue but also the right to fight smuggling by levying fines and confiscations. "Otherwise, if joint action with foreign countries in cases of confiscation and fine were still necessary," Wang asked rhetorically, "how could it be called complete autonomy?"[47]

Along with monopolizing the legal authority to prosecute smuggling, the Nationalist government also sought to expand its territorial jurisdiction to cover remaining foreign concessions.[48] Effectively "asserting sovereignty through policing," the Nationalists continued late Qing law enforcement initiatives by "vigorously and aggressively" pursuing opportunities to supplant the jurisdiction of extraterritorial authorities with a Chinese police force.[49] Following the Nationalists' lead, the Maritime Customs also sought to extend its reach by creating a legal framework that would facilitate operations within foreign concessions. An important battleground in the fight against extraterritoriality was Shanghai, the city that registered the highest levels of smuggling and was most compromised by the fragmented sovereignties of foreign concessions, such as the International Settlement and the French Concession. During the early 1930s, officials debated ways to effect interdiction in these extraterritorial enclaves before exploiting a technicality in existing import regulations that gave the agency the right to inspect firm records and ensure that duties were properly paid.[50] Invoking this legal justification, the Maritime Customs concluded an unofficial agreement with the foreign-run Shanghai Municipal Council in 1932 that, upon notifying the council, agents could raid businesses within the International Settlement suspected of harboring smuggled goods.[51]

Once again, fighting smuggling provided a vehicle for the Nationalists and their agents to project the authority of the central state. But such assertive anti-smuggling policing aroused opposition from many quarters, foreign and domestic. Foreign powers, in particular, balked when Nationalist China unilaterally abrogated the Joint Investigation Rules. The United States rejected the Nationalists' expansive interpretation of "tariff autonomy" in the Sino-American Tariff Treaty and insisted that the U.S. Court for China continue to exercise jurisdiction over American nationals accused of smuggling.[52] Great Britain clung to the original interpretation of the Treaty of Tianjin, which recognized Chinese prerogative to confiscate smuggled goods but not to fine British nationals.[53] Japanese diplomats closely followed Nationalist China's aggressive campaign at fighting smuggling and reported on legislative efforts such as the promulgation of the Preventive Law.[54] As the preeminent foreign power in China, Japan sought to uphold the treaty port order and complained that Chinese actions like the abrogation of the Joint Investigation Rules violated both the spirit and letter of existing treaty agreements.[55] Meanwhile, a number of well-publicized raids within the International Settlement led foreign consuls to assert their nationals' extraterritorial privileges and object to anti-smuggling operations within foreign enclaves.[56] Articulating their complaints through the colonial discourse of deficiency, foreign consuls declined to assist the Chinese government in any anti-smuggling operation on the basis that China lacked an official law to deal with smuggling. Finally, local Chinese merchants proved equally vehement in their opposition. In a series of petitions publicized in newspapers and forwarded to national government organs, a Shanghai commercial guild objected on behalf of its members to interdiction by customs agents. One petition complained of the raids' disruptive impact on business: "As soon as a store is searched, business immediately comes to a halt and [customers] are frightened."[57] Other petitions complained of the discrimination against Chinese firms without extraterritorial protection, demanded the right of merchants to appeal penalties, and accused the Maritime Customs of "exceeding its authority."[58]

But even in the face of protests, the Nationalists moved forward with their plans to assert central authority over smuggling-related matters. To replace the defunct Joint Investigation Rules, the Nationalist government required companies or merchants who sought to appeal their penalties to deal directly with a new institution, the Customs Penalty Board of Inquiry and Appeal (Haiguan faze pingyi hui). Established in November of 1934 under the Preventive Law, the board provided merchants with a legal forum to appeal penalties levied by the Maritime Customs. Consisting of senior-level officials from the Ministry of Finance and the Maritime Customs, the board reviewed appeals and issued one of three rulings to uphold, modify, or reverse the original penalty. Appellants dissatisfied with the board's rulings could take their cases to the Administrative Court (Xingzheng fayuan), the Nationalists' highest legal body to hear cases regarding administrative agencies' rulings. At least one senior customs official praised the board's efficiency and fairness, noting that its members were "always willing to see the Customs point of view but at the same time they require to be convinced of the justice of the Customs case."[59] The creation of an institution like the board had been a goal of Chinese officials and guilds, who had long agitated for the same privileges foreign merchants enjoyed under the Joint Investigation Rules, such as the right to a formal hearing and to challenge penalties.[60] Legal centralization was thus further realized with unification of different laws and jurisdictions.

Meanwhile, the Nationalist government resumed raids on businesses inside foreign concessions. Customs agents initially pulled back operations in the face of vehement criticisms from businesses, but their actions received support from the highest echelons within the Nationalist government. The Ministry of Finance, for instance, publicly reaffirmed the right of the Maritime Customs to examine firm records, noting that such tactics stopped fraudulent practices, safeguarded national revenue, and protected "legitimate merchants."[61] With the promulgation of the Preventive Law in 1934, the customs officials again negotiated with the Shanghai Municipal Council and foreign consuls to allow its agents to operate within the International Settlement. The agency eventually secured an unofficial agreement that permitted customs agents to raid homes and businesses when armed with a search warrant from the Shanghai No. 1 Special District Court. Customs officials found the agreement "eminently unsatisfactory," since agents could search only shops of Chinese and foreigners who did not enjoy extraterritoriality. Nonetheless, they acknowledged that it was similar to deals other government agencies reached with the council and was the best deal that could be secured under the circumstances.[62]

Customs officials concluded similar arrangements elsewhere with mixed results. In Guangzhou, for instance, customs agents raided a British-owned business in the foreign concession of Shameen (Shamian) Island suspected of evading duties on foreign alcohol, but they were unable to do anything other than levy a nominal fine on the firm's owner.[63] In Tianjin, unrestricted entry into foreign concessions by customs agents would not be fully realized until after extraterritoriality was formally abolished.[64] In the meantime, agents maintained close surveillance on various smuggling concerns operating in the city's foreign concessions. Intelligence reports revealed that these firms—mostly Chinese and Japanese firms in foreign concessions with estimated operating capital from CN$1 million to CN$2.5 million each—ran very profitable businesses importing and selling smuggled sugar, artificial silk, and other products.[65] Such problems, in any case, did not stop agents from executing raids and thereby projecting Nationalist authority into foreign concessions when possible. Looking back at interdiction operations at the end of 1936, the Shanghai commissioner reported intermittent difficulties.[66] Yet the agency continued to enforce the Preventive Law in both the International Settlement and French Concession even without the assistance of the municipal council or French authorities.[67]

Anti-smuggling legal reforms thus helped consolidate the Nationalists' legal authority. New institutions, such as the Customs Penalty Board of Inquiry and Appeal, with their formalized procedures of adjudication helped China yet again showcase itself as a "modern" nation worthy of exercising full territorial sovereignty. As Li Chen notes, "Attempts to abolish foreign extraterritoriality continued to be a most powerful rallying call among the Chinese to 'modernize'/'Westernize' their legal and political systems to regain sovereignty and international respectability."[68] One senior Nationalist official made this link explicit when he proclaimed that China now had a dedicated court for its citizens to challenge decisions rendered by the Maritime Customs—just as citizens in Europe and the United States could do with their own customs.[69] Foreign Minister Wang Jingwei reinforced this point in a conversation with a British diplomat, noting that the new anti-smuggling regulations were promulgated "with the aim of bringing the provisions of Chinese law in this matter more into line with modern requirements, such as are adopted in other countries."[70] Creating Western-style institutions and procedures on par with their foreign counterparts was an important strategy for the Nationalists to deflect the colonial discourse of deficiency that maintained China could not effectively deal with smuggling because it lacked positive laws, "modern" laws, or a competent central government.[71] Finally, the mandate that smuggling-related disputes had to be processed through new legal channels and institutions signaled the Nationalists' intention to limit jurisdictional shopping by appellants. Smuggling, in the minds of Nationalist officials, would henceforth be a routine, *domestic* law enforcement issue adjudicated exclusively by the Chinese central government rather than a *diplomatic* issue subject to external interference.

Again, such efforts by Nationalist China paralleled efforts by other semicolonial polities seeking to reverse the extraterritorial privileges of foreigners through legal reform.[72] Measured against the Westphalian ideal of full territorial sovereignty, the Nationalists' accomplishments in contesting extraterritoriality through aggressive policing appear modest, even unimpressive. Yet if scholars are correct in their assertion that sovereignty has always been variegated, layered, and tenuous, then the progress made by the Nationalists in effecting this transition from jurisdiction over *persons* to jurisdiction over *territory* appears quite remarkable.[73] This transition was never fully realized during the Nanjing Decade, but suppressing smuggling did provide ample, consistent opportunities for the Nationalists to contest the legacies of legal imperialism and project their authority into foreign-controlled enclaves in ways their predecessors were unable to do.

POLICING MARITIME BORDERS

Another important agenda on the Nationalists' anti-smuggling campaign was control of China's maritime borders, which required regulating, monitoring, or even prohibiting the movement of vessels along the seaboard. Policing the littoral was another important expression of national sovereignty, since foreign powers in the past dispatched their own navies to suppress illicit maritime activities on the China coast when domestic authorities were ostensibly unable to do so.[74] Maritime smuggling generally occurred through two vectors: on large vessels such as steamships and on small vessels like junks and motorboats. Progress at fighting smuggling on board the former was slow but steady because authorities could identify owners and hold them accountable through financial sanctions. The same, by contrast, could not be said for fighting smuggling on board the latter; owner-ship of smaller craft was difficult to trace and they were too numerous to monitor. To remedy this problem, the Nationalists throughout the Nan-jing Decade authorized the Maritime Customs to modernize its maritime assets. A construction program was initiated in 1931 to expand the agency's fleet from seven obsolete pre–World War I steamers to eighty-six vessels of various size, speed, and maneuverability manned by a crew of 1,500 men by 1937. A scheme to divide the coast into "spheres of action" was instituted. Ships were outfitted with radio, and communication between vessels at sea and stations on land improved considerably when a network of wireless stations stretching along the coast became operational in 1934.[75] To ensure that vessels could defend themselves against armed smugglers, they were equipped with upgraded weapons like the Lewis automatic machine gun.

The Nationalists paired these technical tools of border control with a new regulatory framework to secure China's maritime borders. By the 1930s, China had already been deeply engaged in ongoing global debates and conferences defining the status of territorial waters in international law. Yet these discussions produced no firm consensus since most countries recognized three miles from the coast as the minimum zone of control but differed in designating their own maximum zone of control.[76] These ambi-guities afforded China some interpretative latitude in deciding which international norm to use as justification for its own claims. In 1931, in the midst of ongoing disputes with Japan over coastal fishing rights, the National Assembly announced that it recognized the three-mile limit as the extent of China's maritime territorial claim but simultaneously desig-nated a contiguous twelve-mile anti-smuggling zone.[77] Moreover, it charged the Maritime Customs with the responsibility to patrol China's entire coastline and conferred on the agency "the right of exercising any preventive measures it may consider necessary for the protection of its rev-enue" within the anti-smuggling zone. New regulations also urged the agency to follow the "internationally accepted practice of 'hot pursuit,'" whereby vessels suspected of violating Chinese laws along the coast might be pursued into the open seas.[78] The twelve-mile maritime anti-smuggling zone was codified three years later with the promulgation of the Preventive Law.[79]

To bolster the Chinese position, senior officials from the Ministry of Foreign Affairs prepared an extensive research report that canvassed a wide corpus of international laws and treaties. Citing seminal jurists of international law (including Henry Wagner Halleck, Francis Taylor Piggott, and Lassa Oppenheim), the report first emphasized that all maritime countries have historically claimed the right to police their shores in the name of fighting smuggling. It then surveyed the relevant tariff and maritime customs laws of other countries and found wide variations on the size of maritime anti-smuggling zones, ranging anywhere from three to twelve miles. In light of such evidence, officials concluded: "It is obvious that our country's designation of a twelve-mile anti-smuggling zone is truly not unprecedented."[80] If Rebecca Karl is correct that Chinese intellectuals and policy makers from the early twentieth century onward increasingly read their nation's situation in a global context, then Ministry of Foreign Affairs officials clearly did the same in justifying China's maritime claims—drawing from global conversations to delineate its borders and exercise its prerogative to fight smuggling.[81]

In the course of fighting smuggling, Nationalist China mobilized prevailing understandings of international law for Chinese benefit. It asserted territorial claims by basing them on international conventions while exploiting existing ambiguities. Indeed, because of differences in designating maritime jurisdictions, Nationalist China's assertion of its twelve-mile maritime anti-smuggling zone—unlike its abrogation of the Joint Investigation Rules—did not meet with uniform resistance. Great Britain maintained its recognition of three miles as the maximum extent of Chinese maritime territorial jurisdiction.[82] Japan, which had been monitoring Chinese intentions as early as 1930, protested what it viewed as China's selective interpretation of international norms and later dispatched its navy to discourage Chinese preventive vessels from venturing beyond the three-mile limit.[83] The United States, by contrast, did not explicitly endorse

China's claim but did implicitly accept it. When the American legation wanted to issue a protest to the Ministry of Foreign Affairs regarding China's claim, it was overruled by the State Department, which discovered that the United States itself claimed a similar twelve-mile anti-smuggling zone along its coasts.[84]

Meanwhile, other new rules sought to regulate domestic maritime activities and render movement more legible to the central state, as imperative scholars like James Scott have identified for many modernizing states.[85] In another bid to realize greater commercial control and fight smuggling, the Nationalist government in January 1931 ordered the Maritime Customs to assume control of all "extra-fifty-*li* Native Customs" stations. Such stations fifty *li* (roughly eighteen miles) outside of treaty ports had long collected duties on the domestic junk trade while operating independently of the Maritime Customs.[86] To enhance official control over junks, the Nationalist government also introduced the Customs Regulations for the Control of Seagoing Junks (Haiguan guanli hanghai minchuan hangyun zhangcheng). Promulgated in 1931 and revised in 1934, the regulations required small vessels and junks to register with their local customhouse, carry licenses and passbooks, and report to specified stations.[87] Owners also had to brand their vessels with their registration number and a single Chinese character signifying the port of registration. Violation resulted in a fine or confiscation of cargo or even of the vessel itself. From 1932 to 1937, more than 37,000 vessels up and down the coast submitted to this process and registered with their local customs station.[88]

Introduction of such regulations essentially segmented different forms of maritime movement into "legal" and "illegal" categories. This top-down state effort clashed with longtime, ongoing commercial practices. Not surprisingly, violation of the new regulations on maritime movement was a frequently contested issue in cases adjudicated by the Customs Penalty Board of Inquiry and Appeal. In December 1934 off the coast of Guangdong, for example, a customs patrol boarded the junk *De'anli* (*Tehanlee*) after it made some suspicious and evasive maneuvers. Agents searched the junk and uncovered discrepancies between its manifest and cargo.

Cross-referencing the junk's logs with customs records, they discovered that the vessel had been at sea for two weeks—a suspiciously long time given the short distance between its origin and destination. The junkmaster, when confronted with the evidence, admitted that the vessel had docked at the French concession of Guangzhouwan, discharged part of the original cargo, and took on board foreign goods—all violations of Article 11 of the Revised Junk Regulations that prohibited trade with "foreign territories" (*guowai difang*) without authorization. As a result, the junk and its entire cargo were confiscated. Two months afterward, Huang Yousan and fellow cargo owners appealed the penalty. In addition to questioning whether the entire cargo could be legitimately confiscated, they also protested the junk's seizure. The boat had been sailing a commonly traversed route, they argued, one that many had used for decades: "Ask any navigator or local persons and without exception they will acknowledge this."[89] Their claim, in essence, was that the artificial boundaries delineated and enforced by the state did not accord with local practices. How, then, could they have been "smuggling?" The board carefully reviewed Huang's protest but ultimately dismissed it, given that there was no question that the *De'anli* traversed foreign waters as defined by regulations. In so doing, it not only upheld the original penalty but also reaffirmed the principle that national regulations took precedence over local practices.[90]

This case—and others along the Chinese seaboard[91]—encapsulates the long-running conflict created by two countervailing processes stretching back to the early modern era: official efforts to territorialize the sea and commercial interests that resist this territorialization.[92] Such schemes at "marking water" required more than new technologies projecting state reach: they also required a new regulatory framework that defined appropriate venues for commercial activity. New laws, furthermore, compelled the master of the *De'anli* to collect, maintain, and report the junk's movements—the very evidence on which state agents ultimately relied to determine the extent of violations and levy the appropriate penalties. Greater state legibility enhanced the state's capacity to enforce its prerogatives in the courtroom, thereby routinizing its authority. More fundamentally, challenges from litigants like Huang inadvertently helped legitimize the same laws and institutions he was contesting. After all, whatever his actual attitude toward Nanjing, Huang had to submit to its procedures and institutions if he were to find redress. That is, he had to play by the new rules, thereby further reifying them.

Contests over new legally defined arenas of commerce also illustrate how enduring ties within regional economies were disrupted—but not severed—by new restrictions. Merchants often challenged regulations for marking water by pointing out that the boundaries drawn on maps and enforced by the government did not accord with local economic realities. These incidents highlight the divergence between two competing understandings of trade—one "legitimate" (defined by customary practices), one "legal" (defined by state fiat). Although backed by formidable state power, the latter did not descend untrammeled on the former but was frequently contested both inside and outside the courtroom. More significantly, cases adjudicated by the board underscore how boundaries were difficult to delineate and recognize, given the many foreign concessions and colonies that dotted the Chinese seaboard. As Janice Thomson reminds scholars, boundaries—far from being "given, permanent, or even natural"—are actually "arbitrary, contested, and ever-changing" and intricately intertwined with the sovereign claims of modern nation-states.[93] Nationalist attempts to define and enforce China's maritime borders highlight this malleable quality of boundaries. The proliferation of new laws gradually, even abruptly, restricted ongoing practices and patterns of exchange. Such changes bred resentment, certainly, but they also bred confusion. And authorities were certainly aware of this problem. One official observed that while some individuals were motivated by the desire to evade duties, many others were "not smugglers in the true sense of the word, but rather seem[ed] to be ignorant of the new procedure, and [were] carrying on as they did before."[94] Indeed, it is clear that one unintended consequence of the war on smuggling was—ironically enough—more smuggling, created by tightening strictures on movement.

CONSEQUENCES: INTENDED, UNINTENDED

How effective was Nationalist China's campaign against smuggling? One tangible measure comes from the total value of fines and confiscations. Starting at approximately CN$2.6 million in 1930, fines and confiscations rose threefold to CN$7.9 million in 1934 before declining in the years leading up to the Second Sino-Japanese War.[95] Many of the penalties were collected at larger ports, but reflecting the expanding geography of interdiction, fines and confiscations collected at smaller ports were also considerable.[96] Officials celebrated rising fines and confiscations as signs of progress. One senior customs official, for instance, boasted that the increases demonstrated the agency's success and efficacy in preventive work.[97] The Ministry of Finance and senior Nationalist officials echoed such commendations.[98]

But to reiterate concerns expressed by specialists, historical data on crime do not always accurately measure the efficacy of enforcement and may obfuscate the direction of causality between more crime and more enforcement. Smuggling certainly increased with higher tariffs incentivizing duty evasion, as well as with more regulations restricting many behaviors once deemed legal. It would increase further still with rising geopolitical tensions and more punitive laws. Ongoing disputes with Japan in late 1935, in particular, gave way to a full-blown crisis in early 1936. Smuggling in North China grew to alarming proportions with the encouragement of the Japanese army and cooperation of separatist regimes. Customs stations in Tianjin, along the Shandong coast, and on the Manchurian border all reported being inundated by brazen trafficking. Along with national sovereignty and public order, government finances came under threat. The Maritime Customs issued multiple warnings to the Ministry of Finance in mid-1936 that the decline in revenues was serious enough to undermine the Nationalists' ability to service its debts and indemnities.[99] Flagrant Japanese support for smuggling further inflamed anti-Japanese sentiments throughout China. Stories of Taiwanese and Korean "vagrants" (*langren*) colluding with "traitorous Chinese" (*Hanjian*) and "treasonous merchants" flooded the media and scandalized the public. The *Shen Bao Weekly* article "Northeast China's Startling Amount of Smuggling" reported how smuggled sugar, cotton yarn, rayon, and other products "too many to enumerate" made their way from Tianjin and Beiping (Beijing) to nearby provinces in northern and central China and eventually to the Lower Yangzi. It concluded on an ominous note: "Although the Ministry of Finance has now decided to solve the problem through diplomacy and rigorous enforcement of inspections, whether it can truly stamp out smuggling in North China by vagrants and traitorous Chinese remains an open question."[100]

As before, the Nationalist government responded to this new upsurge in trafficking by intensifying interdiction, ordering the Maritime Customs to beef up patrols in North China and dedicate a new unit, the Chief Inspection Bureau (Fangzhi zousi zong jicha chu), to fight smuggling throughout China's extensive railway network. And once again, the government introduced more laws. While still treating run-of-the-mill duty evasion as an administrative offense, it now criminalized the transaction of smuggled goods as akin to the transaction of stolen goods.[101] It also promulgated the emergency measure Revised Provisional Code Governing Punishments for Evasion of Customs Duty (Xiuzheng chengzhi toulou guanshui zanxing tiaoli), which criminalized duty evasion for select high-value and frequently trafficked foreign products including sugar, rayon, and kerosene. The new law also prescribed longer prison terms and heavier fines for individuals committing, attempting, or even assisting in smuggling. Under certain conditions, smuggling could be punished as a capital offense: those leading and inciting violence while resisting arrest or "conspiring with foreigners or rebels" in evading duties could be sentenced to life in prison or even death.[102] Nationalist China's campaign in one sense conforms to what legal scholars have termed "overcriminalization," the phenomenon whereby criminal law is increasingly applied to regulatory offenses.[103]

Fines and confiscation data were problematic for other reasons. Besides raising questions of accuracy and causality, these figures also obscure serious social conflicts and other unintended consequences created by ramped-up enforcement. Nowhere was this more evident than in the uneven application of justice. The new regulations permitted officials to inflict significant fines on suspected smugglers and confiscate not just the smuggled goods but also the vessel of transport. The Maritime Customs also instructed officials to negotiate with the offender or pursue fines in civil court if payment was not forthcoming. In theory, heavier punishments discouraged smuggling by raising the financial stakes involved. This was certainly the view of officials who saw smuggling as a "business" with its own economic logic.[104] To be sure, such penalties had serious and painful financial repercussions—even for individuals or firms that could absorb such losses. In practice, however, punishments were often meted out disproportionately. In some cases, fines levied or duties evaded actually exceeded the market value of the confiscated goods. The offender thus had an incentive to simply abandon the goods, write off the associated expenses, and cease further dealings with the Maritime Customs.[105]

The efficacy of heavier fines as a form of deterrence was also mixed. Unlike some merchants accused of smuggling who could afford to contest their penalties, small-time smugglers who made a precarious living shuttling small amounts of goods between ports simply had no means to pay the financial penalties. Many smugglers were women who expertly leveraged prevailing social taboos and notions of feminine weakness to their advantage. As one commissioner reported, it was "futile" to sue these petty runners given that they could not afford to pay fines of any kind.[106] Those who could not or would not pay had their cargoes or even their means of livelihood confiscated. To cite but one example, sampan owners in Xiamen caught collecting smuggled goods tossed from steamships prior to docking were fined anywhere from CN$15 to CN$30. Those unable to pay usually had their vessels destroyed.[107] Officials were certainly aware of this tiered system of justice. In a confidential letter to his superior, one commissioner admitted that while the small operators who were paid to transport illicit goods were often caught and punished, the actual owners of the cargo remained beyond the reach of the law.[108] Even popular literature captured this prevailing sentiment. In a 1930s play about illicit trade, for instance, outraged villagers resent seeing their brethren thrown in jail for petty trafficking while two local merchants enjoy impunity and profits from smuggling on a far larger scale. Seething at the injustice, they exclaim: "The gentry get rich while we get prosecuted!"[109]

Incarceration was the fate for many petty smugglers, although its administration was not always uniform. In some cases, local courts meted out harsher penalties in accordance with new punitive measures introduced after mid-1936. Along the coast, customs agents and the press reported suspected smugglers being tried, convicted, and sentenced to penal servitude.[110] In other cases, prosecution sometimes moved very slowly. Prosecuting smugglers remained a low priority for many local courts, since duty evasion threatened the revenues of the central government rather than those of the local government. In one southern port, for instance, a commissioner lamented the backlog of more than eight hundred smuggling cases in the local court: "The possibilities of grave injustice to the accused—whose offenses may not warrant an imprisonment term as long as the period which elapses between being handed over for trial and actual trial—are evident."[111] Moreover, other practical constraints compounded administrative indifference. Many cash-strapped local governments, as Xiaoqun Xu points out, faced mutually reinforcing incentives to avoid formal and lengthy prosecutions since jailing and feeding defendants was a significant financial burden.[112] Prosecuting the growing volume of smugglers in local courts, in essence, represented an unfunded central mandate that local magistrates understandably wanted to avoid.

Not surprisingly, local authorities sometimes found more expedient ways to deal with suspected smugglers. Some officials simply released prisoners after a short stay in jail. At one port, the local police informed customs officials that smugglers remanded to its custody had to be released, "on the plea of lack of space to keep them and lack of funds to feed them." As one commissioner observed, scarce resources encouraged local officials to dispense this sort of "quick justice": "In such cases there is no alternative but to treat the short [jail] term as a punishment in lieu of fine and to let offenders go."[113] Some magistrates avoided accepting suspects altogether. After the passage of the Preventive Law, a commissioner and a magistrate in southern China instituted a pilot program to prosecute captured smugglers. The scheme, however, was quickly suspended when the volume of suspects transferred from the former overwhelmed the resources of the latter. As the commissioner reported, the magistrate was initially cooperative in accepting the first batches of suspects, but he later declined to take in more: "Once he accept[ed] [the suspects], he must charge them, a course which [took] three days and he [had] no room in his prison to keep them for so long."[114] Another unintended consequence of the war on smuggling and its concomitant legal reforms was thus the uneven administration of justice, which highlighted the lingering incongruence between uniform regulations from the center and varied realities at the local level. State power certainly expanded with the fight against smuggling, but at considerable cost.

* * *

To fully appreciate the legal ramifications of Nationalist China's war on smuggling, let us return to the case of Yu Guangbo, the Shandong villager arrested during a raid that discovered contraband sugar. After fleeing his captors, Yu embarked on a long legal journey to seek redress. The district court hearing Yu's complaint ruled that customs agents violated Chapter 23 of the 1935 Republican Criminal Code for inflicting bodily injury (*shanghai zui*), a decision subsequently upheld by other provincial courts.[115] The Maritime Customs, for its part, charged Yu with smuggling under the Preventive Law, confiscated the sugar, and imposed the maximum fine of CN$1,000. Agents identified labels on the bags of sugar that bore the names of a company in Dalian and a fishing vessel as ipso facto evidence of smuggling since existing regulations permitted neither imports from Japanese-occupied Dalian nor goods shipped by fishing trawlers. Agents also produced signed statements from two village elders affirming that smuggled sugar had been unearthed from homes. In light of the evidence, the Customs Penalty Board of Inquiry and Appeal affirmed the penalties and rejected Yu's appeal.[116]

A tenacious Yu, however, appealed yet again, this time taking his case all the way to the Administrative Court. In reviewing the case, the court noted that despite the bags' foreign labels, agents failed to offer sufficient evidence countering Yu's claim that he purchased the sugar at an auction of confiscated goods. (Judges, it turned out, proved no better than customs agents in distinguishing between ordinary consumer goods legally imported from those illegally imported.) The court also threw out other evidence attesting to Yu's guilt after village elders confessed that they signed their statements under duress. Eight years after the original incident, the court overturned the Maritime Customs' original ruling and penalties.[117]

The case of Yu Guangbo—and those of many others—must be viewed in the context of expanding central state power during the Nanjing Decade. On the one hand, litigants like Yu could and did skillfully use new regulations and institutions to challenge state authority. On the other hand, Yu's "crime" was a product of newly promulgated laws that defined his purchase and possession of foreign sugar as illegal. New drivers of interdiction compounded his ordeal. Sanctioned by a new institutional mission, empowered by new laws, and incentivized by financial rewards, state agents brought the war on smuggling into ever more private venues. And regardless of their success, legal challenges by Yu—and many others—unwittingly reinforced state prerogative to impose official definitions of legal behavior by submitting themselves to the judgment of the court. The fight against illicit trade thus not only serves as an example of the state creating the very crime it was combating—it also serves as an example of the state's ability to compel compliance from otherwise reluctant individuals by constructing a pervasive legal system. State coercion, in other words, was implemented through the force of arms and the authority of law, both of which were greatly enhanced by the war on smuggling.

4

SHADOW ECONOMIES AND POPULAR ANXIETIES

The Business of Smuggling in Operation and Imagination

N MARCH 1935, the Chinese Maritime Customs Service dispatched officer Wang Huamin and an assistant on a monthlong expedition. Their mission was to investigate conditions in Hangzhou Bay, just south of Shanghai, which had emerged as another coastal trafficking hot spot starting in the early 1930s. The pair traveled incognito, Wang posing as a "Shandong smuggler with plenty of capital" and the assistant as a "Shanghai gangster." They went on to interview a colorful cast of characters, including local officials professing varying degrees of sympathy for the Nationalist government's anti-smuggling campaign, merchants harmed by or profiting from illicit trade, and boatmen boasting of their ability to evade customs patrols "with ease." In the course of his investigation, Wang unearthed valuable intelligence not just on local conditions but also on elaborate networks linking regional merchants with faraway suppliers. Some junks, he reported, sailed from as far north as Japanese-occupied Dalian in the dead of night, taking circuitous routes to avoid detection. Others waited offshore for days on end until given the all-clear signal to land at coastal villages without reporting to the local customhouse. Their cargo: rayon, sugar, cigarette paper, and other highly taxed products that fetched outsized profits on the market. Coolies, "always available" for a reasonable price, loaded the illicit goods onto fleets of trucks bound for distribution centers in Ningbo. After more sorting, the goods were forwarded to their final destinations in Hangzhou and Shanghai. At various nodes in the supply chain, smugglers took the necessary precautions: securing deposits from boatmen as collateral against potential losses, paying tribute to pirates for protection, and purchasing cooperation from local officials with a cut of the profit.

Wang's findings were specific to one locale, but they were broadly mirrored across the Chinese littoral during the Nanjing Decade. State and smuggler at the time were engaged in a never-ending game of cat and mouse, with the latter's creative evasions challenging the former's tightening strictures. As previous chapters have illustrated, smuggling—organized or otherwise—enjoyed a long history on the China coast. Individual runners, organized gangs, and even whole communities traded narcotics, weapons, and other commodities. The illicit economy reported by Wang, however, represented something new, an inadvertent product of assertive domestic policies regulating unpredictable global flows. Higher tariffs introduced by Nationalist China suddenly made trafficking everyday consumer products profitable—despite the vast distances and complex coordination involved. As Wang himself noted, the comparative gains from trafficking traditional contraband such as narcotics were still attractive, but "the incentive to smugglers to discard other forms of smuggling and engage in evading Customs duty is [now] very strong."[1]

This chapter shifts the top-down perspective of lawmaking to explore bottom-up practices of lawbreaking. It begins by tracing how new policies transformed three commodities—rayon, kerosene, and sugar—from everyday consumables to profitable contraband. It then examines ways smuggling effectively operated as a "business," with variegated business models, supply chains, and resistance tactics against official interdiction. Finally, it explores the growing, popular uneasiness over the smuggling epidemic through a deep reading of press reports, political cartoons, and literary fiction. The specter of illicit trade and its threats to the national economy worried state and public alike, but it also generated anxieties among nationalistic elites that intersected with existing social anxieties over issues of nation, gender, and class. A survey of popular writings, moreover, reveals how such ambivalence was directed not just at traffickers and "treasonous merchants" but also at women smugglers and even state agents themselves. By looking at how the war on smuggling was viewed, experienced, and understood by merchants and the wider public, then, this chapter reconstructs the broader impact of bold state intervention in everyday life beyond the codification of laws and promulgation of policies.

NEW PROFITABLE TRAFFICKING: RAYON, KEROSENE, AND SUGAR

Nationalist China relied on what economist Arthur Young calls a "highly regressive" tax system to fund its day-to-day administration and state-building agenda.[2] Besides tariffs, the central government levied various indirect taxes—excise, consolidated, and stamp—that fell disproportionately on consumers and businesses. Financial exigencies undoubtedly drove the introduction of such punitive fiscal policies, but so too did other considerations. As economic historian Kubo Toru notes, the "tariff policy was not pursued merely as a means of securing a source of revenue for the Nationalist government, but was considered as an effective means of achieving China's economic development through the import-substitution industrialization strategy, and was promoted as such."[3] Indeed, disciplining consumption was fundamental to realizing the regime's goal of economic control and Sun Yat-sen's vision of an industrialized China. Subsequent campaigns like the 1934 New Life Movement—the Nationalist party's attempt to inculcate Chinese society with militaristic virtues of self-sacrifice, discipline, and patriotism—reinforced official attempts to curb the consumption of seemingly frivolous imports.

Nationalist China accordingly subjected a wide range of consumer imports to heavy taxes and strict regulations, but three commodities in particular became the most-frequently trafficked because of the strong demand and outsized profits they commanded. The traffic of each illustrates a different logic underpinning its trade and how Nationalist policies stimulated the creation of vast underground economies. One article was rayon, artificial silk valued by clothing producers who were forced to rely on clandestine markets to stave off price pressures brought about by higher tariffs. The fabric was first invented and commercially produced in the late nineteenth century, but it was not until the 1920s that large-scale manufacturing took off from 33 million pounds worldwide in 1920 to 926 million pounds in 1935. The United States was the world's leading producer throughout this period, but Japan quickly turned itself into the world's second-largest producer by 1933 despite being a latecomer to the industry.[4] China was not a producer but a consumer of rayon, with its imports rising dramatically during the latter half of the 1920s and peaking at almost 2.9 million yards in 1929.[5] Artificial silk was gaining widespread popularity because it held many advantages over natural silk, a substitute good. One was price: throughout the twenty-five-year period from 1911 to 1936, rayon remained consistently cheaper than silk thanks to relentless advances in technology and manufacturing.[6] Another plus was versatility: rayon could be manufactured in different sheens, dyed in many colors, and used in a wide range of clothing, from outerwear to underwear and everything in-between. It was thus more amenable than natural silk in meeting rapidly changing consumer tastes. "Fashion is the order of the day," a 1933 article in the *China Weekly Review* declared, noting that Chinese consumers enthusiastically embraced modern clothing styles for the same reasons their counterparts around the world did. "Since the fabrics of synthetic silk are not only cheap in price but also brilliant in luster, they naturally appeal to the psychology of the buying public."[7]

Chinese industries were especially hard-hit by this secular shift away from natural silk, traditionally one of China's largest exports but already suffering from stiff international competition since the turn of the twentieth century.[8] Filatures, further devastated by the one-two punch of changing domestic tastes and depressed international demand, agitated for official assistance. The Nationalist government responded by raising tariffs on rayon piece goods to 10 percent in 1928, 45 percent in 1930, and

80 percent in 1934.[9] It also announced plans to construct a new state-operated rayon factory, another step toward realizing its industrialization program. While aiming to protect a depressed domestic industry and a symbol of Chinese material culture, the Nationalist government also sought to encourage the domestic production of rayon. Most importantly, it wanted to stem one of the largest imports from its geopolitical rival Japan.

On paper at least, new tariffs made foreign rayon uncompetitive, and imports steadily declined throughout the 1930s. Surveying the market in early 1936, the National Economic Council (NEC) estimated that imported rayon cost CN$389 per hundred kilograms, with CN$117 accounting for production costs and CN$272 for import duties.[10] Domestic rayon, by contrast, cost CN$220 per hundred kilograms—almost 44 percent cheaper than imported rayon. "Therefore," the NEC report concludes, "present tariffs on rayon are more than sufficient to protect domestic rayon industries; there is no urgent need to for revisions."[11] Looking back at the development of China's rayon textile industry, Kubo Toru notes that "it is clear that tariffs fulfilled the role of protecting and promoting the development of industrial production based on Chinese capital."[12]

Yet the costs and benefits of new policies were unevenly distributed among state, producer, and consumer. High tariffs indirectly hurt consumers by raising retail prices, but they directly hurt producers who relied on artificial silk as a substitute for natural silk. Weavers, in particular, supported official efforts to create a domestic rayon industry in the future but wanted lower tariffs to offset high costs in the meantime. The Chinese Industrial Federation and the Shanghai Silk and Satin Guild in 1934 separately petitioned the government to reduce duties on rayon and argued that lower prices for a critical input would make their members' products more competitive on the market. The response from the Ministries of Industry and Finance was polite but firm: "Because import duties on rayon are related to the relief of the domestic silk industry, the request cannot be granted."[13]

Unrelenting economic pressures and unsympathetic official policies thus made cheaper, smuggled rayon yarn comparatively attractive, if not outright essential, to many businesses. Whether arriving in packages thrown overboard from steamships prior to docking, cargoes ferried by junks, or even parcels sent by post, smuggled rayon was eagerly snapped up by consumers and producers.[14] Brands like Heavenly Bridge (Tianqiao), Golden Tri-Horses (Jin san ma), and Beautiful Woman (Meinü) produced in Dalian commanded the highest premiums.[15] Typical buyers included businessmen like Shen Baosheng and Shen Baoqing, proprietors of the Shaoxing-based weaving company Shen Qing Ji, which depended on cheap rayon for operations. Their illicit purchases only came to light when a boatman they hired confessed to delivering forty-seven bags of smuggled rayon after he was arrested en route by the police.[16] Not every buyer of smuggled goods was caught, so the brothers' appearance in the historical record was exceptional. Yet their reliance on smuggled rayon was anything but. As a writer surveying the market in late 1934 noted: "It is an open secret that a large percentage of our rayon imports has come to this port through illegal channels. Thus . . . our consumption of rayon has been actually on the increase instead of on the decrease as the Customs figures indicate."[17] The Nationalist government itself later admitted as much, noting that the decline in rayon yarn imports was more than offset by the increase in smuggling.[18]

Another frequently smuggled commodity was kerosene, which enjoyed relatively inelastic market demand by urban and rural consumers alike. Lighting countless homes, businesses, and streets since its introduction in major Chinese cities during the 1870s, kerosene quickly supplanted vegetable oil as China's illuminating oil of choice and breaking the "tyranny of darkness" by revolutionizing nightlife.[19] Imports rose from almost 31 million gallons in 1890, peaking in 1928 at almost 263 million gallons, most of which came from the United States.[20] Much of that amount, in turn, came from Standard Oil, which pioneered the production of kerosene and quickly dominated the Chinese market in the late nineteenth century. In the following decades, it built a vast, vertically integrated supply chain that achieved impressive economies of scale.

Standard Oil paired this extensive physical infrastructure with an equally extensive retail network. It retained a core staff of Western managers and Chinese professionals to coordinate imports and handle accounting but relied on an army of Chinese agents to advertise, distribute, and sell kerosene. Working on commission, these agents and their subagents leveraged their native-place ties and local knowledge to effectively peddle kerosene at periodic rural markets and grocery stores. They even accommodated poorer customers by selling kerosene in minute quantities, one scoopful at a time. The company also sold—or even gave away—cheap but reliable lamps stamped with its Chinese name, Mei Foo (Meifu) and other marketing messages like "Burn Standard Oil Kerosene." To stem price wars and avoid ruinous competition, Standard Oil forged cartel agreements with rivals entering the China market starting at the turn of the twentieth century.[21] Such tactics helped American kerosene reach, penetrate, and eventually dominate markets well outside of treaty ports. A survey conducted in 1935 estimated that 54 percent of Chinese families in the countryside regularly bought kerosene.[22] Far from an object of luxury for urban elites, kerosene was available to, consumed by, and essential to even the poorest peasants.

In the early part of the Nanjing Decade, the kerosene market in China was essentially an oligopoly with artificially high prices and inelastic market demand. To fiscalize this demand, Nationalist China raised duties on imported kerosene to 40 percent in 1931 and 110 percent in 1934.[23] For the cartel, new tariffs exacerbated slumping economic conditions and plunging silver prices during the 1930s, which depressed the buying power of Chinese consumers. For smugglers, by contrast, new tariffs magnified potential profits by widening the price differential between legally imported and illegally imported kerosene. Traffickers soon flooded markets along the China coast with smuggled foreign (primarily Japanese) kerosene from Dalian, Taiwan, and Hong Kong. Because of its relative bulk, kerosene was commonly trafficked in large quantities on board junks and discharged at deserted beaches away from urban ports. The coastal hinterland was the point of entry for smuggled kerosene and was thus the market where legitimately imported kerosene first fell out of favor. For the cartel, its most valuable markets were also its most vulnerable. So pervasive and damaging was smuggling that the oil companies moved to cut prices just a year after introducing concerted price increases.[24]

Cartel members consistently pushed their own governments to apply diplomatic pressure on Japan to halt the trafficking. At the same time, they peppered the Chinese government with urgent appeals. Standard Oil in particular relayed directly to the Maritime Customs reports from its agents on the unimpeded, untaxed flow of kerosene along the Fujian coast. Illicit goods carried on motorboats and junks bypassed customs stations and were unloaded ashore, these reports note, where they filtered into rural marketing networks. Thereafter, individual hawkers carried small lots of this smuggled kerosene for sale in villages and eventually in towns and cities. Not surprisingly, this illegally imported kerosene retailed at much lower prices than its legal competitor. According to a Standard Oil Chinese agent in early 1934, the former was priced from CN$6.00 to CN$6.80 per tin on the open market. The latter, which included duties and local taxes, was priced from CN$8.48 to CN$10.28—a difference of 40 to 50 percent. "Under the circumstances," an exasperated company representative implored, "our agents at these points request that you give the subject your best attention by taking immediate action with the proper authorities, to stop the smuggling at once."[25] Whatever its outcome, this particular instance of trafficking was far from unique and serves as another example of an illicit economy created by restrictive state policies and strong consumer demand.

The third principal contraband of the Nanjing Decade was white sugar, whose clandestine trade best exemplified ongoing tensions between central and local authorities over which side should exercise greater control over the economy. As one of the three industrially processed "white goods"—the other two being white flour and white rice—white sugar became an integral part of the Chinese diet by the turn of the twentieth century.[26] But virtually all this sugar was imported since China did not have any modern refineries until the late 1930s. Moreover, smallholder farmers lacked the economies of scale to produce sugar cheap in price and uniform in quality for refining. Thus, domestic sugar—previously exported widely from Guangdong to communities on the China coast and markets worldwide—could neither keep pace with shifting consumer tastes nor compete with cheaper foreign sugar from Southeast Asia, Hong Kong, Taiwan, and North America.

Reviving domestic sugar production motivated the Nationalist government to levy some of its most prohibitive tariffs. Duties soared dramatically to 11 percent in 1928, 34 percent in 1930, 80 percent in 1932, and 137 percent in 1934.[27] Adding assorted excise taxes and local taxes, duties stood well above 200 percent in some localities.[28] As with rayon, the Nationalist government also wanted to nurture a domestic sugar industry by supporting the construction of modern factories with public funds. A 1935 NEC report employed the same language as in the "tariff problem" debate to justify import substitution by declaring the government's goal as stemming the "unmended leakage" of Chinese wealth revealed in the chronic trade imbalance. And reflecting growing global awareness on the part of policy makers, the report also noted that Chinese tariffs—as high as they might have been—were in line with or even slightly lower than those of other countries.[29] New tariffs resulted in a dramatic decline in the import of sugar, from 14 million piculs in 1928 to 4.5 million in 1934.[30] Meanwhile, they also nurtured the Chinese sugar industry, with at least six modern refineries completed in Guangdong alone by 1936.[31]

The provenance and legal status of sugar were difficult to determine once it entered China. Many traffickers sought to pass off foreign sugar as native sugar, which could be shipped within China at much lower duties. Other government policies inadvertently made this tactic even more effective. High tariffs encouraged domestic producers to improve the quality of their sugar, and government-sponsored modern refineries commenced operations after 1934. Many merchants were caught between state and smuggler. Shipments from sugar-producing regions in Guangdong to Shanghai, in particular, were frequently detained by the Maritime Customs under suspicion that smuggled foreign sugar was being passed off as native sugar. The problem actually extended as far back as the early twentieth century, when Chaozhou merchants frequently protested that their domestically produced sugar was misclassified by the Dutch Sugar Standard, a visual examination standard, and hence assessed higher duties.[32]

Disputes became more acute when polarization, a chemical procedure adopted by the Maritime Customs in 1932 to more accurately distinguish among different grades of sugar, suggested that domestically produced sugar was actually smuggled foreign sugar due to the presence of crystals ostensibly produced only by "modern" refineries that China then did not have. Merchants, through their local guilds, protested to both the Maritime Customs and the national government.[33] Meanwhile, customs officials continued confiscating shipments based on the results of polarization tests even as they admitted that complaints about misclassification were "not altogether unjustified."[34] "These cases of foreign sugar mixed with native sugar are never ending," an exasperated official wrote at the end of 1937, after years of disputes with local merchants.[35]

Sugar laundering was certainly widespread. But it was most systematically practiced by separatist regimes that challenged the Nationalists' claim as the legitimate, central government of China. The Guangdong provincial government under the general Chen Jitang, in particular, enjoyed de facto independence from Nanjing's authority and pursued its own "economic reconstruction" programs by building local refineries to revive local sugar production.[36] At the same time, provincial officials and military also engaged in "official smuggling," where they imported goods under the cover of provincial business without paying import duties or securing permission from Nanjing. Before it introduced provincial monopolies and opened provincial factories in 1935 and 1936, the Guangdong government imported, repackaged, and resold sugar from Hong Kong as "native" sugar. The practice was ostensibly a stopgap measure designed to satisfy local demand until new sugar factories were completed, but the profits from "smokeless sugar" (*wuyan tang*)—so called because the sugar was not locally produced but simply relabeled—were nonetheless substantial. A bag of illegally imported sugar, for instance, could be resold in Guangzhou for more than three times the original price—still roughly competitive with legally imported sugar inclusive of duties.[37] As one customs report notes: "Of the enormous profits, half were turned over to General [Chen Jitang] and half were devoted to the purchase and erection of provincial sugar [factories]. It is therefore apparent that the provincial sugar [factories] were very largely, if not entirely, paid for out of Maritime Customs revenue diverted from the Central Government."[38]

"Official smuggling" of sugar occurred less frequently—or at least less visibly—with the fall of Chen Jitang's regime and the subsequent assertion of control over Guangdong by Nanjing in 1936. Yet its practice highlighted the strange ways new tariff policies realigned political incentives throughout the country. Both the competing regimes in Guangzhou and Nanjing wanted higher tariffs for similar reasons—promoting domestic sugar production by warding off foreign competition. But the former sought to realize provincial goals by circumventing national constraints imposed by the latter. The loss of tariff revenues hit national, rather than local, coffers. Sugar smuggling thus stood at the intersection of two distinct, conflicting agendas. Its practice was an exercise of political independence by Guangzhou, while its suppression was an assertion of national sovereignty by Nanjing. The struggle to contain this trafficking underscores how fighting smuggling was part and parcel of the center's agenda to exercise more control over the local.

THE BUSINESS OF SMUGGLING

"Smuggling," wrote a customs commissioner, "is a business. Like all businesses it will be carried on so long as, and no longer than, the profits to its owners are considered worth the risks entailed."[39] Indeed, smuggling essentially operated under the same logic as trade, with the same drive to maximize profits and minimize costs. It was the legal framework that ultimately distinguished one from the other—and that very legal framework was undergoing tremendous changes after 1928. Meanwhile, the decision to participate in smuggling—as buyer, transporter, or seller—was a function of complicated considerations that were neither completely uniform nor neatly delimited by specific industries or geographies. Some businesses willingly turned to illicit markets for their needs; others resisted as best they could. Responses varied according to individual preferences and market conditions, yet the evidence reveals faint outlines of several patterns. Manufacturers, retailers, and importers with long-standing operations, for instance, already invested significant resources establishing their supply chains and feared the influx of cheaper smuggled goods. Many actively voiced their complaints through their local guilds, which monitored the activities of their rank-and-file and disciplined, censured, or at least shamed any members caught trafficking. Guilds in Guangzhou and Tianjin, for instance, directly petitioned customs officials to stem the illicit trade of sugar and even volunteered information that might prove useful to preventive efforts: means of transport, points of entry, and more.[40] Aggrieved businesses big and small applied pressure on the Maritime Customs in less direct ways. Dealers in Shanghai and Hong Kong who managed a thriving trade importing ginseng from the United States and reexporting it to Overseas Chinese communities in Southeast Asia, for example, felt threatened by the upsurge in smuggling that sought to evade tariffs that stood at 40 percent by 1930.[41] They responded by petitioning senior Nationalist officials, who in turn forwarded their complaints to the Maritime Customs, requesting action.[42] Even industrialists like Liu Hongsheng—China's "match king" (*huochai dawang*)—had to appeal for relief from the government when the flood of smuggled Japanese matches battered business and frustrated his ongoing efforts to forge a nationwide cartel.[43]

Indeed, smuggling did not affect all business equally. Large market incumbents like Liu, for instance, were particularly vulnerable because the visibility and scale of their operations made evading tariffs costlier than simply paying them. Moreover, the advantages in cost and efficiency they derived from their extensive supply chains proved less flexible in countering nimbler smugglers and their evanescent networks. Large foreign firms were also vulnerable. The vestigial extraterritorial protections they enjoyed—even if not already vigorously challenged by a new regime—offered little protection against smuggling. Foreign businesses initially resisted the new taxes imposed by Nationalist China but ultimately agreed to pay taxes only to Nanjing, a quid pro quo Arthur Young characterized as "the freedom from the burdensome and often arbitrary exactions and bribery that previously impeded their operations."[44] As the aforementioned examples of kerosene smuggling demonstrate, foreign businesses like Standard Oil also had to appeal to Chinese authorities to clamp down on smuggling. Even Japanese companies—many of them ostensible beneficiaries of illicit trade—expressed similar sentiments. The zaibatsu Mitsui and Mitsubishi, for instance, saw their respective businesses "go into precipitous decline" (*jizhuan zhixia*) at the height of the 1936 North China smuggling epidemic. Whereas monthly sales once averaged CN$3 million, it plummeted to a low CN$200,000—a startling decline of more than 90 percent—as the firms' legitimately imported stock sat unsold in warehouses.[45] Like other companies undersold by smuggled goods, Mitsui and Mitsubishi agitated for more rigorous enforcement, going so far as to urge Japanese authorities to cooperate with Chinese customs officials in interdicting illicit traffic.[46] The oversupply of contraband in North China—which left even smugglers in a precarious financial position by the end of 1936—only compounded Mitsui's and Mitsubishi's woes.[47] In many ways, then, the threat of smuggling made strange bedfellows of established incumbents— Chinese and foreign, big and small.

For many other businesses, however, the wide disparities between prices of smuggled and non-smuggled goods were simply too lucrative to ignore. Smuggling in such cases was thus as much a defensive strategy as it was a profit opportunity. Residents of the village Xuwen in southeast China, for instance, turned to smuggling to help revive the fortunes of an area devastated by intermittent warfare and economic depression. Stores began doing a brisk trade in high-quality foreign goods at "bargain prices" from Hong Kong and the nearby French concession of Guangzhouwan. Teahouses and inns, so rare just a few years prior, now lined the streets and hummed with activity—the tangible signs of economic recovery.[48] This "period of prosperity" (*fanrong de shihou*) for the town, unfortunately, came at the expense of neighbors like Hainan Island, which housed a customs station and was heavily patrolled. As their businesses "withered" (*diaoling*) in the face of competition, it was not long before Hainan merchants themselves "heeded the call of smuggling" (*wen le zousi de fengsheng*) and began selling illicitly imported goods.[49] The situation was similar in the north, where officials reported that some merchants in Tianjin had turned to dealing in smuggled commodities: "These brokers were men who had previously dealt in legal sugar, artificial silk and piece goods. When their legal business was destroyed, however, they had no alternative but to deal in smuggled products. One cannot really blame them."[50] Relentless price pressure—exacerbated by smuggling—was a powerful motivation for businesses to evade duties.

Besides the drive for profit, illicit enterprises shared similar practices and organization as those of their licit counterparts. Whatever the commodity trafficked, smuggling in many cases effectively operated as a business with organized logistics and retail channels connecting consumers and suppliers on an ongoing basis. The sophisticated supply chain described by Wang Huamin in Hangzhou Bay was replicated many times over along the coast. As one journalist reported from Chaozhou in northeast Guangdong, for instance, smuggling linked inland retailers with coastal suppliers, with the former contacting the latter with orders and coming to a mutually acceptable price. The supplier bore all the risks prior to delivery, and if losses were incurred during transport, the buyer assumed no responsibility. Payment was made on delivery by check or money order, which was cashed once the buyer telegraphed the supplier that the goods had been received. The trafficking was divided along urban-rural lines. Suppliers—who possessed capital and access to foreign goods—tended to hail from cities, while transporters—who supplied the necessary labor—tended to hail from the countryside.[51] In another account from Shandong, rayon shipped on junks from Dalian was landed at Zhifu and peddled on city streets the same night. When discovered by customs agents, traffickers simply relocated to ever more "secluded" (*pijing*) areas to unload their wares—another classic example of the "balloon effect" whereby interdiction simply displaces rather than eliminates the targeted activity.[52]

Elsewhere, smuggling operated on different business models, where buyers sought out smuggled goods instead of waiting for smuggled goods to come to them. In Guangzhou, the manager of a medicine store admitted, upon being questioned by customs officials, that his supplies came from runners heading daily to Hong Kong on trains and steamships.[53]

Further south on the Leizhou Peninsula, one official reported merchants offering commissions, initially as high as 20 percent but falling to 15 percent and eventually to 7 percent when intense competition among suppliers counterbalanced the strong demand for smuggled goods.[54] To lend these imports a veneer of legality, shippers included paperwork mixed with accurate and inaccurate information. One firm, for instance, imported clocks and watches through legitimate channels but was later discovered to have produced invoices under-declaring their true value by as much as 40 percent.[55] Side industries sprang out of systematic efforts to evade official detection. To cite but one case, officials on an inspection trip in Hong Kong to verify invoices from a company discovered that it was a "bogus concern consisting of one man only." The owner of the so-called firm kept no records and openly admitted that his entire "business" was devoted to producing receipts with misleading or even false information.[56]

As the example of sugar smuggling demonstrates, trafficking consumer products was profitable partly because it was difficult to detect. Unlike narcotics or weapons, consumer products were commonly, openly, and freely consumed. Authorities thus faced considerable difficulties distinguishing which goods were smuggled and which were not. The question of legality, after all, rested not on the goods themselves or how they were used but how they were imported. The admission by two local officials interviewed by Wang Huamin during his investigation illustrates this dilemma of accurately distinguishing between goods that paid the required duties and those that did not: "Their chief concern about passing junks is to see that no prohibited articles and arms are carried. The question of smuggling never bothered them and they have no exact idea of how to distinguish between smuggled goods and duty-paid commodities."[57]

Illicit trade operated under the same logic as licit trade. Yet the former differed from the latter in one important respect: the higher risks involved. Thus, businesses engaged in smuggling sought to hedge against various hazards. Some firms sought to minimize potential losses by distributing cargo across multiple transport vessels, reasoning that the scale of profits would still exceed any losses from confiscation. The risk of confiscation itself, however, could not be completely eliminated, especially in an era of ramped-up enforcement. Such was the fate that befell Xu Xueliang's father and three uncles. The "four brothers" (*xiongdi siren*) had operated stores selling shoes and assorted goods in Zhoucun on the Shandong Peninsula since the first years of the Republic. As early as 1931, the town was already an important consumer of smuggled rayon for the local weaving industry. As Xu recalled, his father and three uncles, "seeing this opportunity, resolved to take a chance to earn an 'easy fortune.'" In 1934, his uncle took out a bank loan and traveled to Dalian to purchase a boatload of silk. After successfully bringing the cargo back to Zhoucun, the family was able to turn a profit of more than ten thousand yuan. A year later, his uncle secured another bank loan and arranged to have two boats successively bring back their cargoes of silk, calculating that only one boat needed to return safely for the family to break even. Unfortunately, authorities intercepted both shipments and confiscated all the goods. When news of the seizures reached home, the bank pressed for repayment of the loan. With their capital tied up with the confiscated shipments, the four brothers subsequently liquidated their stores' entire inventory, declared bankruptcy, and divided the family's assets (*fenjia*).[58]

Unlike the Xu brothers, other merchants guarded against the risk of loss by employing their own protection, drawing from local militias or demobilized soldiers. One Fujian-based smuggling network, for instance, employed more than three hundred people and operated more than thirty boats trafficking commodities across the Taiwan Strait. To counter interdiction, it equipped couriers with more than two hundred rifles in its arsenal.[59] Other operations, by contrast, simply allied with local civil and military officials willing to resist central authority, offering a cut of the profit in exchange for protection. Silk importers from the Xu family's hometown of Zhoucun, for instance, paid the local army six yuan per box to escort their shipments—a fee still lower than import duties levied by the central government. Paying off local authorities, however, did not always shield businesses from official predation. The Taiwanese Wei Rongtai, who operated the large smuggling firm Jin Long Xing (Jinlongxing yanghang), paid a local "tax" to Jinmen officials on assorted commodities like sugar and kerosene in lieu of national tariffs. When a local police unit was cut out of the action, it seized one of Jin Long Xing's shipments and arrested two of its clerks, calling them "Chinese traitors" (*Hanjian*).[60]

The experience of the Xu brothers also demonstrates how profits and risks from smuggling could be greatly amplified by leverage—that is, borrowing more capital. As a 1936 Ministry of Finance report noted, it was not uncommon for financial institutions in many localities to issue loans to fund smuggling enterprises or accept smuggled goods as security.[61] One customs search party, for instance, discovered four major banks in a mid-sized town that had advanced loans amounting to roughly CN$157,000 to local merchants. The collateral used for the loan turned out to be more than 6,600 bags of smuggled white sugar, prized for their high market prices and long shelf life.[62] Banking associations in Shanghai and Tianjin issued public statements warning members against accepting smuggled goods as collateral, thereby underscoring the prevalence of this practice.[63]

Besides capital and labor, smuggling also required cross-border partnerships linking Chinese retailers and foreign suppliers. The Zhongyuan Trading Company (Zhongyuan shanghang), for example, was established in January 1936 and did brisk business selling smuggled Japanese goods in Qingdao. Besides Song Rujiu, the storefront manager, the firm had two other important partners: the supplier Niu Fengchi, who supplied goods from Osaka, and the post office employee Ren Ruishan, who exempted all packages to Zhongyuan from inspection. Song also received supplies from Dong Fuxiang, who—using capital raised by three other partners—smuggled rayon, sugar, and other goods back to China from Dalian. One reporter offered vivid details on this traffic between Dalian and North China, in which small-time merchants like Dong were likely participants: "Every night after dark . . . Chinese go to the shops [in Dalian] and lay in small supplies all sorts of proprietary articles, from tinned vegetables and fruits to chewing gum or whiskey. Small orders all of them. The goods are crammed into a sack and the buyer hurries off ultimately to catch a train or a boat to take him to his profitable market. His goods travel as personal baggage and the only time to stop him is when he crosses the border into China or arrives at one of its ports."[64] The illicit operations came to an end only when the local Qingdao police caught Song purchasing fifty-two bolts of smuggled rayon from Dong. Song and Dong, leaders of their respective enterprises, received the longest jail sentences, while their associates received lesser sentences proportionate to their involvement.[65]

Another method to tap foreign connections was for Chinese businesses to hire foreigners. Since its founding in 1930, the Nicot Products Company (Changtai yan gongsi), for example, had systematically submitted fraudulent receipts to the Maritime Customs that underreported the value of imported cigars and thus underpaid duties. The company engaged in complicated bookkeeping to cover its tracks, paying suppliers in separate remittances through separate banks. Customs officials first detected the fraud in 1933, but the company responded by requesting suppliers to direct their shipments to Qingdao, where an agent forwarded them to Shanghai by rail. Nimbly adjusting to changing conditions, the company continued to obfuscate its complex supply network until 1936, when customs agents finally shut it down. After raiding the firm and concluding its investigation, the Shanghai Customs sought not only to recover the duties evaded (CN$13,050) but also to collect a fine twice that amount (CN$26,100) for the fraud. Lin Youzhou, the firm's Chinese owner of record, appealed the penalty, arguing that the company originally belonged to P. C. Boon, a Belgian national now deceased. Lin claimed that he was a mere investor who advanced capital to the firm while Boon managed day-to-day operations, asserting: "The responsibility for Boon's own fraudulent practices should not be pinned onto a third party ignorant of the facts in this matter." As evidence, Lin produced documents from the Belgian consulate in Shanghai and advertisements from Chinese newspapers that purported to list Boon as the company's owner. Yet exhaustive and incriminating evidence unearthed from the raid contradicted Lin's claims of merely being a passive investor. Accounts showed that Boon, from the firm's founding in 1930 to his death in June 1936, was indeed responsible for importing the cigars, corresponding with foreign suppliers, and submitting fraudulent receipts to the Maritime Customs. They also, however, showed Boon drawing monthly payments of CN$420 (later reduced to CN$150), suggesting that the late Belgian was the company's employee rather than its owner. Given the weight of the evidence, both the Customs Penalty Board of

Inquiry and Appeal and the Administrative Court ruled against Lin and permitted the original penalties to stand.[66]

In the case of the Nicot Products Company, Lin sought more than just overseas connections when he hired Boon—he also sought extraterritorial protection. Firms had long recognized the value of extraterritoriality as a business asset and sought to exploit China's fragmented sovereignty for profit. Indeed, many Chinese merchants who dealt in smuggled goods exploited extraterritoriality to gain favorable access to supplies and minimize the risk of prosecution: claiming multiple nationalities, moving their businesses to foreign concessions, or partnering with foreign nationals.[67] But such tactics became more difficult to execute as the Nationalist government sought to compel foreign nationals accused of smuggling to deal directly with its legal institutions as part of its anti-smuggling campaign. While not always successful, Nationalist legal reforms did compel businesses like the Nicot Products Company to submit to its procedures and implicitly recognize the authority of the central government.

COUNTERMEASURES: OBFUSCATION, EVASION, AND RESISTANCE

Besides securing financing and protection, smugglers also adopted countermeasures to more directly undermine, evade, or defeat state interdiction. Despite the abundant and technologically sophisticated resources amassed by the state, merchants, runners, and assorted organizations were clearly able to marshal resources of their own, frustrating repeated efforts to compel them to comply with regulations and pay duties. The overall impact of such countermeasures is difficult to determine, but they nonetheless offer tangible examples of how elaborate, bottom-up tactics were effectively, cheaply, and asymmetrically deployed to counter the official, top-down war on smuggling. The common theme running through these examples, to borrow a metaphor employed by historian Eric Tagliacozzo, is the "waltz" between state and smuggler—the dialectical relationship where each measure adopted is in turn met with a countermeasure in a seemingly endless cycle.[68]

In contrast to petty traffickers, who sought to evade preventive measures individually, organized traffickers sought to do so systematically. To counter the Maritime Customs' new fleet, for instance, smugglers employed elaborate teams of lookouts to monitor interdiction on both land and sea. As one customs commissioner reported, spies exercised "extreme vigilance" in their surveillance: "No sooner does a [search] party leave a station than signals are flashed and cannon fired to give the alarm."[69] In some cases, smugglers were even able to match the resources of the state. The unimpeded flow of weapons along the coast equipped smugglers and even whole villages with the means to violently resist interdiction. Nationalist China did not just lack a monopoly on the use of force—it also lacked a monopoly on advanced technology. Customs officials quickly realized, for instance, that smugglers in certain areas nullified the advantages the agency initially enjoyed from its new wireless network. On the coast of Fujian, for example, provincial officials counted thirty-five wireless stations built by one smuggling concern and its many branches to coordinate their operations.[70] Elsewhere, officials uncovered a wireless station "in the middle of [a] smuggling district" and warned local personnel that outside parties could eavesdrop on their radio communications.[71]

Smugglers challenged another important pillar of interdiction: information. The Maritime Customs had long relied on informants as part of its preventive efforts and offered rewards based on the value of seized goods. The upsurge in smuggling and growing urgency to suppress it led the agency to expand its system of rewards and even to create a dedicated intelligence service to hire informants (both Chinese and foreign) on a retainer basis. Mirroring the construction of this elaborate intelligence network, however, was the growing effort to defeat it. The most direct, brute method was to silence the channels of information by intimidating informants themselves. The sheer volume of tips authorities received suggests that many informants still believed that monetary rewards, or perhaps moral satisfaction, still outweighed the risk of personal harm. Yet the risks were real, since such informers threatened potentially lucrative profits. In a letter to authorities, for instance, one merchant was willing to come forward with information on major smuggling routes across the Hong Kong border but hesitated to reveal more: "This humble merchant is weak, and [since] the bandits can retaliate, [I] therefore dare not point out their names and addresses."[72] One commissioner, lamenting the recent dearth of actionable intelligence, blamed the maddening silence on rumors that an informant had been killed by smugglers, noting that "this news [had] naturally frightened other would-be informers."[73] Two other informants, both steamship crew members, suffered similar fates when their treacheries were uncovered. One was thrown overboard. The other was locked away in a cabin and later disappeared without a trace.[74] Reports also abounded in the popular press that "snitches" (*xianmin*) were targets of reprisals. The *Shen Bao* revealed how several informants had been murdered at the hands of smugglers who were furious that their activities had been uncovered.[75]

Smugglers also compromised intelligence channels in less violent ways. Officials often expressed exasperation at being inundated with information of dubious quality. One raid executed at a shop supposedly having a significant stash of illicitly imported medicines uncovered instead only one account book with some questionable records: "As has occurred on previous occasions, the information which seemed to come from a very reliable source was grossly exaggerated."[76] Misinformation was also a problem. After a few successful raids in Tianjin, for instance, *Shen Bao* reported on instances of smugglers feeding the Maritime Customs false or misleading information to help divert attention elsewhere.[77] In addition to wasting time and resources, such misinformation certainly exacerbated tensions with various local communities already wary of cooperating with an ever-more intrusive agency. Meanwhile, the system of rewards was exploited by those willing to play both sides. One customs employee recalled how enterprising individuals served as both smuggler and informant, depending on which role was more profitable in a given situation.[78] Such manipulation probably did not consume a significant part of the Maritime Customs' anti-smuggling budget, but it did have other deleterious consequences. Officials were concerned that long delays and smaller-than-expected rewards discouraged would-be informants. One commissioner urged his counterpart at another port to issue the rewards due his informant ("one of our few reliable informers"): "He is becoming very discouraged by the delay in receiving his fees and I fear that unless he is given something on account he will cease to give valuable information."[79]

Finally, smugglers found unexpected opportunities to profit from other forms of interdiction. To help recoup expenses and pay informants, officials often held public auctions at customhouses to dispose seized goods. To generate the widest possible range of interest, they advertised auctions through public notices (*qishi*) in local newspapers (figure 4.1). Customs officials, however, quickly learned that such events attracted a host of interested parties. Local officials, acting on behalf of provincial governments that imposed their own surtaxes, attended auctions to "make their own arrangements with purchasers concerning the payment of provincial taxes after the goods leave Customs premises."[80] Smugglers themselves, meanwhile, also attended and colluded to buy back seized goods at artificially low prices. The practice was so pervasive that a Xiamen commissioner stopped holding auctions in his area due to "the tendency of local bad characters to form a ring to bid low and to intimidate those outside the ring from taking part." Instead, he sent seized goods to Shanghai for sale.[81]

Even the proper disposal of seized goods created its own dilemmas. Auctioned goods, in particular, frequently filtered back into legitimate markets where they were later resold by retailers at low prices even after markup. The problem was especially serious for domestic match companies, which were negotiating to form a nationwide cartel during the 1930s even as they labored under the new consolidated tax introduced in 1931 and intense competition from smuggled Japanese matches. In 1934, Liu Hongsheng, head of the China Match Company and the China Match Manufacturer's Association, petitioned the Ministry of Finance to urge the Maritime Customs to destroy, rather than auction, the seized matches. Traffickers, he also noted, had learned to forge labels used by officials to identify auctioned matches and thereby laundered smuggled matches as auctioned matches.[82] Liu's claim that auctioned goods were indistinguishable from

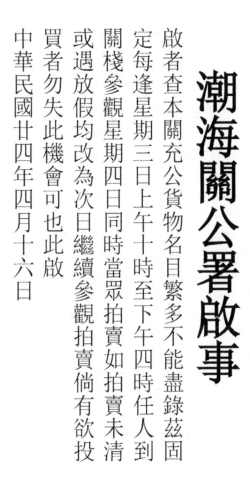

潮海關公署啟事

"Shantou Customs Office Announcement:

We have the honor to inform [the public] that the goods confiscated by the Customs are too numerous and cannot be enumerated. Every Wednesday from ten o'clock in the morning to four o'clock in the afternoon, [the public] is invited to view [the items to be auctioned] at the Customs warehouse. Thursday during the same time, a public auction will be held. If goods are not entirely auctioned off or the date of auction falls on a public holiday, the auction and public viewing will continue the following day. Those who are interested and would like to bid, do not let this opportunity slip away.

Sixteenth Day, Fourth Month, Twenty-Fourth Year of the Republic of China"

Source: XR, April 20, 1935, 2

FIGURE 4.1

Advertisement for Public Auction by Shantou Customs

smuggled goods had some merit. In one case, the Customs Penalty Board of Inquiry and Appeal was forced to reverse a penalty imposed by the Hangzhou Customs on the merchant Lin Guifang. Lin demonstrated that a shipment of Japanese Heavenly Bridge rayon seized by customs agents was actually purchased at an auction held by the Wenzhou Customs.[83]

Even customs officials themselves, in other words, were not always able to ascertain the legal status of auctioned commodities.

POPULAR RESPONSES TO SMUGGLING

Frank Dikötter might well be correct in his assertion that "price ruled the market in China."[84] That is, when making their purchasing decisions, many Chinese consumers and merchants in the 1930s voted with their wallets, frequently placing price over nationalism. Yet such rationalization does not gainsay the importance of nationalism or the anxieties illicit trade generated. Popular writings reveal how nationalist critics shared the same concerns of the central government, viewing illicit commerce as a menace to the nation's finances, sovereignty, even survival. Moreover, the growing volume and increasing visibility of smuggling implicated deep-seated social anxieties over the new role of women as petty traffickers. Price considerations and nationalistic sentiments were not mutually exclusive—even if one was frequently valued over the other.

Elite response to illicit trade assumed different rhetorical forms. One common trope that resonated with public fears was smuggling-as-economic threat. The outbreak of the smuggling epidemic in the 1930s coincided with the apogee of the National Products Movement (Guohuo yundong). A shifting alliance of government officials, businessmen, and activists three decades in the making, this movement sought to restrict access to foreign goods and enforce consumption of Chinese goods. Accurately or otherwise, the movement's activists and sympathizers viewed the battle between "national products" (*guohuo*) and smuggled goods in zero-sum terms, the growth of one coming at the expense of the other. Smuggling undermined their call for nationalistic consumption by making cheap and plentiful foreign goods, thereby weakening Chinese allegiance to Chinese products. It also accentuated existent concerns of Chinese industries being decimated by foreign competitors (figure 4.2).[85] Moreover, activists feared that the demise of national products threatened to have

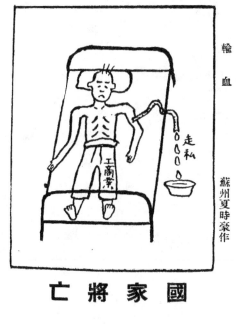

FIGURE 4.2

"Blood Transfusion" (*Shuxue*)

The sickly man of "industry and commerce" (*gongshangye*) is being bled slowly to death by "smuggling" (*zousi*). The caption reads, "coming death of the nation" (*guojia jiang wang*). The cartoon sends an unambiguous message of illicit trade's repercussions to the national economy.

Source: Zhongguo manhua (China cartoons), no. 8 (1936)

wider ripple effects—retailers would go bankrupt, factories would shutter, workers would be unemployed, and Chinese citizens would become foreign subjects (figure 4.3). National products, in this dystopian vision, were but the first dominos to fall in the face of virulent smuggling.

Another common trope was to liken smuggling to foreign invasion. With the country seemingly unable to assert itself on the battlefield or at the diplomatic table, nationalistic activists had long sought to harness the buying power of consumers as a weapon against foreign imperialism.

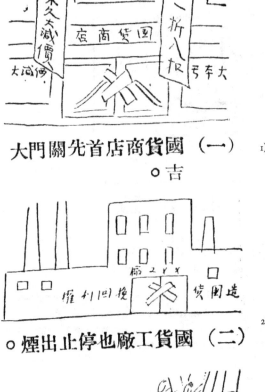

假使走私無法制止

廈門星光影業公司丁白作

"If Smuggling Cannot Be
Stopped"

（一）國貨商店首先關門大吉。

1) "First, 'national products'
stores close down for
good."

（二）國貨工廠也停止出煙。

2) "Then, 'national products'
factories also stop
producing."

（三）失業工人大請願。

3) "Unemployed workers
petition [i.e., strike]."

FIGURE 4.3

"If Smuggling Cannot Be Stopped" (*Jiashi zousi wufa zhizhi*)

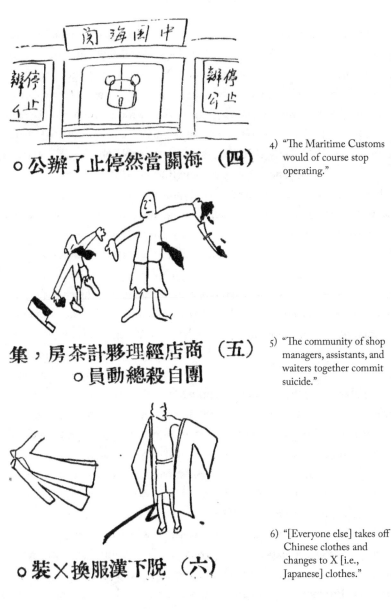

（四）海關當然停止了辦公。

4) "The Maritime Customs would of course stop operating."

（五）商店經理夥計茶房，團自殺總動員。

5) "The community of shop managers, assistants, and waiters together commit suicide."

（六）脫下漢服換×裝。

6) "[Everyone else] takes off Chinese clothes and changes to X [i.e., Japanese] clothes."

FIGURE 4.3 (continued)

The cartoon shows the disastrous ripple effects of smuggling on the Chinese economy and nation. In order to avoid censorship, the Chinese press employed "X" or "certain country" (*mouguo*) to refer to Japan.

Source: Zhongguo Manhua (China cartoons), no. 10 (1936)

Essentially extending the "war of commerce" ideology to the marketplace, they now imagined consumers as "soldiers" on a new battlefield in the long-running war against imperialism.[86] Their primary target was Japan, whose goods faced numerous boycotts due to the country's expanding footprint on the Chinese mainland from the introduction of the Twenty-One Demands in 1915 to the seizure of Manchuria in 1931. Anti-Japanese sentiment rose higher still throughout the 1936 North China smuggling crisis. Stories of Japanese-backed smuggling flooded the press and scandalized the public. Even ostensibly nonpolitical magazines like the *Young Companion* (*Liangyou*), which catered to female readers with news on fashion trends and celebrity gossip, devoted photo spreads of scenes from the crisis in North China.[87] Besides potentially destroying domestic industries, Japanese-backed smuggling also exacerbated what Karl Gerth calls the symbol of China's lost sovereignty and enduring weakness—the trade deficit—and threatened to roll back hard-won gains from tariff autonomy.[88] Trafficking was thus portrayed as a violation of Chinese sovereignty, a portent of more disaster (figure 4.4). From this perspective, petty smugglers were not merely a public nuisance but the first wave of a coming invasion.

Popular antipathy against smuggling was directed not only at external threats but also at internal shortcomings. Not infrequently, critics condemned trafficking as another symptom of the nation's moral deficiency. Corrupt officials and conniving gentries were frequent targets of this enmity, yet no one better embodied the smuggling-as-moral-failure archetype than the "treasonous merchant" who knowingly purchased, shipped, or peddled smuggled goods. Once linked to profiteering or dishonesty, the epithet was now directed at any businessman who ostensibly pursued personal profits at the expense of national welfare. China had long reviled merchants for their greed and deviousness, but as Karl Gerth notes: "The National Products Movement . . . added a new and popular layer to this image by depicting merchants as *treasonous*. By selling foreign products, 'treasonous merchants' undermined the health of Chinese industries, and, by extension, the Chinese nation."[89] The epithets "Chinese traitor" and "treasonous merchant," in fact, were frequently and interchangeably used

走私三部曲

（一）已往

（二）現今

（三）未來

周志良作

FIGURE 4.4

"Trilogy of Smuggling" (*Zousi sanbu qu*)

Each panel of the cartoon corresponds to a phase in Japanese-backed smuggling. The top panel ("past," *yiwang*) shows how smugglers have surreptitiously crossed into China under the cover of night with their bags of "illicit" (*si*) goods. The center panel ("present," *xianjin*) shows the trafficking now brazenly conducted in middle of the day, with smuggled goods (still marked with "illicit") fortifying and shielding an invading army. The bottom panel ("future," *weilai*) depicts an ominous scenario, when smuggling is transformed from small-time trafficking with individual runners to a large-scale invasion with supply convoys escorted by formidable tanks. The goods are no longer marked as "illicit."

Source: Shidai manhua (Modern Sketch), no. 33 (December 1936): 5. Colgate University Library, Special Collections and University Archives

when discussing smugglers. The cartoon "Another Explanation for the Smuggling Problem" (Zousi wenti de lingyi jieshi), captured this prevailing social attitude linking illicit trade with moral failure (figure 4.5). It identified treasonous Chinese merchants purchasing illicit goods as akin to a john engaging a prostitute. Notably absent are foreign powers or

FIGURE 4.5

"Another Explanation for the Smuggling Problem"
(*Zousi wenti de lingyi jieshi*)

1. "Treasonous Merchant" (*jianshang*) is a prostitute soliciting "National Product" (*guohuo*), an old gentleman with tattered traditional clothes reflecting his comparatively humble status.

2. Dressed in decidedly more modern attire, "Smuggled Goods" (*sihuo*) purchases the services of the grateful prostitute.

3. "National Product" discovers the pair's illicit union.

4. "Treasonous Merchant" and "Smuggled Goods" together beat up "National Product."

Source: Shidai manhua ("Modern Sketch"), no. 33 (December 1936): 21. Colgate University Library, Special Collections and University Archives

agents forcing smuggled goods into China. Instead, as its title suggests, the cartoon offers another explanation—namely Chinese weakness—to account for ongoing smuggling.

The activities of "treasonous merchants" and other traffickers took place outside of the public gaze, and whatever harm they inflicted on the Chinese nation were thus intangible and abstract. The activities of petty smugglers like sailors, travelers, and runners, by contrast, were more intimate for the traveling public and more sensational for the popular press. Smuggling on board steamships was a longtime phenomenon, but it attracted greater attention as trafficking became more profitable and interdiction became more urgent. The ranks of petty smugglers included Chinese from all walks of life as well as "vagrants" (*langren*)—Taiwanese and Korean traffickers who enjoyed extraterritorial protections as Japanese subjects. Foreign runners were no more ferocious than their Chinese counterparts in harassing, resisting, or even beating up inspectors, but their open defiance of Chinese authority made them frequent subjects in archival records and press reports. As a report from Xiamen noted:

> The difficulties we have experienced with the runners from Formosa have been of long standing. On almost every Monday when a Japanese steamer arrives from Keelung, hundreds of Formosan runners are found on board, each carrying from one to ten pieces of the so-called luggage, which contains nothing but "pidgin" cargo . . . Indeed, it is a stupendous task for about ten officers to deal with a mob of, say, three hundred unruly and desperate runners who do not hesitate to obstruct or intimidate the officers, and sometimes resort to violence. Many an unhappy incident is on record, and it is almost hopeless to obtain any redress.[90]

Another "unhappy incident" involved a group of Taiwanese peddlers who surrounded and beat (with baseball bats) twelve customs officers (ten lightly, two seriously) when those officers sought to seize an undeclared package of fountain pens. Reflecting the widespread public interest in smuggling, the incident made headlines in *Shen Bao* in Shanghai.[91]

In response to this explosion of petty smuggling, the Maritime Customs exerted more pressure on steamship companies to better monitor their vessels, crews, and passengers, with heavier fines levied for the discovery of "hides" and presentation of false manifests. The steady stream of penalties provoked a coalition of shippers to lodge a protest in 1931. Among many grievances, they especially balked at shouldering responsibility for monitoring the "large floating population of sailors on the China coast" since they had long outsourced the recruitment, supervision, and management of crew members to compradors or recruitment agencies. The companies also protested that fines, while financially painful, were ultimately ineffective since they "neither enable[d] [the companies] to punish the offenders nor to prevent a repetition of the offense."[92] Nonetheless, they adopted measures to clamp down on smuggling and reduce their financial liability, installing metal grills in ships, wharves, and warehouses to restrict access and prevent hides and strengthening internal controls and monitoring of their crew. Unable to convince the Maritime Customs or the Chinese government to relax fines or introduce harsher legal measures as deterrents, the companies enlisted the help of more sympathetic audiences. At their behest, the colonial government in Hong Kong amended an ordinance to prohibit the import and export of unmanifested cargo to further discourage smuggling.[93] The companies also forwarded monthly updates detailing seizures to customs officials "as evidence of the practical steps . . . taken by [managers] to suppress smuggling from their port by [the companies'] steamers."[94] Crew members or passengers caught smuggling in Hong Kong were either dismissed or tried by local courts and given the option to pay a fine or serve time in prison.[95] They were also required to submit "smuggling deposits" as security, from which companies could draw to pay any financial penalty.[96] Such measures never fully eradicated smuggling on steamships, but they did enhance the state's oversight and reach on a very popular mode of transportation.

Steamships were the arenas where illicit trade and state power clashed most visibly, with ordinary travelers frequently caught in between. Not surprisingly, public scorn reserved for "treasonous merchants" and ragtag traffickers soon extended to customs agents, who were simultaneously portrayed as fighting smuggling with excessive zeal or bumbling incompetence. The most common conflict between passengers and authorities centered on what goods should be subjected to inspection, duties, or even confiscation—the very problem Robert Hart had identified in the nineteenth century. The most vocal complaints against invasive searches and even assaults came from Overseas Chinese travelers and their representative associations. Like chambers of commerce, these organizations forwarded member complaints to various organs within the Nationalist government— including the Ministry of Finance, the Overseas Chinese Affairs Commission, and the Ministry of Foreign Affairs—as well as to the press in China and abroad. In one such protest, two members of the Nanyang Overseas Cooperative Association complained that customs officials at Shantou had seized soap and silk piece goods they brought back from Southeast Asia as gifts for friends and family.[97] Such complaints attracted widespread attention not only due to the heightened sense of Chinese nationalism during the period but also due to the privileged socioeconomic status of some Overseas Chinese travelers.

Newspapers in China and abroad enumerated the indignities suffered by returning emigrants at the hands of customs agents, who reportedly practiced extortion and levied illegal fees.[98] Accusations of malfeasance and abuse did have some basis in fact. One low-level agent at Xiamen, for instance, was discovered to have embezzled funds by overcharging passengers various duties and fees, underreporting the amount collected, and pocketing the difference.[99] A foreign customs official, accused of assaulting a passenger during an argument, was admonished by a commissioner that "never in any circumstances [was he] to lay hands on a Chinese passenger."[100] Yet the agency as a whole was defensive and dismissive of any complaints, asserting that its staff was well trained and could "nearly always" distinguish between runners and "bona fide passengers."[101] Whatever the veracity of such claims, episodes of conflict damaged the prestige of the Maritime Customs and, by extension, the Nationalist government. Especially worrisome were complaints forwarded to local governments or warlord regimes, who viewed bashing the Maritime Customs as an expeditious way to appease an influential lobby, channel nationalist sentiments, and embarrass their Nanjing rival. Merchants in South China and Singapore, for instance, complained of customs "red tape" and abuses upon their return to Shantou not only to the local press but also to the Guangdong separatist regime.[102] The problem became serious enough for the Nationalist government in 1935 to send an envoy to investigate the reports of mistreatment, although complaints continued to be levied against the Maritime Customs for years thereafter.[103] The line dividing a "bona fide passenger" from a "runner" was rarely as sharp as customs officials claimed. An emigrant returning to his or her native place, bearing gifts for relatives and acquaintances, was as likely to be accused of smuggling as a runner disguising merchandise as personal belongings to evade duties. Such a problem had been an inescapable part of maritime travel at least since the birth of the treaty port system, but it became more acute as stricter enforcement sharpened the tensions between state reach and private space.

The intensified state crackdown also threw the gendered dimensions of trafficking into sharp relief. Smuggling by women had been commonly reported by government and press alike even before the turn of the twentieth century. The phenomenon only became more widespread—or at least more visible—during the 1930s. Officials, reporters, and travelers all described how ports along the China coast were filled with poor women making precarious livings as petty traffickers of assorted consumer goods, particularly sugar. Many such runners wielded social conventions as weapons, exploiting, for instance, their role as mothers. Reports surfaced that some babies carried by women passengers were not actually babies at all but sugar carried in bags fashioned in the shape of children to fool the undiscerning inspector: "Artificial limbs were attached to the body, and the head was formed by a small bag of sugar inside a coconut shell covered by a woolen cap complete with tassel."[104] Feigning pregnancy was another favored ruse. One traveler employing this tactic was caught with bundles of watches tied across her stomach: "Suspicion was aroused by the woman's movements which seemed to be unduly active."[105]

The bold subversion of social expectations worried officials. The unexpectedly fierce resistance women runners put up, in particular, challenged prevailing notions of feminine weakness. As a customs report noted, "They are specially difficult persons to deal with as they fight, scratch and tear the uniforms of our Officers and when goods have been taken from them have frequently come wailing round the Custom House causing disturbance."[106] Supposed feminine wiles also led officials to preach greater vigilance. An issue of the Maritime Customs magazine *Customs Echo* (*Guansheng*) featured a translated article entitled, "Girl Smugglers" (Fansi de guniang), which surveyed the many instances of "delicate and pretty girls" (*xianruo xiuli de guniang*) leveraging their beauty and youthful innocence as they "bewitched" (*hunxiao*) unassuming inspectors to smuggle narcotics, precious stones, and assorted contraband across Europe. Losses to government revenues and threats to public order from such "dreadful ruses" (*kewei de guiji*), the article asserted, were incalculable but nonetheless real. Appended at the end was a commentary by the translator, a Chinese customs official who urged colleagues to "guard against deception while on duty" (*zuo fuwu shi fangbei shou meng*) and bemoaned ways women everywhere "enjoyed better advantages than us men" (*dou jiao wobei nanzi zhan pianyi*).[107] The translator thus implicitly aligned himself with the worldwide brethren of customs agents, imagining solidarity not only over their shared professional responsibilities but also over their experiences as men.

Aggressive state efforts to crack down on women smugglers created their own set of problems. Women travelers being improperly subjected to invasive searches by male officers—be they Chinese or foreign—was an accusation frequently levied against the Maritime Customs.[108] Officials consistently denied such charges, but public outcry and the new Preventive Law nonetheless impelled them to hire more women searchers.[109] Compliance varied. Some customhouses on the Hong Kong–Shenzhen border and at railway stations, for example, had already employed women searchers before the 1930s.[110] Customhouses at Xiamen and Shantou, major transit points for Overseas Chinese emigrants, were comparatively tardy. The former, repeatedly borrowing women searchers from local authorities, reported hiring a woman searcher of its own on a provisional basis in early 1935.[111] The latter added a woman searcher on its staff (also provisionally) in early 1934 to search women passengers and their quarters and lavatories on steamships. This particular searcher proved quite effective. As she participated in many searches, she racked up seizure rewards that represented more than thirty times her official wage. Unsurprisingly, her success quickly attracted resentment from her male colleagues.[112]

Violence arising from aggressive interdiction against women frequently made sensational headlines. Some incidents inflamed public opinion and generated negative publicity for authorities. A Shantou newspaper reported how the "beast-like ferocity" (*rulang sihu*) of customs officials led to the tragic death of a runner.[113] When a steamer from Hong Kong docked at Shantou on August 8, 1935, one Mrs. Zhang (née Chen), was to board a small craft that pulled alongside the ship. She was supposed to be taken to another dock where she could unload her goods far away from the customhouse. But when she suddenly saw some customs officers boarding the steamer, she ran away and jumped to the craft below. The force of her landing, unfortunately, rocked the small boat and threw Mrs. Zhang and a few others into the water. Several months pregnant and weighed down by the heavy coat concealing her bags of sugar, she drowned. Her body went unrecovered.[114]

The public's conflicted attitude toward women runners and state power is neatly captured in a 1937 newspaper essay entitled "Smuggling Yet Again" (Ye shi zousi). The author begins by recounting how witnessing repeated scenes of women with bellies stuffed with bags of smuggled sugar running to and fro, day and night, aroused his anger and disgust. "Shameless things! Chinese traitors!" he cursed. Later when he saw a runner caught, bloodied, and hauled away by authorities, he exclaimed with approval: "She deserved it! Who told her to engage in such shameless, shady business?" Yet such self-righteousness proved far from unyielding. Already uneasy from hearing news of smugglers who died after their small boat capsized, the author was shaken further after seeing another group of women carrying their crying children and illicit goods while fleeing from the authorities.

Like Mrs. Zhang, one unfortunate woman drowned during pursuit after she slipped into a nearby river. The pathetic scene aroused the sympathies of onlookers who bemoaned the terrible risks taken by these women runners for negligible gains. It also led the author to rethink his position: "Ah! Such affairs occur all too often. It is too pitiful. Past anger transforms into endless dreariness. The shadow of suffering envelops my heart. Are they doing this willingly? Of course they are doing this to live! The tide of unemployment and the forces of poverty force them to do what they cannot avoid doing: selling out their own people. I believe how truly serious this problem is!"[115]

In his lament, the writer clearly recognized that socioeconomic conditions were as responsible for driving petty smuggling as personal greed. Yet the tone is one of helpless resignation. The repeated, distressing sight of women traffickers was but a symptom of deeper ills afflicting the Chinese nation. If, as Gail Hershatter rightly notes, women's venture into exposed public spaces during the early twentieth century already "merited notice and some anxiety," then women's participation in the smuggling epidemic and state efforts to crack down only exacerbated such social apprehensions.[116]

The explosion of petty trafficking and the very visible and seemingly casual manner in which it was practiced scandalized the public and stoked fears of lawlessness breaking down the social order. The political cartoon "Smuggling in Shantou" (Zou si zai Shantou) in the magazine *Modern Sketch* (*Shidai Manhua*) accurately—if exaggeratedly—connected the chain of sugar smuggling on board steamships from trafficking to consumption (figure 4.6). It mocked a host of characters: Taiwanese "vagrants" and Chinese petty smugglers working side by side in the pursuit of illicit profit; "dirty poor women" as both victims and agents of trafficking; and indifferent customs agents more interested in putting up a show of authority than actually combating smuggling. The effete upper-class passengers are especially singled out for censure. Not only are they clueless about the ongoing hubbub and the invisible plight of poorer passengers below deck, but they are also the primary consumers of the smuggled sugar in their tea. Such opprobrium reflects the cartoonist's awareness of

FIGURE 4.6

"Smuggling in Shantou" (*Zousi zai Shantou*)

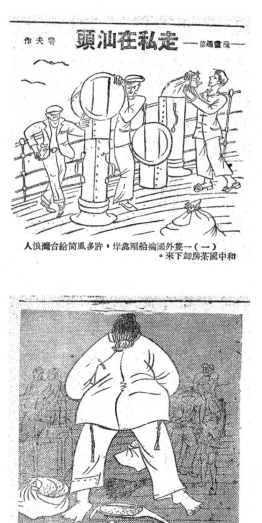

作夫曾 走私在汕頭 —漫畫連作—

（一）一隻外國輪船剛靠岸，許多風筒給台灣浪人
和中國茶房卸下來。

1) "As a foreign steamship nears the shore, the many ventilators begin unloading [the smuggled goods] to Taiwanese vagrants and Chinese tea-boys."

（二）一袋蔬一袋的私貨，分裝在一批髒
髒的窮婦人的肚子上，一個女孩子被浪人督促
快裝，竟嚇得哭起來！

2) "Bag after bag of smuggled goods are divided and stuffed into the bellies of dirty poor women. A young woman pressed by the vagrants to speed up suddenly cries in fright!"

FIGURE 4.6 (continued)

3) "The women board a boat lying low at the tail end of the ship and hide themselves in the cabin before a vagrant commandeers the ship for escape."

4) "They say that some tidewaiters come wearing snow-white uniforms, lacquer-bright leather shoes, and off-centered Chevalier-style caps. Some appreciate the confused sentiments of gawking commoners; some whistle 'Song of the Fisherman' while strolling on the deck."

Note: "Chevalier-style" (*Xifulai shi*) refers to Maurice Chevalier, a French movie actor known for his trademark boater hat. "Song of the Fisherman" (*Yuguang qu*) comes from a 1930s Chinese movie.

FIGURE 4.6 (continued)

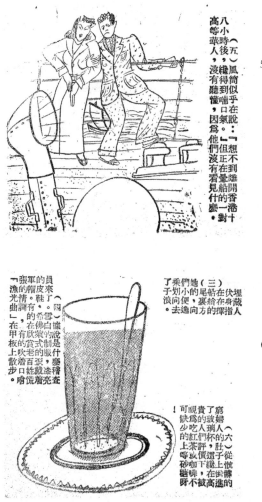

5) "The ventilators seem to say: 'Who would have thought that after eighteen hours leaving Hong Kong, we can finally get some air.' But the seasick upper-class Chinese couple can't understand because they don't see a thing."

6) "From the belly of filthy women and dumped into a glass cup: high-grade sugar, in the eyes of elites, is something black tea and coffee cannot afford to be without!"

FIGURE 4.6 (continued)

Source: Shidai manhua ("Modern Sketch"), no. 35 (February 1937): 18. Colgate University Library, Special Collections and University Archives

Chinese consumers contributing to the smuggling epidemic. And even the selection of the cartoon's setting is not arbitrary. Shantou, as this chapter shows, was a notorious center of trafficking on board steamships and a perpetual site of conflict between state and traveler. In the cartoon, as in real life as imagined by the public, illicit behavior implicated everyone and transcended all lines of identity—national, class, gender, and political allegiances.

Smuggling as a subject also appeared in other media. Literary fiction on trafficking, in particular, was widely read and consumed, spanning various genres and attracting different audiences. Some were short stories like "The Smugglers' Cave" (Zousihuo ren de dong), which appeared in the magazine *Children's World* (*Ertong shijie*). Two siblings, an older boy Cheng Er and a younger girl Mei Gu, uncover the titular hideout along a seaside cliff during a picnic as they wander away from their father, Mr. Peng. Before the pair can exit the cave, they are forced to take refuge deep within when a gang of smugglers returns with a bound prisoner. As the afternoon turns to dusk, the siblings surreptitiously untie the prisoner, who turns out to be none other than their own father. Freed, he quickly calls for assistance and chases the smugglers away. The story ends with a proud Mr. Peng congratulating his children: "They have fled, but we seized their smuggled goods—thanks to you two!"[117]

"The Smugglers' Cave" highlights the heroism of the siblings in many ways. The children's courage in freeing their father and saving the day are certainly commendable. (Their actions also offer a modern twist on traditional notions of filial piety.) But even more praiseworthy is the precocious political consciousness they exhibit. As Cheng Er exclaims upon seeing the wooden chests and alcohol barrels in the cave: "This must be a place hiding the goods of people who smuggle and want to evade taxes!"[118] He thus immediately links his serendipitous discovery to its larger implications for the nation. The story presents an exemplary, if overly didactic, message for its young readers: anyone could and should do their own small part to fight smuggling and thereby protect national finances.

Smuggling also became the subject of a 1936 eponymous one-act play by Hong Shen (1884–1955), the American-educated dramatist hailed as China's "founding father of realist theater."[119] "Smuggling" (Zousi) centers on the tense confrontation one evening between an armed gang of sugar traffickers who arrive in a small North China village and a restaurateur, Mrs. Li, who is pressed to serve them after her husband flees. Much of the gang seems content to wait quietly for the arrival of their unnamed leader ("the boss"). The lone exception is the trafficker Jia Yunxing, who loudly boasts of his ill-gotten gains, conspicuously consumes the smuggled white sugar, and continually menaces Mrs. Li with his gun as he becomes increasingly inebriated. The play's climatic scene occurs when the gang's boss—dressed in foreign clothes that hint at his true origins—enters the restaurant. In the heat of an argument, the boss smashes the treasured Li family heirloom (a Qianlong-era pot) and threatens Mrs. Li with rape, provoking a distraught Mrs. Li to seize Jia's gun and shoot him. Other villagers quickly arrive in force and confront the gang. They arrest the drunken Jia, despite his protests of innocence and threats of calling on his foreign backers. The play concludes with the villagers vowing henceforth not only to stop traffickers from entering the village but also to renounce the consumption of Japanese white sugar.[120]

In subsequent years, Hong produced other dramas like "Foreign White Sugar" (Yang baitang) and "Salt Fish Doctrine" (Xianyu zhuyi) that also took illicit trade as their main theme. Written to "probe and expose social problems in realist form," his plays fit squarely within the 1930s "national defense literature" (guofang wenxue) movement, which attracted writers of all political allegiances to make national defense the central theme of their work in the face of Japanese aggression and in response to Communist leader Mao Zedong's call for political unity.[121] As Hong himself explained in the preface to his 1937 drama collection: "In today's China, regardless of which artistic field you are in . . . what we need to represent are the tyrannical actions of the enemy, and what we want to reflect are the anti-Japanese sentiments of the populace."[122] Despite changes to accommodate censorship of unfavorable mentions of Japan, the play clearly broadcasts its anti-Japanese message. Indeed, Japanese presence clearly pervades every aspect of the play, from the origins of the sugar to Mrs. Li's recollections of bandits pillaging the village to the identity of the gang's boss. The audience undoubtedly connected the drama with Japanese aggression, not to mention the contemporaneous North China smuggling crisis. So sharp was its political message that the play was frequently performed in the early war years, even as it was forced to shut down by the Shanghai Municipal Council on more than one occasion.[123]

Along with Hong's other dramas, "Smuggling" reflects the prevailing public distaste for illicit trade as both an act of venality and treachery. It also reflects something more: widespread antipathy for state authority and modern consumption. Both China's war on smuggling and consumers' reverence for foreign goods are presented in an unfavorable light. In a conversation peripheral to the play's overall plot, gang member Cheng Jinde boasts of how he once challenged not only policemen but also Maritime Customs agents, beating up five of them with his gang of three. His justification is essentially a commentary on popular attitudes toward interdiction: "These customs agents wear official uniforms yet regularly treat people with great cruelty!"[124] Meanwhile, Jia's ostentatious consumption of sugar—mixing it with his tea—has a decidedly foreign provenance. "I learned it from the boss," he declares, before Mrs. Li, the unpretentious villager, replies in bewilderment: "I have never seen drinking tea with sugar."[125] Finally, Cheng's casual comments about the superiority of foreign goods hint at the broader damage done to the Chinese economy by smuggling: "Who doesn't crave cheap [goods]? My mother and sister buy this printed cloth to wear because it's cheaper and better than our local cloth. [And besides] our village doesn't even produce local cloth anymore."[126] Like the cartoons "Another Explanation for the Smuggling Problem" and "Smuggling in Shantou," Hong's play implicitly mocks the unthinking adoption of a foreign habit and the amoral purchase of foreign goods by Chinese consumers as primary drivers of trafficking. Just as buying smuggled goods was likened to soliciting prostitution, Hong and like-minded intellectuals implied, smuggling was a moral issue in which Chinese consumers bore some culpability.

* * *

Inverting the state-centered perspective on the war on smuggling reveals the broader social responses to the expansion of state power in everyday life. It also highlights the fuzzy line dividing the legal and the illegal economy and ways the two frequently interpenetrated. Far from uncritically accepting official visions of regulatory nationalism or being helpless in the face of aggressive interdiction, many individuals, merchants, and organizations found creative ways to circumvent tightening strictures and profit in a new regulatory environment. Tactics and degrees of resistance varied. Some went as far as resorting to force of arms while many others challenged the state in less direct and more quotidian ways: creating counter-surveillance networks, exploiting legal loopholes, colluding at customs auctions, and so forth. Such widespread forms of evasion certainly highlight the war on smuggling's limits but do not necessarily denote its failure. Smugglers had to engage in elaborate ruses and rely on complex networks precisely because new tariffs were high enough, new regulations were strict enough, and interdiction was meddlesome enough to make extra efforts at evasion necessary. Legal and illegal trade shared a similar logic but ultimately differed in cost structure, potential profits, and degree of risk.

Meanwhile, as illicit trade became more visible and widespread, it occupied an increasingly prominent and problematic position in the popular imagination. Just as stakes in "the tariff problem" debate encompassed more than just state finances, so too did the outcry over the smuggling epidemic encompass more than just public lawlessness. In an array of writings, cartoons, and even fiction, nationalistic critics consistently inveighed against the consumption of smuggled goods and its broader harm to the Chinese nation. Their targets included almost every participant of the underground economy—"vagrants," "treasonous merchants," "Chinese traitors," and even ordinary consumers. Critics were certainly aware of how government policies, socioeconomic conditions, and foreign imperialism fostered the conditions for smuggling, but they were also quick to identify individual greed and other moral failings of Chinese society as culprits. At the same time, critics directed their outrage at customs agents for executing their new anti-smuggling mandate harshly, arbitrarily, or ineffectively. Such sentiments invariably grew from the expansion of state power that brought state agents into new venues and intimate spaces. And of course there was the visible and problematic archetype of the woman runner, who was simultaneously imagined as victim and enabler of the smuggling epidemic. Public discourse on illicit trade thus offers a window into ways everyday trafficking and interdiction fostered popular ambivalence and other anxieties in this moment of Nationalist state-building.

5

ECONOMIC BLOCKADES AND WARTIME TRAFFICKING

Clandestine Political Economies Under

Competing Sovereignties

I N JUNE 1942, the newly inaugurated American intelligence agency, the Office of Strategic Services (OSS), issued a confidential report entitled "Trade Between Occupied China and Free China." Frequently and interchangeably employing the terms "smuggling" and "trade," it detailed the flourishing, regularized commercial intercourse between ostensible adversaries. This extensive traffic helped alleviate chronic shortages in foodstuffs, consumer goods, and raw materials behind both sides of the front lines, despite nearly five years of hostilities and the introduction of numerous economic blockades. Nationalist officials—depending on the commodity and locale—reportedly adopted a range of responses, from fighting, to tolerating, to abetting this wartime commerce. Under such circumstances, the line separating "smuggling" from "trade" was understandably blurry. At the end of one copy of the report is a handwritten comment: "There is so much confusion in the above as to what 'smuggling' really is."[1]

The scrawled note neatly captures the ambiguities surrounding the practice of smuggling during the Second Sino-Japanese War (1937–1945). Confusion over what constituted "legal" or "illegal" trade was not limited to this reader alone. As the conflict escalated, each side haphazardly constructed its own "economic blockades" (*jingji fengsuo*) to isolate the other and thereby limit commerce trading with the enemy. On paper and in practice, however, these blockades were far from absolute, and the numerous exceptions they made for trading across front lines further muddled the definition of smuggling. In accounting for wartime trafficking, contemporary observers pointed to avarice, treachery, and other moral failings of smugglers and officials as the primary culprits. Frequent references to "treasonous merchants" or "Chinese traitors" in popular and official discourse reflected this antipathy. Later writers also pointed to wartime smuggling as yet another manifestation of the endemic corruption that foreshadowed the Nationalists' loss of legitimacy and eventual collapse.[2] These critiques certainly had merit. Official connivance did help drive wartime trafficking. So did individual greed. But wartime smuggling was not exclusively the product of incompetence or venality, for the historical evidence reveals its complex dimensions and conflicted meanings. Beyond the untold death and destruction it wrought, war fractured, disrupted, and displaced existing sources of authority and patterns of exchange. It burred and even erased territorial bounds of authority as the Nationalists, the Japanese, the Japanese-sponsored puppet regimes, and countless other parties—including the Communists, local governments, and guerrilla armies—fought on and off the battlefield. In this fluid and uncertain environment, wartime realities made the clear-cut categorization of "legal" and "illegal" impossible to sustain. Indeed, who was the ultimate arbiter of legality in the face of overlapping and competing claims to legitimate authority? And what did smuggling really mean in this context? Trading with the enemy? Or simply connecting supply and demand for desperately needed commodities?

In considering these questions, this chapter traces the ambiguous meaning of wartime smuggling. It chronicles how Nationalist China's economic blockades were initially defined in the fog of war and eventually redefined—again and again—to suit changing exigencies. As the conflict dragged on, the imperative of victory slowly gave way to the imperative of survival. To examine the actual practice and logic of wartime trafficking, the chapter follows various smugglers and their cargo across frontlines, identifying the tactics of evasion under unprecedented, changing, and inconsistent regulations. Before concluding, this chapter zooms in on the trade in tungsten—the one commodity that was both strictly controlled and frequently trafficked—to explore the unintended consequences of economic controls forged in the crucible of wartime exigencies. If Brett Sheehan is correct that a key feature of the period was the "economy of things," then careful attention to the dynamics of wartime trafficking highlights ways new state strictures—and unceasing attempts to circumvent them—accelerated the flight from money to commodities.[3]

CONSTRUCTING THE ECONOMIC BLOCKADE

The economic blockades that eventually shaped the contours of legal and illegal wartime trade had fortuitous origins. The first phase of the Second Sino-Japanese War erupted with the Marco Polo Bridge Incident on July 7, 1937, culminating with the Nationalists' retreat to Chongqing in late 1938. During this one-and-a-half-year period as the Japanese overran North China, occupied major coastal ports, and ejected the Nationalists from Central China, the battle lines separating the two sides constantly shifted. Neither the Nationalists nor the Japanese originally anticipated a protracted conflict, let alone eight years of brutal warfare.[4] Reflecting such expectations and uncertainties during this first phase of war, economic policies were haphazardly and provisionally promulgated by each side. Whether by design or accident, holes in the blockades were present from the beginning.

The restrictions the Nationalists introduced varied in scope, but all sought to limit the movement of goods that could potentially "aid the enemy" (*zidi*)—a category that became ever more expansive as the war dragged on. The first priority was adequate security of food supplies. In the opening weeks of the war, the government prohibited the export of wheat abroad and to Manchuria. It also ordered the Maritime Customs Service to report any coastwise shipments—especially shipments to six northern ports that "appear[ed] excessive" or seemed "unusual" in any way.[5] Regulations were repeatedly adjusted and expanded until the government finally introduced a more comprehensive ban on the export of foodstuffs—the Provisional Code Governing Punishments for Supply of Foodstuff to the Enemy (Shiliang zidi zhizui zanxing tiaoli)—on August 31, 1937, as the battle of Shanghai raged. During the ongoing "period of emergency," the sale of foodstuffs to the enemy was punishable by death. Even exporting food was considered akin to aiding the enemy (table 5.1).[6] Other commodities quickly came under similar restrictions. Scrap metal, the movement of which had already been regulated prior to the war, was

TABLE 5.1 MAJOR WARTIME TRADE REGULATIONS

DATE OF PROMULGATION	REGULATION
August 1937	Provisional Code Governing Punishments for Supply of Foodstuff to the Enemy (Shiliang zidi zhizui zanxing tiaoli): Made sale of foodstuffs to enemy punishable by death. Large-scale export of foodstuffs also were considered to be smuggling and punishable by death.
October 1938	Regulations Governing the Prohibition of Enemy Goods (Chajin dihuo tiaoli): All goods originating from the enemy—including its colonies, as well as factories and areas under its control—prohibited from import.
October 1938	Regulations Governing the Prohibition on the Transport of Goods to Aid the Enemy (Jinyun zidi wupin tiaoli): Goods "sufficient to increase the enemy's strength" prohibited from export.
October 1938	Emergency Law on the Management of Agriculture, Mining, Labor, and Commerce (Feichang shiqi nong kuang gong shang guanli tiaoli): Placed strategic commodities like tungsten under government control.
March 1939	Measures to Inspect the Transport to Shanghai of Prohibited Goods to Aid the Enemy (Jinyun zidi wupin yun Hu shenshe banfa): Exempted goods to and from Shanghai's foreign concessions and "friendly nations" from embargoes.
May 1942	Regulations Governing the Control of Importation and Exportation of Cargo During Wartime (Zhanshi guanli jinkou chukou wupin tiaoli): Reduced number of contraband. Permitted wide range of goods to be imported and exported under license or without restrictions altogether.

prohibited from being shipped abroad or coastwise domestically.[7] Resin, mercury, bamboo, hemp, ramie, and even seaweed—commodities deemed essential to the war industries of Nationalist China and imperial Japan— were likewise prohibited from export.[8] With the promulgation of these ad hoc policies, the definition of smuggling was slowly but steadily enlarged to include the movement across enemy lines of goods vital to the domestic war effort—even as those lines and categories were still fluid during this opening stage of the conflict.

At the same time it sought to restrict trade, the government also worked to contain disruptions from the conflict and thereby retain popular support at home and abroad. Even as they tightened the movement of food-stuffs, for example, the Nationalists specifically exempted rice and wheat from new domestic inter-port duties introduced to raise revenues during the war, since these commodities were deemed important to the livelihood of the people.[9] Other exemptions were made in the name of supporting the economy by encouraging Chinese businessmen to maintain operations in both free and occupied China.[10] Favorable treatment extended even to relatively modest businesses with no apparent connections to the war effort. The Shanghai Lace and Embroidery Merchants' Guild, for instance, successfully appealed to the Ministry of Finance to "protect the handicraft industry" by exempting its members' shipments from inter-port taxes.[11] Officials entertained but ultimately shelved proposals to "improve the balance of payments by curtailing imports which can be dispensed with in time of war," for fear that such policies would deal another blow to already fragile business confidence and alienate other foreign powers whose support China was desperately courting during the conflict.[12] Uncertainties during the opening phase of hostilities clearly tempered policy responses. Rather than introducing restrictions wholesale, the government initially built the economic blockade commodity by commodity. It then carved out various exemptions and conferred favorable duty treatment to balance competing priorities.

The Maritime Customs, meanwhile, was charged with enforcing a growing number of complex, inconsistent prohibitions at the same time its own geography of enforcement dramatically contracted. The agency's status as a foreign-managed institution continued to shield it from out-right seizure by the Japanese until the outbreak of the Pacific War (1941–1945). Yet it was not entirely immune to the fallout from ongoing hostili-ties. Customs officials, in particular, had to curtail patrols and shutter stations as open warfare made many areas too dangerous for regular opera-tion. Most detrimental for the agency was the deterioration and even destruction of its technical assets. Wartime reports were replete with accounts of customs patrols and vessels coming under fire by the Japanese. One of the more notable incidents occurred in November 1937, when the Japanese military seized ten customs vessels docked in the Huangpu River as it tightened its encirclement of Shanghai in the wake of Nationalist retreat.[13]

Changes in the level of fines and confiscations reflect the adverse impact of the war on both trade patterns and preventive capacities (table 5.2). After the 1936 North China smuggling crisis, the Maritime Customs intensified its preventive efforts along the Great Wall and around Tianjin. As a result, fines and confiscations in the region held steady through the first half of 1937. They were on pace to match the levels of prior years, according to an official, but hostilities "completely shattered" such gains.[14] The Chief Inspection Bureau (CIB), established in 1936 specifically to combat smuggling on major railways and highways in North and Central China, experienced similar problems in 1937 and was shuttered by the end of 1938. Fines and confiscations in Shanghai, long the highest among all ports, fell dramatically after mid-1937 as open warfare erupted in many parts of the city and its vicinity. In addition to its adverse impact on trade, the war seriously constrained local customs operations and "all active pre-ventive work came to an end except on the pontoons and at the wharves along the International and French Bunds."[15] Preventive work in Guang-dong proved comparatively more resilient since South China was largely spared of the worst fighting until the 1944 Ichigō Campaign. As patrols at sea became more restricted, local stations focused their efforts in other venues. In Shantou, for instance, officials intensified their campaign against smuggling on board steamships.[16] In the Pearl River Delta, land patrols continued apace despite increasing dangers from the twin threat of war

TABLE 5.2 FINES AND CONFISCATIONS BY REGION, 1932–1938 (THOUSANDS OF $CN)

REGION	1932–1936 AVERAGE	1937 FIRST HALF	1937 SECOND HALF	1937 TOTAL	1938 TOTAL	1938/ 1932–1936 (%)
North China ports	1,935.2	975.6	560.1	1,535.8	427.9	-77.9
Yangzi ports	181.1	35.3	40.2	75.6	159.4	-12.0
Shanghai	1,316.8	504.1	109.2	613.4	401.2	-69.5
Mid-coastal ports	1,026.5	182.9	64.9	247.8	187.1	-81.8
Guangdong ports	1,700.6	879.6	554.6	1,434.2	1,224.7	-28.0
Interior land stations	54.8	21.9	17.8	39.7	71.2	29.9
Chief Inspection Bureau (CIB)	307.8*	188.4	44.6	233.0	43.2	-86.0
Total	6,461.3**	2,787.8	1,391.5	4,179.3	2,514.7	-61.1

Source: Calculated from SHAC, *679/1/4135,* PN (various).

Note: North China ports: Great Wall stations (1934–1936), Longkou, Qingdao, Qinhuangdao, Tianjin, Weihaiwei, Zhifu; Yangzi ports: Changsha, Chongqing, Hangzhou, Hankou, Jiujiang, Nanjing, Shashi, Suzhou, Wanxian, Wuhu, Yichang, Yuezhou, Zhenjiang; Mid-coastal ports: Fuzhou, Ningbo, Sandu, Wenzhou, Xiamen; Guangdong ports: Beihai, Guangzhou, Jiangmen, Kowloon, Lappa, Leizhou (1936), Nanning, Qiongzhou, Sanshui, Shantou, Wuzhou; interior land stations: Longzhou, Mengzi, Simao, Tengyue.

*CIB not established until 1936. Data from 1936 only.

**Average of totals from 1932–1936, not the total of 1932–1936 averages, plus 1936 CIB data.

and banditry. As a result, fines and confiscations in Guangdong during 1938 fell only one-third from their average levels from 1932 to 1936—a modest decline compared to other regions during the same years.

By late 1939, the agency's preventive secretary reported that the Japanese had shut down the Maritime Customs' entire wireless coastal network and "immobilized, destroyed, or seized" much of the agency's fleet. His remarks summarize the new constraints under which the agency was operating:

> With the occupation of large tracts of territory including the main coast ports and the blockade of the remainder, the fiscal zone under Chinese Government control is now virtually bordered by one vast land frontier which stretches the entire length of China and which constantly fluctuates according to the progress of hostilities. The Customs task of protecting such a frontier would be difficult enough in peace time but is made infinitely more so by war conditions . . . Furthermore, the Customs have [sic] not only to protect revenue interests but to endeavor to enforce a number of new prohibitions and restrictions on imports and exports which have been introduced as war measures to maintain China's economic stability.[17]

Ongoing hostilities and the deterioration of technical assets made effective enforcement of regulations extremely difficult, if not impossible. If the Maritime Customs steadily expanded its geography of enforcement during the Nanjing Decade, then the war slowly pushed the agency back to its traditional jurisdiction at treaty ports.

DEFINING THE ECONOMIC BLOCKADE

After the Nationalists lost the battle of Wuhan and subsequently retreated to Chongqing in October 1938, the conflict entered its "war of attrition" phase. Entrenched in western China, the Nationalist government opted for decentralized warfare instead of direct engagement against superior

Japanese forces. It opened new fronts by establishing guerrilla armies and ten war zones throughout China. It also launched a campaign of terrorism and assassinations in major cities like Shanghai against the Japanese and Chinese collaborators. For their part, the Japanese initiated limited land campaigns that focused on capturing "points and lines"—strategic locales or routes. Lacking sufficient manpower to hold their territorial gains, the Japanese relied heavily on unrelenting aerial bombardment to break morale. The air raids punished but did not prevail, for they failed to achieve their stated objective in forcing a settlement with Nationalist China. While this phase of the war still very violent, neither side achieved any major breakthroughs until the Japanese army's massive Ichigō Campaign of early 1944 that devastated Nationalist forces across central and southern China.

During this period of decentralized warfare, the Nationalists also turned to economic warfare, attempting to restrict trade yet encountering unforeseen obstacles. Initially, economic blockades were more comprehensive and more absolute in the kinds of commodities prohibited. On October 27, 1938, less than a week after the fall of Wuhan, Chongqing introduced two sets of regulations aimed at limiting commercial traffic between free and occupied China. Regulations Governing the Prohibition of Enemy Goods (Chajin dihuo tiaoli) outlawed the import of all "enemy goods" (*dihuo* or *chouhuo*), defined as products originating from the enemy, its colonies, or factories and occupied areas under its control. The corresponding Regulations Governing the Prohibition on the Transport of Goods to Aid the Enemy (Jinyun zidi wupin tiaoli) outlawed the export of goods that "could increase the enemy's strength" (*zuyi zengjia diren zhi shili zhe*). Punishments for offenders include fines, penal servitude (six months to life), and even death in certain circumstances.[18] Subsequent judicial rulings reaffirmed the new and broader definitions of smuggling. In response to queries from provincial and military officials, the Judicial Yuan, Nationalist China's constitutional court, ruled that merchants, soldiers, and inspectors who sold prohibited goods to the enemy or even abetted their transport could be punished in accordance with the prohibitions.[19]

Managing this blockade was the new Ministry of Economic Affairs (MOEA, Jingji bu). Charged with the responsibility for defining what constituted an "enemy good," it established a dedicated Committee on Economic Blockade Against the Enemy (Duidi jingji fengsuo weiyuan-hui), which coordinated with local Committees on Prohibiting Enemy Goods (Chajin dihuo weiyuanhui), local governments, Maritime Customs stations, chambers of commerce, guilds, and factories to enforce prohibitions in nonoccupied areas.[20] Already granted sweeping powers to nationalize preexisting enterprises and establish new state-owned enterprises, the MOEA now imposed bureaucratic guidance in managing the everyday flow of commodities for the war effort.[21] Its expansive role was underpinned by different motives. Ideologically, the MOEA's management of blockades represented another step for Nationalist China to more fully realize the ideals of economic control articulated by its founding father Sun Yat-sen. At the same time, wartime exigencies fueled official imperatives to mobilize national resources and discipline everyday consumption in the name of achieving victory. Conserving essential commodities both limited contact with the enemy and deprived new Japanese-financed "development companies" in occupied areas of raw materials from the interior.[22] Most importantly, prohibiting unnecessary commercial intercourse with occupied China staunched the hemorrhaging of valuable specie and foreign exchange—all of which free China desperately needed to purchase essential imports; fund the government and military; and arrest inflationary pressures.

Government correspondences commonly referenced cases of draconian punishments meted out for trafficking.[23] Yet such frequency and harshness did not fully translate into more effective deterrence. Indeed, despite the sweeping nature of the new blockade, smuggling remained vibrant during this relative lull in the war. As economic conditions on both sides deteriorated, shortages of almost every commodity—from daily necessities, to luxury products, to industrial components—proved increasingly acute. From a macro perspective, the overall geography of wartime smuggling was similar to its prewar counterpart (map 5). Except for trade across the

Burmese border, imports and other manufactured goods still flowed from coastal entrepôts into the Chinese interior where they were exchanged for specie, raw materials, and other foodstuffs. Yet from a micro perspective, according to Keith Schoppa, "war displaced and transformed the prewar trading system" by forcing traffickers to bypass economic blockades, damaged infrastructure, and dangerous battlefields.[24] Rerouting commercial corridors enhanced the relative importance of both marginal hinterlands and colonial enclaves as links between occupied and unoccupied areas. Although referring to Zhejiang province specifically, Schoppa's observation applies across the Chinese littoral generally. Islands like Zhoushan, Jinmen, and Nan'ao just off the coasts of Ningbo, Xiamen, and Shantou, respectively, were transformed from smuggling hubs before the war to critical transshipment centers during the war. Meanwhile, ports like Shanghai, Hong Kong, Macao, and Guangzhouwan served as "lifelines" between free China and the outside world, as their colonial status staved off immediate occupation by the Japanese.

One reason why the blockade proved so porous was that the definition of smuggling continuously shifted. As government economist Cheng Yu-kwei (Zheng Yougui) notes, Nationalist China's "wartime trade policy with respect to imports underwent several modifications and reversals to suit the changing situation."[25] Such modifications took on many forms. Nationalist China still exempted certain goods from the blockade for the sake of necessity, just as it had done during the pre-1938 phase of the war. In response to a query from inspectors in the Hunan-Hubei area, for instance, the Ministry of Finance ruled that goods such as razors, scissors, hair clippers, and rubber solution for tires could be imported regardless of origins.[26] Other modifications were made ad hoc in specific locales. Upon the receipt of intelligence that the Japanese were purchasing large amounts of charcoal along the coast and in occupied areas, for example, the government resurrected a temporary ban on the exportation of charcoal to Zhejiang.[27] Policy variations, exceptions, and inconsistencies were the understandable results of official efforts to meet fluid circumstances, yet they further complicated the meaning of smuggling by selectively permitting

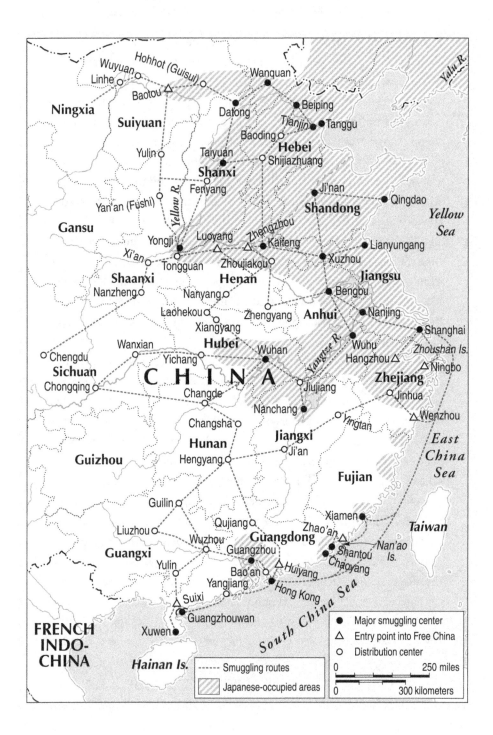

Ningxia

Wuyuan
Linhe
Hohhot (Guisui)
Baotou
Suiyuan
Yulin
Wanquan
Datong
Beiping
Tianjin
Tanggu
Baoding
Hebei
Taiyuan
Shijiazhuang
Shanxi
Fenyang
Ji'nan
Shandong
Qingdao
Yellow
Sea
Yan'an (Fushi)
Gansu
Yongji
Luoyang
Zhengzhou
Kaifeng
Lianyungang
Xi'an
Tongguan
Zhoujiakou
Xuzhou
Shaanxi
Henan
Jiangsu
Nanzheng
Nanyang
Bengbu
Laohekou
Zhengyang
Anhui
Nanjing
Xiangyang
Shanghai
Wanxian
Hubei
Wuhan
Wuhu
Zhoushan Is.
Chengdu
Yichang
Hangzhou
Ningbo
Sichuan
CHINA
Jiujiang
Zhejiang
Chongqing
Changde
Nanchang
Jinhua
Changsha
Yingtan
Wenzhou
Hunan
Jiangxi
East
China
Sea
Guizhou
Hengyang
Ji'an
Fujian
Guilin
Xiamen
Taiwan
Liuzhou
Qujiang
Zhao'an
Wuzhou
Guangdong
Nan'ao
Guangxi
Guangzhou
Shantou
Is.
Yulin
Bao'an
Huiyang
Chaoyang
Yangjiang
Hong Kong
FRENCH
INDO-
CHINA
Suixi
Guangzhouwan
South China Sea
Xuwen
Hainan Is.

Yalu R.
Yellow R.
Yangtze R.

● Major smuggling center
△ Entry point into Free China
○ Distribution center
----- Smuggling routes
▨ Japanese-occupied areas

0   250 miles
0   300 kilometers

MAP 5

Wartime Smuggling Networks, ca. 1940

This map is produced by combining two maps: one showing Japanese-occupied areas, one showing major smuggling networks between free and occupied China as detailed by Nationalist China intelligence reports. It provides a schematic representation of land and riverine smuggling networks but does not purport to show all routes, particularly aerial routes. Wartime exigencies meant that smuggling routes and occupied areas were much more fluid than the map's static lines and boundaries suggest.

Map of Japanese-occupied areas from Department of History, US Military Academy (USMA), http://www.usma.edu/history/sitepages/chinese%20civil%20war.aspx (accessed August 9, 2017). Original map of smuggling network from IMHA, 18-26-01-003-01; modified version from Lin Meili, "Kangzhan shiqi de zousi huodong yu zousi shizhen" (Smuggling activities and smuggling markets during the War of Resistance period), in *Jinian qiqi Kangzhan liushi zhounian xueshu yantaohui lunwen ji* (Collection of essays from academic conference to commemorate the 60th anniversary of the July 7 War of Resistance), ed. Jinian qiqi Kangzhan liushi zhounian xueshu yantaohui choubei weiyuanhui (Taipei: Guoshi guan, 1998), 2:52

trade with the enemy. While not mutually exclusive in the official imagination, immediate survival took precedence over future victory.[28]

More importantly, the blockade's efficacy rested primarily on categories of "occupied areas and factories," "enemy goods," and "goods to aid the enemy" (*zidi wupin*), all of which were defined in lists issued by the MOEA. Updated irregularly, such "enemy goods lists" (*dihuo biao*) cataloged the growing number of commodities prohibited from import into free China. The lists also enumerated the provinces, prefectures, and other localities that had "been forcefully controlled by the enemy" (*bei diren baoli kongzhi*). Transporting goods to or from such areas was also strictly banned. Not surprisingly, classifying a prohibited commodity or an occupied area was a difficult task. One major obstacle confounding effective enforcement was the ever-changing geography of the war. Maps of wartime China with their static frontlines and shaded areas belied the complex and fluid realities on the ground. The number of counties on lists of occupied areas prohibited from trading with free China, in particular, constantly fluctuated (table 5.3). Some occupied localities, such as the northeastern provinces in

Manchuria, were restricted entirely from commercial intercourse with free China almost immediately after the outbreak of hostilities. Other localities, by contrast, were later added to and deleted from the lists within a relatively short period. Further complicating the definition of an occupied area, the lists permitted some trade with counties that bore notations such as "county seat excluded" (*xiancheng chuwai*) to reflect that they were only partially occupied.

Other exemptions were explicitly carved out to protect economic activities in strategic locales. Shanghai, in particular, was classified as an occupied area by late 1938. Yet its foreign concessions—the city's "solitary island" (*gudao*)—continued to serve as major nodes in free China's economic lifeline. Merchants who depended on the Shanghai market quickly petitioned officials to relax regulations blockading the city.[29] In response, the government introduced a new law in March 1939—less than five months after instituting the economic blockade—permitting limited commercial intercourse between free China and Shanghai. Measures to Inspect the Transport to Shanghai of Prohibited Goods to Aid the Enemy (Jinyun zidi wupin yun Hu shenhe banfa) exempted Shanghai's foreign concessions from the blockade. It also permitted the export of goods from free China required by the city's factories, "friendly nations'" (*youbang*) businesses, or denizens' livelihood. Businesses or factories that wished to purchase prohibited goods to sell to their counterparts in Shanghai had to obtain a certificate (*zhengming shu*) from their local chamber of commerce or the Shanghai Municipal Chamber of Commerce.[30]

The government expanded these exemptions further. Whatever their status, ports like Shanghai and Hong Kong were critical to the Nationalists' war effort since they served as major sources for manufactured goods and foreign commodities—both prohibited and permitted. Accordingly, the government was reluctant to shut down free China's remaining tenuous links to the coastal economy and global markets. Such reluctance persisted even after December 1941, when Hong Kong and all of Shanghai fell to the Japanese. In response to a query submitted by officials for an update on the status of goods from the newly occupied ports, the Ministry of Finance responded:

TABLE 5.3 NUMBER OF PREFECTURES, COUNTIES, AND MUNICIPALITIES BY PROVINCE CLASSIFIED AS OCCUPIED AREAS AND PROHIBITED FROM TRADING WITH FREE CHINA, 1938–1941

PROVINCE	DECEMBER 1938	APRIL 1939	JUNE 1939	AUGUST 1939	JANUARY 1940	NOVEMBER 1940	SEPTEMBER 1941
Anhui	32	31	24	19	27	28	31
Fujian	2	2	2	3	3	3	6
Guangdong	9	7	10*	10*	15*	18*	23*
Guangxi	—	—	—	—	1	8	N/A**
Hebei	70	70	70	70	126	126	126
Henan	33	32	32	32	33	37	40
Hubei	28	27	30	29	29	33	33
Hunan	2	2	2	2	2	2	2
Jiangsu	43	52	52	51	51	58	59
Jiangxi	7	7	13	12	13	11	10
Shandong	52	65	65	65	73	75	77
Shanxi	57	57	58	58	66	69	83
Suiyuan	12	12	12	12	14	14	14
Zhejiang	14	14	14	15	15	17	23

Source: Tabulated from *JJ* (various).

Note: Dates refer to when lists from the Bureau of Economic Affairs were issued. Other occupied provinces (entire): Chahar, Heilongjiang, Jilin, Liaoning, Rehe. Other occupied municipalities: Nanjing, Beiping, Qingdao, Shanghai.

*Includes Hainan Island and all its counties (not individually enumerated).

**All counties along the China-Vietnam border from Longzhou in Guangxi to Lang Son in French Indochina (not enumerated).

Since the outbreak of the Pacific War, Shanghai, Hong Kong, and other areas have fallen to the enemy. Unavoidably, factories and business in these areas have been hijacked by the enemy. Yet at the present, goods in the rear areas are in short supply. For the sake of stabilizing prices and supplying the needs of the military and the people, all goods from factories and business in Shanghai, Hong Kong, and other areas—other than those already specified by this bureau as "enemy goods"—may be imported [into free China].[31]

In another ruling, the Ministry of Finance ordered officials to continue permitting goods carrying national products certificates (*guohuo zhengming qingdan*) issued by the Shanghai Chamber of Commerce to pass—even after the city's fall to the Japanese.[32] Unfavorable wartime circumstances forced the government to adopt pragmatic measures that helped meet desperate needs, yet created and enlarged more holes in the blockade.

Tracing goods from enemy-controlled factories was a harder task still. The MOEA's enemy goods lists publicized the identities of enemy-controlled businesses and the brand names or trademarks of products from those firms.[33] Such lists were compiled to help inspectors identify enemy goods, yet their efficacy was limited in practice for many reasons. First, some products from enemy-controlled factories did not actually have a brand or trademark. As a result, the enemy goods lists listed the trademark (*shangbiao*) of these products as simply "unknown" (*buxiang*). Second, the dizzying array of brands produced by a single company or factory made it difficult for anyone to keep track of what came from where. The number of brands of matches from Liu Hongsheng's Great China Match Company (Da Zhonghua huochai gongsi) placed on the enemy goods list after the company's factories in occupied China were seized by Japanese authorities in September 1938, for instance, totaled more than seventy.[34]

Compounding the confusion was the fact that certain products had multiple points of origin. Guben, for instance, was a popular brand of soap owned by the Five Continents Company but produced in different factories. While the Guben soap produced by the Japanese Fats and Oils Company's (Nippon yushi kaisha) factory in Shanghai's Xujiahui district was strictly banned, the Guben soap produced by the Five Continents' new temporary factory in the International Settlement was specifically excluded from the prohibition.[35] Products from the Shenxin Cotton Textile Company (Shenxin fangzhi gongsi), owned by the prominent industrial capitalist Rong family, also proved difficult to differentiate. Fifty-two of the company's brands produced by the five Shanghai mills under Japanese control were placed on the enemy goods list. Yet the brands produced by the company's two other mills in the International Settlement and still controlled by the Rong family were explicitly excluded from the list.[36] Official attempts by economic blockades to segregate goods based on national origins were thus complicated not only by wartime realities but also by survival strategies by Chinese businesses pursued to protect assets, relocate production, or reinvent themselves as foreign companies.[37]

Nationalist officials themselves complained of how complex regulations and ever-changing classifications proved difficult to enforce. In a July 1940 telegram addressed to President Chiang Kai-shek, Zhejiang provincial chairman Huang Shaohong recounted numerous problems with the blockade. Huang, for instance, claimed that inspection of goods moving between Shanghai and unoccupied areas in adjacent provinces was simply too cumbersome—even with certificates from the Shanghai Municipal Chambers of Commerce attesting to the legality of shipments. Other rules, like a Ministry of Finance requirement to settle all transactions with Shanghai-based businesses by money transfer, did not clearly stipulate the actual steps for compliance. "Greatly varied and frequently changing regulations," Huang asserted, fostered illicit trade by creating confusion among the people, opportunity for the crafty, and frustration for the ignorant.[38] Others echoed similar misgivings. A government investigation team visiting the front lines, for example, reported on the problems local inspectors faced in identifying goods from enemy-controlled factories. Cotton textiles or fabric were especially vexing for inspectors since they often did not carry a trademark or brand name identifying their origins.[39] In a special issue on "eradicating enemy goods" (genjue dihuo), the publication Battlefield (Zhan Di) presented a series of articles that laid out the rationale behind wartime commodity controls as well as ongoing problems with their compliance. The articles appealed to nationalist sentiment by pointing out the harm done by smuggling to the war effort and exhorting: "Compatriots, wake up! Don't buy enemy goods!" Directing their ire primarily at the longtime bugbear "treasonous merchants," the articles also warned of the draconian punishments for evading the blockade by reprinting the prohibitions on trade with occupied China in their entirety. Yet despite the tough talk, the articles betray a sense of anxiety in their descriptions of the blockade's inability to stem the tide of smuggled goods. One author who visited the frontlines in northern Henan witnessed case after case of ordinary people ("blind to righteousness") trafficking smuggled goods and admitted that enforcing the blockade was "truly one of the most difficult [tasks]."[40]

Effectively conceding that the blockade was impractical and the shortages of everyday commodities too urgent, Chongqing gradually relaxed restrictions before revamping them altogether. The definition of smuggling was loosened as restricting the enemy's access to critical commodities— still an important concern—was eclipsed by the urgency to relieve free China's own dire shortages. In June 1939, the government announced new regulations that limited contraband imports to 168 items, most of which were luxury or semi-luxury goods.[41] In August 1940, Chiang Kai-shek himself reiterated this policy in a meeting of senior Executive Yuan officials: "In all rear areas, essential goods may be supplied with enemy goods for the sake of convenience. For unnecessary luxuries—regardless of whether they are enemy goods or national goods—they are categorically prohibited from import."[42] Almost two years later, in May 1942, the government promulgated Regulations Governing the Control of Importation and Exportation of Cargo During Wartime (Zhanshi guanli jinkou chukou wupin tiaoli), which further narrowed categories of prohibited goods and permitted the rest to be imported or exported under license or without restrictions altogether. Cotton, silk, and foodstuffs including sugar, fruit, and meat were removed from prohibited lists and could now be imported freely upon payment of duties. Raw materials such as tungsten, wood oil, and tea were permitted for export under the direction of government agencies. Luxury goods that wastefully consumed precious foreign exchange—foodstuffs such as sea cucumbers, birds' nests, and shark fins or Japanese products such as sake and porcelain—remained banned from import. Meanwhile, items deemed critical to funding and sustaining the war effort—precious metals, machinery, and foodstuffs such as rice, wheat, and cereals—remained banned from export.[43] Most significantly, the new measures made no mention of the origin or destination of products, a silence that reflected a more permissive stance by the government in trading with occupied China. The new policy, according to a confidential government report, was designed to deal with the shortcomings of past policies by simultaneously encouraging the import of "sorely lacking" (*qique*) civilian and military commodities while eradicating the import of luxuries and narcotics. If trading with the enemy was unavoidable, the report noted, it was better to trade wood oil, hog bristles, and timber—the exchange of which would "not hurt our side or benefit the enemy"—than trade necessities such as foodstuffs, precious metals, and strategic raw materials.[44]

Not coincidentally during this phase of the war, the Nationalist government itself also sought to actively coordinate trafficking. In a June 1940 report submitted to the Executive Yuan, the Transport Control Bureau (Yunshu tongzhi ju) and the Ministry of Transportation (Jiaotong bu) jointly proposed a new plan under the slogan "preventing smuggling, exploiting smuggling" (*fangzhi zousi liyong zousi*). As its name suggests, the program was aimed at preventing smuggling that was harmful while harnessing smuggling that was necessary for Nationalist China's war effort. Such efforts, the report vowed, would "destroy industries in enemy territories, fight for the idle capital of the people, mobilize the campaigns of noncompliance among the masses in occupied territories, and isolate the economic flows between occupied and nonoccupied territories."[45] Much of this officially sponsored trafficking came under the control of Chiang Kai-shek's spymaster Dai Li, who built an extensive smuggling network through the Transportation Control Bureau and other official agencies such as the Supervisory Office (Jiancha chu) and the Smuggling

Prevention Bureau (Jisi shu). Wartime smuggling helped fund the Nationalists' intelligence and military operations throughout occupied China. Yet it became so profitable that Dai's network soon attracted competitors from within the Nationalist government, like Chiang Kai-shek's brother-in-law and one-time finance minister H. H. Kung.[46] Official participation in clandestine trade further underscores how the boundaries separating legal from illegal were blurred or even erased during wartime as conditions on the battlefield and changes in policies recalibrated the relative profitability of smuggling.

Changes in policy also coincided with the breakup of the Maritime Customs. The agency had already suffered serious constraints on its operations since mid-1937, but its institutional integrity came under severe stress when the outbreak of the Pacific War in December 1941 removed all implicit Western protection it enjoyed. Japanese forces quickly captured many stations at major ports including Shanghai, Guangzhou, and Tianjin. These captured stations formed the core of the "Bogus Customs" (Wei Haiguan), now staffed with Japanese officials at key senior posts and reporting to the Wang Jingwei puppet regime. Meanwhile, customs officials who made their way to free China or remained stations that had not fallen to the Japanese formed the core of the reconstituted Maritime Customs reporting to Chongqing. The Nationalists charged the reconstituted Maritime Customs to open new stations in the interior and collect the wartime consumption tax (zhanshi xiaofei shui), effectively reviving the lijin tax that was abolished nearly a decade earlier. Combined with its breakup and the rise of competing agencies, the Maritime Customs "lost its primacy among revenue-policing and anti-smuggling organizations during the war."[47]

Driven by the twin impetuses of wartime exigencies and institutional changes, the definition of smuggling was transformed once more. This about-face in official attitude is neatly captured in a 1941 article "Developing the Work of Counter-Smuggling" (Zhankai fan zousi gongzuo) in the magazine Battlefield, which had published a special issue denouncing smugglers and "treasonous merchants" only a year earlier. Opening with the rhetorical question, "What is counter-smuggling?" the article explained how the new government policy was designed to mobilize the "patriotic feelings" (*aiguo xin*) of merchants and smugglers and thereby break the enemy's blockade. Aroused, the people and "patriotic merchants" (*aiguo shangren*) of occupied areas would help guerrilla forces "rescue" (*jiu*) urgently needed materials for transport into free China. Aware that counter-smuggling and smuggling "employ the same methods and take the same form," the article took pains to differentiate the two by pointing out how the latter is primarily conducted by "merchants who wish to satisfy their selfish demands and go against the interest of the nation's people." After ruminating on the efficacy of various tactics to break the enemy blockade and warning of the need to strictly supervise existing smugglers in conducting counter-smuggling, the article concluded with the following statement: "At present, the air of smuggling has filled the entire country. Supposing we can genuinely make use of smugglers to break through the enemy's blockade and execute counter-smuggling activities, not only can we obtain essential goods and trade nonessential goods for foreign exchange, we can also solve the serious problem of smuggling currently affecting public finances."[48]

In other words, given the prevalence of smuggling already, the government might as well turn an acute problem into a potential solution to solve widespread shortages and thereby help the war effort. This attitude was echoed in a December 1943 report, which recommended that the government "should mobilize state organs and reward merchants to use all kinds of methods to procure as many goods as possible in war zones and occupied areas to relieve material shortages in [unoccupied areas]."[49] With the promulgation of new, more permissive policies, the distinction between enemy and nonenemy goods became further blurred. More than ever, the definition of smuggling was now a function of a complicated calculus involving the category of the commodity, payment of duties, and the identity of the buyer and seller. And given the chaos of war and the inconsistency of regulations, it was a problem that was often difficult to solve.

DEFYING THE ECONOMIC BLOCKADE

Wartime smuggling was undoubtedly a dangerous enterprise, particularly during the early years of the conflict, when both sides still confronted one another on the battlefield. Junks running the blockade between Hong Kong and China in the years leading up to December 1941, for instance, frequently came under fire by the Japanese navy.[50] Yet at the same time, wartime smuggling was also pervasive. As the conflict's stalemate stabilized fronts between free and occupied China, trafficking became relatively easier. According to one firsthand account: "The trade over the lines was constant, with rice, salt, and various raw materials going out; cloth, cigarettes, and luxuries coming in. A shrewd trader could make a profit of four to five hundred per cent by one trip across the front and back."[51] Nationalist government intelligence reports described the "guesthouses" (*zhaodaisuo*) operating at the edge of occupied areas attracting would-be smugglers with alcohol, tobacco, gambling, and prostitution, in addition to smuggled goods.[52] Even ostensible adversaries got into the act, as Chinese and Japanese armies traded sorely needed supplies in defiance of their respective governments.[53] Indeed, opportunities multiplied for enterprising individuals and organizations to traverse battle lines for profit. But how was wartime smuggling actually practiced? What were the tactics of evasion? And how were wartime regulations exploited for profit and survival?

Aside from taking new routes, traffickers had to make other creative accommodations to circumvent ever-changing blockades. One tactic was to launder "enemy goods" as "national goods," a long-standing practice that became more widespread after the outbreak of hostilities in 1937. Enemy goods or goods from occupied areas were often repackaged or relabeled to fool inspectors already laboring under the difficult task of keeping track of kaleidoscopic lists of prohibited products. Gu Zhutong, commander of the third war zone that included the Lower Yangzi region, noted that as soon as a commodity entered the enemy goods list, "it was also not difficult for the enemy to make superficial changes [to the packaging] as the situation demanded."[54] So common was the practice, in fact,

that whole industries sprang up to repackage goods from abroad or occupied China for sale in free China. Many repackaged goods came from
Shanghai and Hong Kong, which retained links to foreign markets as well
as the industrial capacity to repackage high volumes of goods during most
of the war. Regulatory loopholes made Hong Kong a particularly attractive
venue for this business since customs regulations did not require importers
from the colony to declare their products' true origins.[55] Already a longtime transshipment hub between China and the rest of the world, Hong
Kong during wartime experienced a sizeable influx of goods manufactured
in Japan and other prohibited areas that were eventually repackaged and
reexported to free China.[56] Prohibited goods were laundered in other ways.
Japanese cotton yarn, for instance, was repackaged in Shanghai and shipped
to factories in Hong Kong. Manufacturers obtained national products certificates verifying the "Chinese" origins of their piece goods before shipping them to markets in free China and Overseas Chinese communities in
Southeast Asia. After such practices came to light, local guilds temporarily
suspended issuing the certificates, although a chairman admitted: "Currently, because sources of cotton yarn are mixed up, distinguishing [their
origins] is truly not an easy task."[57]

Repackaging was active not just at large coastal ports like Shanghai
and Hong Kong but also at other locales. Counties around Wuhan, for
instance, repackaged goods from the occupied city and shipped them up
the Yangzi for sale at Shashi and beyond.[58] Along the Anhui-Henan border, goods from occupied areas were stamped with labels such as "Jardine,
Matheson & Co." to take advantage of the exclusion of English goods
from the blockade. Such goods, in turn, were funneled into central and
southern China.[59] Along the coast, smuggling grew active with the retreat
of the Maritime Customs' preventive fleet. The town of Shenjiamen on the
island of Zhoushan off the coast of Ningbo, for instance, was a hot spot
for fishing, piracy, and smuggling. During the war, it emerged as a major
transshipment center with a thriving industry devoted to repackaging
cigarettes, clothing, and sugar. Island residents stocked up on low-priced
Japanese goods at the Shanghai bazaars euphemistically called "fish markets." After returning to Shenjiamen, they relabeled the goods to disguise

their origins and shipped them on vessels heading to parts of free China. The traffic was so extensive, according to a 1940 article, that "most enemy goods passed off as products coming from Chinese factories at markets in the interior came from Shenjiamen."[60]

While repackaging facilitated the passage of prohibited goods across blockades, it did not dampen their appeal. Indeed, counterfeit "American" and "Chinese" goods from Shanghai were eagerly snapped up by consumers despite widespread awareness that they were actually Japanese goods. One such product was Baya'er, a brand of soap the MOEA classified by as an enemy good and prohibited from import into free China. The soap did not list its factory's name and address but featured two fashionable Chinese women along with an advertisement—in English—declaring that it was made with unadulterated minerals selected through the latest foreign artisanal and scientific methods. Further raising the MOEA's suspicions was a note that the soap was "most suitable for use in Japanese climate and waters."[61] Businesses in China have long had to balance competing market demands by highlighting the indigenous origins of their products while "tap[ping] into the allure of the foreign, with its associations of power and superior quality at a lower price."[62] The continued popularity of products like Baya'er soap shows how the "allure of the foreign" remained a potent selling point. Consumption during the war, as was the case before the war, did not necessarily value nationalism exclusively above other considerations.

Besides exploiting the confusion over the ever-shifting taxonomy of "enemy goods" or "occupied areas," smugglers defied the economic blockade in more direct ways. According to a Chinese writer who toured occupied China, smuggling in war zones broadly fell into several categories, including what he called "protecting" (*hu si*) and "releasing" (*fang si*). Such practices were already prevalent before the war, but according to the writer they became especially widespread with the retreat of central governmental authority and the emergence of local armies, puppet regimes, and other bandits filling the resulting power vacuum. "Protecting" referred armed groups escorting smuggled goods heading in or out of free China. The deterioration of public order and attendant uncertainties during wartime necessitated armed protection for transport, and many groups including guerrilla armies, demobilized soldiers, local bandits, and village defense teams offered such protection.[63] Even some Nationalist soldiers themselves jumped into the business. While the government sanctioned some coordinated trafficking, it did not look kindly on uncoordinated trafficking and issued numerous pronouncements warning of harsh punishments against "unworthy government soldiers" (*buxiao guanbing*) colluding with smugglers.[64] In one case, Chiang Kai-shek himself ordered commanders in the Four Counties area (Siyi) near the Pearl River Delta to crackdown on government soldiers working with smugglers.[65] Well-equipped, these redoubtable convoys not infrequently clashed with customs patrol teams or other Nationalist soldiers trying to enforce the blockade.

A government intelligence report commented that large-scale smuggling (*da guimo de zousi*) during such chaotic conditions was possible only with armed escorts.[66] The smuggler Huang Keng, for instance, rose from a "hoodlum without an honest profession" before the war to a leader of a major syndicate in Guangdong during the war by making use of armed trafficking. Employing more than a thousand carriers and almost five hundred armed men, Huang's organization trafficked numerous prohibited commodities between Guangdong, Guangxi, and the French treaty port of Guangzhouwan—specie, foodstuffs, and raw materials. Huang also astutely forged diverse partnerships. Local merchants and gentry, for instance, provided business connections as well as capital, including a three-story hotel that served as the organization's headquarters and place of entertainment (complete with gambling and prostitution) for "guests" who filled orders for smuggled goods. They even supplied a steamship (*Da baoshi*, "Big Jewel") that shuttled between Hong Kong, Guangzhouwan, and India loaded with goods. For their part, local government officials and military officers offered political cover as well as legal sanction, such as transit passes that permitted unfettered movement of goods across the region and effectively "legalized" the organization's activities. "By day, they were a government army," recalled one official familiar with the case, but "by night they were a smuggling protection convoy." The scale of Huang's operations became so notorious that the Nationalist government finally issued secret orders in late 1941 to a local military commander to put an end to them.

Although Huang was eventually arrested and executed, some of his business partners emerged from his fall unscathed.[67] Smuggling in the region—armed and otherwise—continued unabated throughout the war.

Another tactic of trafficking in war zones was "releasing," which referred to the practice of inspectors, soldiers, and officials who controlled checkpoints permitting the passage of smuggled goods. Releasing exemplified the devolution of central government authority during the war. As the Maritime Customs was being progressively pushed back to its traditional jurisdiction at treaty ports at the same time the war's frontlines moved into the interior, enforcement of the blockade and responsibility for inspection fell to local governments, chambers of commerce, and guerrilla armies.[68] Bribery was the most common manifestation of releasing. In some instances, the practice of paying off inspectors became so routinized that it was more accurate to label it "taxation" rather than bribery. Government investigators reported that soldiers stationed at checkpoints along the Yellow River accepted payment from fishermen in exchange for passing their cargoes of prohibited goods.[69] An American official reported that certain Nationalist military officers stationed on the quiet frontlines had become wealthy by taxing smugglers who were shuttling between both sides.[70] In some cases, inspectors issued or sold various types of official passes. Besides transit passes, such permits included domestic sales permits (*neixiao zheng*) and disbursement permits (*shusan zheng*). The former were issued to facilitate the sale of commodities that could earn foreign exchange.[71] The latter were issued by local governments to scatter goods that might otherwise be bombed or seized by the enemy. Often, these permits ended up in the hands of smugglers who used them to import, export, or reexport prohibited and restricted commodities.

But venality was only one driver behind releasing. Wartime exigencies often compelled local officials to countenance trafficking across front lines. In response to acute food shortages, for instance, military officials in some areas permitted smuggling as long as smugglers included grain in their shipments.[72] The need for revenues forced other localities to make similar accommodations. As previous chapters noted, preventing smuggling had always been a low priority for many local governments, given that import

duties accrued to the central government. But devolution of fiscal authority during the war recast the fight against smuggling as an opportunity for
local governments to alleviate their own dire financial conditions by suppressing or permitting smuggling. One province in 1940 piggybacked on
the national government's regulations prohibiting the import of enemy
goods by promulgating its own rules on the inspection of imports and
exports. Ostensibly introduced to "stamp out smuggling and ensure that
no military or consumer products flowed to the enemy," the local regulations also levied a provincial "inspection fee" on all goods to make up for
the wartime loss of tax revenues.[73] The jockeying over revenues was intense.
One county chamber of commerce reported to a visiting investigation team
that the coast of Guangdong was full of inspection or tax collection stations
established by various agencies vying for a share of revenues—an Excise
Tax Bureau, Business Tax Bureau, provincial Anti-Smuggling Bureau,
Special Tax Bureau, and local military checkpoints.[74] The predation
became so bad in certain instances that calls emerged for the central government to reassert its taxing monopoly. One customs station in an unoccupied part of Guangdong reported that local merchants had expressed
interest in the agency reopening one of its stations because "all sorts of
'Inspection Parties' and soldiers [were] making prey on goods coming in as
smuggled goods."[75]

Without direct control over inspection, the government was well aware
of the potential for abuse. The regulations creating the first Nationalist
blockades in 1938, for instance, already contained several clauses declaring
releasing, "harboring" (*baobi*), or any type of fraud committed by a local
official responsible for inspection punishable by life imprisonment or even
death.[76] But as the war dragged on, the problem became so pervasive that
the Military Commission had to order both the Ministry of Finance and
the Ministry of Military Administration to introduce more regulations forbidding the practice. Promulgated in 1942, the Rules Prohibiting the Release
of Smuggled Goods on Payment of Duty (Jinzhi duiyu zousi huowu
zhengshui fangxing banfa) stipulated that seized contraband was not to be
passed in lieu of payment under any circumstances. Other commodities
that were supposed to be under government control—such as foreign

exchange, narcotics, and materiel—were to be handed over to agencies responsible for their disposal in accordance with existing regulations. Instructions accompanying the rules from the two ministries stated that while evading restrictions on trafficking contraband was considered to be far more harmful than evading duty, both categories of smuggling "violated the government's decree on the economic blockade against the enemy and produced an enormously harmful effect on wartime finances."[77]

As the Nationalists tinkered with their economic blockades throughout the war, their rivals engaged in similar endeavors. The Japanese instituted their naval blockade of coastal China in 1937, while puppet regimes in North and Central China introduced their own economic blockades by late 1941. The policies of these puppet regimes mirrored those of the Nationalists, vesting responsibility for enforcement in provincial and county governments. These local governments, in turn, established their own "economic blockade committees" (*jingji fengsuo weiyuanhui*). Generally, food and material vital to the Japanese war effort were prohibited from export, while luxuries, narcotics, and anything else that would be exchanged for Nationalist currency and thereby stoke inflation in free China were permitted.[78]

Competing sovereignties encouraged merchants, travelers, and traffickers to shop for legal protection sanctioning their movements. Some Chinese steamship companies, for instance, relied on a prewar practice to secure safe passage: paying hefty fees to their Western counterparts to register their vessels as foreign and thereby enjoy "presumed immunity from seizure and detention by the Japanese navy."[79] Other vessels employed more primitive tactics, flying the national flag in free China but flying the puppet regime flag in occupied China to advertise different allegiances.[80] Others acquiesced to the authority of new regimes as the unavoidable cost of doing business. Fishermen and coastal merchants, for instance, purchased transit passes from the puppet Shanghai municipal government and thereby secured legal permission to dock at other occupied ports. Their counterparts in the Pearl River Delta also obtained transit passes from Japanese military authorities in Guangzhou and Hong Kong and rerouted supply networks through occupied areas.[81] Nationalist military officials reported that these merchants were the primary vectors of smuggled goods between free and occupied China due to their unfettered mobility.[82]

Intelligence reports were replete with cases of merchants subcontracted by the Japanese or their proxies to procure raw materials and foodstuffs. For violating the blockade by trading with the enemy, such merchants were accordingly labeled as "smugglers" or even "traitors" by the Nationalists. Profit-minded merchants rushed to meet the military needs of the enemy by purchasing tungsten, scrap metal, hemp, and precious metals from the interior and shipping them to Hong Kong for sale to Japanese buyers. This pattern of goods moving across battle lines only grew more extensive as the war dragged on and economic conditions deteriorated. In fact, the Japanese came to rely more and more on the services of Chinese commercial agents to procure essential commodities for their troops and occupied areas. At Shantou, for instance, acute shortages and limited military reach forced the Japanese to hire local merchants to purchase foodstuffs and raw materials from nearby counties.[83] Further north around occupied Xiamen, merchants did brisk business purchasing grain from the unoccupied rural interior in exchange for narcotics. To protect their shipments, the merchants engaged the services of the local military and police.[84] Besides foodstuffs, the Japanese also hired Chinese merchants to purchase from the interior raw materials such as resin, quicksilver, and tungsten—all of which were important components in war industries but whose export was prohibited without explicit permission from the Nationalist government.

One group that proved particularly adept at playing all sides was the "puppet pirates" along the Zhejiang-Fujian coast. So called for their collaboration with the Japanese and puppet regimes, the puppet pirates were a diverse lot who performed a variety of interrelated functions in governance and commerce. One was tax collection. The pirates were deputized by the Japanese and the Wang Jingwei regime to collect taxes on goods destined for free China at several designated stations on islands off the coast. Another was providing armed escort. Besides operating their own profitable trade in narcotics and other commodities, the puppet pirates offered protection to anyone who needed to move goods across frontlines. When the

Japanese naval blockade early in the war severed direct transportation routes between Shanghai and Ningbo, for instance, merchants turned to the pirates for assistance smuggling cigarettes and sugar.[85] When the Nanjing puppet regime imposed new restrictions on trade with Shanghai, merchants from Zhejiang and Jiangsu fanned across the city's hinterlands to purchase cotton and hired the pirates to ship their goods to Wenzhou despite the high cost of transport.[86] Pirates also collected tolls to facilitate the passage of shippers, travelers, and merchandise along the coast. Steamers from Shanghai loaded with consumer goods called regularly at locales like Shenjiamen on Zhoushan, where they were met by Fujianese merchants from the south who paid the pirates a hefty fee for the passage north.

The political loyalties of the puppet pirates were always suspect. Some, like the legendary female pirate Huang Bamei, who operated off the coasts of Zhejiang and Jiangsu, allied themselves with different sides in response to the shifting fortunes of war.[87] And in the final years of the war, the Japanese even arrested and executed a number of pirate leaders when they signaled a willingness to work with Nationalist China.[88] But whatever the degree of collaboration with the enemy, puppet pirates and smugglers themselves held more nuanced attitudes on the significance of their actions. As one American observer reported in 1944 on his conversations with them: "The trade affects the view of the people engaged in it. Some frankly hope the war will continue so that their trade will not be interrupted. Others are in the business because the Chinese Government has asked them to go into it. Most consider themselves loyal Chinese, trying to help get needed materials into China. They feel that China gets more benefit from Japan and that they are playing Japan for a sucker."[89]

Such testimonies could be dismissed as self-serving justifications. Yet the attitude of these traders—"they don't like to be called smugglers," wrote the observer—also highlights the complex moral calculus of wartime smuggling. Material shortages and economic deterioration adversely affected everyday life and enervated the war effort. Regulations on all sides were steadily relaxed until smuggling effectively meant unlicensed trade in a handful of commodities or the outright evasion of duties. Moreover, smuggling was no longer viewed exclusively as a social menace, acquiring new meanings in the popular imagination and official discourse. Trading with the enemy, while still offensive to nationalistic sensibilities and potentially harmful to the war effort, was practiced by almost everyone—guerrilla armies, merchants, peasants, and even elements within the Nationalist government itself. Trading with the enemy was also practiced by the Communists, whose wartime behavior has often been favorably compared to the Nationalists' by contemporary observers and historians alike.[90] Seen in this light, what was really "smuggling," when everyone was doing it?

TUNGSTEN SMUGGLING IN PEACE AND WAR

The most-frequently smuggled items during the conflict included foodstuffs, consumer goods, and raw materials—necessities for both survival and war. But no commodity was better situated at the nexus of state controls and wartime trafficking than tungsten. Indeed, the ore appeared frequently in wartime records on smuggling because it was both the most valued and most regulated article during the conflict, a strategic resource for states and a form of currency for everyone else. With the highest melting point of any known metal, tungsten has wide industrial and military applications for cutting and shaping refined steel. It also serves as a key ingredient in heat-resistant armaments and electricity-conducting filaments. Countries including Bolivia, Portugal, and the United States held sizeable deposits of tungsten during the early twentieth century, but China held the most abundant reserves in the world.[91] Domestic demand for this important metal was limited until the outbreak of the Second Sino-Japanese War, since Chinese industries were relatively underdeveloped and did not make use of tungsten in large volumes. Foreign demand, by contrast, was strong if volatile. World War I stimulated the Chinese tungsten mining industry, with most ores exported to Great Britain and the United States.[92] After falling off dramatically during the 1920s, foreign demand for Chinese tungsten rebounded during the global rearmament of mid-1930s. Well into the 1940s, tungsten was pledged as security by Nationalist China in many credit and bartering agreements with Germany, the Soviet Union, and the United States.[93] Due to its critical role in industry, military, and diplomacy, tungsten was proclaimed by one writer to be "the first among all metals."[94]

The growing recognition of tungsten's economic and strategic value led to a concomitant tightening of regulations in China. Controls were first introduced starting in the late 1920s by the provincial governments of Guangdong and Jiangxi, where the country's largest tungsten deposits were located. They were further tightened and finally centralized in 1936, when the Nationalists—fresh from ejecting the Communists from Jiangxi and toppling the Chen Jitang separatist regime in Guangdong—charged the National Resources Commission (NRC) to manage the mineral wealth of the two provinces. The NRC's mandate was to exercise both a monopoly and a monopsony over tungsten and other strategic minerals. It established new Tungsten Mining Administration offices throughout the southern provinces to purchase ores from miners and sell them to foreign customers.[95] Prior to NRC management, merchants who wanted to export tungsten could do so freely as long as they paid a tungsten mining tax (*wu kuang juan*) and an export tax.[96] Under NRC management, miners were required to sell their ores at official prices to central state agents, and merchants were required to apply for permits to transport their ores. The outbreak of war in 1937 interrupted plans to expand this network but accelerated ambitions to centralize controls. Shortly after its retreat to Chongqing in October 1938, the Nationalist government promulgated the Emergency Law on the Management of Agriculture, Mining, Labor, and Commerce (Feichang shiqi nong kuang gong shang guanli tiaoli) along with prohibitions on the purchase of enemy goods. Among other stipulations, the new law placed strategic commodities like tungsten under the management of the MOEA and prescribed penal servitude and financial penalties for individuals who earned private profits through speculation and hoarding.[97] The new law was certainly driven by wartime exigencies, but it also represented a culmination of Sun Yat-sen's ideal of state-led technocratic development for the Chinese nation's benefit. Tungsten, in the official imagination, was a national resource too important to be left in private hands.

Despite extensive restrictions on the books, the channels of supply proved extremely leaky on the ground. Problems began at the source. After declaring a national monopoly on tungsten in 1936, the Nationalist government fenced off deposit areas and established on-site central purchasing offices. Yet actual production at individual mines in northern Guangdong and southern Jiangxi remained free from official control, with deposit areas divided into small independent holdings and the miners difficult to supervise.[98] Many miners surreptitiously sold some of ores they unearthed to dealers who paid more than the low official price offered at central purchasing offices. Whether legally or illegally sold, the tungsten was transported along inland rivers or highways to coastal ports including Guangzhou and Shantou.[99] Thereafter, it made its way to colonial enclaves like Hong Kong, which was the primary entrepôt for tungsten until the Pacific War cut off coastal trade. An investigative report by the NRC in early 1937 detailed this sophisticated market. Orders from foreign buyers were filled when Chinese sellers stockpiled sufficient supplies. Upon delivery, the buyer had three days to decide whether to accept or reject the tungsten; the seller in the interim could not resell the ore to a third party but could raise the original price if the market moved in his favor. Once the deal was consummated, both sides engaged a chemist to inspect the tungsten and certify its quality before readying it for export.[100]

Neither the buyer nor the seller, however, expressed any concerns over the legal status of the tungsten, which was not prohibited from export by the Hong Kong government until September 1939 when war erupted in Europe. Not surprisingly, a significant proportion of the Chinese tungsten sold abroad came through unofficial—that is, illicit—channels. Comparing the discrepancies between Chinese export data and foreign import data, an economist estimated that smuggled tungsten comprised 15 percent of all Chinese tungsten exported to foreign countries in 1934, rising to 16 and 34 percent in 1935 and 1936, respectively.[101] In some areas, the proportion was even higher. The 1937 NRC report, for instance, estimated that 40 to 50 percent of all tungsten sold in the northeast Guangdong port of Shantou came from illicit sources.[102] After its retreat to Chongqing, the Nationalist government still sought to maintain some modicum of control over mining through vestigial Tungsten Mining Administration offices scattered across unoccupied parts of Jiangxi and Guangdong. Yet trafficking only accelerated throughout the war. A British businessman in late 1939 reported from his conversation with a Japanese colleague that fleets of Chinese junks smuggled into Hong Kong two hundred tons of tungsten per month.[103] A 1941 report by the research department of the South Manchurian Railway Company (Mantetsu) confirmed the vibrancy of the tungsten traffic, noting that the metal was the most valuable commodity smuggled into Hong Kong.[104] The scale of the traffic led one magazine to proclaim: "The era of opium smuggling is over; the era of tungsten smuggling has taken its place and flourished."[105]

While certainly hyperbolic, the magazine's declaration nonetheless underscored how smuggling tungsten struck a chord with nationalistic elites who already took a dim view of illicit trade and its concomitant ills. It even became the subject of another 1937 one-act play by the dramatist Hong Shen. "Tungsten" (Wu) tells the story of two entrepreneurs in Guangdong seeking to profit from strong foreign demand as well as strict domestic regulations on the mineral. The venal gentry Lin Zicai and the shady businessman Zheng Dezhong together run a lucrative operation in tungsten arbitrage: buying low from miners at government-fixed prices and selling high to foreigners at market prices. Each brings something to the partnership: Lin leverages his social standing to manipulate ignorant villagers and hapless officials while Zheng exploits his managerial position at a large Sino-foreign joint venture to secure extraterritorial protection and overseas customers. The pair's operation is certainly illegal. In the play, as in real life, tungsten is a government monopoly. The pair's operations, however, is also treasonous. The smuggled tungsten is sold to Japan, which used it to manufacture weapons ultimately used against China. Meanwhile, the miners who engage in the dirty and dangerous work of unearthing the tungsten despair at how the cost of living is fast outpacing the low prices they receive. They also resent the disproportionate punishment inflicted on their brethren desperate enough to engage in their own "smuggling"— that is, selling the tungsten they mined to unofficial channels for a mere few yuan above the government price. Matters come to a head when outraged miners uncover Lin and Zheng's scheme and the extraordinary profits they reaped at others' expense. The play ends with Lin and Zheng receiving their comeuppance as they are hauled by the villagers to the local magistrate and made to account for their treacherous business.[106]

"Tungsten"—like Hong's other plays and works of "national defense literature"—captures the antipathy of nationalistic elites toward smuggling. In the eyes of critics like Hong, nothing better embodied greed and treason than the sale of a strategically critical commodity to an enemy of the Chinese nation. But the play also accurately illustrates the operations of the underground market for tungsten, the details of which were confirmed in subsequent government reports. It identifies, for instance, the fundamental reason Lin and Zheng were able to reap sizable profits from their venture: the chronic gap between official prices and market prices. The former always lagged behind the latter, since insatiable wartime demand exerted upward pressures on global prices while precarious finances limited what the government could pay. Nationalist attempts to ameliorate the problem by offering higher prices were limited in effectiveness. Official prices remained well below black market prices even after the NRC in 1941 authorized payments of 40 to 60 percent above official prices for tungsten sold in localities near occupied areas.[107] This disparity only widened into a chasm as the war dragged on. The market price of tungsten at US$69 in early 1943, for instance, was more than three times the official price of Chinese tungsten, fixed at US$21.19 per ton from 1941 through 1944.[108] Official attempts to cap the price of tungsten thus all but encouraged sellers to turn elsewhere for buyers.

Hong's play accurately pinpoints Japan as the primary customer of smuggled tungsten. In the play, as in real life, Japan engaged numerous contractors to secure adequate supplies of tungsten for its own war effort. Some were foreign nationals like Portuguese merchants. Leveraging their extraterritorial status and their home country's neutrality during the war, they established front companies in Macao and Guangzhouwan to funnel materiel from unoccupied to occupied China.[109] Others were Chinese middlemen like Zhang Wendong. A Guangdong native described as "one of the leading lights in the business of smuggled" tungsten, Zhang scoured the province for ores on behalf of Japanese backers who financed his ventures. Originally an employee of Mitsui's Hong Kong office, he later served as manager of the Macao-based Jincheng Company and supplied the Japanese military with grains and other supplies, in addition to tungsten.[110] His contribution to the Japanese war effort was serious enough to warrant the Nationalist government declaring Zhang a "traitor" and ordering his arrest after the war.[111] Besides leveraging their proximity to mines, Japanese agents like Zhang successfully outmaneuvered their Nationalist counterparts in buying up tungsten because they were authorized to pay markedly higher prices. In 1943, for example, agents paid anywhere from CN$5,000 to CN$7,000 per picul, or five to seven times Nationalist China's fixed price of CN$1,000 per picul.[112] Agents were also authorized to barter for tungsten with sorely needed—and highly desired—Japanese consumer goods. In one instance late in the war, puppet troops sailing from Hong Kong to Haifeng on the northeast Guangdong coast exchanged cotton cloth for tungsten on terms very favorable to smugglers.[113]

Trafficking siphoned a strategically valuable commodity that could be traded for purchase credits and—more perniciously—directed it into enemy hands. Nationalist China accordingly pursued various tactics to stem the leakage of tungsten. On the diplomatic front, for instance, the government in November 1938 assigned exclusive tungsten export rights to the Pekin Syndicate, a British consortium. A letter from the NRC to the syndicate elaborated on the aim of the agreement: "We hope that you being the owners of the Sole Export Rights will make energetic protests through your Governments against any interference with them by Japanese [and] will give as much publicity as possible to the completely unjustified interference in your Rights by the Japanese."[114] The Nationalists thus sought to align foreign interests with those of China's, although their attempts to partially outsource the policing of tungsten exports to the British were foiled after the outbreak of the Pacific War. On the domestic front, the government introduced a raft of anti-smuggling measures like imposing harsher punishments for soldiers engaged in trafficking and requiring shippers to produce official certification attesting to the tungsten's origins.[115] Wartime conditions, however, militated against effective enforcement. Writing in 1941, Huang Bowen, head of the Tungsten Mining Administration's office in Guangdong, blamed a host of elements behind tungsten trafficking, including the absence of "national ideology" (*guojia sixiang*) among the people and even the coastal geography of the province. While viewing tungsten smuggling as primarily a moral problem, Huang nonetheless recognized other underlying factors driving the traffic. Because the government lacked sufficient manpower, its anti-smuggling strategy had to focus more on stopping the source of trafficking inside mining areas and less on interdicting illicit shipments in transit. Even official orders to halt mining in occupied zones or areas near the frontlines became "dead letters" (*juwen*).[116] The very guerrilla armies, demobilized soldiers, local bandits, and village defense teams notorious for their practice of "protecting" (i.e., armed smuggling) asserted de facto authority in mining areas and tenaciously resisted government orders to close any financially lucrative ventures.[117] Outgunned, outmanned, and overstretched, the central government experienced considerable difficulties enforcing its writ.

Meanwhile, the fundamental economics of tungsten mining also fostered smuggling among the miners themselves, many of whom were local farmers who relied on mining for seasonal work. Like their fictional counterparts in Hong's play, countless real-life miners and their families smuggled the tungsten they unearthed to supplement their meager incomes and thereby make ends meet. Such low-level trafficking had been a longtime problem, but wartime deprivations only exacerbated the pressures for survival. In a 1942 report, for instance, the Tungsten Mining Administration's Guangdong Office admitted that "because official prices were too low, miners were unable to make a living" and understandably mined and transported tungsten for sale to the enemy.[118] A 1944 British report echoed such observations, noting how communities that relied on tungsten mining as their sole source of livelihood continued their operations "irrespective of the ultimate purchasers."[119]

Given how Nationalist authorities concentrated their meager anti-smuggling resources at monitoring mining sites, those caught in the already-frayed regulatory net were rarely armed gang members or well-connected individuals like Zhang Wendong. Instead, they were more likely to be petty traffickers like nineteen-year-old Second Sister Ou and twenty-four year-old Big Sister Chen. The two panners worked at the Shenmentou mine in western Guangdong, filching some of the tungsten they rinsed and selling it to the middleman Zhang Si for CN$60 per kilogram, or roughly three times the official price of CN$20. Zhang, in turn, bought the ore and resold it to Zheng Zhangyuan, another middleman. Ou, Chen, and Zhang transacted twice before they were arrested and interrogated by the local Tungsten Mining Administration office in March 1944. Remanded to the local court, they were charged with violating the 1938 Emergency Law on the Management of Agriculture, Mining, Labor, and Commerce, which invested in the MOEA the supreme authority to prohibit the import or export of specified goods.[120] (Zheng, the other middleman, was shot as he resisted arrest and died before he was charged.) The records do not reveal the ultimate legal fates of the three defendants.[121] They do, however, reveal how the long supply chain of illicit tungsten began with low-level traffickers like Ou and Chen and middlemen like Zhang and Zheng. They also reveal how Nationalist China, while too weak to take on organized smuggling in unoccupied zones, was still strong enough to enforce its legal authority in cases like those of the three traffickers. In wartime, as in other times, those at the lowest rungs of the socioeconomic ladder often bore the disproportionate brunt of anti-smuggling enforcement from a badly battered but still redoubtable regulatory regime.

* * *

The meanings of smuggling changed throughout the Second Sino-Japanese War as wartime exigencies and uncertainties led Nationalist China to adopt a range of inconsistent and contradictory policies. Such policies, in turn, produced many unintended consequences. Tighter central control over the wartime economy, designed to make better use of scarce goods for the war effort, exacerbated material shortages that only smuggling could alleviate. Extensive economic blockades, aimed at severing ties between belligerents, created new gaps for everyone to exploit. Together with wartime deprivations, economic controls tightened the interdependence between free China and occupied China. Depending on the time, place, and commodity, trading with the enemy might be strictly banned, tacitly permitted, or actively encouraged. Under such conditions, smuggling underwent so many redefinitions that its signifier as a crime became fuzzy or even meaningless. Ineffectual leadership, rampant corruption, and treasonous venality certainly helped drive wartime smuggling, but they could not exclusively account for it.

Indeed, smuggling in wartime China appears less exceptional when viewed within a comparative context. Surveying five hundred years of conflicts in world history, political scientists Jack Levy and Katherine Barbieri show how "trading with the enemy" was a fairly common phenomenon. Juggling other priorities besides achieving victory, belligerents have rarely been willing or able to sever economic ties with one another. In some cases, the costs of cutting trade with the enemy exceeded the benefits. In other cases, third-party considerations—avoiding alienating potentially helpful neutrals or other nonbelligerents—complicated efforts at plugging holes in wartime blockades. Finally, state capacity to monitor and interdict illicit trade typically degraded during wartime when resources and attention were diverted to meet more pressing threats. This was especially the case for weak states or poorly organized armies that relied on external sources for arms, food, and supplies. Desperate conditions thus created "clandestine political economies of war" that blurred the line between fighting and commerce.[122]

The long Sino-Japanese conflict certainly created many such clandestine political economies. The retreat of central authority, the rise of competing sovereignties, and the deterioration of living conditions all opened more opportunities to skirt fuzzy legal boundaries and added greater urgency to satisfy desperate demand. But just as there were transformations, there were also continuities. The logic animating wartime smuggling's underlying dynamics, in particular, traced its roots well before the conflict to bold economic interventions by the Nationalists during the Nanjing Decade. The imposition of wartime controls and attendant problems simply confirmed the long-running trajectory of economic control in modern Chinese statecraft. The end of the conflict, moreover, did not spell the end of wartime controls, which survived in different guises through the Chinese Civil War and beyond despite their many problems. So unshakable was the official commitment to economic control that neither the Nationalists nor the Communists would envision a modern Chinese economy without the very visible hand of the Chinese state.

6

STATE REBUILDING AND NEW SMUGGLING GEOGRAPHIES

Restoring and Evading Economic Controls
in Civil War China

O N MAY 7, 1948, officers from the Chinese Maritime Customs Service boarded the steamship *Shengking* (*Shengjing*), which had just arrived in Shanghai from Hong Kong. A routine inspection uncovered an assortment of ordinary consumer products hidden throughout the ship's cabins—nylon stockings, woolen socks, and construction nails. Required duties were not paid on any of the items. Nor were they listed on the ship's manifest or even permitted for import. No one witnessed the goods being stashed away before docking, but suspicion quickly centered on two sailors who purportedly had access to the cabins with the hidden goods. The officers detained the pair and transferred them with a full report of their investigation to the Shanghai Local Court. The suspects faced imprisonment if they were convicted, but the prosecutor released them less than three weeks later on May 25 after they were further interrogated. The prosecutor justified the release due to the absence of direct evidence and the relatively minor value of the smuggled goods involved.[1]

Around the time of this incident, in early 1948, the outcome of the Chinese Civil War (1946–1950) still hung in the balance. The decisive military campaigns in North and central China were still months away, but international and domestic attention already focused on the escalating conflict between the Nationalists and the Communists. The smuggling on board the *Shengking*, by contrast, was a routine affair that merited little attention from the public. Almost every facet of the incident was pedestrian, from the goods trafficked to the suspects arrested. So too was the vector of the trafficking. Steamships plying the Hong Kong–Shanghai route had long served as channels for smuggled goods. Yet the incident still encapsulates the many aspects of smuggling during the civil war: a volatile economy and tightening regulations that once again made trafficking ordinary consumer products profitable. This confluence was a product of forces old and new. Smuggling in the years after the Second Sino-Japanese War was similar to smuggling during the Nanjing Decade. On water, goods still arrived at coastal ports by steamships, motorboats, and junks. On land, they made their way into cities and villages by foot and trains. Smuggling's scale, however, was magnified by conditions inherited from wartime—a shattered economy, civil strife, and weakened authority. The new postwar geopolitical order further complicated state efforts to crack down on smuggling. As legal international trade in theory could only be conducted with the sanction of states, the ambiguous relations Nationalist China enjoyed with the governments of a defeated Japan and an independent Korea created opportunities for merchants unconstrained by diplomatic fictions to (re)connect supply and demand. In the face of these new challenges, the Nationalist government relied on the Chinese Maritime Customs Service to assume its traditional role policing and taxing trade. But like the rest of the Nationalist government, the agency also emerged from the war considerably weakened. With material assets destroyed by years of conflict and staff discipline eroded by the deteriorating economic and political situation, it struggled to shoulder heavier responsibilities enforcing more expansive state strictures.

Research on the period from 1945 to 1949 has long sought to account for Communist victory or Nationalist defeat.[2] By focusing on diplomatic intrigues and military vicissitudes, however, it is easy to overlook the ways the Nationalist regime tried to reassert its authority in the face of the daunting challenges to reconstruction. It is also easy to overlook how consumers and merchants managed to go about their everyday business and weather the economic and political uncertainties that, only in retrospect, led inexorably to Communist victory in 1949. Turning attention to the Nationalists' ongoing campaign against smuggling during this period affords perspectives from both above and below to explore enforcement and evasion of trade regulations in the politically and economically fluid postwar environment.

What were the drivers of smuggling during this era? How did state and individual alike respond to shifts in domestic needs, geopolitics, and global economic currents? To answer these questions, this chapter first examines the macroeconomic context during the Civil War that made smuggling a necessity for consumers and merchants and its suppression an imperative for the Nationalist government. It then turns to the messy picture of state control over trade through an examination of the Maritime Customs' postwar experience. On the one hand, wartime destruction degraded the agency's postwar enforcement capabilities and limited its reach. On the other hand, the legal reforms undertaken as part of the war on smuggling during the Nanjing Decade finally reached their fruition, permitting the agency to move into new legal spaces with support from local officials and unconstrained by extraterritoriality. Before concluding, this chapter reconstructs the postwar geography and practice of smuggling by surveying different trafficking hot spots along the coast—all of which were created in part by an emergent geopolitical order superimposed on long-standing patterns of exchange.

NEW CONTROLS AND ECONOMICS OF SMUGGLING

The end of the Second Sino-Japanese War in August 1945 was almost a pyrrhic victory for the Nationalists, who faced the daunting task of rebuilding a China devastated after years of war. In addition to fending off an insurgent challenge from the Communists, the Nationalists also faced formidable economic challenges at war's end—reconnecting the economies of free and occupied China, reviving war-torn agricultural and industrial production, alleviating shortages, and asserting control over territories such as Manchuria and Taiwan that were once under Japanese rule. In the war's immediate aftermath, the Nationalists liberalized the economy by abolishing wartime regulations rendered unnecessary by peace, including the economic embargoes and other trade restrictions with occupied China. Except for luxury goods and products from countries that did not have official diplomatic relations with China (e.g., Korea and Japan), the government permitted industrial materials for rebuilding the economy and daily necessities to be imported without prior approval. Foreign aid offered by the United Nations Relief and Rehabilitation Administration (UNRRA) was funneled into China by the Chinese National Relief and Rehabilitation Administration (CNRRA) duty free. By all accounts, the government believed that relaxing import restrictions would help ease shortages of consumer goods and thereby relieve inflationary pressures that had been building throughout the war.

The war-ravaged economy, however, required substantial imports to satisfy its needs. In the words of one senior-level Nationalist official, "The economy of China had been so thoroughly disrupted during war and occupation that large-scale imports of all kinds were needed to effect a postwar readjustment." Moreover, wartime austerity created pent-up demand for consumer goods that could not be satisfied solely by domestic production. The transportation infrastructure linking coastal metropoles with their hinterlands suffered serious damage during the war and was still not operating at full capacity after the war. As a result, demand for imports had "swollen enormously" and quickly depleted the government's foreign exchange reserves.[3] Most importantly, escalating conflict with the Communists and a badly fractured tax base forced the government to resort to deficit financing and meet revenue shortfalls through the printing press.

Together, these policies created a vicious cycle that quickly led to runaway inflation, causing breathtaking leaps in prices in cities throughout China. In Shanghai, for instance, wholesale prices surged 545 percent during 1946 and another 1,367 percent during 1947.[4] Hyperinflation eroded buying power at an alarming rate and encouraged desperate consumers to find ways to dispose of their increasingly worthless currency. While economic volatility might have benefited an "irresponsible" cohort of profiteers, speculators, and high-level government and military officials who leveraged their connections for personal gain, inflation's deleterious impact was felt keenly across class lines. The poor were naturally hard-pressed to keep pace with rising prices, while the middle class saw the value of its hard-earned savings erode. Shopkeepers suffered losses as profits from goods sold could not cover the cost of replacing their inventory. Civil servants, teachers, and others who lived on fixed salaries were also hard-hit by inflation.[5] Even the rich were not immune, for they experienced "relative hardships" in buying food and indulging in leisure. "People therefore raced to buy goods—any kind of goods—before their money lost what little value it still retained. This rapid circulation of the currency added fuel to the inflation."[6] The "economy of things" that emerged at the depths of wartime deprivation thus persisted through the chaos of postwar reconstruction.

In response to the deteriorating economic situation, the government reversed course starting in 1946 by reasserting control over the economy to halt inflation (table 6.1). Besides laws punishing speculators and hoarders, the government also promulgated a series of Emergency Economic Measures (Jingji jinji cuoshi fang'an) in February 1947 aimed at regulating foreign trade. One measure targeted the flow of capital by prohibiting private transactions of foreign exchange and precious metals. Limiting the availability of foreign exchange, the government believed, would restrict the currency available to purchase nonessential imports. Another measure targeted the flow of goods by tightening permissive import policies. The Temporary Foreign Trade Regulations (Jinchukou maoyi zanxing banfa)—promulgated in March 1946, revised in November the same year, and made permanent in August 1947—revived wartime economic controls by reestablishing a classification scheme to distinguish among different classes of imports. Machinery and other industrial equipment badly needed for postwar reconstruction could be imported with few restrictions. Some luxury goods were permitted for import provided that a 50 percent surtax atop existing tariffs was paid. Other luxury goods such

TABLE 6.1 MAJOR POSTWAR TRADE REGULATIONS

DATE OF PROMULGATION	REGULATION
March 1946	Temporary Foreign Trade Regulations (Jinchukou maoyi zanxing banfa): Divided imports into three categories—free imports, licensed imports, and prohibited imports. Some luxury articles were permitted for import through payment of a 50 percent luxury surtax above existing tariff rates. Total number of prohibited articles was 22. Exports subjected to examination by Customs and required a certificate issued by appointed banks testifying that foreign exchange would be surrendered.
November 1946	Revised Temporary Foreign Trade Regulations (Xiuzheng jinchukou maoyi zanxing banfa): All imports—except for items prohibited, required no foreign exchange, or valued less than US$50—may be imported with license. Board for the Temporary Regulation of Imports created to oversee licensing and coordinate regulations. Quotas established and permits allocated to trade associations and guilds, which in turn distributed them to members.
February 1947	Emergency Economic Measures (Jingji jinji cuoshi fang' an): Prohibited gold speculation and foreign exchange circulation.
August 1947	Foreign Trade Regulations (Jinchukou maoyi banfa): Import licensing system and regulations prohibiting gold speculation and foreign exchange circulation maintained. Board for the Temporary Regulation of Imports renamed to Import-Export Board to reflect its role regulating the flow of all commodities.
March 1948	Regulations Governing the Punishment of Smuggling (Chengzhi zousi tiaoli): Smuggling criminalized and punishable by penal servitude or death.

as sea delicacies, silk piece goods, and cosmetics—virtually the same items enumerated by wartime regulations—were strictly prohibited. Everything else in between these categories—from raw materials to everyday consumer products—could be imported within quotas established by the government. The regulations created a Board for the Temporary Regulation of Imports (later renamed the Export-Import Board) to oversee imports, issue permits, and adjust quotas. The permits themselves were often allocated to various trade associations such as guilds or chambers of commerce, which in turn distributed them among different firms within their respective industries. Firms had to register with the board, apply for permits, and submit their receipts and contracts for inspection before their goods were released. To compel participation in this scheme, the government barred unregistered firms from applying for permits.[7]

The government further constricted the channels of legitimate trade by reducing import quotas. As its supply of foreign exchange reserves steadily eroded, the government correspondingly reduced import quotas from US$172 million during February–July 1947 to US$42 million during September 1948–March 1949—a decrease of more than 75 percent.[8] Lower quotas naturally made importing by legal means more difficult. Yet even if import permits were available, their method of top-down allotment exacerbated imbalances in supply and demand. Large firms held a surfeit of licenses that often exceeded their actual needs. Small firms and petty traders, by contrast, proved reluctant to register with the government or apply for import permits. This was especially the case for small-time merchants, like farmers who sold produce and livestock along border regions as well as owners of general stores (*zahuodian*) who stocked a general line of merchandise and did not require large volumes of any one particular import to resupply their inventories.

Nationalist officials strongly believed that preventing smuggling and stemming capital flight were critical to arresting the economy's downward spiral and reasserting state authority. A senior Central Bank of China official, for instance, commented that the "key to success or failure" (*chengbai dishi guanjian*) of the new economic regulations rested on controlling the illicit flow of goods and capital, particularly from South China.[9] The government, however, had a difficult time enforcing the complex regulations as it struggled to contain the structural driver of inflation: deficit financing to fund the ongoing civil war with the Communists. Meanwhile, high duties continued to encourage smuggling. Tariffs stayed at prewar levels until August 1948, when the government doubled or even tripled existing rates to further protect domestic industries.[10] Yet it was the new controls on trade—combined with chronic shortages of goods and an unstable economy—that truly created opportunities for private profit during this period. Observers quickly detected this new shift in the economics of smuggling. As the Kowloon commissioner reported, "The main incentive to smuggling was not the evasion of payment of duty but the evasion of trade controls."[11] One writer noted how quotas and other restrictions on imports made the application process onerous and smuggling relatively attractive. Under such market conditions, merchants were naturally "unwilling to suffer losses" (*buyuan chikui*) and dumped their quickly depreciating Chinese currency for badly needed imports, thus accelerating the vicious cycle of inflation.[12]

New restrictions necessitated new strategies of evasions. Importers who wanted to obtain licenses were especially desperate since they had to apply directly with the Central Bank of China in Shanghai—an inconvenience, if not an impossibility, for many merchants elsewhere. Exporters, for their part, were required to surrender any foreign currencies they earned to government-designated banks in return for Chinese *fabi*, which was rapidly losing value. To accommodate the needs of merchants, the Central Bank of China later amended regulations, permitting satellite branches in southeastern Chinese ports to issue import licenses for merchants unable or unwilling to apply in person at Shanghai. To circumvent such requirements, many merchants purchased surplus permits then openly traded on the market. Customs officials along the Hong Kong border, for instance, discovered that permits initially issued to facilitate local "traditional petty trade" quickly became "valuable negotiable documents" that were being "freely sold at a high premium and made use of in lieu of Import Licenses to cover the importation of large quantities or commercial goods."[13]

Other merchants exploited holes in the regulatory net's geographical coverage by conducting business in ports exempt from the regulations or where formal state presence was limited. One popular strategy was shipping foreign goods to one port not covered by the regulations before reshipping them as "domestic" goods to another port covered by the regulations. In one instance, a group of Hong Kong merchants chartered a wartime landing craft, the *Guoquan* (National Sovereignty), to transport cotton yarn, radios, refrigerators, and other electrical appliances to Qinzhou, a port at the Gulf of Tonkin's northern end not covered by the regulations at the time. The goods were then transported by land to the interior city of Nanning, where they were sorted for distribution further inland. Buoyed by the venture's success, the merchants launched another expedition by chartering the *Guoquan*'s sister ship, the *Guochu* (National Foundation). This time, however, the scheme was uncovered; a customs patrol boat caught the *Guochu*, towed it back to Hong Kong, and detained its entire cargo.[14] So pervasive were such practices, in fact, that the government eventually banned transshipments of imported goods from ports such as Guangzhou to Shanghai.[15] Exporters, meanwhile, shipped their goods to frontier regions or other sparsely populated areas without a government-appointed bank to avoid losses that came with surrendering foreign currencies for increasingly worthless Chinese *fabi*.[16]

Such strategies of evasion were neither easy nor cheap. Many merchants, according to official reports, grudgingly adhered to the regulations due to the time and cost consumed in circumventing them. Nonetheless, the calculus of smuggling still paid off, particularly from mid-1946 onward as inflation accelerated and encouraged Chinese consumers to spend their rapidly depreciating *fabi* for relatively more valuable imports. For many, the costs of evading trading restrictions were high, but the profits to be earned proved higher still. The impetus behind smuggling—pecuniary motivations aside—also rested on another logic according to one journalist: "Those who smuggle raw materials or even those who join armed smuggling organizations in resisting the Maritime Customs' preventive efforts do not acknowledge they are engaged in smuggling. Instead, they call it 'underground trading' (*dixia maoyi*). What they are saying is that they are not unwilling to pay customs duties. Rather, they are saying that even if they paid customs duties, the government would still not permit them to import [their goods]."[17] The interviewees' justification for their actions could correctly be interpreted as self-serving; the same journalist who reported the incident, in fact, dismissed "underground trading" as de facto smuggling. Nonetheless, their attitude also highlights how strict controls once again created conflicting notions of legitimate trade between state and merchant. Moreover, "smuggling" was a label that still carried enough moral connotations that these merchants justified their actions as circumventing what they viewed to be an unjust law.

POSTWAR INTERDICTION

As was the case before the Second Sino-Japanese War, the Nationalist government relied on the Chinese Maritime Customs Service to enforce its foreign trade regulations after 1945. The Maritime Customs that emerged from the conflict, however, was a changed institution. At the top, the agency was now headed by the Inspector General Lester Knox Little, an American, and Deputy Inspector General Ding Guitang (Ting Kui-t'ang), the highest-ranking Chinese in the service. British influence declined, Japanese influence eradicated, and the agency no longer enjoyed the implicit foreign support it had during the heyday of the treaty system.[18] Finally, customs duties—while still sizeable—waned in relative importance, comprising approximately 20 percent of central government revenue during the postwar years versus 50 percent during the Nanjing Decade.[19]

More consequential to the fight against smuggling was the agency's changing arena of control and the condition of its material assets. Resumption of control and surveillance over coastal trade unfolded unevenly across time and geography after Japan's surrender (table 6.2). From December 1941 to August 1945, coastal customs stations had been managed by the Japanese-sponsored "Bogus Customs" (Wei Haiguan). After the surrender, the Executive Yuan initially forbade the takeover of any puppet institutions without written permission from a newly formed, high-level government committee. An exception, however, was eventually made for organs such as the Customs, Salt Administration, and banks to resume operations as soon as possible. As a result, customs officials were able to quickly initiate the recovery of many formerly occupied stations. Stations at several major coastal ports, including Shanghai and Guangzhou, resumed operations by September 1945. Deputy Inspector General Ding, who spearheaded the takeover effort with a senior staff, found the Shanghai Customs on the

TABLE 6.2 DATES OF LOSS AND RECOVERY OF COASTAL CUSTOMS STATIONS, 1937–1946

REGION AND CUSTOMS STATION	JAPANESE OCCUPATION	BOGUS CUSTOMS TAKEOVER	NATIONALIST CUSTOMS TAKEOVER
NORTH CHINA			
Qinhuangdao	July 1937	December 1941	November 1945
Tianjin	August 1938	December 1941	November 1945
Longkou	February 1938	December 1941	Communist control
Zhifu	February 1938	December 1941	Communist control
Weihaiwei	March 1938	December 1941	Communist control
Qingdao	January 1938	December 1941	October 1945
LOWER YANGZI			
Hankou	October 1938	December 1941	September 1945
Jiujiang	July 1938	1943	Shuttered
Wuhu	December 1937	March 1943	Shuttered
Nanjing	December 1937	June 1942	September 1945
Jinjiang	December 1937	1943	Shuttered
CENTRAL COAST			
Shanghai	November 1937	December 1941	September 1945
Suzhou	December 1937	1943	Shuttered
Hangzhou	December 1937	1943	Shuttered
Ningbo	April 1938	May 1943	September 1945
SOUTHERN COAST			
Xiamen	May 1938	December 1941	October 1945
Shantou	Jun 1939	December 1941	September 1945
Guangzhou	October 1938	December 1941	September 1945
Kowloon	December 1941	December 1941	September 1945
Jiangmen	March 1939	December 1941	September 1945
Sanshui	October 1938	Shuttered	Shuttered
Qiongzhou	February 1939	December 1941	1946

Source: Inspectorate General of Chinese Customs, *The Trade of China* (Shanghai: Statistical Department of the Inspectorate General of Customs, 1946), vol. 1.

Bund and other offices throughout the city in good condition, with archives and most properties undisturbed.[20] Conditions at other offices varied. The Shantou Customs, for instance, was in a similar condition as the Shanghai Customs, with archives still well preserved and properties in good condition.[21] The Shanhaiguan station at the border of North China and Manchuria, by contrast, was in complete disorder; looters had ransacked its office and warehouses and made off with bicycles and petty cash.[22]

Stations elsewhere did not resume operations until late 1945, if at all. In North China, stations proved more difficult to reopen, given that the Nationalists had no military presence in the region at the end of the war. Oftentimes, customs officials had to wait until Nationalists and American troops secured the area before they could move in. The Qinhuangdao Customs near Shanhaiguan, for instance, did not reopen until November 1945, when American marines finally reestablished order after the Japanese surrendered and Soviet troops and the Communist Eighth Route Army departed.[23] Meanwhile, stations at the Shandong Peninsula ports—Longkou, Zhifu, and Weihaiwei—were taken over by the Communists and never returned to Nationalist control. Finally, stations at smaller ports such as Jinjiang, Hangzhou, and Suzhou were deemed too unimportant to reopen. Their overhead costs were "hardly commensurate with [their] minor services," and their staff was urgently needed at larger ports such as Shanghai.[24]

Officials estimated that if prewar tariffs were to remain in place, postwar preventive efforts required at least the same level of resources available back in 1937.[25] In some places, particularly ports where heavy fighting was limited, the Maritime Customs' material assets emerged relatively unscathed. In Tianjin, for instance, one officer reported during an inspection tour in late October 1945 that wharves, warehouses, and other navigational aids "remained in the same manner as before during the war until the Japanese surrender."[26] In general, however, the technical infrastructure painstakingly built during the Nanjing Decade suffered a far worse fate. The celebrated coastal system of lights and network of radio towers that coordinated interdiction on land and seas, for example, were severely damaged. The Maritime Customs' fleet of preventive vessels fell from seventy-three in 1937 to twenty-two in 1946—a decline of 70 percent.[27] What vessels were still in operation were dedicated to the more urgent task of rebuilding the economy than fighting smuggling.

The agency made many efforts to repair damaged infrastructure and to reconstitute the maritime fleet by repurchasing and repurposing surplus wartime vessels, but the agency never fully recovered its prewar strength. Not surprisingly, this degradation of material assets hampered preventive work after the war. The shortage of vessels forced the agency to concentrate patrols in smuggling hot spots such as the Pearl River Delta and leave other areas less patrolled. The Fujian coast—despite the region's long history as an active smuggling frontier—was one such casualty of this neglect wrought by the agency rationing limited resources in the postwar era. The Xiamen commissioner, for instance, complained that his office was often "in the dark" regarding smuggling from Hong Kong and other ports due to the lack of preventive vessels to monitor and interdict such trafficking.[28] The Fuzhou commissioner readily concurred with his colleague's grim assessment. Despite widespread rumors of smuggling in his district, his land-bound officers were unable to take action, "tied down as they have no craft for use in investigation."[29] If the technologies of surveillance empowered the state to "see" during the Nanjing Decade, their destruction undeniably occluded official vision in the postwar era.

Even in ports where the Maritime Customs resumed operations, preventive efforts were often geographically circumscribed and limited to wharves. Stations at strategic choke points or far-flung commercial routes remained closed even in areas where the main office had already resumed operations. More than a year and a half after the war, for instance, many customs stations scattered throughout the Pearl River Delta remained closed, with preventive vessels in short supply.[30] Raids on remote villages—a tactic of interdiction so common during the 1930s—became less frequent as limited resources constrained the agency from extending its reach. Finally, even as the agency had its hands full combatting the usual smuggling on land and sea, it had to reckon with new modes of smuggling. The growing prevalence of air travel after the war, in particular, forced the agency to stretch resources still further to monitor smuggling by air.

In addition to deteriorating material assets in the postwar years, the Maritime Customs also faced the problem of eroding staff discipline. Relaxing enforcement for monetary gain became an increasingly attractive option for many employees, who were just as adversely affected by the economy's free fall and hyperinflation's pernicious effects as the general public. Their plight is documented in the many petitions they submitted to their superiors calling for financial relief, which often found a sympathetic audience. Deputy Inspector General Ding, who received one such petition from his staff in late 1945, noted that many employees who once willingly endured "hardships of life" during the war for the sake of their country were now "rather restive" on account of the rising cost of living, from daily necessities to tuition for their children.[31] Even when the agency introduced measures to alleviate financial hardships (e.g., raises, loans, subsidies) hyperinflation quickly negated these palliative efforts. For instance, less than four months after receiving a raise, employees in April 1947 petitioned yet again for an immediate adjustment of their pay and loans to help them through ongoing difficulties. As the recipient of the request admitted: "It is unnecessary for me to say that their financial difficulties are genuine."[32]

Under such conditions, some employees turned to exploiting their official positions for personal gain. Not infrequently, the suppression of smuggling benefited the enforcers of commercial restrictions, in China as elsewhere.[33] While not an uncommon problem in the agency's long history, corruption became especially problematic in the postwar years.[34] Questions of ethics aside, corruption was also a survival strategy for frontline employees to profit from the opportunities created by the combination of stringent trade controls and unrelenting demand for imports. In one spectacular case, four customs agents extorted businessmen from six firms for payoffs in exchange for permission to import shipments. When the scheme came to light, the government sought to make an example of those involved, taking a hard line by sentencing the businessmen to prison terms of various lengths for bribery and executing the customs agents for corruption.[35] While the incident exemplifies how an insecure state sought to discipline its employees, it also highlights how new regulations accorded frontline enforcers considerable latitude in implementation and opened numerous opportunities for profit by transforming import permits into a commodity to be traded and sold. It is difficult, if not impossible, to determine the degree of corruption among the rank and file and its measurable consequences for the suppression of smuggling. Yet what is clear is that the specter of malfeasance remained much on the minds of senior-level officials who took care to highlight even relatively minor instances of staff members' incorruptibility in discharging their duties.[36]

Hyperinflation compounded economic woes and dulled another weapon in the agency's arsenal of enforcement. Fines remained the primary tool of punishment for customs officials, but in an economy where money was rendered meaningless at breathtaking speed, financial penalties quickly lost their punitive function. The maximum fine of CN$2,000 leviable under the Preventive Law had remained unchanged since its introduction in 1934 and proved already inadequate after years of wartime inflation by 1945.[37] The first adjustment in fines came in August 1945, when the government permitted agencies such as the Maritime Customs to levy fines of up to fifty times the rate stipulated by law, or CN$100,000.[38] A subsequent adjustment came more than a year later, in November 1946, when fines were ratcheted up one hundred times the official rate, or CN$200,000.[39]

Yet postwar hyperinflation easily outpaced these halting increases in penalties. The maximum fine of CN$100,000 introduced in August 1945 translated to roughly CN$289 at 1937 prewar price levels. The subsequent adjustment to CN$200,000 failed to even keep up with rising prices in the intervening months, as it translated to a mere CN$38 at 1937 prewar price levels (table 6.3).[40] Not surprisingly, commissioners up and down the coast peppered the inspector general with complaints about the inadequacy of fines even after the upward adjustments. They were also not mollified by the inspector general's pledge to secure governmental permission to raise fines yet again—this time one thousand times the official rate. The Shanghai commissioner, for instance, dismissed the new penalties as "farcical" and called for fines to be raised to at least three thousand times prewar levels in order to "have a salutary effect on would-be smugglers."[41] The Shantou commissioner went further in his complaints, calling for fines to

TABLE 6.3 MAXIMUM NOMINAL AND REAL FINES LEVIABLE,
1937–1948

DATE	A: FINE LEVIABLE (CN$)	B: PRICE INDEX (MID-1937 = 1)	C: 1937 EQUIVALENT (CN$)
Mid-1937	2,000	1	2,000
August 1945	100,000	346	289
November 1946	200,000	5,318	38
August 1948	400,000,000	4,927,000	81

Sources: Column A from SHAC, 679/1/28024, IG Circular No. 6711 (August 23, 1945); No. 6937 (November 5, 1945); and SHAC, 679/1/26925, IG Circular No. 7352 (August 10, 1945). Column B taken from Shanghai general wholesale price index from Wu, *Jiu Zhongguo tonghuo pengzhang shiliao*, 160–2. Column C calculated by dividing Column A by Column B.

Note: Price Index for August 1945 taken from September 1945.

be raised to six thousand times prewar levels, given the "armed and dangerous resistance" often encountered in the course of suppressing smuggling.[42] A final adjustment in August 1948, made on the eve of the gold yuan's introduction, raised fines up to an astounding 200,000 times the official rate, or CN$400 million.[43] This adjustment, however, translated to only CN$81 at 1937 price levels, highlighting yet again how hyperinflation stayed far ahead of increases by government decree.

With slow-moving regulations failing to keep pace with fast-changing economic circumstances, pressures for more flexibility in levying punishments welled from the bottom up. As a result, many commissioners began adopting more liberal interpretations of the law and taking expedient measures. The Shanghai commissioner, for instance, supplemented inadequate fines by confiscating vessels used in smuggling and "reselling" them immediately to their former owners for a nominal sum.[44] Implicitly acknowledging the agency's inability to offer a more effective solution, the inspector general approved this "tentative measure" after the fact and permitted commissioners at other ports to follow Shanghai's example.[45] More significantly, the inspector general also approved of a Guangzhou commissioner's aggressive enforcement of the Preventive Law to levy fines of up to three times the value of smuggled goods in addition to the maximum fine for infractions by steamship operators.[46]

NEW LEGAL FRAMEWORK OF ENFORCEMENT

While degraded material assets and deteriorating economic conditions hampered anti-smuggling work, the denouement of the treaty port legal order finally clarified the legal dimensions of interdiction. External constraints on the authority of the Chinese state—already forcefully challenged or even dismantled outright during the Nanjing Decade—had been completely eliminated after the abrogation of the unequal treaties in 1943. With the shift from jurisdiction over persons to jurisdiction over territory complete, Nationalist law enforcement organizations were finally able to execute their duties without formal territorial or diplomatic restrictions. Official efforts against smuggling benefited from this legal transformation, as customs agents moved into new venues and called on the assistance of local authorities as never before.

New domestic laws also redefined interdiction in this era. During their discussions on using law to deter and deal with would-be smugglers, customs officials debated ways to make smuggling a criminal offense that would warrant more than just monetary punishments.[47] Smuggling had been treated as an administrative offense, but it was temporarily criminalized back in 1936 when the government promulgated the Revised Provisional Code Governing Punishments for Evasion of Customs Duty (Xiuzheng chengzhi toulou guanshui zanxing tiaoli).[48] The measure was renewed annually until 1944, when it was allowed to expire. Now that the government increasingly viewed rampant smuggling as an existential threat to state control and economic stability, it criminalized the transgression yet again by promulgating the Regulations Governing the Punishment of Smuggling (Chengzhi zousi tiaoli) in March 1948. The new regulations called for penal servitude of up to five years for engaging in smuggling, defined as importing or exporting "goods over which the Government has decreed a special control, or goods which are liable to the payment of Customs duty." The harshest penalties—life imprisonment or death—were reserved for smuggling ringleaders and those who employed armed resistance. Just as had done more than ten years prior, in 1936, when it criminalized smuggling in response to the Japanese military-backed smuggling crisis, the government introduced the new strictures in another atmosphere of crisis to demonstrate a tougher line against violators and assert its prerogative to exercise tighter control over the economy.[49]

Promulgation of new laws criminalizing smuggling encouraged customs officials to once again remand apprehended smugglers to local authorities for prosecution. Customs leadership in particular ordered commissioners to avoid sending "trifling cases" or cases with weak evidence and no "fair chance of conviction" for prosecution. And while customs officials retained the sole prerogative to levy fines or effect confiscations, they were instructed to leave penalties regarding penal servitude to the court's discretion.[50] The incident involving the two Cantonese sailors described at the beginning of the chapter was one of many cases governed by the new legal framework criminalizing smuggling that divided responsibility between interdiction and prosecution between the central government and the local government, respectively. Such cases exemplified the increasing prevalence of coordination between the central government and local law enforcement agencies, something often difficult to secure during the Nanjing Decade.

Meanwhile, the end of extraterritoriality and the promulgation of the Regulations Governing the Punishment of Smuggling meant that foreigners suspected of smuggling appeared as defendants in criminal cases for the first time. Prosecution of these cases reveals not just foreign connections to the hidden illicit economy of postwar China but also sheds light on the workings of the Nationalist legal machinery during its last days on the mainland. One such case, unfolding over the course of 1948, was that of Nicholas Panaitescu (aka Nick C. Pan, aka Pan Naide, aka Pan Naidisheng). The Romanian national, operating a women's clothing store at the edge of the former International Settlement, came to the attention of customs officials who discovered his name among telegrams uncovered from another case involving smuggled antibiotics and adrenalin. Panaitescu and several foreign accomplices were later arrested in a raid and provided statements attesting to the nature of his business, which retailed women's clothes since 1941 but recently operated a profitable side venture purchasing smuggled Western medicines wholesale and reselling them to pharmacies in smaller lots at considerable markups.[51] The case was then transferred to the Shanghai Local Court, where prosecutors cited evidence produced by the Maritime Customs in charging Panaitescu with violating the Regulations Governing the Punishment of Smuggling. During the trial, prosecutors called on his accomplices to testify and offered as evidence receipts for imported medicines that bore no seal showing taxes or duties paid.[52]

Almost three months after the raid on August 4, 1948, the Shanghai Local Court found Panaitescu guilty of knowingly selling smuggled medicine. In reaching its judgment, the court relied on the prosecution's evidence and witnesses' testimonies. The court also dismissed arguments by Panaitescu's lawyer that the Regulations Governing the Punishment of Smuggling were inapplicable since the purchase of the smuggled medicine was made prior to the law's promulgation. Panaitescu was sentenced to four months of penal servitude, although he accepted the option of paying a fine of CN$10,000 for each day of the sentence and was eventually released in October 1948.[53] The decision effectively reaffirmed the principle— embodied in the Preventive Law—that authorities could prosecute based on when the smuggling was uncovered, rather than when the offense was committed.

While the case of Nicholas Panaitescu reveals how foreigners in China tapped into illicit supply chains, the case of another would-be smuggler sheds light on larger global commodity flows in which China was but a node. On October 9, 1948, the steamship *California* arrived in Shanghai from San Francisco and Guam en route to Korea and Japan. A routine search of the ship uncovered eighty-one boxes and seventy-four bags of saccharine hidden in the cabin of the American deck engineer Martin J. Joyce. The saccharine was not listed on the ship's manifest, and sugar was a commodity under the purview of government import regulations. Joyce himself did not deny ownership of the saccharine, admitting in his statement to the Maritime Customs, "I assume the responsibility of the [saccharine] which was concealed in the double lining of my cabin." After further investigation, customs officials confiscated the saccharine, levied a fine, and transferred the case to the Shanghai Local Court, where prosecutors charged Joyce with smuggling.

In a statement submitted to the court, Joyce's legal counsel explained that the saccharine was entrusted to his client by a friend to bring to Japan and was never intended to be smuggled into China. In addition to demonstrating his client's intent, Joyce's counsel also argued that the Regulations Governing the Punishment of Smuggling were inapplicable in this case. Customs officials had already confiscated the saccharine and fined Joyce for the infraction, the statement noted, but more importantly, Article 25 of the bilateral 1946 Sino-American Treaty of Friendship, Commerce, and Navigation permitted transshipment of goods by Chinese and American nationals through the United States and China, respectively. Article 25 also exempted transshipments from customs duties.[54] In its judgment, the court determined that Joyce's actions fell under the purview of the 1946 treaty and ordered the deck engineer released. The court did, however, note that the Regulations Governing the Punishment of Smuggling would have certainly applied had smuggling been demonstrated to have occurred.[55]

In one sense, the cases of Panaitescu and Joyce merely illustrate how foreigners were prosecuted after the end of extraterritoriality in China. But in another sense, they indicate something more, specifically how the Nationalist government realized its long-held goal of making the prosecution of smuggling on Chinese territory a domestic, rather than a diplomatic, concern. None of this meant that cases for Chinese nationals and foreigners were processed equally.[56] But despite their different outcomes, the two cases were processed in a manner agreeable to Nationalist notions of Chinese sovereignty. They were both handled by domestic institutions (rather than diplomatic institutions) with a central government institution (the Maritime Customs) successfully coordinating with a local government institution (the Shanghai Local Court). That Nationalist rule on the mainland soon ended should not obscure how the centralization of legal authority—the cherished goals of Chinese officials since the late Qing—finally bore fruit during these chaotic times.

POSTWAR SMUGGLING GEOGRAPHIES: KOREA AND JAPAN

In addition to tightening state controls, new borders also exacerbated postwar smuggling. The collapse of the Japanese colonial empire in 1945 redrew the political geography of East Asia. Manchuria and Taiwan reverted to Chinese sovereignty. Korea gained its independence on paper but remained under international trusteeship and began fragmenting into two competing regimes. Trade between China proper and its newly recovered territories, previously international, was now domestic. Trade between Japan and its former colonies, once intra-empire, was now international. Trade routes that once crisscrossed continental and maritime East Asia were now bisected by newly reconfigured national boundaries. The emerging battle lines in the escalating civil war between the Nationalists and Communists further muddled this picture.

Diplomatic and commercial relations between a victorious China, an independent Korea, and a defeated Japan were still under negotiation in the war's aftermath. Hostilities ceased but relations had yet to normalize. Japanese and Koreans, for instance, remained classified as "enemy nationals" by the Allies. Postwar geopolitical reconfiguration effectively created zones of illegal trade. In theory, international trade could only be sanctioned between states on a bilateral basis. Undermining this diplomatic fiction, however, were longtime patterns of commerce that did not reorient themselves as quickly as changes in political geography and could not be channeled through new boundaries. Thus, as official trade was haltingly reestablished, unofficial trade in the form of smuggling quickly flourished.

With respect to Korea, Nationalist China permitted only limited state-sponsored bartering until it established official relations with a new government that would presumably be formed after the period of international trusteeship concluded. Korea's problematic place in the former Japanese colonial empire and the new postwar East Asian order, however, made normalizing relations a complicated prospect. Before the war, Korea was a major source of smuggled Japanese goods, and Koreans were—both in public and official imagination—notorious traffickers, especially since they enjoyed extraterritorial privileges as Japanese colonial subjects. After the war, the Korean Peninsula remained a conduit for Japanese goods not only to Nationalist China but also to Communist-occupied areas in Manchuria and North China. A November 1947 memorandum from the Ministry of Finance, for instance, pointed to Korean "outlaws" (*youmin*) responsible for smuggling Japanese goods through North China and Shanghai.[57]

Moreover, dire postwar economic conditions encouraged smuggling. Besides products such as rayon and lumber, Korean specialties such as ginseng and sea delicacies (e.g., shark fins and sea cucumbers) were among the few exportable commodities that could be quickly traded for foreign goods or currencies. The Allied occupation authorities allowed the provisional South Korean government to issue export permits for these commodities, but they were the very ones classified by the Nationalist government as luxury goods and expressly banned from import under the Foreign Trade Regulations.[58] Thus, despite limited approval granted by Allied occupation authorities for Korean businesses to export their products, private Sino-Korean trade remained largely illegal from the perspective of the Nationalists.

Reports from the press and the Maritime Customs nonetheless detailed resilient economic ties between China and Korea. As one newspaper article in 1948 noted, "Trade between the peoples of China and Korea—although still not officially permitted since the end of the war—has also never been really severed."[59] A Tianjin Customs official, meanwhile, described one pattern of smuggling in the north where vessels from Korea declaring themselves to be returning to China plied a profitable route circling the Yellow Sea. Merchants brought goods from Korea and exchanged them along the North China coast at Tianjin as well as Communist-controlled ports on the Shandong Peninsula. After returning to Korea, they changed their vessels' name and registration before returning to Tianjin with more goods.[60] Farther south along the Zhejiang coast, where smuggling from the north was common well before the war, a Ningbo Customs official reported the seizure of a vessel laden with sea delicacies "direct from Korea."[61]

While the Nationalist government encountered difficulties cracking down on this traffic, it still caught many who supposedly traded with Korea in contravention of regulations. The Chinese-Korean community, whose livelihood was threatened by restrictions on commerce between China and Korea, made many appeals to the government and the public regarding their plight. In one petition submitted to the Nationalist government and reprinted in the popular press, Chinese-Korean merchants complained of how trade restrictions bankrupted many of their members as the Maritime Customs refused to release their merchandise for export or import. Moreover, since the agency treated all imports from Korea as smuggled goods, the petitioners confessed that their fellow merchants took desperate measures evading restrictions: "Some evaded inspections altogether [by unloading their goods] beyond the Wusong Harbor."[62] "Some purchased transit passes and took advantage of the night to slip past the Maritime Customs. Some falsely listed Shanghai merchants as the cargoes' owners. Some transshipped their goods from another Chinese port to Shanghai—all in the hopes of avoiding punishment and protecting their cargo."[63]

Meanwhile, other merchants bristled at the indiscriminate nature of enforcement. The owners of the junk *Nee Cheng Hsing*, for instance, formally protested the Maritime Customs' seizure of their vessel and cargo outside of Shanghai in early 1947 on suspicion that they had sailed to Korea. The vessel itself, they averred, landed only at Zhuanghe on the Liaodong Peninsula and never touched Korea. Moreover, they claimed they could not adhere to the prewar Customs Regulations for the Control of Seagoing Junks to report their movements since no customs stations or government offices were available in the vicinity.[64] Finally, according to the petitioners, the only evidence that purportedly substantiated the vessel's journey to Korea—invoices prepared by Korean firms—had an understandable explanation. Zhuanghe then was "in a state of confusion" after the Nationalists ejected the Communists from the area, and the junk owners feared retribution during their return voyage: "[Any] true indication that the vessel sailed from [Zhuanghe] might cause immense trouble and difficulties to the owners on board if the vessel should be intercepted during the voyage by the communists." As a result, the junk owners used invoices "purposely prepared" by Korean firms to disguise their cargoes' origins.[65] In other words, to avoid potential harassment by the Communists, the junk owners claimed they held invoices to (falsely) demonstrate that they landed at Korea rather than Nationalist-controlled Zhuanghe.

Whatever the veracity of their claims, the petitioners revealed some characteristics of Sino-Korean commerce at this time. In asserting how they were different from the many other merchants "charged with smuggling [and] unauthorizedly [sic] importing goods from Korea," the appellants implicitly alluded to the widespread nature of this problem. In admitting to using fake invoices due to their fear being harassed by the Communists, the appellants also highlighted one strategy of self-protection. The merchants of the *Nee Cheng Hsing*—perhaps like so many of their brethren who plied the Sino-Korean trade—looked for ways to legalize their activities for multiple authorities, a form of insurance in doing business amid shifting circumstances on the battlefield and at the diplomatic table during this era of uncertainty.

The ambiguities surrounding Sino-Korean commerce that rendered the movement of the *Nee Cheng Hsing* as smuggling were eventually clarified as the Nationalist government relaxed restrictions on private trade with Korea. First, vessels owned by Chinese nationals and Chinese-Koreans were permitted to return to China with Korean goods, provided such imports did not violate the Foreign Trade Regulations.[66] Channels of legitimate trade were further widened in April 1948, when the Nationalists established formal diplomatic relations with the new South Korean state and permitted Korean vessels from South Korea to dock at Shanghai and Tianjin.[67] The government soon opened two additional ports—Keelung and Kaohsiung—in response to acute shortages of fertilizer in Taiwan. An important driver of the decision was the island's tight prewar economic ties with colonial Korea, which the government explicitly acknowledged in its orders justifying the relaxation.[68]

In contrast to normalizing Sino-Korean relations, normalizing Sino-Japanese relations proved far more difficult. As with Korea, Nationalist China sanctioned limited, government-to-government bartering but continued to prohibit private trade with Japan. The government held firm to this position even after the Supreme Commander for the Allied Powers (SCAP) announced that it would lift restrictions on Japanese foreign trade in August 1947. Public opinion in China also overwhelmingly opposed normalizing trading relations with Japan. Reflecting the general public mood, an editorial in *Shen Bao* inveighed against China reopening trade with Japan before reparations were paid and a peace treaty ratified.[69] Aside from nationalist sensibilities and fresh memories of Japanese imperialism and wartime atrocities, opposition to Sino-Japanese economic rapprochement rested on another logic. Many worried that Japan would dominate the Chinese economy and flood the market with its goods, as it had done before 1945. One journalist spoke of the "Nippon-phobia" (*kong Ri bing*) pervasive among a public that had not forgotten the outsized role of Japan in smuggling.[70] Chinese economists voiced concerns about a potential "economic invasion" (*jingji qinlüe*) from Japan.[71] A leading Shanghai businessman expressed fears that reopening trade with Japan would only make the ongoing problem of smuggling worse by making legitimately imported Japanese goods difficult to distinguish from their smuggled brethren—even as he admitted that foreign trade controls had been ineffective thus far.[72]

Such fears were likely overblown, given the precarious state of the postwar Japanese economy. But they were nonetheless very real in the minds of the Chinese government and public alike, both of whom paid inordinate attention to the illicit influx of Japanese goods. As Sino-Japanese trade was officially limited to government-to-government bartering in the immediate postwar years, imports from Japan made up less than 1 percent of total imports to China—a dramatic contrast to the Nanjing Decade when similar figures fluctuated in the high teens.[73] Unofficially, however, Sino-Japanese trade through smuggling was far more robust than the statistics suggested. One writer, for instance, noted how the public had but scan current newspaper headlines to be "startled" (*chumu jingxin*) by the scale of the problem. Reports from the media called attention to how Japanese products, from manufactures like cotton piece goods to the popular medicine Jintan, reappeared on the Chinese market after a long absence despite official sanctions against their import.[74]

Even with the retreat of Japanese presence from mainland East Asia, Japanese goods nonetheless continued to find their way into Chinese markets through indirect channels. As noted earlier, Koreans were high-profile carriers of Japanese goods, before and after Nationalist China relaxed its restrictions on trade with Korea and Korean goods. Another important conduit for Japanese smuggling was the Pearl River Delta, particularly Hong Kong. Like Nationalist China, Hong Kong limited trade with Japan on a government-to-government basis in the immediate aftermath of the war. Unlike Nationalist China, however, the colony reversed this policy starting from 1946, permitting private trade with Japan. Japanese manufactures were still in demand throughout Asia and thus served as the currency with which to trade for badly needed and expensive goods such as western medicine and sugar. As a result, Hong Kong and Japan quickly renewed their prewar commercial ties. Trade between the two spilled over into China, whose government still maintained no formal relations with Japan yet whose consumers badly wanted Japanese goods.[75]

POSTWAR SMUGGLING GEOGRAPHIES: SOUTH CHINA

The entry of Japanese goods into China through the Pearl River Delta once again highlighted the region's pivotal role as China's smuggling entrepôt. By 1945, nearly all foreign concessions and colonies along coastal China had been abolished, leaving Hong Kong and Macao as the only remaining political spaces independent of direct Chinese government authority. Toward China, the two colonies were restricted in what they could legally import and export. Toward Japan, Korea, and other global markets, however, they traded with fewer constraints. The Janus-faced positions of Hong Kong and Macao meant that the two colonies remained China's primary source and destination of smuggled goods, since would-be smugglers could profit from differences between regulatory regimes. New postwar regulations, combined with the Chinese economy's urgent demand for imports, only raised the profits to be earned through evading detection by authorities.

The nature of smuggling was a function of the proximity to Hong Kong and the mode of transportation. On water, steamships that departed from Hong Kong were filled with passengers and crews bringing all sorts of consumer goods that fetched high profits due to ongoing trade restrictions and shortages in China. One journalist provided an estimate of the revenues earned and expenses incurred by individual smugglers trafficking ordinary consumer products such as cosmetics, nylon stockings, and woolen piece goods between Hong Kong and Shanghai (table 6.4). Though impressionistic and sensitive to market conditions such as fluctuations in the cost of goods and speed of turnover, the suggestive figures highlight the economics of petty maritime smuggling. The cost of goods made up the largest proportion of expenses. The cost of travel, by contrast, was comparatively low, given the regularized steamship traffic between Hong Kong and

TABLE 6.4 ESTIMATED REVENUES AND EXPENSES BY INDIVIDUAL STEAMSHIP SMUGGLERS

	ITEM	HK$
Revenues		800
Expenses		
	Cost of Goods	400
	Passage to Shanghai	60
	Passage to Hong Kong	30
	Hotel (2 days)	15
	Meals and Expenses	50
	Total Expenses	555
Net Profit		245

Source: FR, May 5, 1948, 4:8, 449.

Shanghai that accommodated travelers of all kinds. Finally, the figures also suggest that petty smugglers earned profits sufficient to eke out a modest living that could purchase a basket of consumer necessities in Shanghai.[76]

Smuggling on other routes also proved profitable. Vessels regularly shuttling between Hong Kong and Guangzhou remained especially notorious for trafficking by their crews and passengers. In three separate spectacular incidents on the steamship *Wusueh* (*Wuxue*) during March, August, and October 1947, for instance, customs search parties in Guangzhou uncovered an assortment of smuggled goods worth roughly CN$106.7 million, CN$122.8 million, and CN$344.8 million, respectively, elaborately hidden in cabins throughout the vessel. Despite hyperinflation, the outsized value of the seizures on board the *Wusueh* still attracted attention from the public and the government. The illicit cargoes were a mishmash of ordinary consumer products, sharing no similarities other than being prohibited from import by postwar trade regulations—cosmetics, nylon, woolen piece goods, Western medicine, ginseng, dyes, and many other items. Their diversity attests to the stringency of regulations excluding a wide range of commodities from import through legitimate channels. They also show how strong demand for all foreign goods ensured smuggling remained very profitable.

Customs officials confiscated all the smuggled goods and levied penalties of CN$312.5 million, CN$368.7 million, and CN$1.12 billion, respectively—each fine equaled roughly three times the value of each seizure, as an aggressive application of the Customs Preventive Law warranted. Since the culprits could not be identified or had absconded, responsibility for discharging the fines fell to the *Wusueh*'s owner, the China Navigation Company, a subsidiary of Butterfield and Swire. The company appealed all penalties to the Customs Penalty Board of Inquiry and Appeal, the same institution formed in 1934 to adjudicate protests against the Maritime Customs. In all cases, the board rejected the company's assertion that it should be absolved of responsibilities since it did not knowingly permit the smuggling. The board upheld the penalties levied by the Guangzhou Customs and thereby reaffirmed the applicability of the Preventive Law in holding owners of vessels to account for the actions of their crew. In one judgment, the board even scolded the appellant for lax oversight of its crew, noting, "This company can hardly absolve itself in neglecting its supervisory duty."[77]

The case of the *Wusueh* and others illustrate how the legal machinery of the Nationalist government continued to operate during this era of political and economic uncertainty.[78] Moreover, the legal reforms from the Nanjing Decade not only formalized the processing of smuggling cases but also helped hold steamship companies responsible for smuggling on board their vessels. Penalties were also more punitive compared to those levied during the prewar years. Adjusted for inflation, the fines in 1937 price levels were approximately CN$28,300, CN$10,500, and CN$23,000, respectively—huge sums compared to the maximum of CN$2,000 in 1937.[79] Internal reports form the China Navigation Company reveal that company officials were aware that drawn-out appeals allowed galloping hyperinflation to dull the financial sting of fines. Yet they also reveal a company resentful of being held accountable for the actions of its crew by rigorous enforcement of anti-smuggling laws.[80] Indeed, despite the prevalence of steamship smuggling, customs authorities were able to exercise some modicum of control and contain its scope. With its resources overstretched, the agency had to concentrate its enforcement and surveillance efforts at ports, thereby continuing the trend of contracting the geography of enforcement since the outbreak of the Second Sino-Japanese War.

In contrast to its efforts at interdiction on water, the Maritime Customs experienced considerably more difficulties containing trafficking on land. Smuggling by foot and cart remained as prevalent as ever, with farmers and villagers regularly crisscrossing the Sino-Hong Kong border carrying assorted consumer goods along with their produce. More serious was smuggling by rail. The Kowloon-Canton Railway (KCR), in particular, was not just a critical smuggling artery in the Pearl River Delta but also a gateway for smuggling on the Guangzhou-Hankou Railway, which effectively connected the economies of South and Central China. Smuggling on the KCR did not simply involve moving goods from station to station. As trains rolled between Shenzhen and Guangzhou, passengers threw packages of smuggled goods overboard at predetermined locales or times. Waiting along the tracks were fellow carriers who picked up the cargo and distributed it to towns and villages throughout the region. A newspaper described members of one smuggling concern—nicknamed the Flying Packages Clique (Feibao dang)—as seemingly more concerned with profit than with danger while unloading packages on a moving train to Guangzhou.[81] This mode of distribution was also prevalent on steamships, where smugglers threw packages of goods overboard before docking to avoid inspection at ports. The flow of trafficking for railroads like the KCR, however, was not unidirectional. Besides distributing goods, trains were also collecting goods by picking up packages conveyed by foot across the Hong Kong border and transporting them to Guangzhou for sale. Operators allegedly conspired with the smugglers by adjusting the trains' speed to accommodate goods being loaded or unloaded at specific points during the journey.

Petty smuggling had long been a problem on the KCR, but its scale reached alarming proportions after the war. Demobilized soldiers—many of whom were unable to secure adequate employment in the faltering postwar economy—swelled the ranks of traffickers making a livelihood by shuttling prohibited articles across the region. One official's vivid description sheds light not only on the economy of this railborne traffic but also on the outsized role of recently demobilized soldiers as its carriers: "A large number of runners, mostly disbanded soldiers, rushed on board or got off trains at small stations near the terminal stations, taking with them rice, cotton yarn, etc., on the outward trip [toward Kowloon] and salt, kerosene oil, glass plates, etc., on the inward one [toward Guangzhou]. They swarmed over the coaches, sat on the top of the wagons and threw the train into such a disorder that even its running was endangered."[82]

A former managing director of the Guangdong Provincial Bank and a longtime observer of the South China economy estimated in 1948 that more than three thousand demobilized soldiers and petty traders (*xiao shuike*) were engaged full-time in smuggling on the KCR, while another two to three million directly or indirectly made their living from this illicit traffic.[83] The same year, another writer offered similar estimates on the number of traffickers and provided addition details on their background and motivations: "After the war's conclusion, some of these [smugglers are soldiers] forgotten by their country. They are not willing to engage in banditry but can only rely on this path for their livelihood. In addition, some [smugglers] are locals familiar with the area and are using their physical strength to make a living. Others are good people returning from exile in the interior [during the war]. [They] want to farm but have no land, want to work but have no employment. [They] can only engage in smuggling between Guangzhou and Hong Kong."[84]

The scale of smuggling and individual motivations behind the activity are difficult to verify. Yet they are nonetheless suggestive of the railway's large role in the smuggling economy of the Pearl River Delta, given a deteriorating postwar economy unable to absorb surplus labor. Smuggling on the KCR, in fact, became so regularized that even rice and flour, whose profit-to-volume ratios were comparatively lower than that of lighter consumer goods because of their bulk, became major articles of trafficking. In two separate instances during the summer of 1946, for example, customs agents intercepted shipments of 235 and 344 bags of smuggled flour conveyed to Guangzhou from Hong Kong by rail.[85] As one report noted, "The fact that goods of bulky nature as in the forgoing cases were even smuggled into [Guangzhou] in large quantities shows how flagrant smuggling by rail was being undertaken by smugglers."[86]

The reach of smuggled goods by land from Hong Kong extended well beyond the Pearl River Delta. Other vectors of long-distance illicit trade linked Hong Kong with interior and maritime China. On May 31, 1948, for instance, customs officials together with the Hangzhou municipal police intercepted a shipment of assorted smuggled goods—rayon, wool, and cellophane—at the Hangzhou station along the Zhejiang-Jiangxi railway. The shipment was escorted by one Yang Jiafu, a thirty-eight-year-old employee of the Southeast Transportation Company (Dongnan yunshu gongsi). Yang pled ignorance: he was told that the shipment contained cotton and dyes and admitted that he had been hired only a few days earlier to deliver the goods to someone in Shanghai. Bolstered by the intelligence officials received, Yang confirmed the goods' long journey originating from

Hong Kong, transshipped to Guangzhou, and transported by land to Ying-tan in Jiangxi where they ended up in Shanghai vis-à-vis the Zhejiang-Jiangxi railway. Yang was transferred to the Shanghai Local Court, where he was later tried, convicted, and sentenced to fifty days of penal servitude under the Regulations Governing the Punishment of Smuggling.[87] Even circuitous land routes, then, proved to be profitable channels of transport at a time when imported goods were in great demand and commanded substantial premiums on the market.

GOLD SMUGGLING: LOCAL DEMAND AND GLOBAL CONNECTIONS

The scale of smuggling in South China became so extensive that it redirected far-flung global supply chains. Such was the case for gold, another frequently trafficked commodity in the Pearl River Delta during the postwar years. The Nationalist government initially imported gold from the United States after the war and sold the precious metal to the public at twice the mark-up through its monopoly, the Central Bank of China. After months of capital flight destabilizing China's balance of payments, the government reversed its policy and banned all private transactions of the precious metal as part of its Emergency Economic Measures in February 1947. Meanwhile, the rapid collapse of the Chinese *fabi* and its eventual replacement, the gold yuan, encouraged Chinese consumers to hold precious metals that would presumably better retain their value. While an understandable defensive investment strategy in the face of galloping inflation, the public scramble for gold accelerated the hemorrhaging of foreign exchange in China as consumers with the wherewithal traded their personal holdings of foreign currencies for precious metals from abroad.

As formal markets were shuttered by government fiat, black markets emerged to meet unsatisfied demand. The source of black market supply was the Pearl River Delta, which had already served as the middle ground where demand from anxious Chinese consumers and supply from eager global dealers converged, since foreign exchange transactions remained legal in Hong Kong and Macao. Panic buying and new restrictions on the mainland accelerated the tempo of this trade and reoriented the global market to satisfy the Chinese demand for gold. Until early 1947, Hong Kong was labeled by one magazine as the modern-day "treasure island," soaking up gold from as far away as the United States and Mexico for eventual sale to China. In 1946, at least 120,000 oz. (8,230 lb.) arrived in the British colony. "Lively buyers" from Shanghai, Guangzhou, Shantou, Xiamen, Hankou, and even Kunming descended on Hong Kong to satisfy the almost insatiable demand for gold throughout China.[88] Each node in the supply chain took a cut—importers reportedly charged a commission of 5 percent while dealers earned a profit between 15 percent and 20 percent.[89]

Hong Kong remained a major center in the postwar global traffic in gold, but the primary pivot soon moved to Macao. The Portuguese colony was a longtime convenient staging ground for smuggling due to its proximity to China, but importing gold in sufficient quantity from distant locales was initially a daunting prospect. Macao was not blessed with the advantages its cross-harbor counterpart enjoyed, namely a modern airfield and a deepwater port to accommodate shipments by ocean-going vessels. Instead, what made Macao an attractive transshipment center for gold in the postwar years were Britain's and Portugal's respective positions within the nascent supranational regulatory regime. Whereas Britain was a member of the newly formed International Monetary Fund (IMF) and bound by the organization's restrictions on gold transactions among member states, Portugal was not a member and hence enjoyed virtually no international restrictions on capital movement.[90] Responding to IMF stipulations and British concerns that the heavy influx of gold would destabilize the pound's exchange rate against the American dollar, the Hong Kong government announced it would limit the import of gold in August 1946 and later ceased issuing permits altogether in April 1947. Its counterpart in Macao, meanwhile, announced that it would issue import permits for 900,000 oz. (61,715 lb.). Financial considerations underpinned the introduction of this policy, as the Macao government charged a fee of one Macanese pataca per ounce for permits it issued.

With the new policy effectively creating profit opportunities from regulatory arbitrage, dealers scrambled to overcome the colony's infrastructural limitations to import as much gold as possible from around the world. One solution they initially settled on was to airlift bullion from abroad into Hong Kong and transport it to Macao. This, however, soon proved to be a risky venture. One plane carrying an estimated 80,000 oz. (5,485 lb.) of gold crashed in eastern Hong Kong. Another plane carrying 33,000 oz. (2,260 lb.) of gold nearly crashed during takeoff.[91] Dealers eventually turned to a more reliable option by chartering Catalina flying boats to haul gold by tens of thousands of ounces to Macao from ports across East and Southeast Asia, including Manila, Bangkok, Saigon, and even as far away as Rangoon and Calcutta.[92]

So active was the Macao traffic in gold that dealers quickly met—and exceeded—the 1947 import quota. Of the 900,000 oz. permitted for import that year, 300,000 oz. entered Macao via Hong Kong, while another 600,000 oz. entered Macao directly. An additional 200,000 oz., however, found its way into the colony with dealers reusing import permits that were not stamped due to administrative oversight, malfeasance, or smuggling. Just as it was the case for permits issued in other locales, an active secondary market also emerged to match the supply and demand for surplus Macao gold import permits. Permits that originally cost one Macanese pataca per ounce were resold (and sometimes resold many times over) for anywhere from 8 to 15 pataca per ounce, a reflection of how profits from the gold trade attracted would-be dealers to pay substantial premiums for the privilege of supplying the Macanese market. While the Macao government eventually raised the cost of permits to 3 pataca per ounce and imposed new restrictions on reselling permits, the trafficking continued.[93] By early 1948, the *Economist* reported that tiny Macao had officially absorbed more gold than any other market in the world, with much of it unofficially destined for China.[94] Some gold legitimately imported into Macao was in turn smuggled back into Hong Kong, where it eventually entered the many illicit trafficking channels to China. Many parties benefited from the traffic. As a 1948 British Foreign Office report observed, "the market is proving highly lucrative to the local government, to the dealer, and also the people who have been manipulating the money exchanges and reselling import licenses."[95]

To crack down on the illicit traffic in the Pearl River Delta, the government concluded separate anti-smuggling agreements with the governments of Hong Kong and Macao in 1948. The agreements permitted the Maritime Customs greater freedom to patrol in the waters of Hong Kong and Macao and exercise stricter surveillance over cargoes.[96] In one sense, the agreements represented a triumph for the Nationalist government, which had long sought to project its control more widely across the Pearl River Delta. Ratification of a similar anti-smuggling agreement with Hong Kong failed in the 1930s due to opposition from Guangzhou merchants. In another sense, however, the agreements had limited practical effect, since the Nationalists would have little time to implement them on the eve of their defeat.

* * *

The difficulties Nationalist China experienced in combatting smuggling were symptomatic of broader challenges it faced in the postwar era. To rebuild an economy that suffered tremendous destruction after eight years of unrelenting warfare, the government initially liberalized foreign trade policies to help alleviate chronic shortages and fight stubborn inflation—conditions inherited from wartime. China's almost-insatiable appetite for imports, however, quickly outstripped the supply of foreign exchange, and the government soon reversed its policies by reintroducing variations of wartime controls on trade. High tariffs remained an important driver of smuggling, but it was these controls that changed the economics of illicit trading yet again since restrictions effectively transformed scores of badly needed consumer products into profitable contraband. The new postwar geopolitical order placed additional legal walls in the middle of traditional trade networks and further encouraged enterprising merchants to circumvent these restrictions. Many merchants engaged in some form of regulatory arbitrage by legitimately importing goods into zones outside of Chinese control like Hong Kong and Macao before funneling them to the mainland.

In the case of Macao, the confluence of strong demand for gold in China and changing regulations in Hong Kong and elsewhere rerouted entire global supply chains to the small Portuguese colony. The speed and scale of the shift highlight the adaptability of smugglers to stay one step (or two or three) ahead of regulations.

While it is tempting to write off this period of Nationalist rule as an unqualified failure, it is also important to recognize that as state authority was undermined, it was also successfully asserted in other ways. When the Nationalists effected the shift in jurisdiction from persons to territory after abolishing extraterritoriality, for instance, customs agents were able to move into new spaces like former foreign concessions and apprehend foreign smugglers for prosecution as part of overall interdiction efforts. Moreover, while trade restrictions were constantly circumvented, the rising number of violations by itself did not suggest that regulations were completely ineffective. After all, merchants and other would-be smugglers had to engage in elaborate and complex evasion tactics precisely because regulations were strict enough to warrant such tactics. Nationalist collapse, therefore, should not completely obscure the overall trajectory of growing state controls, many of which survived past 1949. In Taiwan, the Nationalists simply transplanted their legal system and trade controls onto the island. On the mainland, a new regime formally repudiated Nationalist laws and institutions but actually repurposed them in its own campaigns against illicit coastal trade.

7

OLD MENACE IN NEW CHINA

Symbiotic Economies in the Early People's Republic

N AN ARTICLE published in the January 3, 1951, issue of *People's Daily*, Kong Yuan, director of the China General Customs Administration, proudly recounted the changes afoot in the People's Republic of China (PRC). Within the first year of Communist rule, he claimed, the new government had already devised a foreign trade policy that better served the country's industrial development. Kong's own agency played no small part in this transformation, distinguishing itself from its moribund predecessor by efficiently supervising trade and loyally supporting the revolution. Efforts to remake China's foreign commerce—along with its government, economy, and even culture—were "progressing at full speed" (*feisu jinbu*), according to Kong.

Yet the news in New China was not all rosy. Nor was the break from Old China complete. In recounting his agency's ongoing fight against coastal illicit trade, in particular, Kong struck a decidedly more cautious tone that betrayed concern: "Although the Customs Administration's anti-smuggling work has achieved much success nationwide, the smuggling situation remains serious."[1] Even in the face of ever-tightening state strictures, commodities of all kinds continued flowing freely along the Chinese littoral and filtering into the heartland. Authorities in the early People's Republic, like their predecessors (and successors), fretted over the scale of this problem and its many potential threats. Duty evasion siphoned critical revenues from the state. Contraband running brought undesirable goods into the country. Circumvention of trade controls undermined the command economy. All of this trafficking, according to official rhetoric, maintained China's dependence on foreign imperialists and exposed the country to the vicissitudes of global capitalism. To the leaders of New China, if industry was socialist and commerce was capitalist, then smuggling—illegal and unregulated commerce that ostensibly plagued Old China—was doubly offensive.

But smuggling was not only a threat in the early People's Republic economy; it was also a lubricant that smoothed the frictions generated by the tumultuous transition to socialism. During the formative years of the new order, smuggling helped meet the daily needs of many individuals and firms—private, joint state-private, or state-owned—in the face of chronic material shortages. During the years of famine, smuggling was a survival strategy to put food on the table. Trafficking operated in the shadow of the legal coastal economy, with one supporting the other under the ever-tightening constrains of socialism. At different times, in different places, authorities in Communist China adopted a range of responses to such trafficking—suppression, toleration, and even complicity. Such ambiguity once again demonstrates how commodities trafficked changed in tandem with fluctuating economic and political circumstances.

This chapter examines the ambiguous role of coastal smuggling in challenging and complementing Communist rule during its first decade and a half (1949–1965). This period includes the three "high tides" (*gaochao*) of trafficking before 1978, each driven by major economic changes—postwar recovery (1950–1953), centralized planning (1956–1957), and post-famine recovery (1961–1965).[2] Ostensibly illegal, smuggling was actually pervasive throughout the early People's Republic. It was also diverse in its practices and meanings. Depending on one's perspective, smuggling represented an illicit threat, a campaign target, a business necessity, or a survival strategy. This chapter begins with an overview of Communist China's fear of illicit trade and the ways the new regime kicked off its own war on smuggling by appropriating the institutions and laws from its predecessor while employing novel tactics of its own. It then surveys the vast smuggling economy of merchants, consumers, and travelers moving and selling goods in defiance of domestic trade regulations. In the final sections, it looks at how trafficking alleviated widespread material shortages and supplied the quotidian needs of individuals and firms within the command economy. Given the prevalence of smuggling in the early People's Republic, this chapter shares the contention of Eastern European historians Paulina Bren and Mary Neuburger that "it is almost meaningless to explore 'official' production, consumption, or exchange under communism without simultaneously looking at its 'unofficial' underbelly."[3] A fuller appreciation of everyday life under socialism requires an exploration into the workings of nominally disparate but deeply intertwined economies.

This chapter extends the study's contention that legal and illegal trade were simply two sides of the same coin. In particular, it argues that the nascent command economy and the vibrant underground economy operated symbiotically rather than antagonistically, illustrating how coastal smuggling was embedded in both everyday life and "socialist transformation" during Communist China's formative years. Exploring the scale and scope of this trafficking offers an opportunity to revisit state-economy relations in the early People's Republic. First, by continuing to trace the long afterlife of smuggling after 1949, this chapter adds another perspective on underground economies and evasion of official controls in pre-reform China. Studies on Communist China's "second economy" have identified the widespread semilegal or illegal practices in the countryside undermining state imperatives shortly before 1978 to account for the rapid revival of rural markets after 1978.[4] This chapter on coastal trafficking, by contrast, uncovers the transnational dimensions of the second economy beyond rural China and dates its operation much earlier, to the formative years of the People's Republic. The many ways individuals have trucked, bartered, and exchanged on the margins of legality demonstrate that illicit trade was not merely a result of "corruption" by officials but also "creative accommodations" made by wide swaths of social actors coping with the enormous (and often unintended) consequences of state policies.[5] Second, this chapter illustrates how such survival strategies embodied what

William Kirby calls low-level "patterns of interaction, interpenetration and co-operation across national boundaries that have proved as least as important" as high-level diplomacy in understanding Communist China's foreign engagements.[6] Shifting the focus away from formal diplomatic relations sheds light on otherwise indistinct, informal foreign connections to the command economy and state authority. The dialectical relationship between coastal trafficking and official suppression campaigns highlights the extent of state reach in everyday economic life as well as the persistence of Communist China's ties to capitalist economies after 1949 and beyond.

SMUGGLING AS ILLICIT THREAT, REAL AND IMAGINED

During its formative years, Communist China did not object to engaging in foreign trade per se. As Mao Zedong declared in 1949, "The restoration and development of the national economy of the People's Republic would be impossible without a policy of controlling foreign trade."[7] To first rehabilitate and eventually develop the war-torn economy, Communist China promoted exports that could earn foreign exchange to purchase "necessary" imports. It also harnessed foreign trade to realize geopolitical goals like fostering ties with the Soviet Bloc or meeting military exigencies. Shortly after the outbreak of the Korean War (1950–1953), for instance, high-level leaders including Zhou Enlai and Bo Yibo called for "organized mass smuggling" (zuzhi qunzhong zousi) in South China to circumvent the United Nations embargo to secure desperately needed materiel including fuel, medicine, and industrial hardware.[8] As long as it satisfied any of the new regime's official aims, foreign trade was not only permitted but actively encouraged.

What Communist China criminalized as "smuggling," then, was uncontrolled trade, which in the official imagination eroded tax revenues, stoked capital flight, and menaced public order. Smuggling in post-1949 China did not emerge de novo but actually traced its antecedents to smuggling in pre-1949 China. The two were remarkably similar in their geography, vectors, and operation. A key driver of this durability was continuity in policy. Communist China preserved—and increased—the protective tariffs Nationalist China introduced starting with the Nanjing Decade. The new regime also maintained its predecessor's bold economic interventions, heavily taxing luxuries and strictly regulating commodities deemed unessential for the country's industrialization (table 7.1).[9] More significantly, it introduced a raft of non-tariff restrictions such as an elaborate foreign trade system that required all imports and exports to be licensed and processed through foreign trade bureaus.[10] Anyone who clandestinely imported foodstuffs (e.g., sugar, sea delicacies), consumer goods (e.g., wristwatches), and industrial products (e.g., dyestuff, chemicals), among other commodities, thus avoided paying prohibitive tariffs that reached as high as 250 percent. Anyone who exported precious metals and foreign currencies, meanwhile, circumvented restrictions on foreign exchange, thereby exacerbating the country's unfavorable balance of

TABLE 7.1 TARIFFS FOR FREQUENTLY SMUGGLED
COMMODITIES, NATIONALIST CHINA (1948)
VERSUS COMMUNIST CHINA (1951)

COMMODITY	1948	1951	DIFFERENCE
Cosmetics	120	180	60
Flint	20	120	100
Matches	80	150	70
Nylon and rayon (yarn)	100	150	50
Pencils	40	80	40
Sea cucumber	120	250	130
Sugar	100	80	–20
Watches	70	150	80

Sources: *CI*, 1948; Haiguan guanliju, ed., *Zhonghua Renmin Gongheguo haiguan jinchukou shuize* (Import and export tariffs of the customs of the People's Republic of China) (Beijing: Zhongyang renmin zhengfu haiguan zongshu, 1951).

Note: Duties as a percentage of wholesale value (ad valorem). Data for 1948 are general tariff rates (*guoding shuilü*). Data for 1951 are the general import tariff rates (*putong jinkou shuilü*).

payments position and depriving the government resources to purchase what it considered "useful" imports. High tariffs and intricate regulations—originated by the Nationalists but expanded by the Communists—mediated supply and demand and thereby underpinned the financial calculus of smuggling.

The geography of smuggling was another continuity that survived the 1949 divide. As was the case in Nationalist China, major channels of trafficking in the People's Republic still coursed through coastal cities like Shanghai, Tianjin, Xiamen, Shantou, and Guangzhou. The primary sources of smuggled goods still came from the colonial enclaves of Hong Kong and Macao, which remained as China's conduits to global markets even at the height of the Cold War. In the fifteen years from 1950 to 1965, the Customs Administration recorded 468,249 cases of smuggling and confiscated more than 131 million yuan worth of goods nationwide.[11] Reflecting the geography of trafficking and enforcement, the Pearl River Delta made up nearly two-thirds of cases during the same period (table 7.2). Even as the new People's Republic sought to consolidate its continental borders in the west, its maritime frontiers in the east remained porous to unsanctioned commerce.

Communist China shared Nationalist China's concerns over smuggling's pernicious effects on the economy. Yet it was also more concerned than its predecessor over smuggling's pernicious effects on governance. As an "antagonistic contradiction" (*diwo maodun*) in the imagination of some officials, smuggling embodied all sorts of threats to the revolution.[12] First, it subverted the Communists' idealized vision of socialist transformation, where city and countryside worked in concert to create a self-sufficient national economy. Second, it maintained Communist China's dependence on the hostile capitalist bloc and thereby hindered the regime from realizing the geopolitical aim of "leaning to one side" in the Cold War. Finally, smuggling potentially challenged the new order itself. During the "century of humiliation" before liberation, as officials consistently reminded the nation, smuggling violated China's sovereignty, destabilized the government, and destroyed native industries. Now it was ostensibly practiced by China's enemies and other counterrevolutionaries who brought into the country

TABLE 7.2 SMUGGLING CASES APPREHENDED BY
CHINA CUSTOMS, 1950–1965

REGION	CASES	% OF TOTAL
Pearl River Delta	283,198	60.5
Guangdong*	37,412	8.0
Fujian	69,252	14.8
Shanghai	13,307	2.8
Qingdao	1,137	0.2
Tianjin	2,664	0.6
Dalian	2,322	0.5
Other (nationwide)	58,957	12.6
Total	468,249	—

Sources: Su Shifang, ed., *Dangdai Zhongguo haiguan* (Contemporary China's customs) (1992; reprint, Hong Kong: Xianggang zuguo chubanshe, 2009), 449; Guangdong sheng difang shi zhi bianzuan weiyuanhui, ed., *Guangdong sheng zhi: haiguan zhi* (Guangdong provincial gazetteer: customs gazetteer) (Guangzhou: Guangdong renmin chubanshe, 2002), 270–71; Fujian sheng difang zhi bianzuan weiyuanhui, ed., *Fujian sheng zhi: haiguan zhi* (Fujian provincial gazetteer: customs gazetteer) (Beijing: Fangzhi chubanshe, 1995), 179–80; Shanghai haiguan zhi bianzuan weiyuanhui, ed., *Shanghai haiguan zhi*, 390–91; Shandong sheng difang shi zhi bianzuan weiyuanhui, ed., *Shandong sheng zhi: haiguan zhi* (Shandong provincial gazetteer: customs gazetteer) (Ji'nan: Shandong renmin chubanshe, 1997), 512; Tianjin haiguan bianzhi shi, ed., *Tianjin haiguan zhi* (Tianjian customs gazetteer) (Tianjin: Tianjin haiguan bianzhi shi, 1993), 207–8; Dalian haiguan zhi bianzuan weiyuanhui, ed., *Dalian haiguan zhi* (Dalian customs gazetteer) (Beijing: Zhongguo haiguan chubanshe, 2005), 125.

Note: Other (nationwide) calculated subtracting sum of coastal cases from total. Pearl River Delta includes the Guangzhou, Jiulong, and Gongbei Customs. Fujian includes the Xiamen and Fuzhou Customs. Data for Xiamen until 1961 include seizures via post. Data unavailable for Guangzhou 1951–1952, Xiamen 1950, and Fuzhou 1959.

*Not including Pearl River Delta.

anti-Communist propaganda and narcotics to lead the masses astray from the revolutionary path.[13]

To wage its war on smuggling, Communist China blended old institutions with new tactics. During the final years of the Second Sino-Japanese War, the Communists had already operated several customhouses along the North China coast. Within weeks of Japan's surrender in August and

September 1945, they opened new customhouses at Yantai, Weihaiwei, and Longkou to form the core of the "People's Customs" within the Shandong Liberation Area. Throughout the chaos of the Chinese Civil War, the People's Customs struggled to monitor trade between liberated areas and enemy territories. It was also charged with suppressing smuggling, encouraging soldiers and cadres to combat illicit trade with slogans such as "Smuggling means aiding the enemy, aiding the enemy means selling out your country" (*zousi ji shi zidi, zidi jiu shi maiguo*).[14] As the Communists drove farther south, they also assumed more control over the old Chinese Maritime Customs Service, which had taxed, regulated, and policed foreign trade on behalf of successive central Chinese governments—the Qing court, the Beiyang regime, and the Nationalists.[15] The Communists recognized the importance of taking over this important institution. As Mao himself declared in a March 1949 report to the Second Plenum of the Seventh Central Committee, assuming "immediate control of foreign trade and reform[ing] the customs system—these are the first steps we must take upon entering the big cities."[16]

Months of planning thereafter culminated with the creation of the General Customs Administration (Haiguan Zongshu) on October 19, 1949. The new agency, with the old Maritime Customs at its core, was given a new mission to support the regime's aims. Loyal party operatives like Kong Yuan were placed in top leadership positions.[17] Foreign employees of the Maritime Customs who had not already fled were unceremoniously discharged. Chinese employees, who remained at their posts even during the Nationalists' steady southward retreat to Taiwan, occupied the rest of the agency's administrative hierarchy. Personnel included not only low-ranking employees but also high-ranking officials like the former deputy inspector general Ding Guitang who were valued (at least initially) for their technical and administrative expertise. Before they resumed their duties, these incumbents participated in reeducation sessions designed to inculcate loyalty to the new order through a mixture of inducements, threats, and magnanimity.[18] Tensions between the two groups were sometimes palpable. New leaders like Kong frequently lambasted the old

Maritime Customs' "corrupt and degenerate style of work" (*tanwu fuhua de zuofeng*), while party investigators uncovered cases of criminal acts and petty corruption within the agency during the Three-Anti Campaign (1951).[19] Meanwhile, holdovers like Ding later complained of being excluded by newcomers from major responsibilities, leaving people like himself with "an office but no authority" (*youzhi wuquan*).[20]

Besides assuming control of an old institution, the new regime also expanded the legal framework created by its predecessor to fight smuggling and broadcast central authority. It officially nullified all Nationalist laws.[21] A closer inspection, however, reveals continuities as well as ruptures between Communist laws and their defunct predecessors. Embodying this coexistence between new and old is the Provisional Customs Law of the People's Republic of China (Zhonghua Remin Gongheguo zanxing haiguan fa). Promulgated in 1951 and replaced only in 1987, the law governed the administration and responsibilities of the new People's Customs for more than three decades. Unlike Nationalist anti-smuggling laws, the Provisional Customs Law explicitly defined smuggling by enumerating violations and categorized their severity by intent and article trafficked. Minor smuggling, which included run-of-the-mill duty evasion and travel beyond designated waters, was punished with a minor fine or confiscation. Major smuggling encompassed serious violations that revealed the perpetrator's intent to harm the nation: using specifically constructed "hides"; employing violent resistance; trafficking narcotics and armaments; counterfeiting government documents; and colluding with government officials.[22] Besides being fined or having the illicit goods confiscated, violators would be transferred to local courts or public security agencies for further investigation and punishment.[23] Instructions to customs and public security officials often referred to such principles, stressing the importance of differentiating between major and minor cases of smuggling and "raising the masses' socialist consciousness" (*tigao qunzhong shehui zhuyi juewu*).[24] Such gradations also widened the scope of discretion for officials in meting out appropriate penalties, which Communist China accused its predecessor of indiscriminately applying.[25]

Other features of the Provisional Customs Law were also built on pre-1949 regulations and procedures. Jurisdictions over minor and major cases of smuggling, for instance, were more clearly delineated between the judiciary, public security, and the Customs Administration. Yet the decision to fine and confiscate remained the sole prerogative of customs commissioners. Furthermore, individuals dissatisfied with the penalties levied by the People's Customs were permitted to appeal their cases in accordance with procedures that echoed those of the old Maritime Customs.[26] The exclusive responsibility of the People's Customs over smuggling cases was among the key features of the new law Kong Yuan explicitly highlighted in a May 1950 nationwide radio broadcast.[27]

While employing inherited Nationalist institutions and laws to fight smuggling, Communist China departed from its predecessor's policies in several distinct ways. As with other campaigns it launched, the new regime did not simply expect passive compliance in the fight against smuggling—it wanted active participation. During the Five-Anti Campaign (1952–1953), for instance, state propaganda encouraged the public to help fight smuggling by pointing to the evasion of customs duties as a prime example of one of the antis (figure 7.1). That smuggling was singled out should not be surprising. "Tax evasion" (toushui loushui) through nonpayment of tariffs or misreporting the value of imports was a longstanding business practice before 1949, and many merchants were thus vulnerable to charges of evading duties, making excessive profits, and owing back taxes. Reports of merchants and other "capitalists" forced to pay back taxes on smuggled goods were common in the popular press.[28] Other forms of mobilization included the various "mass anti-smuggling" (qunzhong fan zousi) campaigns in the late 1950s encouraging the public to "report" (jianju) potential offenses to authorities. In one instance, a Guangzhou resident informed on her neighbor, a "habitual smuggler" who lived a well-to-do life making frequent trips to Hong Kong and returning with large suitcases, despite "having no proper employment."[29] In another instance, a Shanghai wristwatch store employee submitted more than forty reports during the 1950s, leading to 2,000 yuan worth of seizures.[30] Mass anti-smuggling, according to the regime, yielded many arrests that would have otherwise gone undetected. From 1950

FIGURE 7.1

"Severely Punish Lawless Merchants Who Endanger the Nation!"
(*Yancheng weihai guojia de bufa shangren!*)

The cartoon shows targets of the Five-Anti Campaign. From top, left to right: "bribery" (*xinghui*), "tax evasion" (*toushui loushui*), "corner-cutting in workmanship" (*tougong jianliao*), "theft of state property" (*daopian guojia caichan*), and "theft of state economic information" (*daoqie guojia jing ji qingbao*). "Tax evasion" features a merchant pushing his cart of goods past the customs station, thereby avoiding "customs duties" (*guanshui*).

Source: Manhua (Cartoons) 22 (March 1952): 8. Edward Hunter Collection, Chinese Pamphlet Digitization Project. Courtesy of Center for Research Libraries (CRL)

through September 1957, for instance, the Guangzhou, Jiulong (Kowloon), and Gongbei (Lappa) Customs announced that they collectively uncovered more than 41,000 cases of smuggling based on the more than 123,000 letters they received from the public.[31]

In another departure from Nationalist China, Communist China mounted successive outreach programs designed to educate the public on the evils of smuggling. Mirroring ongoing efforts to rectify undesirable social behavior, customs officials across China spearheaded anti-smuggling publicity campaigns by authoring essays in local newspapers, giving lectures over the radio, and showing short public service announcements in theaters.[32] The media also lionized ordinary Chinese whose laudable contributions in the fight against smuggling belied their modest positions. *People's Daily*, for instance, hailed a Shanghai railway inspector who rejected bribes offered from "treacherous merchants" and persevered in the face of repeated beatings from smugglers—thereby doing his small part protecting the nation's revenues.[33] Finally, the People's Courts held public trials and sentencing rallies for accused smugglers throughout the country. In Guangzhou, an August 1957 public trial with twelve thousand attendees sentenced an individual to eight years of penal servitude for consistently misrepresenting his travel plans (e.g., visiting relatives or attending funerals) in trafficking goods between Hong Kong and Guangzhou. Other defendants received sentences of from four to five years of penal servitude, save for one who was sentenced to six months for providing information on other smugglers.[34] In Shanghai, a March 1958 anti-smuggling sentencing rally had 1,800 attendees, most of whom were merchants and the target of the event's message. In addition to high-level court and customs officials, "representatives of the people" also made statements supporting serious punishments and expressing willingness to cooperate with the government in suppressing smuggling.[35] Other government agencies like the Ministry of Foreign Trade encouraged the People's Court to hold similar events to "help the masses recognize smuggling's harm to the nation."[36]

Other programs were more expansive in scope. Officials organized many "anti-smuggling exhibitions" (*fan zousi zhanlanhui*) throughout the country, the largest of which was held in the Guangzhou from November

1957 to January 1958 and jointly sponsored by the Guangzhou, Jiulong, and Gongbei Customs. The exhibition aimed to "concretely and systematically" present smuggling's one hundred year history to visitors from local residents to Chinese visitors from Hong Kong and Macao. Along with photographs and charts, the exhibition also featured more than six hundred displays of items confiscated by authorities: tin cans concealing saccharine, water bottles storing wristwatches, and a radio transmitter purportedly used by Nationalist spies.[37] Strong attendance for the exhibition (716,000 visitors), combined with the government's concern about the increasing seriousness of illicit trade, prompted other cities to host their own anti-smuggling exhibitions. The 1958 Shanghai exhibition attracted more visitors (800,000) despite running a month shorter than its Guangzhou counterpart. It also featured a satirical play—"Under the X-Ray" (Zai X guang xia)—performed by the Shanghai Municipal People's Theater Company.[38] Whether using inanimate displays or performance art, the exhibitions sought to impress on visitors the continuing threat illicit trade posed to national sovereignty. The efficacy of these campaigns is questionable—smuggling, after all, continued unabated throughout the Maoist era and beyond. Yet such didactic efforts represented a marked departure from the techniques of governance under the Nationalists, who never attempted such programs at countering smuggling. Moreover, they accorded perfectly with the revolutionary state's goals of cultivating an ethic of volunteerism among the people and encouraging officials to "combine punishment with education" (chengban yu jiaoyu xiang jiehe).[39] The fight against smuggling was yet another example of the new regime's belief that sociopolitical and economic transformations could be realized through mass mobilization.[40]

LEGAL LOOPHOLES AND PROFIT OPPORTUNITIES

Who were the smugglers at the other end of these campaigns in this post-1949 era? The anti-smuggling rhetoric of Communist China, which like its

Nationalist predecessors articulated the fight against trafficking in the language of nationalism by linking the illicit pursuit of profit to the damage it inflicted on the welfare of the Chinese people. The same epithets "treasonous merchants" and "bandits" (*tufei*) aimed at smugglers before 1949 were still employed thereafter. The Communists, however, expanded the public vocabulary to describe those who purportedly collaborated with foreign imperialists and the "Chiang Kai-shek bandit gang" (*Jiang feibang*) in undermining the laws, borders, and sovereignty of the People's Republic. The new labels they affixed on smugglers—"lawless traders" (*bufa shangren*), "lawless capitalists" (*bufa zibenjia*), "rotten capitalist" (*yulan zibenjia*), "feudal remnants" (*fengjian canyu*), and "counterrevolutionary" (*fan geming fenzi*)—reflect the regime's belief that private economic motivations were ultimately inseparable from insidious political aims.[41] This alarmist rhetoric painting Manichean pictures of illicit trade's threats was employed in both public pronouncements and government correspondences. A report from the Ministry of Foreign Trade to the State Council, for instance, notes: "The nature of smuggling activities is not just an economic issue [but] also a political issue. Its essence is a struggle between socialism and capitalism."[42] In the official imagination, then, smugglers were not merely committing an economic crime that reduced the efficiency of the new command economy; they were committing a political crime that potentially undermined the new revolutionary order itself.

The historical evidence, however, reveals that smugglers were actually a heterogeneous lot motivated less by politics and more by economics. Indeed, the desire to exploit regulatory loopholes and remedy widespread shortages created by the transition to socialism itself was not limited to any specific individuals or groups. As was the case in Nationalist China, the identities of smugglers in Communist China were as diverse as the commodities they trafficked. Residents of frontier towns, coastal villages, and remote islands traversed porous borders to profit from price disparities and material scarcities on the mainland. Traffickers in the interior then funneled goods by rail and post. Some operated legitimate fronts, like the thirty-seven smuggling rings in northeast Guangdong masquerading as inconspicuous "handicraft cooperatives," "stationery factories," or "watch factories" that supplied assorted consumer goods to Shanghai, Fuzhou, Xiamen, and Wenzhou.[43] Some operated with official connivance, like the Guangzhou "female smuggling king" (*nü zousi dawang*) Gao Yamei, who did brisk business ferrying goods between China and Hong Kong from before 1949 until her arrest in 1952. Importing more than 25,000 watches, Western medicines, ginseng, and mechanical pencils, while exporting more than 200 *liang* of gold, Gao operated a vast smuggling network stretching across the Pearl River Delta from Shenzhen to Guangzhou.[44] Speculators—euphemistically called "cattle" (*huangniu*)—made trafficking practically a full-time profession, constantly seeking to profit from arbitrage opportunities in both rationed and smuggled goods.[45] For others, trafficking was a temporary expedient to make ends meet during economically uncertain times. Shao Maotang and four partners, for instance, led typical lives for smugglers in the early 1950s, peddling watches, batteries, and assorted foreign goods across Guangzhou, Shanghai, Tianjin, and Harbin. A decade later, they led unremarkable lives as factory workers and shopkeepers, leading Shanghai Customs officials who uncovered their offenses to recommend minor financial penalties rather than jail time as punishment.[46]

Everyone could potentially practice smuggling, then, but certain individuals attracted particular attention for doing so. Overseas Chinese (*huaqiao*)—a wide category that encompassed travelers from Hong Kong and Macao or returnees (*guiqiao*) from Southeast Asia—were often portrayed in government correspondences and popular media as prominent carriers of illicit goods, given their mobility and access to foreign markets.[47] From the late Qing through the entire Republican period, Overseas Chinese freely traveled between China and the rest of Asia, potentially leveraging their mobility and legal status to move smuggled goods. War, revolution, and decolonization starting from the 1940s, however, ended this long era of unrestricted mobility and forced millions of transnational families to choose between remaining in their adopted country or returning to their ancestral homeland. Yet Communist China preserved and even systematized the legally privileged status of Overseas Chinese, according returnees intending to resettle in China "special treatment" (*youdai*) with preferential access to jobs, housing, and other social services. This policy was aimed at encouraging remittances and soliciting contributions from the vast Overseas Chinese community to the mainland's modernization, but it incidentally created liminal spaces for smuggling. Regulations, for instance, permitted returnees to enter China with some personal effects duty free but some returnees arrived with "personal effects" that far exceeded the duty-free limit: stockpiles of razor blades, lighter flints, pens, knives, bicycles, and other Western consumer goods.[48] Overseas Chinese visitors from Hong Kong and Macao, meanwhile, exploited similar loopholes, especially after 1956 when travel restrictions and duty-free limits on personal effects were relaxed.[49] A 1957 Guangdong Customs report estimated that of the Overseas Chinese visitors from Hong Kong and Macao, 33 percent were on legitimate business (e.g., tourism, commerce, or visiting relatives), 26 percent were profiteers bringing in goods for sale in the mainland, 40 percent were itinerant peddlers who relied on smuggling for a living, and 1 percent were counterrevolutionaries plotting political sabotage.[50] Almost two-thirds of visitors, in other words, were suspected of engaging in one kind of nefarious activity or another. Putting aside the veracity of such figures, officials certainly cast a wary eye toward most Overseas Chinese travelers, even as the People's Republic formally welcomed returning "compatriots" (*tongbao*).

Officials had reasons to worry. In China, Overseas Chinese who wanted to dispose of their personal effects were required to sell them to state-run companies or "purchasing stations" (*shougouzhan*).[51] Yet the prices offered at these stations—based on wholesale prices plus any tariffs levied—were usually far lower than prices offered by nonofficial buyers. As some Overseas Chinese who relied on selling their personal effects to pay for their living expenses on the mainland complained, "The renminbi we get after [our goods] are purchased is not enough to buy similar goods on the market."[52] Unable to profitably sell their goods through legal channels, many Overseas Chinese instead turned to black markets with sophisticated distribution and retail networks. Returnees in Fujian, for instance, could engage any one of the estimated 300 "middlemen" (*jingjiren*) who brokered the sale of smuggled jewelry, Western medicines, foodstuffs, and other assorted merchandise to buyers in Shanghai, Tianjin, and Beijing.[53] Travelers in the Pearl River Delta, meanwhile, disposed of their smuggled wristwatches and fountain pens at hotels and other guesthouses, where reliable managers tapped local connections to find willing customers.[54] Finally, Overseas Chinese were also vectors of capital flight, working with Hong Kong remittance agencies (*yinhao*) to send gold, silver, jewelry, and currencies abroad in explicit defiance of state strictures.[55] Many travelers and returnees thus sought to profit (or even survive) by taking advantage of their politically privileged and separate status as well as their ties to foreign markets. Despite official exhortations that continued well into the 1960s encouraging them to turn instead to state-run units, many Overseas Chinese continued to rely on illicit channels to meet their needs.[56]

Knowledge of such petty smuggling tactics circulated widely among Overseas Chinese communities not only through word of mouth or popular press reports but also through travel guides. One guidebook, *Things to Know Returning to Native Village and Returning to Hong Kong* (*Huanxiang fan Gang xuzhi*), dispensed travel advice that spanned the spectrum of legality. Along with helpful information on train schedules and customs regulations, it also offered legally dubious answers to frequently asked questions including: "How to safely sell off wristwatches and fountain pens?" and "How to rescue your gold jewelry from the mainland and bring it back to Hong Kong?"[57] For proffering such advice—which was blatantly illegal—the book was banned in China and denounced by *People's Daily* as Nationalist propaganda designed to "stir up smuggling" (*shandong zousi*).[58] The origin of the guide is unclear, but its many descriptions of trafficking in the mainland were undeniably accurate. Reports from both the popular press and internal government correspondences confirmed that guesthouses were indeed havens for illicit peddling and critical channels in the smuggling pipeline.[59] Literature like *Things to Know* served less as an incitement to smuggle and more as a reflection of a sizeable Overseas Chinese readership that hungered for practical advice on profiting from cross-border arbitrage.

Other groups that received widespread attention for their alleged propensity to smuggle were ethnic minorities—particularly Uighurs and

Huis. Military conquest of the west and the creation of autonomous regions during the 1950s brought minority areas under the rule of the People's Republic. While some Han Chinese cadres and settlers made their way west, some minorities moved eastward to coastal cities and soon attracted official attention for being major carriers of illicit goods. Unlike their overseas Chinese counterparts who leveraged their access to foreign markets, ethnic minority smugglers carved out a niche as traffickers who nimbly moved goods between cities. In February 1957, for instance, the Shanghai Customs arrested eighty-six Uighur and Hui merchants operating a network that brought smuggled goods from Guangzhou to Shanghai before transshipping them to far-flung cities including Wuhan, Chongqing, Ji'nan, Tianjin, and Shenyang.[60] Similarly spectacular cases testified to their extensive geographical reach and mobility.

Like Overseas Chinese, ethnic minorities enjoyed a politically privileged status that complicated law enforcement efforts. To help consolidate the Chinese nation-state during the 1950s, the regime adopted conciliatory policies like favorable legal treatment and tax relief toward minorities. In the Principles for Customs Organization issued by the State Council in December 1950, for instance, "minority nationalities and residents in frontier regions" exchanging commodities of daily necessities in small volumes were explicitly permitted to pass in and out of China untaxed.[61] Meanwhile, top leaders including Mao himself explicitly denounced the widespread "Han chauvinism" (da Han zhuyi) that presumably poisoned relations between the Han majority and other ethnic minorities.[62] In an attempt to best adhere to such top-down directives, officials pursued several strategies balancing competing imperatives when dealing with ethnic minority smugglers. Some sought to demonstrate leniency. A Ministry of Foreign Trade report, for instance, affirmed that ethnic minority smugglers should be strictly dealt with but recommended that their punishments be a bit lighter than the punishments levied against Han smugglers. The State Council forwarded the report throughout the government, thereby implicitly endorsing the recommendation.[63] Others pushed for relocation with the assumption that removing ethnic minority residents from cities would also remove the smuggling problem. In Guangzhou, instructions for a 1957 anti-smuggling campaign ordered that any ethnic minority smuggler caught should have their goods confiscated but otherwise be sent home, with money for travel expenses if necessary.[64] In Shanghai, officials implored their Xinjiang counterparts to encourage the city's Uighurs to return west but to no avail. Few left and those who did quickly returned to Shanghai or simply relocated their operations to another city.[65]

Even government officials themselves attracted considerable opprobrium for engaging in smuggling. The Three- and Five-Anti Campaigns in particular exposed many cases of local officials exploiting state-sanctioned trafficking during the Korean War for private gains. A cadre stationed in Macao to purchase strategic materials for the Central Military Commission, for instance, was discovered to have forged receipts to avoid paying tariffs on foreign goods he purchased for personal use. Other officials used private firms as fronts and even engaged in armed smuggling (*wuzhuang zousi*) by employing soldiers to import nonstrategic materials such as watches, pens, and sugar. More than fifty government units—many of them military—engaged in similar forms of duty evasion, according to statistics compiled by the Guangzhou Municipal Tax Bureau in 1951.[66] The problem became so acute at one point that General Ye Jianying, then in charge of Guangdong, arrested more than five hundred cadres and army officers for trafficking.[67] Such incidents unfolded around the same time that the 1952 Statute of Penalties for Corruption added smuggling as a violation.[68] Compared with its treatment of other traffickers, the regime tended to be less lenient with officials accused of smuggling for personal gain, since their actions compromised its revolutionary aims and eroded its prestige.

SOCIALIST SHORTAGES AND CAPITALIST GOODS

For the regime, coastal trafficking was unregulated commerce that threatened governance. For everyone else, it helped meet quotidian needs within the emerging command economy. As it was the case in other socialist economies, bureaucratized production in China created what scholars have called "planned disequilibrium."[69] Mismatches between supply and demand that were fundamental—and not aberrant—features of command economies led to chronic shortages of consumer goods often neglected by planners. The First Five-Year Plan (1953–1957) was no exception, creating widespread material scarcities in both city and countryside despite being universally hailed for rapidly developing heavy industries and helping the country recover from wartime devastation. The plan's geographical biases, moreover, exacerbated austere conditions along the Chinese littoral. The central leadership "deliberately chose to redistribute human and invest-ment resources from the advanced to the poorer regions," thereby relocat-ing China's industrial center of gravity to the interior and leaving coastal enclaves more reliant on commerce for their development.[70] In theory, trade with the socialist bloc should have helped Communist China over-come shortages by serving as the "last resort to make up for scarcities and sell surpluses."[71] In practice, socialist commerce often suffered from what William Kirby calls "built-in disadvantages" serving as disincentives to exchange: bilateral trade agreements that were inflexible and the Soviet model that reinforced inherent biases toward autarky.[72]

In this environment, everyone—consumers and producers—had to improvise around state plans. Well-known tactics like bartering and hoarding employed by cadres, team leaders, and plant managers helped overcome mismatches in supply and demand.[73] Less attention, however, has been paid to ways smuggling helped ameliorate shortages in the Chi-nese littoral created by the transition to the command economy and the early Cold War foreign trade regime. Smuggling effectively connected China with far-flung markets and made available a range of consumer goods government channels could not adequately supply. Outlets in Shang-hai, for example, did brisk business selling foreign wristwatches, cosmet-ics, silk scarves, socks, and assorted plastic products—all trafficked from abroad via Guangdong (Guangzhou, Foshan, and Shantou), Fujian (Xia-men and Fuzhou), and Wenzhou. Suppliers included unemployed indi-viduals, petty merchants, housewives, ethnic minorities, and Overseas

Chinese who sold the "personal effects" they brought into China duty-free.[74] Smuggled consumer products continued to be openly peddled in Shanghai markets well into the 1960s, even after various anti-smuggling campaigns, while similar black markets operated in other cities including Guangzhou and Tianjin.[75] They attracted buyers from all walks of life, and even visiting foreigners could not resist their allure. Soviet technical advisers and their families stationed in China during the 1950s, for instance, reportedly used their generous salaries from the Chinese government to snap up smuggled foreign goods unavailable back home.[76]

Among all smuggled consumer articles, wristwatches proved especially popular. Already the "ultimate object of desire" before 1949, watches retained their allure thereafter as one of the "big three" consumer items (*san dajian*) that conferred significant social status.[77] They were also valued as "gifts" that could be used to curry favor with officials, even cadres ostensibly hostile to products from "imperialist America."[78] So insatiable was the demand that it easily survived the Three-Anti and Five-Anti Campaigns targeting ownership of luxury goods and other forms of "corruption."[79] Meanwhile, small size made the clandestine transport, distribution, and sale of watches immensely profitable. Dealers in Hong Kong supplied mainland China and the rest of Asia with watches genuine (imported duty-free from Europe) and fake (manufactured locally).[80] Throughout the Maoist era and beyond, smuggled watches were widely available, retailed not only at stores, bazaars, parks, teahouses, and guesthouses but even on the factory floor. Authorities in Shenyang, for instance, uncovered several smuggling rings in factories throughout the city. Peddlers had been permitted by factory foremen to sell watches from faraway Guangzhou and Shanghai in exchange for "petty favors" (*xiao'en xiaohui*). With profits allegedly reaching 100 percent, some factory workers even sought to abandon their full-time occupations and engage in wristwatch trafficking instead.[81] That such an officially stigmatized commodity could be so easily procured reveals the persistence of consumer demand in defiance of state ideology and highlights the extent and durability of extensive smuggling networks linking coast and interior to supply that demand.

Along with consumers, producers were also eager buyers of illicit goods. Hamstrung by shortages of raw materials and key inputs, many of them turned to the black markets. The trafficking of tungsten carbide cutters, valued for their high heat resistance and durability, exemplified the symbiotic relationship between the command economy and the illicit economy. Under Soviet technical tutelage during the 1950s, Chinese factories were encouraged to replace older lathes and adopt tungsten cutters in their production lines. Domestic cutters at the time were produced solely at the Dalian Iron and Steel Factory, while foreign cutters were imported through local trade bureaus from the Soviet Union, West Germany, Japan, and Sweden. Distribution of cutters was coordinated through planning, but as the First Five-Year Plan kicked into high gear, demand quickly outstripped supply. Indeed, government reports confirmed widespread shortages of industrial equipment and metal hardware in early 1956, but shortages of cutters were most acute.[82] In Shanghai, large factories received cutters directly from central planners. Small factories, including joint state-private enterprises, received their cutters indirectly from central planners through branches of the Shanghai Municipal Hardware Company. Large factories ostensibly had first priority for cutters but frequently received far fewer than they needed. The Shanghai Electric Motor Factory, for instance, required at least 16 kilograms (32 *shijin*) worth of cutters for its operations but were allocated only one-third of that amount. To make up for the shortfall, the factory turned to the Shanghai Municipal Hardware Company, thereby placing downward pressures on other factories and creating a ripple effect throughout the market. A 1957 report noted that the Shanghai Municipal "Hardware Company's normal supply is already far insufficient to satisfy market requirements, causing strained conditions where demand exceeds supply. Consequently, the 'free market' (*ziyou shichang*) has become active. Because [the allocation of] steel cutters is managed by the central state, cutters from the so-called free market all come from smuggling."[83]

"Free markets" for cutters in cities like Shanghai were actually nodes within a larger network that stretched throughout the country and mapped along the same vectors for all smuggled goods. From Hong Kong and

Macao, where supplies were plentiful and almost unrestricted, Overseas Chinese smuggled foreign cutters (primarily Swedish) into China across the border to Shenzhen and Guangzhou. There, merchants (many of them ethnic minorities) purchased the cutters and shipped them throughout the country, where they were then sold to local retail outlets like branches of the Shanghai Municipal Hardware Company before finally filtering into official supply channels. Reflecting this geography of smuggling, black market prices for cutters were highly correlated with distance from Hong Kong. The further away from the British colony, generally, the higher the premium commanded (table 7.3). This traffic was very active. An April 1957 report by the Jiulong Customs, for instance, noted that along the Hong Kong border tungsten cutters had just displaced wristwatches as "first place among all smuggled articles [and] it is obvious that the situation is becoming more serious with each passing day."[84] Shanghai, a major destination for smuggled cutters, attracted eager buyers near and far. Factories throughout the northeast as well as the Yangzi River Delta dispatched agents to scour the city and secure desperately needed inputs for their own production. Buyers and sellers reportedly converged at the New Asia Hotel to hash out deals.[85] Supplies otherwise scarce or unavailable in the command

TABLE 7.3 BLACK MARKET PRICES FOR TUNGSTEN CARBIDE CUTTERS, CA. 1956

LOCATION	PRICE	DIFFERENCE FROM HK	
	RMB	RMB	%
Hong Kong	125	—	—
Guangzhou	320–450	195–325	56–106
Shanghai	860	735	488
Tianjin	760	635	408
Wuhan	700	575	360
Northeast	900	775	520

Source: SHMA, B6/2/286, "Diaocha tanhua wugang daotou zousi de chubu cailiao" (June 11, 1957), in Shanghai Customs to Shanghai Municipal People's Committee.

economy, then, were plentiful in the underground economy thanks to smuggling.

Tungsten carbide cutters were far from the only producer good that stood at the ambiguous intersection between the nascent command economy and the active illicit economy. Government reports consistently employed the phrase "supply falls short of demand" (*gong bu ying qiu*) when explaining the widespread reliance by factories on a host of smuggled commodities. Nylon—a necessity in the production of toothbrushes, stockings, and other products—was frequently smuggled into the mainland from Hong Kong on board fishing trawlers and purchased by retailers for resale. Cocoa—used in the manufacture of sweets—was in such short supply that factories throughout China eagerly snapped up illicitly imported stocks from Hong Kong. In 1956, one *jin* of cocoa commanded 17 yuan on the black market, a huge premium over the prevailing Hong Kong price of 1.27 yuan per *jin*. Yet buyers had few alternatives since no cocoa whatsoever was available at the official price of 14 yuan per *jin*.[86] Besides state-owned enterprises (SOEs), according to reports, buyers of these smuggled goods included "underground factories" (*dixia gongchang*). These small economic units were mostly private businesses eking a shaky existence during the transition to socialism as they operated on the margins of the law and faced intense pressures to join state-sponsored cooperatives. Smuggling helped extend their precarious survival by offering alternative supply channels after being systematically excluded from legitimate ones. It thus underpinned what Lynn White regarded as these factories' critical role in the command economy: "easing production bottlenecks that the economic planners had not anticipated."[87]

Officials worried that participation in the illicit economy, particularly by SOEs, had other pernicious effects. Since SOEs were rapidly becoming the biggest companies during the 1950s, their potential role in boosting demand for smuggled goods was not trivial. As a Ministry of Foreign Trade report noted: "There are some enterprises and commercial units sending agents to border regions or black markets to purchase high-priced foreign commodities, [thereby] greatly stimulating the development of smuggling and the flow of foreign goods into the interior. There are some employers of government offices who purchase smuggled foreign goods for personal use, [thereby] assisting in the sale of smuggled goods."[88]

Even more worrisome was how SOEs helped legitimate black market trade. Foreign luxuries like wristwatches and other consumer products were easily identifiable. Other illegally imported commodities were far less conspicuous in revealing their origins. "The problem that currently exists," as one customs report noted, "is that there is no way to distinguish between smuggled [goods] and non-smuggled [goods]."[89] This ambiguity afforded every participant in the smuggling chain—from traffickers to retailers to buyers—some plausible deniability, claiming they were ignorant of the goods' legal status. One report quoted a common refrain from smugglers that neatly encapsulates this attitude: "If state-owned [companies] purchase [smuggled] goods, how can it be called illegal?"[90]

SMUGGLING AS SURVIVAL STRATEGY

As was the case with the First Five-Year Plan, state interventions during the Great Leap Forward (1958–1962) and after created new incentives for smuggling. The introduction of the grain monopoly and collectivized agriculture led to devastating famine across China. Suffering was widespread but not always passively borne. As Jeremy Brown observes, some peasants retaliated against state restrictions by peddling foodstuffs hoarded during successive waves of collectivization and roving between city and country.[91] Other peasants resorted to smuggling, the organization of which changed in response to famine and market shortages. Customs gazetteers often employed the euphemism "domestic economic hardships" (*guonei jingji kunnan*) to account for the resurgence of illicit trade during this period.[92] Wristwatches remained popular articles of trafficking, but reflecting ongoing agricultural shortages, the most frequently smuggled commodities during this period were desperately needed ones. Sugar, for instance, commanded substantial premiums on the black market. A 1962 Shanghai Customs report recorded that foreign sugar, sold in Hong Kong for 3–4 yuan per pound, was illicitly sold in China for around 120 yuan per pound—roughly forty times the cost.[93] Central government relaxation of private rural marketing after 1960 gave smuggling an additional boost. Promoted by Chen Yun and supported by the "marketeers and bureaucrats" faction then ascendant in the aftermath of the Great Leap, the new policy sought to relieve famine but also stimulated more black market activities.[94] In the face of widespread trafficking, officials grumbled that peasants confused "free markets" with "the freedom to buy and sell anything" (*yangyang dou ke ziyou maimai*).[95]

Like previous rounds, this round of smuggling implicated the usual suspects—Overseas Chinese, ethnic minorities, speculators, and itinerant peddlers.[96] Yet it was the participation by coastal communities that most attracted official attention. From the late 1950s through the early 1960s, authorities detected an upsurge of trafficking by communes and production teams who "relied upon their favorable location" (*pingjie dili*) to crisscross borders.[97] In some villages, 80 to 90 percent of residents were estimated to have engaged in smuggling.[98] Even before the Great Leap, illegal crossings into Hong Kong and Macao by coastal peasants—whose ranks included nominally reliable Communist party branch members and production team leaders—were already a widespread, "serious situation" (*qingkuang hen yanzhong*).[99] Dire conditions during the Leap only stimulated more illicit movement. An incident in the Pearl River Delta typified this problem. At the height of the Great Leap on June 1, 1959, a customs patrol apprehended three commune members in a newly built junk loaded with assorted foreign goods from Hong Kong returning to Fuyong Village in Bao'an County. The villagers funded their week-and-a-half journey and purchases with Hong Kong dollars remitted by overseas relatives. While commune leaders disavowed their claims, the apprehended villagers insisted that the new boat was intended for the commune's use and that the purchases were sanctioned by the village party branch secretary. Further investigation revealed that this journey was not the first instance of cross-border smuggling. In fact, the villagers made at least another trip to Hong Kong a year earlier. Underscoring the frequency of such trafficking, the Guangzhou Customs candidly admitted in its summary of the incident: "It is our understanding that every county along the coast has similar cases."[100] Communes in Maoist China pursued many "informal strategies" to enhance their collective welfare.[101] Besides altering the size of production teams, engaging in speculation, and withholding goods and services, cross-border trafficking was certainly a key tactic employed in response to new changes in the countryside.

Within coastal communities, fishermen attracted official opprobrium for their "insufferably extreme arrogance" (*qiyan feichang xiaozhang*) and "very low political consciousness" (*sixiang juewu hen di*). A Ministry of Foreign Trade report noted that fishermen frequently disregarded border controls and evaded inspections, sometimes even resorting to violence by beating up anti-smuggling officers. Communist China had not always been implacably hostile to such mobility across porous borders. At the height of the Korean War, for example, the regime actually encouraged coastal communities to ferry strategic materials from abroad and rewarded many fishermen handsomely for circumventing the United Nations embargo. But a decade of centralized planning meant such trafficking was no longer welcome, or at least no longer useful to Beijing. The Ministry of Trade, which helped coordinate "strategic smuggling" during the early 1950s, complained of trawlers "brazenly" (*gongran*) moving smuggled wares between Hong Kong and Guangzhou by the late 1950s.[102]

Aside from blaming bad attitudes, officials also recognized more fundamental reasons fostering the antipathy of coastal communities and fishermen toward state authority. Long before 1949, coastal villagers thwarted official efforts to regulate maritime commerce, fishing, and movement since "maritime nomadism" had been a long-standing feature of life in the region.[103] After 1949 at the height of the Cold War, they were subjected to even more restrictions, forbidden from sailing to Hong Kong, Macao, and Taiwan to fish and trade.[104] State imperatives thus kicked off a vicious cycle of new strictures, more evasion, and more suppression. As before, anti-smuggling efforts provoked resentment as much as they curtailed trafficking. Officials from the Guangdong Provincial Bureau of Border Defense, for instance, candidly admitted that overly strict confiscations of cargo in trawlers often did not distinguish between personal goods and smuggled goods, thereby "harming the masses" (*shanghai le jiben qun-zhong*) and breeding hostility to authorities.[105] The creation of new fishing cooperatives and communes, meanwhile, raised the volume of catches but deepened the dissatisfaction of some fishermen, who responded by surreptitiously selling their catches for higher market prices in Hong Kong rather than at lower official prices in China.[106] Desperate conditions during the Great Leap Forward compelled others to brave the dangers of crossing the Taiwan Straits to fish or seek relief.[107] Fishermen were not alone in seeking better prices for their harvests, but unlike peasants in the interior, they were better able to exploit their mobility and proximity to markets outside China to profit from fundamental price disparities inside the country.

Fishermen and communities along the China coast may not have always practiced a "culture and agriculture of escape," to borrow James Scott's description of peasants in upland Southeast Asia resisting state incursions.[108] Yet their frequent exploitation of physical and political geographies to evade official controls of all sorts proved no less frustrating to Chinese state authorities. Indeed, as previous chapters demonstrate, many fishermen ignored or circumvented official boundaries segmenting coastal waters by maintaining the same patterns of commerce they had practiced since well before the birth of the People's Republic. Seamlessly straddling different regulatory spaces, they engaged in an array of survival strategies—fishing, trafficking, and everything in between—in accordance with the circumstances and under the cover of practicing their livelihood. To exploit multiple sovereignties in the Pearl River Delta, for instance, many based themselves in the traditional smuggling havens in the outlying islands of Hong Kong. Yuen Wah Chiu (Yuan Huazhao), a Guangzhou native who had lived on Lantau Island for decades, was one such famed smuggler who "was well-known and well-respected by all those who earn their living in underground or semi-underground way in the whole of the Pearl River Delta." While Yuen had retired by the 1950s, his younger counterparts from other islands continued plying this trade, which in the description of one Hong Kong official "alter[ed] in nature according to the laws, restrictions and controls enforced by the Chinese, British and

Portuguese governments at the mouth of the Pearl River . . . Commodities var[ied], but there [was] always something worth smuggling from somewhere to elsewhere. In 1948 it was gold; in 1950 fuel oil; and so on."[109] Another article that could be added to this list was foreign currency. Along with Overseas Chinese, fishermen served as a critical conduit of capital flows from South China to Hong Kong on behalf of remittance agencies well after 1949.[110]

Examining the Cold War tensions across the Taiwan Straits, Michael Szonyi notes that fishermen were "objects of special regulatory concerns" given their mobility in the liminal and contested space spanning the Chinese littoral.[111] In the official imagination, fishermen were simultaneously viewed as vulnerable, gullible, unreliable, and intractable. Yet the complex motivations of coastal communities belied such broad descriptions. Willfully or not, they flouted regulations imposed from without and engaged in smuggling throughout the Maoist period and beyond.[112] Problems with economic centralization—compounded by the disasters of the Great Leap Forward—only propelled them to further disregard state strictures. Ongoing trafficking by coastal communities in the face of famine once again underscores smuggling's moral ambiguity—as a form of resistance, indulgence, and survival.

* * *

A long-standing phenomenon, coastal smuggling both hurt and helped the People's Republic. With ample justifications, the new regime—like its counterpart before 1949 and successor after 1978—feared illicit trade's many pernicious effects on governance, economy, and society. Smuggling deprived the state of revenues it might have otherwise collected through tariffs. It undermined laws and policies designed to give the government a monopoly over foreign trade and thereby realize official visions of an idealized, socialist China. Yet coastal trafficking served different purposes for different actors at different times. For all its real and purported harm, smuggling also helped smooth China's socialist transition by ensuring continued access to global markets during the regime's formative years.

While it did not fully satisfy material shortages, smuggling ameliorated the pressing circumstances of its practitioners. Profit—and even survival—was made possible by illicit trade.

In her survey of the Soviet and Eastern European experience, Maria Łoś argues that the primary economies inspired by Marxist ideology create a parallel second economy operating in defiance of that very ideology.[113] China was no exception in this regard, for its nascent command economy and vibrant illicit economy coexisted symbiotically rather than antagonistically. In the early People's Republic, illicit coastal trade was fostered in part by both the "failure" and "success" of the transition to the command economy. On the one hand, central planners' neglect of light industries and disastrous policies like the Great Leap Forward created the material scarcities and pent-up demand for foreign goods that smuggling helped satiate. On the other hand, the smuggling of producer goods like tungsten cutters and nylon was created by the overall success of crash industrialization programs like the First Five-Year Plan. Yet China's economy and cross-border connections onto which new socialist constraints were grafted stimulated what one might call smuggling with Chinese characteristics. The elaborate "special treatment" policy, in particular, created a parallel system accommodating Overseas Chinese to encourage financial contributions and political loyalty to the new Chinese state. The economic transnationalism at the heart of the People's Republic's treatment of Overseas Chinese certainly helped "breach the Cold War cordon" to foster surprising connections between Communist China and the capitalist world ostensibly severed after 1949.[114] Such connections, however, brought their own unintended and unwanted consequences for central planners, serving as an example of how socialist policies of exchange also worked against the construct of the economy as a wholly state-managed domain.

Exploration into coastal smuggling and official efforts to suppress it also places continuities and ruptures across the 1949 divide into sharper focus, thereby underscoring Joseph Esherick's contention that the Communist Revolution was "a watershed, not an unbridgeable chasm."[115] The post-1949 Chinese political order was undeniably different from its pre-1949 predecessor, and that difference was partly reflected in the new regime's approach to combatting smuggling: employing mass campaigns, holding public exhibitions, and other didactic techniques designed to educate as much as punish. Yet Communist China's war on smuggling was built atop Nationalist China's institutions and laws—re-staffed, reorganized, and repurposed but still bearing the indelible marks from the past. The commodities and logistics of trafficking might have changed after 1949, but the geography and vectors of trafficking were remarkably similar to those before 1949. Indeed, even after a convulsive revolution followed by successive disruptive campaigns, smuggled goods *still* made their way through colonial enclaves and traffickers *still* exploited legal ambiguities that conferred different gradations of privilege on different groups of individuals. Economic patterns and social practices—along with state policies and institutions—could thus be counted among the survivors of the 1949 divide despite official efforts to remake them.

CONCLUSION

F ROM THE MID-NINETEENTH through the mid-twentieth centuries the war on smuggling on the China coast fitfully but inexorably amplified state power. Extensive, protracted campaigns against illicit trade helped expand state capacity, centralize legal authority, and transform economic life. The ways different regimes taxed, regulated, and policed trade illustrate how new legal categories and rules further extended state control over different sectors of society and economy. Changes in official policies, in particular, remade the underlying economics of exchange, which in turn shifted the relative profitability of smuggling. The boundaries of legal commerce were thus in constant motion, defined and redefined to suit prevailing official imperatives.

Evading state strictures and taxation on commerce has been (and remains) an enduring phenomenon in human history. Yet it is remarkable how policies by successive regimes steadily widened the definition of smuggling in modern China and thereby narrowed the scope of legal trade, movement, and consumption. Throughout the treaty port era, the smuggling that frequently warranted the most official attention was the traffic in a handful of contraband, such as narcotics or weapons or government monopolies such as salt. With the introduction of higher across-the-board tariffs starting in 1928, however, the gap in prices for ordinary goods legally imported and those illegally imported diverged dramatically, providing opportunities for retailers of smuggled goods to drastically undercut competitors who paid the required duties on the goods they sold. During and after the Second Sino-Japanese War, economic and military exigencies—combined with an unwavering commitment to realizing economic control—drove the introduction of new regulations. The panoply of permits, licenses, and quotas strictly limited or outright prohibited access to consumer goods, thereby creating severe shortages. Such strictures did not end with the Nationalists' retreat to Taiwan but lived on in different guises in the subsequent decades of communist rule. Indeed, the transition toward the command economy essentially expanded on the many controls already introduced before 1949 and remade institutional incentives for illicit trade.

This gradual accretion of state power was not met with passive acceptance, however. Facing higher prices and circumscribed choices at the marketplace, numerous consumers, merchants, and communities turned to the underground economy for relief. Not infrequently, they resisted official attempts at disciplining consumption and commerce, confounding state interdiction by evading tariffs, circumventing strictures, and exploiting regulatory loopholes. Such resistance was certainly widespread and, at times, intense. But if the disparate voices of smugglers, consumers, and officials embedded within various historical sources are any indication, this resistance was not necessarily born of ideological antipathy directed specifically at any one regime. Instead, it was often the result of more material concerns: profit and, in some cases, survival. And even other instances of violating state strictures—like crossing newly enforced borders or overlooking newly promulgated regulations—were less purposeful and more inadvertent, driven in part by the aggressive expansion of state control that created new "crimes" seemingly overnight. With respect to analyzing the state-centered discourse of illegality, scholars must be alert to implicitly accepting its assumptions of ipso facto illegality as well as recognizing its relationship with state power.

That successive official campaigns failed to absolutely stop coastal smuggling did not mean that they absolutely failed to be consequential.

Indeed, the history of Chinese state-building demonstrates that while many projects fell short of fully realizing their creators' visions, they nonetheless produced dramatic changes in generating economic dislocations, sparking social strife, and reconfiguring political authority. From the perspective of Chinese authorities, suppressing illicit trade met many aims of state-building by safeguarding critical revenues, protecting domestic industries, restricting undesirable flows, or realizing ideological goals. The drive to realize a more active role for the central state in the economy was a long-cherished goal throughout modern China. Such a goal traces its genesis to the late Qing but was taken for granted by later policy makers and elites who firmly believed that individual consumption could—and should—be disciplined for collective welfare by state fiat. Fighting smuggling, in the official imagination, contributed to the vision of a modern, economically unified China. Besides fortifying fiscal health or unifying the national economy, suppressing illicit trade brought other benefits in governance. In asserting their prerogative to police trade within China's borders and in extraterritorial enclaves, Chinese authorities also used the fight against smuggling to assert their authority and sovereignty. Smuggling by foreigners, dealt with through diplomatic channels from the mid-nineteenth century, was eventually dealt with through domestic channels with the creation of new institutions and the formalization of legal procedures by the Nanjing Decade. Many of these state-building ideals had been percolating in official and public discourse from the late Qing through the early Republic. Yet it was Nationalist China that began translating them into practice and Communist China that maintained them through the rest of the twentieth century and beyond.

Studying China's war on smuggling thus clearly highlights the same imperatives that spanned different eras. But some of these imperatives were certainly not unique to China's leaders. With some variations, the policies successive Chinese regimes pursued in suppressing unsanctioned trade shared many similarities with those pursued by governments elsewhere throughout history. Reliance on customs duties for funding was a condition common to many modernizing states, as was the desire to assert control over the economy and nascent national borders. And to defend their source of funding and assert their sovereignty across territories of control, many modern states waged their own wars on smuggling that were no less violent, no less intrusive than China's. At different points in their respective histories, the governments of other countries (including England, France, and the United States) launched repressive campaigns against illicit trade that not only protected valuable revenues but also extended the reach of central authority.[1] Campaigns against illicit trade and the resistance they provoked are thus not exclusively a Chinese story but a global one.

Yet crucial differences remain. What distinguished modern Chinese regimes from their counterparts, of course, was that the Chinese were trying to build a modern state while laboring under the legacies of foreign imperialism, political instability, and a hostile geopolitical environment. Fighting smuggling was thus necessarily imbricated with other state-building projects particular to modern China. It helped reclaim some elements of sovereignty ceded by the unequal treaties, namely Chinese jurisdiction over foreign enclaves and foreign sojourners on domestic soil. It also helped project central authority that had been steadily attenuated since the late nineteenth century and support the construction of a modern state with unprecedented capacity to tax and regulate commerce. Above all, it helped realize an ideological imperative critical to many modern Chinese officials and thinkers: a greater role for the state in guiding the economy. Studying China's war on smuggling thus enables us to place China within a broader comparative context by identifying the parallels it shared in the state-building process elsewhere. At the same time, it also enables us to avoid accepting Western states as normative models by appreciating the constraints specific to modern China's experience.

SMUGGLING AND INTERDICTION IN REFORM ERA

The war on smuggling and the contest over the role of the state in the economy thus enjoy a long history on the China coast. And despite dramatic changes inaugurated since the reform era, this history reverberates in China today. As the country emerged from the throes of the Cultural Revolution (1966–1976), a new government committed the country to a radically different course of economic development. At first glance, the transition away from the command economy combined with the introduction of new "open door" policies might have dismantled parts of the regulatory infrastructure built during prior decades that greatly incentivized smuggling. Instead, coastal smuggling exploded during the reform era, catapulting itself to the forefront of official and public attention.[2] Reforms freed southern coastal provinces from central controls to attract foreign investment in new special economic zones (SEZs) stipulating fewer regulations on imports and exports. The creation of a nascent market economy helped spearhead China's integration into the global economy. But it also provided plenty of legal cover for illegal trade, and the southeast coast where reforms were first introduced quickly reemerged as the epicenter of trafficking.[3] Watches, televisions, stereos, VCRs, and other consumer electronics flowing into China were exchanged for traditional medicines, foodstuffs, and specie—transactions that avoided taxation, circumvented regulations, or violated prohibitions. So pervasive was coastal smuggling that a March 1982 issue of *People's Daily* featured a front-page story celebrating one Fujian fishing community for *not* taking advantage of its geography and mobility to traffic in assorted consumer goods like neighboring communities did.[4] Abstaining from smuggling during this era of economic opening, in other words, was far more newsworthy than engaging in smuggling itself.

Driving the revival of coastal smuggling was the confluence of increasingly robust demand, artificially prohibitive prices, and relatively constrained supply. Rising "aspirations for material goods and a more diverse life style" impelled a burgeoning Chinese consumer class to acquire the accoutrements of modern consumption and furnish their homes with the hardware of late modernity, thereby transforming items once considered unattainable luxuries into daily necessities.[5] With Western-style consumption in post-Mao China no longer officially prohibited or socially stigmatized, demand for consumer goods of all kinds soared. Yet consumers found few legitimate outlets to satisfy their needs because consumer goods were still undersupplied in the transitional economy, which was still primarily oriented toward producing intermediate goods. At the same time, the anticonsumption bias of earlier foreign trade policies remained, with punitive duties pricing legitimately imported and highly desired goods beyond the reach of many ordinary Chinese consumers.[6] Finally, many post-1978 reforms slowly loosened economic controls in some sectors but retained vestigial restrictions in many others, particularly regarding foreign trade.[7] Reforms effectively erected administrative barriers separating two radically different economies within China and created significant distortions in prices as well as mismatches in supply and demand.

Coastal smuggling enjoyed a dramatic resurgence after 1978. Yet the economics underpinning this new smuggling wave undoubtedly mirrored those of past smuggling waves. And while the conditions of reform were certainly particular to the post-Mao moment of market transition, they also shared unambiguous similarities with conditions that fostered smuggling in prior eras. Indeed, just as in the past, smuggling helped redress the stark imbalances in supply and demand by funneling desirable foreign goods to the rest of China. The symbiosis between the official and unofficial economies in the early People's Republic thus lived on in the early reform era, bridging the command and market economies separated by governmental fiat. Overseas Chinese, still accorded favorable legal treatment similar to that accorded under the defunct *youdai* policy, traveled to China bringing clothes, electronics, and even automobiles ostensibly as "gifts" for relatives but often instead ended up for resale. Fishermen, still taking advantage of porous borders, trafficked assorted consumer goods and appliances between China, Hong Kong, and Taiwan under the cover of fishing. State-owned enterprises, still leveraging their favorable status to engage in regulatory arbitrage, colluded with foreign businesses to exploit SEZ loopholes, importing raw materials and consumer goods duty-free and well above prescribed quotas before selling "surpluses" on black markets throughout the country. New rules designed to restructure the economy thus simultaneously, if inadvertently, revived old incentives for profit.

News of sensational cases of smuggling circulated widely in China, tapping into deep-seated, long-held anxieties among the public and officialdom over the pernicious effects of freewheeling commerce. More importantly, they widened the growing divide between the "radical" and "conservative" wings of the reformist coalition and exacerbated infighting at the highest levels of government. In the eyes of conservatives, the explosion of smuggling and other economic crimes signaled an erosion of party discipline and embodied all that was wrong with the reforms: their pace, scale, and even purpose. Conservative discontent reached a boiling point by January 1982, when Chen Yun, architect of the command economy and the most senior statesman sympathetic to opponents of radical reform, joined the chorus critical of problems with the SEZs and called for decisive action, declaring, "With regard to the serious perpetrators of economic crimes, I want to severely punish a few, imprison a few, and even execute those guilty of the most heinous offenses."[8] The scandalous nature of the offenses was so "astonishing" (*zhen jing*), according to one witness, that even some reformers had to concede to the severity of the problem.[9] Not surprisingly, smuggling became a prime target of virtually all major campaigns in the early reform era, including the Campaign Against Economic Crimes (1982–1983), the Anti-Spiritual Pollution Campaign (1983–1984), and the Strike Hard Campaign (1983–1984).[10] Conservative backlash and public crackdowns never fully derailed the open door policy, but concerns over smuggling undoubtedly exacerbated the volatility in policy swings between reform and retrenchment throughout the 1980s. Once again, smuggling proved to be more than just a minor law enforcement problem. It sparked widespread apprehension and intersected with the most critical questions confronting the political and economic reforms in the post-Mao era. How much and how fast should China open itself to foreign trade? And what can the government do to balance competing priorities, particularly engaging with the global economy while maintaining control over the domestic economy?

But if the outburst of smuggling seemingly undermined state authority and deepened official anxieties in the reform era, it also provided ample opportunities for the central government to reassert control. As the fight against smuggling eventually resumed—and intensified—during the 1990s, it also facilitated official attempts to lay the institutional foundations for a more resilient, unified market economy. Economics and politics added to the urgency of the fight. By 1998, it was estimated that smuggling deprived the central government of tens of billions of yuan in revenue annually and flooded the domestic market with cheap foreign electronics, automobiles, oil, and even steel. Meanwhile, the prestige of the party and the regime as a whole was damaged by a number of spectacular cases that implicated officials and businesses with semiofficial ties.[11] President Jiang Zemin and Premier Zhu Rongji made stemming illicit trade an important priority in their program to enforce party discipline and curb corruption. Kicking off a new campaign by personally attending a July 1998 national anti-smuggling meeting convened by the Chinese Communist Party Central Committee and the State Council, the pair oversaw a massive crackdown focused particularly on the southeast coastal provinces.[12] More critically, the crackdown targeted smuggling committed by officials with a divestiture drive that forced numerous military, law enforcement, judicial, and other state organs to liquidate nonofficial businesses, focus on their core missions, and thereby avoid potential conflicts of interest. Neither smuggling nor corruption, of course, was ever fully extinguished; sensational stories of both continued to garner public attention into the twenty-first century. Yet the smuggling crisis, according to the political scientist Dali Yang, provided the necessary political impetus to accelerate long-desired reforms that helped "revamp the relations between state and business, rationalize the state, and level the economic playing field."[13]

Meanwhile, institutions and legal tools were refashioned throughout the reform era to fight smuggling. The Customs Administration underwent successive reforms to better monitor and enforce new trade policies from the center. Once again prioritizing the regulation, taxation, and policing of foreign trade, Beijing elevated the agency in 1980 to a ministry-level department reporting directly to the State Council. More critically, it reversed the administrative decentralization effected during the Cultural Revolution, when responsibility for anti-smuggling devolved to local provincial governments.[14] The reconstituted Customs Administration was granted sweeping authority to review applications for imports and held nationwide conferences strategizing anti-smuggling work on the coast.[15] The agency's mission also benefited from new legal reforms that formally defined and criminalized smuggling while detailing punishments for traffickers and their accomplices.[16] During the anti-smuggling drive of the 1990s, Beijing effected significant personnel changes, purging compromised officials and installing trusted administrators. It also sought to enhance the institutional integrity and efficacy of the Customs Administration with new reforms and resources.[17] Such concerted efforts sent an unambiguous signal that fighting smuggling was once again an important concern and a national imperative.

As was the case before 1978, then, fighting smuggling after 1978 proved critical to efforts by the central state to broadcast its authority and realize more effective control throughout different sectors of the economy. Today, China has dismantled much of the old command economy, (re)emerged as global economic powerhouse, and lowered trade barriers since joining the World Trade Organization (WTO). Yet Beijing still has not relented its war against smuggling. As one Customs Administration official stated at the dawn of the twenty-first century, "Smuggling has become a serious problem, which has undermined national foreign trade management, caused great losses to State tax incomes, and led to unfair competition in the market."[18] Employing language that administrators from past regimes themselves might have used, the official's declaration betrays state anxieties over the multiple threats trafficking represented to governance and economy. At the same time, the statement implicitly reaffirms the prerogative of Chinese authorities to suppress unsanctioned trade to realize broader imperatives—namely, creating a stronger state with unrivaled authority to tax, regulate, and monitor the economy.

But if the sustained fight against coastal smuggling epitomizes the perennial commitment of China's leaders to control commerce for national goals, then the persistence of coastal trafficking serves as another reminder of the durability of "deviant" social and economic behaviors once thought to have been eradicated before the reform era and flourished thereafter. The prevalence of activities like smuggling before 1978 shows how the second economy and other "unofficial" forms of commerce were not, contra previous assertions, "products of the current economic reform policy."[19] In considering the degree to which the second economy of post-1978 China may be attributed to "structural factors" or "disorganization that all attempts at reform inevitably bring in their wake," the historical perspective this book offers suggests it was more the former than the latter.[20] When the People's Republic was confronted by successive waves of smuggling crises after 1978, a vibrant underground economy on the coast had already been operating for decades, if not for centuries. Reforms might have amplified the scale of smuggling and transformed the relative profitability of articles trafficked, but they certainly did not create smuggling de novo. Seen in this light, the explosion of smuggling after 1978 represents more a continuity than a departure, a contest between smugglers defying official controls over the economy on the one side and the Chinese state with its overriding imperative to fiscalize, discipline, and police commerce for national goals on the other. And judging from the spate of news stories about coastal smuggling coming out of contemporary China, this contest is unlikely to end anytime soon.

CHARACTER LIST

aiguo shangren	愛國商人
aiguo xin	愛國心
ban zhimindi	半殖民地
baobi	包庇
Baoshun yanghang	寶順洋行
bei diren baoli kongzhi	被敵人暴力控制
benshu tongbing	本屬同病
boshang nihuo	舶商匿貨
bufa shangren	不法商人
bufa zibenjia	不法資本家
buxiang	不詳
buxiao guanbing	不肖官兵
buyuan chikui	不願吃虧
Caizheng bu	財政部
cangni sihuo	藏匿私貨
Chajin dihuo tiaoli	查禁敵貨條例
Chajin dihuo weiyuanhui	查禁敵貨委員會
Changguan	常關
chengbai dishi guanjian	成敗得失關鍵
chengban yu jiaoyu xiang jiehe	懲辦與教育相結合
Chengzhi zousi tiaoli	懲治走私條例
chouhuo	仇貨
chumu jingxin	觸目驚心
chuqi	出奇
cizhimindi	次殖民地

da guimo de zousi	大規模的走私
da Han zhuyi	大漢主義
daopian guojia caichan	盜騙國家財產
daoqie guojia jingji qingbao	盜竊國家經濟情報
Da Qing lüli	大清律例
Da Qing xianxing xinglü	大清現行刑律
dayi	大異
diaoling	凋零
dihuo	敵貨
dihuo biao	敵貨表
diwo maodun	敵我矛盾
dixia gongchang	地下工廠
dixia maoyi	地下貿易
dou jiao wobei nanzi zhan pianyi	都較我輩男子占便宜
Duidi jingji fengsuo weiyuanhui	對敵經濟封鎖委員會
fan geming fenzi	反革命分子
fan zousi zhanlanhui	反走私展覽會
fang si	放私
fangzhi zousi liyong zousi	防止走私利用走私
Fangzhi zousi zong jicha chu	防止走私總稽查處
fanrong de shihou	繁榮的時候
Feichang shiqi nong kuang gong shang guanli tiaoli	非常時期農礦工商管理條例
feisu jinbu	飛速進步
fengjian canyu	封建殘餘
fenjia	分家
gaochao	高潮
genjue dihuo	根絕敵貨
gong bu ying qiu	供不應求
gonghang	公行
gongran	公然
gongshangye	工商業
guanjin	關津
guanshui	關稅
guanshui wenti	關稅問題
guanshui zizhu	關稅自主
Guan-wu Shu	關務署
gudao	孤島
guiqiao	歸僑
guofang wenxue	國防文學
guohuo	國貨
Guohuo yundong	國貨運動
guohuo zhengming qingdan	國貨證明清單

guojia jiang wang	國家將亡
guojia sixiang	國家思想
guonei jingji kunnan	國內經濟困難
guowai difang	國外地方
hai yu minsheng	害於民生
Haiguan	海關
Haiguan faze pingyi hui	海關罰則評議會
Haiguan guanli hanghai minchuan hangyun zhangcheng	海關管理航海民船航運章程
Haiguan jisi tiaoli	海關緝私條例
Haiguan Zongshu	海關總署
haijin	海禁
Hanjian	漢奸
hu si	護私
huangniu	黃牛
huaqiao	華僑
Huixun chuanhuo ruguan zhangcheng	會訊船貨入官章程
Huixun zhangcheng	會訊章程
Humen tiaoyue	虎門條約
hunxiao	混淆
huochai dawang	火柴大王
huzhao	護照
Jiancha chu	檢察處
Jiandu	監督
Jiang feibang	蔣匪幫
jianju	檢舉
jianshang	奸商
jiantu	奸徒
Jiaotong bu	交通部
jieji	接濟
Jinchukou maoyi zanxing banfa	進出口貿易暫行辦法
Jingji bu	經濟部
jingji de yapo	經濟的壓迫
jingji fengsuo	經濟封鎖
jingji fengsuo weiyuanhui	經濟封鎖委員會
Jingji jinji cuoshi fang'an	經濟緊急措施方案
jingji qinlüe	經濟侵略
jingjiren	經紀人
Jinyun zidi wupin tiaoli	禁運資敵物品條例
Jinyun zidi wupin yun Hu shenhe banfa	禁運資敵物品運滬審設辦法
Jinzhi duiyu zousi huowu zhengshui fangxing banfa	禁止對於走私貨物徵稅放行辦法
Jisi shu	緝私署

jiu	救
jizhuan zhixia	急轉直下
junhuo qixie danzhao	軍火器械單照
Junyong qiangpao qudi tiaoli	軍用槍砲取締條例
juwen	具文
kecheng	課程
kewei de guiji	可畏的詭計
kong Ri bing	恐日病
langren	浪人
lijin	釐金
loubao	漏報
louzhi	漏巵
maoyi lunzhe	貿易論者
maoyi tongzhi	貿易統制
Meifu	美孚
minsheng	民生
minshi youxiao bufen	民事有效部分
neixiao zheng	內銷證
nishui	匿稅
nü zousi dawang	女走私大王
panjie jianxi	盤結奸細
pijing	僻靜
pingjie dili	憑藉地利
pohuai shehuizhuyi jingji zhixu zui	破壞社會主義經濟秩序罪
qingkuang hen yanzhong	情況很嚴重
qique	奇缺
qishi	啟事
qiyan feichang xiaozhang	氣焰非常囂張
Quanguo jingji weiyuanhui	全國經濟委員會
qunzhong fan zousi	群眾反走私
Riji	日籍
rulang sihu	如狼似虎
san dajian	三大件
sekimin (Jp.)	籍民
shandong zousi	煽動走私
shangbiao	商標
shanghai le jiben qunzhong	傷害了基本群眾
shanghai zui	傷害罪
shangzhan	商戰
shengshi xiong'e	聲勢兇惡
Shiliang zidi zhizui zanxing tiaoli	食糧資敵治罪暫行條例
shougouzhan	收購站

shuangguizhi	雙軌制
shuike	水客
Shuiwu chu	稅務處
shuiwu si	稅務司
shusan zheng	疏散證
si	私
sichu waijing ji weijin xiahai	私出外境及違禁下海
sixiang juewu hen di	思想覺悟很低
Siyan zhizui fa	私鹽治罪法
tanwu fuhua de zuofeng	貪污腐化的作風
Taigu lunchuan gongsi	太古輪船公司
tigao qunzhong shehui zhuyi juewu	提高群眾社會主義覺悟
tongbao	同胞
tongzhi jingji	統制經濟
tongzhi zhuyi	統制主義
tougong jianliao	偷工減料
toushui loushui	偷稅漏稅
tufei	土匪
Wei Haiguan	偽海關
weijin huowu	違禁貨物
weilai	未來
wen le zousi de fengsheng	聞了走私的風聲
wu kuang juan	鎢礦捐
wuqi	武器
wuyan tang	無煙糖
wuyi	無益
wuzhuang zousi	武裝走私
X guo	X國
Xian xinglü	現刑律
xiancheng chuwai	縣城除外
xiangfu erxing	相輔而行
xianjin	現今
xianmin	線民
xianruo xiuli de guniang	纖弱秀麗的姑娘
xiao shuike	小水客
xiao'en xiaohui	小恩小惠
xiaoguo	小國
xinghui	行賄
Xingzheng fayuan	行政法院
xiongdi siren	兄弟四人
Xiuzheng chengzhi toulou guanshui zanxing tiaoli	修正懲治偷漏關稅暫行條例

yanfei	鹽匪
yanghang	洋行
yangyang dou ke ziyou maimai	樣樣都可自由買賣
yangyao	洋藥
yapian zui	鴉片罪
yiding zeli	議定則例
Yingshang Yihe yanghang	英商怡和洋行
yiwang	已往
youbang	友邦
youdai	優待
youmin	莠民
youzhi wuquan	有職無權
yulan zibenjia	魚爛資本家
Yunshu tongzhi ju	運輸統制局
zahuodian	雜貨店
zangwu zui	贓物罪
Zanxing xin xinglü	暫行新刑律
Zhanshi guanli jinkou chukou wupin tiaoli	戰時管理進口出口物品條例
zhanshi xiaofei shui	戰時消費稅
zhaodaisuo	招待所
zhen jing	震驚
zhengming shu	證明書
zhengshui	徵稅
Zhonghua Remin Gongheguo zanxing haiguan fa	中華人民共和國暫行海關法
zhunyun huzhao	準運護照
Zhuzhang shuifa pingdeng hui	主張稅法平等會
zibenjia	資本家
zidi	資敵
zidi wupin	資敵物品
Ziyuan weiyuanhui	資源委員會
zong shuiwu si	總稅務司
zousi	走私
Zousi fanzui zhencha ju	走私犯罪偵查局
zousi ji shi zidi, zidi jiu shi maiguo	走私即是資敵，資敵就是賣國
zuo fuwu shi fangbei shou meng	作服務時防備受朦
zuo geguo de nuli	做各國的奴隸
zuo geguo de zhimindi	做各國的殖民地
zuyi zengjia diren zhi shili zhe	足以增加敵人之實力者
zuzhi qunzhong zousi	組織群眾走私

NOTES

ABBREVIATIONS USED IN CITATIONS

Archival Sources

AH   Academia Historica (Guoshi guan), Taipei

GDPA   Guangdong Provincial Archives (Guangdong sheng dang'an guan), Guangzhou

GMDR   National Defense Supreme Commission Archive (Guofang zuigao weiyuanhui dang'an), Zhongguo Guomindang Records, Hoover Institution Archives, Stanford University. Citation by collection, reel number, and document number.

HKPR   Hong Kong Public Records Office (Xianggang zhengfu dang'an chu)

IMHA   Institute of Modern History Archives (Zhongyang yanjiuyuan jindaishi yanjiusuo dang'an guan), Academia Sinica, Nan'gang

JSSIII   China Navigation Company, Butterfield and Swire, School of Oriental and African Studies (SOAS), London. Citation by file, box, and document number.

NBCK   Neibu cankao (Internal reference), Universities Service Centre for Chinese Studies, Chinese University of Hong Kong

SHAC   Second Historical Archives of China (Zhongguo di'er lishi dang'an guan), Nanjing

SHMA   Shanghai Municipal Archives (Shanghai shi dang'an guan)

TJMA   Tianjin Municipal Archives (Tianjin shi dang'an guan)

Diplomatic Sources

FO   British Foreign Office, National Archives

FRUS   Foreign Relations of the United States. Citation by year, volume, and page number.

NGB *Nihon Gaikō Bunsho* (Documents on Japanese foreign policy). Citation by collection, volume, part, and document number.

TAC MacMurray, John Van Antwerp. *Treaties and Agreements with and Concerning China, 1919–1929.* Washington, D.C.: Carnegie Endowment for International Peace, 1929.

TCF Inspector General of Customs. *Treaties, Conventions, Etc., Between China and Foreign States.* 2nd ed. 2 vols. Shanghai: Statistical Department of the Inspectorate General of Customs, 1917.

Legal Sources

CCC *The Chinese Criminal Code and Special Criminal and Administrative Laws.* Translated by the Legal Department, Shanghai Municipal Council. Shanghai: Commercial Press, 1935.

DLC Xue Yunsheng. *Duli cunyi chong kan ben* (Lingering doubts after reading the substatutes, newly edited version). 5 vols. Edited by Huang Jingjia. Taipei: Chinese Materials and Research Aids Service Center, [Qing] 1970. Statutes and substatutes cited by serial number.

DXA *Da Qing xianxing xinglü anyu* (Remarks on Criminal Code of the Great Qing Currently in Use). Edited by Shen Jiaben. 37 vols. Beijing: Falü guan, 1909. Citation by volume, chapter, page, and leaf.

FGH *Zhonghua Renmin Gongheguo fagui huibian* (Collection of regulations from the People's Republic of China). Compiled by Guowuyuan fazhi ju, Zhonghua Renmin Gongheguo fagui huibianji hui. Beijing: Falü chubanshe, 1955–2005. Citation by volume (year) and page.

FLH *Zhongyang renmin zhengfu faling huibian* (Collection of laws from the People's Central Government). Compiled by Zhongyang renmin zhengfu fazhi weiyuanhui. Beijing: Falü chubanshe, 1949–1954. Citation by volume and page.

HFH *Haiguan faze pingyi hui zhangze yi'an huibian* (Compilation of the regulations and motions of the Customs Penalty Board of Inquiry and Appeal). Edited by Haiguan faze pingyi hui (Customs Penalty Board of Inquiry and Appeal). Publisher unknown, 1936. Citation by case and page number.

KJF *Kang Ri zhanzheng shiqi Minguo zhengfu jingji fagui* (Collection of economic laws and regulations of the Nationalist Government during the War of Resistance). Edited by Chongqing Shi Dang'anguan. 2 vols. Beijing: Dang'an chubanshe, 1992. Citation by volume and page number.

XFH *Xingzheng fayuan huibian* (Compilation of rulings by the Administrative Court). Edited by Xingzheng fayuan (Administrative Court). 1948. Reprint, Taibei: Chengwen chubanshe, 1972. Citation by case and page number.

ZFD *Zhonghua Minguo fagui daquan* (Complete collection of laws and regulations of the Republic of China). Edited by Xu Baiqi. 5 vols. Shanghai: Shangwu yinshu guan, 1937. Citation by volume and page number.

ZHL   Zhonghua Minguo zanxing xin xinglü (Republic of China New Criminal Code Temporarily in Force). From *Zhonghua liu fa* (Six Codes of China). Shanghai: Shangwu yinshu guan, 1927. Citation by volume, chapter, statute, and page number.

Chinese Maritime Customs Service Materials

CG   *Customs Gazette*, Shanghai

CI   Inspectorate General of Customs. *Customs Import Tariff of the Republic of China.* Shanghai: Statistical Department of the Inspectorate General of Customs, 1928, 1930, 1934, 1948.

DIO   Inspectorate General of Customs. *Documents Illustrative of the Origin, Development, and Activities of the Chinese Customs Service.* 7 vols. Shanghai: Statistical Department of the Inspectorate General of Customs, 1937–1939.

GN   *Guansheng* (Customs echo), Shanghai. Citation by volume, issue, and date.

PN   Preventive secretary's notes (Jisi ke tongqi). SHAC. Citation by note number.

SR   Smuggling report (Jisi baogao). SHAC. Citation by date and page number.

Other Sources

DJH   *Diwei jingji huibao* (Collected intelligence on the economic conditions of the enemy and puppet regimes). Edited by Zhongyang diaocha tongji ju tezhong jingji diaocha chu. Chongqing. Citation by issue, date, section, and page number.

DJQ   *Diwei jingji qingbao* (Intelligence on the economic conditions of the enemy and puppet regimes). Edited by Jingji Bu Mishuting. Ziyuan weiyuanhui jingji suo jiu shi. Reprinted in Kangzhan shiqi diwei jingji qingbao (Intelligence on the economic conditions of the enemy and puppet regimes during the War of Resistance). 2 vols. Beijing: Quanguo tushuguan wenxian suowei fuzhi zhongxin, 2009. Citation by issue and date of original, followed by volume and page number of reprint.

JJD   *Zhonghua Renmin Gongheguo jingji dang'an ziliao xuanbian: duiwai maoyi juan, 1958–1965* (Select documents and materials on economic affairs of the People's Republic of China's economic archives: foreign trade, 1958–1965). Edited by Zhongguo shehui kexue yuan and Zhongyang dang'an guan. Beijing: Jingji guanli chubanshe, 2011.

MDZ   *Zhonghua Minguo shi dang'an ziliao huibian* (Compilation of historical archival materials of the Republic of China). Edited by Zhongguo Di Er Lishi Dang'an Guan. Nanjing: Jiangsu guji chubanshe, 1991. Citation by part, volume, subject, number, and page number.

Newspapers and Periodicals

Citation by date and page plus additional information when noted.

CP   *China Press*, Shanghai

CW   *China Weekly Review*, Shanghai

DG   *Dagong bao*, Hong Kong

DZ   *Dongfang zazhi*, Shanghai. Citation by volume and issue.

FR   *Far Eastern Economic Review*, Hong Kong. Citation by volume and issue.

GS   *Gongshang ribao*, Hong Kong

GZ   *Guangzhou Minguo ribao*, Guangzhou. Citation by sheet and page.

HQ   *Huaqiao ribao*, Hong Kong

HZ   *Huazi ribao*, Hong Kong. Citation by sheet and page.

JF   *Jiefang ribao*, Shanghai

JJ   *Jingji bu gongbao*, Nanjing/Chongqing. Citation by volume and issue.

NF   *Nanfang ribao*, Guangzhou

NH   *North China Herald*, Shanghai

RM   *Renmin ribao*, Beijing

SB   *Shen Bao*, Shanghai

SC   *South China Morning Post*, Hong Kong

SF   *Sifa gongbao*, Nanjing. Citation by issue.

XR   *Xinghua ribao*, Shantou

YZ   *Yinhang zhoubao*, Shanghai. Citation by volume and issue.

ZD   *Zhandi*, Chongqing. Citation by issue.

ZH   *Zhonghang yuebao*, Shanghai. Citation by volume and issue.

ZY   *Zhongyang ribao*, Nanjing

INTRODUCTION

1. GDPA, 95/1/1053, Amoy SR (October 1934), 2–4.
2. Frederic Wakeman, "Models of Historical Change: The Chinese State and Society, 1839–1989," in *Perspectives on Modern China: Four Anniversaries*, ed. Kenneth Lieberthal et al. (Armonk, N.Y.: M. E. Sharpe, 1991).
3. See especially Prasenjit Duara, *Culture, Power, and the State: Rural North China, 1900–1942* (Stanford, Calif.: Stanford University Press, 1988); Stephen R. Halsey, *Quest for Power: European Imperialism and the Making of Chinese Statecraft* (Cambridge, Mass.: Harvard University Press, 2015); Philip A. Kuhn, *Origins of the Modern Chinese State* (Stanford, Calif.: Stanford University Press, 2002); Huaiyin Li, *Village Governance in North China: Huailu County, 1875–1936* (Stanford, Calif.: Stanford University Press, 2005); Kenneth Pomeranz, *The Making of a Hinterland: State, Society, and Economy in Inland North China, 1853–1937* (Berkeley: University of California Press, 1993); Julia C. Strauss, *Strong Institutions in Weak Polities: State Building in Republican China, 1927–1940* (Oxford: Oxford University Press, 1998); R. Bin Wong, *China Transformed: Historical Change and the Limits of European Experience* (Ithaca, N.Y.: Cornell University Press, 1997); and Xiaoqun Xu, *Trial of Modernity: Judicial Reform in Early Twentieth-Century China, 1901–1937* (Stanford, Calif.: Stanford University Press, 2008).
4. For drug smuggling, see Alan Baumler, *The Chinese and Opium Under the Republic: Worse Than Floods and Wild Beasts* (Albany: State University of New York Press, 2007), and

Edward R. Slack, *Opium, State, and Society: China's Narco-Economy and the Guomindang, 1924–1937* (Honolulu: University of Hawai'i Press, 2001). For salt smuggling, see Zhang Xiaoye, *Qing dai siyan wenti yanjiu* (Research on the salt smuggling problem during the Qing dynasty) (Beijing: Shehui kexue wenxian chubanshe, 2001). Several Chinese-language studies have looked at smuggling but confine their focus to the pre-1949 period or Nationalist rule. See especially Lian Xinhao, *Jindai Zhongguo de zousi yu haiguan jisi* (Smuggling and customs anti-smuggling in modern China) (Xiamen: Xiamen daxue chubanshe, 2011); Qi Chunfeng, *Zhong Ri jingji zhan zhong de zousi huodong, 1937–1945* (Smuggling activities in Sino-Japanese economic war, 1937–1945) (Beijing: Renmin chubanshe, 2002); Son Jun Sik, *Zhanqian Riben zai Huabei de zousi huodong, 1933–1937* (Japan's prewar smuggling activities in North China, 1933–1937) (Taipei: Guoshi guan, 1997); and Sun Baogen, *Kangzhan shiqi Guomin zhengfu jisi yanjiu* (Research on the Nationalist government's anti-smuggling during the War of Resistance period) (Beijing: Zhongguo dang'an chubanshe, 2006). More recently, however, scholars have recognized the potential of examining smuggling to address issues beyond mere criminality. See especially Melissa Macauley, "Small Time Crooks: Opium, Migrants, and the War on Drugs in China, 1819–1860," *Late Imperial China* 30, no. 1 (2009): 1–47; Michael Szonyi, *The Art of Being Governed: Everyday Politics in Late Imperial China* (Princeton, N.J.: Princeton University Press, 2017); Peter Thilly, "Treacherous Waters: Drug Smuggling in Coastal Fujian, 1832–1938" (Ph.D. thesis, Northwestern University, 2015); and the special issue "Binding Maritime China: Control, Evasion, and Interloping," *Cross-Currents: East Asian History and Culture Review*, December 2017, https://cross-currents.berkeley.edu/e-journal/issue-25 (accessed February 1, 2018).

5. *ZY*, December 14, 1933, 3.

6. NBCK, 2427 (March, 3, 1958), 6.

7. Human trafficking in China has been driven less by changes in fiscal and economic policies that are the primary concerns of this book. Instead, trafficking is tied more to cultural practices that underpinned the formation of some Chinese families, as well as immigration laws that restricted international movement. Studies of Chinese human trafficking have generally focused on illegal migration in the contemporary world, although more recent scholarship is looking at historical cases within China. For an example of the former, see Sheldon Zhang, *Chinese Human Smuggling Organizations: Families, Social Networks, and Cultural Imperatives* (Stanford, Calif.: Stanford University Press, 2008). For notable examples of the latter, see Johanna S. Ransmeier, *Sold People: Traffickers and Family Life in North China* (Cambridge, Mass.: Harvard University Press, 2017), and Matthew H. Sommer, *Polyandry and Wife-Selling in Qing Dynasty China: Survival Strategies and Judicial Interventions* (Berkeley: University of California Press, 2015). Piracy, for its part, is fundamentally distinct from smuggling. The efficacy of the former rests on open confrontation and the use of overt violence, while the efficacy of the latter rests on the use of stealth and evasion. For a fuller explanation differentiating the two, see Alan L. Karras, *Smuggling: Contraband and Corruption in World History* (Lanham, Md.: Rowman and Littlefield, 2010), 25–44.

8. See, for instance, J. A. Sharpe, *Crime in Early Modern England, 1550–1750* (London: Longman, 1998).

9. Karras, *Smuggling*, 3.

10. Key exceptions are the Qing dynasty's campaign against the Ming loyalist Zheng Chenggong (ca. 1650–1683) and South China pirates in the early nineteenth century.

11. John K. Fairbank, "Maritime and Continental in China's History," in *The Cambridge History of China*, vol. 12: *Republican China, 1912–1949, Part 1*, ed. John K. Fairbank (Cambridge: Cambridge University Press, 1983), 16.

12. Historical studies on individual treaty ports are too numerous to list comprehensively. For Shanghai, see Gail Hershatter, *Dangerous Pleasures: Prostitution and Modernity in Twentieth-Century Shanghai* (Berkeley: University of California Press, 1997); Hanchao Lu, *Beyond the Neon Lights: Everyday Shanghai in the Early Twentieth Century* (Berkeley: University of California Press, 1999); Wen-hsin Yeh, *Shanghai Splendor: Economic Sentiments and the Making of Modern China, 1843–1949* (Berkeley: University of California Press, 2007); and Frederic Wakeman, *Policing Shanghai, 1927–1937* (Berkeley: University of California Press, 1995). For Tianjin, see Gail Hershatter, *The Workers of Tianjin, 1900–1949* (Stanford, Calif.: Stanford University Press, 1986); Ruth Rogaski, *Hygienic Modernity: Meanings of Health and Disease in Treaty-Port China* (Berkeley: University of California Press, 2004); and Brett Sheehan, *Trust in Troubled Times: Money, Banks, and State-Society Relations in Republican Tianjin* (Cambridge, Mass.: Harvard University Press, 2003) and *Industrial Eden: A Chinese Capitalist Vision* (Cambridge, Mass.: Harvard University Press, 2015). For Guangzhou, see Emily M. Hill, *Smokeless Sugar: The Death of a Provincial Bureaucrat and the Construction of China's National Economy* (Vancouver: University of British Columbia Press, 2010); Seung-joon Lee, *Gourmets in the Land of Famine: The Culture and Politics of Rice in Modern Canton* (Stanford, Calif.: Stanford University Press, 2011); and Michael Tsin, *Nation, Governance, and Modernity in China: Canton, 1900–1927* (Stanford, Calif.: Stanford University Press, 1999).

13. For an overview of the treaty port economy's development and essential features, see Billy K. L. So, "Modern China's Treaty Port Economy in Institutional Perspective: An Introductory Essay," in *The Treaty Port Economy in Modern China: Empirical Studies of Institutional Change and Economic Performance*, eds. B. K. L. So and R. H. Myers (Berkeley: Institute of East Asian Studies, 2011), 1–27. See also Rhoads Murphey, "The Treaty Ports and China's Modernization," in *The Chinese City Between Two Worlds*, ed. M. Elvin and G. W. Skinner (Stanford, Calif.: Stanford University Press, 1974), 17–71.

14. Stated in these terms, fighting smuggling thus satisfied at least three fundamental state capacities: extractive, coercive, and steering. See Theda Skocpol, "Bringing the State Back In: Strategies of Analysis in Current Research," in *Bringing the State Back In*, ed. P. B. Evans, D. Rueschemeyer, and Theda Skocpol (Cambridge: Cambridge University Press, 1985), 3–37; and Shaoguang Wang, "The Rise of the Regions: Fiscal Reform and

the Decline of Central State Capacity in China," in *The Waning of the Communist State: Economic Origins of Political Decline in China and Hungary*, ed. Andrew G. Walder (Berkeley: University of California Press, 1995), 88–114.

15. On the distinction between unregulated ("free") trade and regulated ("fair") trade, see Karras, *Smuggling*, 133–40. On the collective action problem, see Mancur Olson, *The Logic of Collective Action: Public Goods and the Theory of Groups* (Cambridge, Mass.: Harvard University Press, 1965). On the relationship between institutional change and transaction costs, see Douglass C. North, *Structure and Change in Economic History* (New York: Norton, 1981) and *Institutions, Institutional Change, and Economic Performance* (Cambridge: Cambridge University Press, 1990).

16. Charles Tilly, "Reflections on the History of European State-Making," in *The Formation of National States in Western Europe*, ed. C. Tilly (Princeton, N.J.: Princeton University Press, 1975), 6.

17. Karl Marx, *Grundrisse*, trans. Martin Nicolaus (1939; reprint, London: Penguin, 1993).

18. For examples, see Peter Andreas, "Illicit Globalization: Myths, Misconceptions, and Historical Lessons," *Political Science Quarterly* 126, no. 3 (2011): 1–23; Kornel Chang, *Pacific Connections: The Making of the U.S.-Canadian Borderlands* (Berkeley: University of California Press, 2012); Andrew W. Cohen, *Contraband: Smuggling and the Birth of the American Century* (New York: Norton, 2015); Johan Mathew, *Margins of the Market: Trafficking and Capitalism Across the Arabian Sea* (Berkeley: University of California Press, 2016); Cyrus Schayegh, "The Many Worlds of 'Abud Yasin; or, What Narcotics Trafficking in the Interwar Middle East Can Tell Us About Territorialization," *American Historical Review* 116, no. 2 (2011): 273–306; and Eric Tagliacozzo, *Secret Trades, Porous Borders: Smuggling and States Along a Southeast Asian Frontier, 1865–1915* (New Haven: Yale University Press, 2005).

19. Andreas, "Illicit Globalization," 412; original reference from Michael Mann, "The Autonomous Power of the State: Its Origins, Mechanisms and Results," *Archives Européenes de Sociologie* 25 (1984): 185–213.

20. Christopher A. Bayly, *The Birth of the Modern World, 1780–1914: Global Connections and Comparisons* (Oxford: Blackwell, 2004), 247.

21. Adapted from Peter Andreas, who in turn adapted it from Charles Tilly on the relationship between war-making and state-making. Peter Andreas, *Smuggler Nation: How Illicit Trade Made America* (Oxford: Oxford University Press, 2013), 2; Charles Tilly, *Coercion, Capital, and European States, AD 900–1992* (Cambridge, Mass.: Blackwell, 1992).

22. Wong, *China Transformed*, 169.

23. To Prasenjit Duara, these late Qing and early Republican initiatives—"the impulse toward bureaucratization and rationalization, the drive to increase revenues for both military and civilian purposes, the often violent resistance of local communities to this process of intrusion and extraction, and the effort by the state to form alliances with new elites to consolidate power"—were similar to initiatives undertaken elsewhere. Duara, *Culture, Power, and the State*, 2.

24. Nicholas R. Parillo, *Against the Profit Motive: The Salary Revolution in American Government, 1780–1940* (New Haven: Yale University Press, 2013), 25.

25. On the impact of this shift in Qing statecraft on commerce, see Susan Mann, *Local Merchants and the Chinese Bureaucracy, 1750–1950* (Stanford, Calif.: Stanford University Press, 1987); Pomeranz, *Making of a Hinterland*; and Yeh, *Shanghai Splendor.*

26. James J. Sheehan, "The Problem of Sovereignty in European History," *American Historical Review* III, no. 1 (2006): 1–15.

27. Charles S. Maier, *Leviathan 2.0: Inventing Modern Statehood* (Cambridge, Mass.: Belknap Press of Harvard University Press, 2012), 11.

28. Max Weber, *Economy and Society: An Outline of Interpretative Sociology*, ed. G. Roth and C. Wittich (1956; reprint, Berkeley: University of California Press, 1978), 2:904–5.

29. Kuhn, *Origins*, 1.

30. Hendrik Spruyt, "War, Trade, and State Formation," in *The Oxford Handbook of Comparative Politics*, ed. C. Boix and S. Stokes (Oxford: Oxford University Press, 2007), 213.

31. Halsey, *Quest for Power.*

32. Alexander Gerschenkron, *Economic Backwardness in Historical Perspective: A Book of Essays* (Cambridge, Mass.: Belknap Press of Harvard University Press, 1962).

33. Pär K. Cassel, *Grounds of Judgment: Extraterritoriality and Imperial Power in Nineteenth-Century China and Japan* (Oxford: Oxford University Press, 2012).

34. See, for instance, Li Chen, *Chinese Law in Imperial Eyes: Sovereignty, Justice, and Transcultural Politics* (New York: Columbia University Press, 2015), and Teemu Ruskola, *Legal Orientalism: China, the United States, and Modern Law* (Cambridge, Mass.: Harvard University Press, 2013).

35. On policing reforms and their role in state-building, see Tong Lam, "Policing the Imperial Nation: Sovereignty, International Law, and the Civilizing Mission in Late Qing China," *Comparative Studies in Society and History* 52, no. 4 (2010): 881–908, and Wakeman, *Policing Shanghai*. On the role of legal reforms in semicolonial settings, see Lauren Benton, *Law and Colonial Cultures: Legal Regimes in World History, 1400–1900* (Cambridge: Cambridge University Press, 2002); Cassel, *Grounds of Judgment*; Turan Kayaoglu, *Legal Imperialism: Sovereignty and Extraterritoriality in Japan, the Ottoman Empire, and China* (Cambridge: Cambridge University Press, 2010); and Xu, *Trial of Modernity.*

36. William H. Sewell Jr., "A Strange Career: The Historical Study of Economic Life," *History and Theory* 49 (2010): 144. For an overview of this research agenda, see Jeremy Adelman and Jonathan Levy, "The Fall and Rise of Economic History," *Chronicle of Higher Education*, December 1, 2014, http://www.chronicle.com/article/The-FallRise-of-Economic/150247/ (accessed July 28, 2017), and William H. Sewell Jr., *The Logics of History: Social Theory and Social Transformation* (Chicago: University of Chicago Press, 2005). Historians of China, by contrast, have demonstrated a longer, more sustained interest in economic history. See, in particular, Thomas G. Rawski et al., *Economics and the Historian* (Berkeley: University of California Press, 1991), and Thomas G. Rawski

and Lillian M. Li, *Chinese History in Economic Perspective* (Berkeley: University of California Press, 1992).

37. Tagliacozzo, *Secret Trades, Porous Borders*.

38. Willem van Schendel and Itty Abraham, eds., *Illicit Flows and Criminal Things: States, Borders, and the Other Side of Globalization* (Bloomington: Indiana University Press, 2005), 7, 15; emphasis in original.

39. Researchers of the early modern Atlantic World, in particular, have demonstrated how smuggling lubricated—and even made possible—exchange between imperial markets even in the face of tightening mercantilist strictures. See, for example, Bernard Bailyn, *Atlantic History: Concept and Contours* (Cambridge, Mass.: Harvard University Press, 2005); Karras, *Smuggling*; Michael Kwass, *Contraband: Louis Mandrin and the Making of a Global Underground* (Cambridge, Mass.: Harvard University Press, 2014); Linda M. Rupert, *Creolization and Contraband: Curaçao in the Early Modern Atlantic World* (Athens: University of Georgia Press, 2012); and Thomas M. Truxes, *Defying Empire: Trading with the Enemy in Colonial New York* (New Haven: Yale University Press, 2008).

40. Attention to the social, political, and cultural outcomes of the tariff fully accords with research from the field of New Fiscal Sociology, a multidisciplinary research agenda embracing economist Joseph Schumpeter's call to examine taxation at the center of many historical changes. For an overview, see Isaac William Martin, Ajay K. Mehrotra, and Monica Prasad, eds., *The New Fiscal Sociology: Taxation in Comparative and Historical Perspective* (Cambridge: Cambridge University Press, 2009).

41. Such recent studies include Cynthia Brokaw, *Commerce in Culture: The Sibao Book Trade in the Qing and Republican Periods* (Cambridge, Mass.: Harvard University Asia Center, 2007); Sherman Cochran, *Chinese Medicine Men: Consumer Culture in China and Southeast Asia* (Cambridge, Mass.: Harvard University Press, 2006); Elisabeth Köll, *From Cotton Mill to Business Empire: The Emergence of Regional Enterprises in Modern China* (Cambridge, Mass.: Harvard University Asia Center, 2004); Sheehan, *Industrial Eden*; and Madeleine Zelin, *The Merchants of Zigong: Industrial Entrepreneurship in Early Modern China* (New York: Columbia University Press, 2005).

42. For an overview of this debate, see Chi-Kong Lai, "Chinese Business History: Its Development, Present Situation, and Future Direction," *Business History Around the World*, ed. F. Amatori and G. Jones (Cambridge: Cambridge University Press, 2003), 298–316.

43. For the most forceful argument regarding state criminalization of existent customary behavior in the case of early modern England, see E. P. Thompson, *Whigs and Hunters: The Origin of the Black Act* (New York: Pantheon, 1975). For a critique of this interpretation, see Benton, *Law and Colonial Cultures*.

44. Edward Muir and Guido Ruggiero, "Afterword: Crime and the Writing of History," in *History from Crime*, ed. E. Muir and G. Ruggiero (Baltimore: Johns Hopkins University Press, 1994), 227.

1. COASTAL COMMERCE AND IMPERIAL LEGACIES

1. For description of the case along with relevant documents and correspondences between the parties, see Inspectorate General of Chinese Customs, *Foochow: "Taiwan" False Manifest Case* (Shanghai: Statistical Department of the Inspectorate General, 1878).

2. Gang Zhao, *The Qing Opening to the Ocean: Chinese Maritime Policies, 1684–1757* (Honolulu: University of Hawai'i Press, 2013), 99.

3. The ban was originally introduced starting from 1661 to deprive Taiwan-based Ming loyalists led by Zheng Chenggong operation footholds on the mainland. The tollhouse system was a vast network of stations, substations, and checkpoints that dotted China's coastline and rivers, charging a "regular tariff" (*zhengshui*) of 4 percent for imports and other handling and tonnage dues. See Hans Van de Ven, *Breaking with the Past: The Maritime Customs Service and the Global Origins of Modernity in China* (New York: Columbia University Press, 2014), 58–59.

4. The Qing court permitted trade along the coast less to reap economic gains and more to foster political stability in a region that had vigorously resisted Manchu rule only decades before. Security thus took precedence over the economy.

5. Robert J. Antony, *Like Froth Floating on the Sea: The World of Pirates and Seafarers in Late Imperial South China* (Berkeley: Institute of East Asian Studies, 2003), 67–68.

6. Sarasin Viraphol, *Tribute and Profit: Sino-Siamese Trade, 1652–1853* (Cambridge, Mass.: Council on East Asian Studies, Harvard University, 1977). Despite prohibitions, private merchants from southeastern China freely traded at many points between Siam and China by attaching themselves to tribute missions dispatched from Bangkok to Beijing, for instance.

7. Zhao, *Qing Opening to the Ocean*, 177–80.

8. Yen-p'ing Hao, *The Commercial Revolution in Nineteenth-Century China: The Rise of Sino-Western Mercantile Capitalism* (Berkeley: University of California Press, 1986), 15–20.

9. Albert Feuerwerker, "The Foreign Presence in China," in *The Cambridge History of China*, vol. 12: *Republican China, 1912–1949, Part 1*, ed. J. K. Fairbank (Cambridge: Cambridge University Press, 1983), 129.

10. *TCF*, 1:393, Treaty of the Bogue (1843) (Humen tiaoyue), Article VIII. Once it made a concession to one treaty power, China was required by the most favored nation clause to make the same concession to all treaty powers.

11. Pär K. Cassel, *Grounds of Judgment: Extraterritoriality and Imperial Power in Nineteenth-Century China and Japan* (Oxford: Oxford University Press, 2012).

12. *TCF*, 1:412, "Article XXVII—It is agreed that either of the High Contracting Parties to this Treaty may demand a further revision of the Tariff and of the Commercial Articles of this Treaty at the end of ten years, but if no demand be made on either side within six months after the end of the first ten years, then the Tariff shall remain in force for ten years more, reckoned from the end of the preceding ten years; and so it shall be, at the end of each successive ten years."

13. Until the end of the Qing dynasty in 1912, the agency was officially known in English as the Imperial Chinese Maritime Customs. At the risk of anachronism but for the sake of

simplicity, I will use the name Chinese Maritime Customs Service or Maritime Customs when referring to the agency.

14. For more on the agency's origins, see John K. Fairbank, *Trade and Diplomacy on the China Coast: The Opening of the Treaty Ports, 1842–1854* (Cambridge, Mass.: Harvard University Press, 1953); and Van de Ven, *Breaking with the Past.*

15. The only official non-British inspector general was American Lester Knox Little, who served from 1943 to 1950, when he tendered his resignation to the Nationalist government in Taiwan.

16. An important exception was 1941–1945, when the outbreak of the Pacific War created two competing agencies claiming to be the legitimate Maritime Customs: one under the Japanese-sponsored Wang Jingwei government in Shanghai, the other under the "Free China" Chiang Kai-shek government in Chongqing. For further details, see Robert A. Bickers, "The Chinese Maritime Customs at War, 1941–45," *Journal of Imperial and Commonwealth History* 36, no. 2 (2008): 295–311.

17. No other Chinese governmental institution operating during the same period can make a similar claim of longevity or continuity of operations. During the Qing dynasty, it reported to the Zongli Yamen and then to the Ministry of Foreign Affairs after 1901. It later reported to the newly created Revenue Bureau (Shuiwu chu), as part of a government reorganization in 1906, and to the Beiyang government, the Beijing-based successor to the Qing dynasty, until 1928. When the Nationalists defeated the Beiyang government and declared themselves as China's new legitimate central government, their Ministry of Finance (Caizheng bu) placed the Maritime Customs under the jurisdiction of the Guan-wu Shu [Kuan-wu Shu] (Office of Customs Affairs).

18. Liu Cuirong, "Guanshui yu Qing ji ziqiang xinzheng" (Tariffs and late Qing self-strengthening new policies), in *Qingji ziqiang yundong yantaohui lunwen ji* (Collection of essays from academic conference on late Qing Self-Strengthening Movement), ed. Zhongyang yanjiuyuan jindaishi yanjiusuo (Taipei: Zhongyang yanjiuyuan jindaishi yanjiusuo, 1988), 1024.

19. Land taxes totaled roughly 25 million taels; customs duties came in at just under 22 million taels. For more specific data, see Albert Feuerwerker, "Economic Trends, 1912–49," in Fairbank, *Republican China, Part 1*, 63.

20. G. William Skinner, "Regional Urbanization in Nineteenth-Century China," in *The City in Late Imperial China*, ed. G. William Skinner (Stanford, Calif.: Stanford University Press, 1977), 211–20.

21. Catherine L. Phipps, *Empires on the Waterfront: Japan's Ports and Power, 1858–1899* (Cambridge, Mass.: Harvard University Asia Center, 2015), 11.

22. Adam McKeown, "Conceptualizing Chinese Diasporas, 1842 to 1949," *Journal of Asian Studies* 58, no. 2 (1999): 321.

23. Inspectorate General of Customs, *Returns of Trade* (Shanghai: Statistical Department of the Inspectorate General of Customs, 1901), 20.

24. A. D. Blue, "The China Coasters," *Journal of the Hong Kong Branch of the Royal Asiatic Society* 7 (1967): 80–90.

25. Zhao, *Qing Opening to the Ocean*, 119.

26. Inspectorate General of Customs, *Decennial Reports on the Trade Navigation Industries, etc., of the Ports Open to Foreign Commerce in China and Corea, and on the Conditions and Development of the Treaty Port Provinces, 1882–1891*, 1st issue (Shanghai: Statistical Department of the Inspectorate General of Customs, 1893), 598–99.

27. Such gendered dimensions of smuggling were not exclusive to China. For similar tactics of smuggling by women in his survey of Gilded Age America, see Andrew W. Cohen, *Contraband: Smuggling and the Birth of the American Century* (New York: Norton, 2015), 374.

28. *SB*, December 29, 1879, 2.

29. *SB*, December 11, 1885, 2.

30. SHAC, 679/1/26903, Shuiwuchu Dispatch No. 1677 (November 18, 1913), in IG Circular No. 2122 (November 25, 1913).

31. Cai Zhitong, "Wo guo zousi wenti zhi jiantao" (A thorough discussion of our nation's smuggling problem), *Zhonghang yuebao* 12, no. 5 (1936): 2.

32. *TCF*, 1:438, 500.

33. Opium duties made up an estimated 15 percent of the Qing's budget by 1894. See Liu, "Guanshui yu Qing ji ziqiang xinzheng," 1022.

34. Hamashita Takeshi, *Chūgoku kindai keizaishi kenkyū: Shinmatsu kaikan zaisei to kaikōjō shijōken* (Research on the Modern Chinese economy: the Late Qing Maritime Customs finance and open port market) (Tōkyō: Tōkyō daigaku Tōyō Bunka kenkyūjo, 1989).

35. Stanley F. Wright, *China's Struggle for Tariff Autonomy, 1843–1938* (Shanghai: Kelly and Walsh, 1938).

36. SHAC, 679/1/26893, IG Circular No. 449 (April 10, 1889); SHAC, 679/1/26894, IG Circular No. 601 (July 13, 1893); SHAC, 679/1/26894. IG Circular No. 645 (May 7, 1894).

37. Timothy Brook and Bob Tadashi Wakabayashi, eds., *Opium Regimes: China, Britain, and Japan, 1839–1952* (Berkeley: University of California Press, 2000), 11–15.

38. For more on opium smuggling in the Republic, see Alan Baumler, *The Chinese and Opium Under the Republic: Worse Than Floods and Wild Beasts* (Albany: State University of New York Press, 2007), and Edward R. Slack, *Opium, State, and Society: China's Narco-Economy and the Guomindang, 1924–1937* (Honolulu: University of Hawai'i Press, 2001).

39. *TCF*, 1:423, "Rule 3—Contraband Goods. Import and export trade is alike prohibited in the following articles:—Gunpowder, Shot, Cannon, Fowling-pieces, Rifles, Muskets, Pistols, and all other Munitions and Implements of War; and Salt."

40. SHAC, 679/1/26890, IG Circular No. 13 of 1863 (First Series) (February 16, 1863).

41. Jonathan A. Grant, *Rulers, Guns, and Money: The Global Arms Trade in the Age of Imperialism* (Cambridge, Mass.: Harvard University Press, 2007), 31–32.

42. Inspectorate General of Customs, *Decennial Reports, 1882–1891*, 600.

43. Writing in 1894, Hart complained, "The experience of the last 30 years proves that precautions at Treaty ports and against traffic in Arms by Foreign ships are waste of time and labor so long as Chinese junks are not watched with equal care and non-Treaty ports

and long stretches of coast are open to all-comers." SHAC, 679/1/26895, IG Circular No. 629 (January 22, 1894).

44. Inspectorate General of Customs, *Decennial Reports, 1882–1891*, 600–604.

45. Anthony B. Chan, *Arming the Chinese: The Western Armaments Trade in Warlord China, 1920–1928* (Vancouver: University of British Columbia Press, 1982), 74.

46. SHAC, 679/1/26904, IG Circular No. 2436 (November 5, 1915).

47. For an overview of the arms trade in early Republican China, see Chan, *Arming the Chinese*; Chen Cungong, "Minchu lujun junhuo zhi shuru" (The import of arms by the army in the early Republic), *Jindaishi yanjiusuo jikan* 6 (1977): 237–309; and Qi Chunfeng, "Ping jindai Riben dui Hua junhuo zousi huodong" (Review of modern Japan's arms smuggling activities in China), *Anhui shixue*, no. 3 (2002): 58–63.

48. *TCF*, 1:423.

49. The first salt regulations were promulgated during the Spring and Autumn Period (ca. 770–476 BCE). For an overview of regulations before the Qing, see Zhang Xiaoye, *Qing dai siyan wenti yanjiu* (Research on the salt smuggling problem during the Qing dynasty) (Beijing: Shehui kexue wenxian chubanshe, 2001), 1–10.

50. Samuel A. M. Adshead, *The Modernization of the Chinese Salt Administration, 1900–1920* (Cambridge, Mass.: Harvard University Press, 1970), 132–33.

51. For organized salt smuggling, see Winston Hsieh, "Triads, Salt Smugglers, and Local Uprisings: Observations on the Social and Economic Background of the Waichow Revolution of 1911," in *Popular Movements and Secret Societies in China, 1840–1950*, ed. Jean Chesneaux (Stanford, Calif.: Stanford University Press, 1972), and Elizabeth J. Perry, *Rebels and Revolutionaries in North China, 1845–1945* (Stanford, Calif.: Stanford University Press, 1980), 60–62, 104–7.

52. For Nationalist China's efforts to fight salt smuggling and force peasants to buy "official" salt, see Ralph Thaxton, *Salt of the Earth: The Political Origins of Peasant Protest and Communist Revolution in China* (Berkeley: University of California Press, 1997).

53. An especially brutal anti-smuggling campaign was waged by Fang Yao, Regional Commander of the Army of the Green Standard, from 1869 to 1873 in the southeast Chinese region of Chaozhou. For more details, see Melissa Macauley, "Entangled States: The Translocal Repercussions of Rural Pacification in China, 1869–1873," *American Historical Review* 121, no. 3 (2016): 755–79.

54. SHAC, 679/1/26891, IG Circular No. 157 (August 2, 1881).

55. SHAC, 679/1/26893, IG Circular No. 488 (February 18, 1890).

56. See, for instance, *SB*, November 27, 1900, 3.

57. Fu Huiqing, "Shantou haiguan gailüe (1910–1942)" (Summary of the Shantou Customs), *Guangdong wenshi ziliao* 14 (1964): 145.

58. IG Dispatch No. 14 to Canton Customs, April 29, 1867, in *DIO*, 6:197–99.

59. GDPA, 95/1/219, Kowloon Dispatch No. 8151 to IG (September 6, 1917).

60. GDPA, 95/1/1103, Memo (undated).

61. GDPA, 95/1/108, Confidential Semi-Official Memo from Shantou Customs to Kowloon Customs (May 21, 1925).

62. For the incident, see "Er chen wan an," in *DZ*, 5:5, 1908, 25–8.

63. GDPA, 95/1/107, Confidential Semi-Official Memo from Shanghai Customs to Kowloon Customs (May 2, 1928). Emphasis in original.

64. *DLC*, 146-00, 147-00. Translation of chapter titles from William C. Jones, trans., *The Great Qing Code* (New York: Oxford University Press, 1994).

65. Huang Guosheng, *Yapian zhanzheng qian de dongnan si sheng haiguan* (The customs of the four southeast provinces before the Opium War) (Fuzhou: Fujian renmin chubanshe, 2000), 333–4.

66. *DLC*, 141-00, 144-00, 145-00. For an overview of other commodities strictly regulated or prohibited from transport, see Huang, *Yapian zhanzheng qian de dongnan si sheng haiguan*, 249.

67. *DLC*, 225-00.

68. *DLC*, 225-02, 225-03.

69. For piracy before the late nineteenth century, see Antony, *Like Froth Floating on the Sea*; Dian H. Murray, *Pirates of the South China Coast, 1790–1810* (Stanford, Calif.: Stanford University Press, 1987); and Wensheng Wang, *White Lotus Rebels and South China Pirates: Crisis and Reform in the Qing Empire* (Cambridge, Mass.: Harvard University Press, 2014). For late nineteenth-century reports on *anti-piracy* campaigns in the *Peking Gazette*, see *NH*, May 30, 1890, and June 13, 1890.

70. Perry, *Rebels and Revolutionaries*; Mary C. Wright, *The Last Stand of Chinese Conservatism: The T'ung-chih Restoration, 1862–1874* (Stanford, Calif.: Stanford University Press, 1957), 118–19; and Zhang, *Qing dai siyan wenti yanjiu*, 191.

71. *DLC*, 225-01, 225-15, 225-28. Such changes were introduced in the first year of the Guangxu emperor (1875) by Governor-General Shen Baozhen, who sought to assert Qing sovereignty over the newly created province of Taiwan and strengthen its defenses against foreign incursions.

72. The Qing Code consisted of statutes (*lü*) and sub-statutes (*li*). The former were often retained as a formality even after they had become obsolete or had been supplanted by the latter. For more on this legal tradition, see Matthew H. Sommer, *Sex, Law, and Society in Late Imperial China* (Stanford, Calif.: Stanford University Press, 2000), 24–25.

73. *DLC*, 225-00, Jin'an (commentary).

74. *DXA*, 6: Kecheng, 30.1.

75. *DXA*, 6: Kecheng, 26.2–27.1.

76. *DXA*, 6: Kecheng, 29.1–2.

77. For salt, see *DXA*, 6: Kecheng, 1–21. For other commodities, see *DXA*, 6: Kecheng, 22–25. Provincial officials, however, sometimes moved to ban the export of commodities like rice in response to local famine conditions.

78. *DXA*, 8: Guanjin, 8–14.

79. *DXA*, 8: Guanjin, 15–28. Marinus J. Meijer, *The Introduction of Modern Criminal Law in China* (Batavia: De Unie, 1950), 56–57.

80. Philip C. C. Huang, *Code, Custom, and Legal Practice in China: The Qing and the Republic Compared* (Stanford, Calif.: Stanford University Press, 2001), 15–20.

81. *ZHL*, 1:21, 266, 61.

82. *ZHL*, 1:24, 203 and 205, 48.

83. *CCC*, 147–50.

84. SHAC, 679/1/26893, IG Circular No. 413 (April 14, 1888); SHAC, 679/1/26903, IG Circular No. 2218 (June 10, 1914).

85. *TCF*, 1:409, 418.

86. See, for instance, the protest by the Prussian consul at Xiamen in *DIO*, 6:217–22.

87. The Chinese name for the Joint Investigation Rules was usually shortened to *Huixun zhangcheng*. For text of the rules in Chinese and English, see SHAC, 679/1/26890, IG Circular No. 19 of 1868 (First Series) (June 15, 1868).

88. *TCF*, 1:481: "Article IX—It is agreed that in all cases of fines arising out of breaches of Customs regulations, the Superintendent or the Commissioner of Customs may have a seat on the bench and take part with the British Consul in inquiring into the case; and that in all cases of confiscations arising out of breaches of Customs Regulations, the British Consul may have a seat on the bench with the Superintendent or the Commissioner of Customs, and take part in inquiring the case."

89. Cassel, *Grounds of Judgment*. The tradition of allowing alien offenders in China to be punished by officials of their own nationalities stretches back to at least the Tang dynasty (618–907). See R. Randle Edwards, "Ch'ing Legal Jurisdiction over Foreigners," in *Essays on China's Legal Tradition*, ed. Jerome Cohen, R. Randle Edwards, and Fu-Mei Chang Chen (Princeton, N.J.: Princeton University Press, 1980), 222–69.

90. Prince Kung [Gong] to Anson Burlingame (June 13, 1864), FRUS, 1864, 3:435.

91. Kuo Ta-jen [Guo Songtao] to Marquess of Salisbury (June 8, 1876), FO 371/19322.

92. Shu Cheon Pon [Xu Shoupeng] to T. F. Bayard (July 2, 1887), FRUS, 1887–1888, 242–43. Bayard did not contest Xu's interpretation: "The Government of the United States fully recognizes the principles herein set forth, and has no desire to encroach upon the jurisdiction of China in the administration of her customs laws in respect to opium or other contraband merchandise." See T. F. Bayard to Chang Yen Hoon [Zhang Yinheng] (August 30, 1887), FRUS, 1887–1888, 243.

93. *TCF*, 1:418: "Article XLVII—British merchant vessels are not entitled to resort to other than the Ports of Trade declared open by this Treaty. They are not unlawfully to enter other Ports in China or to carry on clandestine Trade along the coast thereof. Any vessel violating this provision shall, with her cargo, be subject to confiscation by the Chinese Government."

94. *TCF*, 1:418: "Article XLVIII—If any British merchant vessel be concerned in smuggling, the goods, whatever their value or nature, shall be subject to confiscation by the Chinese authorities, and the Ship may be prohibited from trading further, and sent away as soon as her accounts shall have been adjusted and paid."

95. *SB*, June 18, 1875, 2, and June 23, 1875, 1–2.

96. *NH*, July 10, 1875, 33.

97. *CG*, April–June 1876, 116.

98. *DIO*, 6:467–74.

99. For resolution of the case, see Wright, *China's Struggle for Tariff Autonomy*, 452–43.

100. SHAC, 679/1/26892, IG Circular No. 247 (October 25, 1883).

101. SHAC, 679/1/26892, IG Circular No. 290 (September 30, 1884), enclosures 3, 4, and 5.

102. SHAC, 679/1/26892, IG Circular No. 290 (September 30, 1884), enclosures 1 and 2.

103. *CG*, 1885 (all issues).

104. SHAC, 679/1/26915, IG Circular No. 4913 (August 4, 1934), 50–51.

2. TARIFF AUTONOMY AND ECONOMIC CONTROL

1. Felix Boecking, *No Great Wall: Trade, Tariffs, and Nationalism in Republican China, 1927–1945* (Cambridge, Mass.: Harvard University Asia Center, 2017), 64.

2. See, in particular, Wunsz King, *China at the Paris Peace Conference in 1919* (New York: St. John's University Press, 1961) and *China at the Washington Conference, 1921–1922* (New York: St. John's University Press, 1963); Stanley F. Wright, *China's Struggle for Tariff Autonomy, 1843–1938* (Shanghai: Kelly and Walsh, 1938); and Arthur N. Young, *China's Nation-Building Effort, 1927–1937: The Financial and Economic Record* (Stanford, Calif.: Hoover Institution Press, 1971).

3. Ching-Chun Wang, "How China Recovered Tariff Autonomy," *Annals of the American Academy of Political and Social Science* 152 (1930): 266.

4. In the negotiations to determine a new tariff schedule, Qing negotiator Qi Ying investigated the duties levied in Guangzhou and found many changes and inconsistencies during the prior century. John K. Fairbank, *Trade and Diplomacy on the China Coast: The Opening of the Treaty Ports, 1842–1854* (Cambridge, Mass.: Harvard University Press, 1953), 117–18.

5. The Qing dynasty surrendered China's tariff autonomy not in a single moment but in successive stages. First, it agreed to the principle of maintaining a "fair and regular tariff" (*yiding zeli*) in the Treaty of Nanjing. Later, it acceded to the 5 percent ad valorem treaty tariff in the Treaty of Tianjin.

6. The major difference was that the treaties explicitly eliminated the irregular "miscellaneous charges and commissions" so hated by foreign merchants. Hans Van de Ven, *Breaking with the Past: The Maritime Customs Service and the Global Origins of Modernity in China* (New Yorker: Columbia University Press, 2014), 58–59.

7. Wang Ermin, *Wan Qing shangyue waijiao* (The diplomacy of the commercial treaties between China and foreign powers during the late Qing period) (Hong Kong: Chinese University Press, 1998), 19.

8. Fairbank, *Trade and Diplomacy on the China Coast*, 117–18.

9. Treaty of Tientsin, "Article XXVII—It is agreed that either of the High Contracting Parties to this Treaty may demand a further revision of the Tariff and of the Commercial Articles of this Treaty at the end of ten years." *TCF*, 1:412.

10. Mary C. Wright, *The Last Stand of Chinese Conservatism: The T'ung-chih Restoration, 1862–1874* (Stanford, Calif.: Stanford University Press, 1957), 271–95.

11. See, in particular, Kenneth Pomeranz, *The Making of a Hinterland: State, Society, and Economy in Inland North China, 1853–1937* (Berkeley: University of California Press, 1993); and William T. Rowe, *Saving the World: Chen Hongmou and Elite Consciousness in Eighteenth-Century China* (Stanford, Calif.: Stanford University Press, 2001).

12. Wen-hsin Yeh, *Shanghai Splendor: Economic Sentiments and the Making of Modern China, 1843–1949* (Berkeley: University of California Press, 2007), 17–27. Other scholars have translated *shangzhan* as "trade war" or "commercial war."

13. Jichuang Hu, *A Concise History of Chinese Economic Thought* (Beijing: Foreign Languages Press, 1998), 258.

14. Wang Ermin, "Shangzhan guannian yu zhongshang sixiang" (War of commerce concept and mercantilist thought), *Zhongyang yanjiuyuan jindaishi yanjiusuo ji* 5 (1976): 25.

15. Susan Mann, *Local Merchants and the Chinese Bureaucracy, 1750–1950* (Stanford, Calif.: Stanford University Press, 1987), 147.

16. Wang Ermin. "Wan Qing waijiao sixiang de xingcheng" (The formation of late Qing diplomatic thought), *Zhongyang yanjiuyuan jindaishi yanjiusuo ji* 1 (1969): 32; and Hu, *Concise History*, 539. Zheng's writings were also translated and circulated widely in Korea and Japan.

17. Zheng Guanying, *Zheng Guanying Ji* (Collected writings of Zheng Guanying), ed. Xia Dongyuan (Beijing: Zhonghua shu ju, [Qing] 2014), 318.

18. Zheng, 319.

19. Zheng, 360.

20. Quoted from Wang, "Shangzhan guannian yu zhongshang sixiang," 29.

21. Zheng, *Zheng Guanying Ji*, 318.

22. Within a decade before its collapse, the Tokugawa shogunate (1600–1868) acceded to the notorious Ansei Treaties (1858) and the Tariff Convention (1866), which fixed rates on all imports and exports at 5 percent ad valorem. Catherine L. Phipps, *Empires on the Waterfront: Japan's Ports and Power, 1858–1899* (Cambridge, Mass.: Harvard University Asia Center, 2015), 66–67.

23. Pär K. Cassel, *Grounds of Judgment: Extraterritoriality and Imperial Power in Nineteenth-Century China and Japan* (Oxford: Oxford University Press, 2012), 148–60.

24. In the Anglo-Japanese Treaty of 1894, Great Britain agreed to relinquish its extraterritorial privileges and restore Japan's tariff autonomy starting in 1899. It was not until 1911, however, that Japan implemented its own tariffs not bound by any treaty. Ting Mien Liu, *Modern Tariff Policies with Special Reference to China* (New York: Alliance, 1924), 29–35.

25. Quoted from Dai Dongyang, "Riben xiugai tiaoyue jiaoshe yu He Ruzhang de tiaoyue renshi" (Japan's treaty revision negotiations and understanding of treaties by He Ruzhang), *Jindaishi yanjiu* 6 (2004): 167.

26. In his 1896 essay "On Raising Taxes" (*Lun jiashui*), Liang focused on tariff autonomy as a key marker of sovereignty denied to China. Ten years later, he elaborated on the significance of the tariff in Sino-Japanese relations. See Liang Qichao, "Lun jiashui" (On increasing taxes, 1896) and "Guanshui quan wenti" (The problem of tariff autonomy,

1906), in *Yin bing shi he ji* (Collected works from the ice-drinker's studio) (Beijing: Zhonghua shu ju, 1989), 1:104, 2:68–76. For a summary, see Lai Jiancheng, *Liang Qichao de jingji mianxiang* (Liang Qichao's economic orientation) (Taipei: Lianjing, 2006), 222–28.

27. Benjamin I. Schwartz, *In Search of Wealth and Power: Yen Fu and the West* (Cambridge, Mass.: Belknap Press of Harvard University Press, 1964).

28. For details of the Chinese delegation at the Paris Peace Conference, see Westel Woodbury Willoughby, *China at the Conference: A Report* (Baltimore: Johns Hopkins University Press, 1922).

29. The authoritative study of tariff negotiations at international conferences is Wright, *China's Struggle for Tariff Autonomy*.

30. Van de Ven, *Breaking with the Past*, 201–4; Wright, *China's Struggle for Tariff Autonomy*, 598–600.

31. Dong Wang, *China's Unequal Treaties: Narrating National History* (Lanham, Md.: Lexington Books, 2005).

32. Feng Sheng, "Chuangkan ci ji qita" (Words for the inaugural issue and other matters), *Guanshui wenti* 1, no. 1 (1928): 2–3.

33. Li was editor of the Commercial Press (Shangwu Yinshuguan) and a prominent academic by this time. See China Weekly Review, ed., *Who's Who in China: Biographies of Chinese Leaders*, 5th ed. (Shanghai: China Weekly Review, 1936), 143. Li's article was one of five articles in the 1925 issue devoted to covering the conference: *DZ*, 22.20.

34. Li Pei'en, "Guanshui zizhu" (Tariff autonomy), in *DZ*, 22.20:34–48.

35. *DZ*, 22.20. See back of front cover for advertisement.

36. Beijing tushuguan, *Minguo shiqi zong shumu (jingji lei)* (Complete catalog of the Republican era [Economics]) (Beijing: Shumu wenxian chubanshe, 1986), 2:960–62. The figure includes three works written by foreign authors but does not include subsequent editions of individual titles. At least seven books bore the generic title of *The Tariff Problem in China* (*Zhongguo guanshui wenti*). Three of these books, in turn, were authored by Overseas Chinese returnees who had received their postgraduate education in the United States. The earliest such study was Zhu Jin's [Chin Chu] 1919 book, which was based on his 1916 dissertation and published "to draw attention to the fact that the revision of tariff treaties [was] one of the engrossing questions in China." For English and Chinese editions, see, respectively Chin Chu [Zhu Jin], *The Tariff Problem in China* (New York: Columbia University Press, 1916), and Zhu Jin, *Zhongguo guanshui wenti* (The Tariff Problem in China) (Zhuzhang guoji shuifa pingdeng hui, 1919).

Another study was by Li Quanshi [Chuan-shih Li], who served as dean of the School of Commerce at Fudan University and received his doctorate in economics. See China Weekly Review, *Who's Who in China*, 456–57. Li's 1936 two-volume work was an updated and significantly expanded version of *A Plea for Tariff Autonomy* in China, a 1921 pamphlet he wrote for "The Chinese Students' Committee on Washington Conference" to persuade delegates the urgency of China's case. For English and Chinese editions, see Chuan-shih Li, *A Plea for Tariff Autonomy in China* (New York:

Chinese Students' Committee on Washington Conference, 1921), and Li Quanshi, *Zhongguo guanshui wenti* (The Tariff Problem in China) (Shanghai: Shangwu yinshu guan, 1936).

37. China Weekly Review, *Who's Who in China*, 593–94.

38. Ma's book was part of the Commercial Press's Universal Library series (*baike xiao congshu*), which sought to "use plain language and interesting methods to introduce indispensable knowledge at an affordable price." Ma Yinchu, *Zhongguo guanshui wenti* (The Tariff Problem in China, 1923) (Shanghai: Shangwu yinshu guan, 1925).

39. Beijing tushuguan, *Minguo shiqi zong shumu (jingji lei)*, 2:960.

40. William C. Kirby, *Germany and Republican China* (Stanford, Calif.: Stanford University Press, 1984), 81.

41. Michael R. Godley, "Socialism with Chinese Characteristics: Sun Yatsen and the International Development of China," *Australian Journal of Chinese Affairs* 18 (1987): 111.

42. Marie-Claire Bergère, *Sun Yat-sen* (Stanford, Calif.: Stanford University Press, 1998), 317–18; Van de Ven, *Breaking with the Past*, 205–7. Sun was motivated by the surplus China's customs revenues yielded after the repayment of foreign loans and indemnities in the years following World War I.

43. Marie-Claire Bergère, *The Golden Age of the Chinese Bourgeoisie, 1911–1937* (Cambridge: Cambridge University Press, 1989), 361. According to Sun, China was no longer threatened by "political oppression" (*zhengzhi de yapo*, i.e., formal conquest of China by foreign powers) given the enormous costs and likelihood of upsetting the regional balance of power.

44. Sun Yat-sen [Sun Zhongshan], *San Min Chu I: The Three Principles of the People* (1924), trans. Frank W. Price (Taipei: China Publishing, 1950), 10.

45. Sun used the example of cloth to illustrate how low tariffs permitted the influx of cheap imports and destroyed native industries, thereby leading many people to being "thrown out of work and [becoming] idlers." Sun, 11.

46. Sun, 10.

47. Sun had long absorbed the writings of late Qing intellectuals. In fact, the wording and ideas in one of Sun's earliest political writings—an 1894 petition submitted to Li Hongzhang—were similar to the writings of Zheng Guanying. Yen-p'ing Hao, "Cheng Kuan-ying: The Comprador as Reformer," *Journal of Asian Studies* 29, no. 1 (1969): 20n35.

48. Boecking, *No Great Wall*, 66–70.

49. Chiang Kai-shek [Jiang Jieshi], *China's Destiny and Chinese Economic Theory* (1947), trans. Philip J. Jaffe (Leiden: Global Oriental, 2013), 55.

50. H. K. T., "Society for the Promotion of Tariff Reciprocity in China," *CW*, December 28, 1918, 128–29; *SB*, December 12, 1918, 10. The society came into being after a conversation between Shanghai merchants and Charles R. Crane, a sympathetic American businessman and diplomat.

51. Isaac William Martin, Ajay K. Mehrotra, and Monica Prasad, eds., *The New Fiscal Sociology: Taxation in Comparative and Historical Perspective* (Cambridge: Cambridge University Press, 2009), 3.

52. For overview of the Nationalist Party's rise, see Lloyd E. Eastman, *The Abortive Revolution: China Under Nationalist Rule, 1927–1937* (Cambridge, Mass.: Harvard University Press, 1974), and C. Martin Wilbur, *The Nationalist Revolution in China, 1923–1928* (Cambridge: Cambridge University Press, 1983).

53. Toru Kubo, "The Tariff Policy of the Nationalist Government, 1929–36: A Historical Assessment," in *Japan, China, and the Growth of the Asian International Economy, 1850–1949*, ed. K. Sugihara (Oxford: Oxford University Press, 2005), 145–76.

54. For text of the treaty, see FRUS, 1928, 2:475–77.

55. All data from Liang-lin Hsiao, *China's Foreign Trade Statistics, 1864–1949* (Cambridge, Mass.: Harvard University Press, 1974). Data do not include the 2.5 percent surtax.

56. Kubo, "Tariff Policy," 151–54. For further details on the Nationalists' 1930s fiscal policies, see Young, *China's Nation-Building Effort*; Albert Feuerwerker, "Economic Trends, 1912–49," in *The Cambridge History of China*, vol. 12: *Republican China, 1911–49, Part 1*, ed. J. K. Fairbank (Cambridge: Cambridge University Press, 1983), 28–127; and Boecking, *No Great Wall*. For an analysis of the new tariff, see Wang Liangxing, "1929 nian Zhongguo guoding shuize xingzhi zhi shuliang fenxi" (Quantitative analysis of the nature of the 1929 Chinese national tariff), *Jindai shi yanjiu* (Modern Chinese history studies) 4 (1995): 209–48. Opium monopolies created by the Nationalists (under the guise of "anti-opium" movements) also helped fund the regime's campaigns against warlord and communist rivals. See Edward R. Slack, *Opium, State, and Society: China's Narco-Economy and the Guomindang, 1924–1937* (Honolulu: University of Hawai'i Press, 2001).

57. Margherita Zanasi, *Saving the Nation: Economic Modernity in Republican China* (Chicago: University of Chicago Press, 2006). On the growing embrace of economic control during the Second Sino-Japanese War, see Morris L. Bian, *The Making of the State Enterprise System in Modern China: The Dynamics of Institutional Change* (Cambridge, Mass.: Harvard University Press, 2005), 180–212.

58. William C. Kirby, "Engineering China: Birth of the Developmental State, 1928–1937," in *Becoming Chinese: Passages to Modernity and Beyond*, ed. W. H. Yeh (Berkeley: University of California Press, 2000), 137.

59. Yeh, *Shanghai Splendor*, 31.

60. Despite differences in their meaning and emphasis, the terms "controlled economic systems" and "planned economic systems" were used interchangeably by scholars during the 1930s. See Bian, *State Enterprise System*, 317n41.

61. See, especially, Barry J. Eichengreen, *Golden Fetters: The Gold Standard and the Great Depression, 1919–1939* (Oxford: Oxford University Press, 1992), and Charles P. Kindleberger, *The World in Depression, 1929–1939* (1973; reprint, Berkeley: University of California Press, 1986).

62. For an excellent overview of contending economic policy prescriptions during the 1930s, see Lee Yu-ping [Li Yuping], "Yi jiu san ling niandai Zhongguo de jiujing jingji konghuang shuo (1931–1935)" (Discussions in China on relieving the economic crisis during the 1930s), *Zhongyang yanjiuyuan jindaishi yanjiusuo ji* 27 (1997): 232–72.

63. H. D. Fong, *Toward Economic Control in China* (Shanghai: China Institute of Pacific Relations, 1936), 35.

64. Li Lixia, "Maoyi tongzhi lun yu Zhongguo maoyi tongzhi wenti" (On economic control and China's economic control problem), *Zhongshan wenhua jiaoyu guan jikan* 4, no. 2 (1937): 482.

65. "Wo guo ying shixing tongzhi maoyi" (Our country should implement trade controls), *Guohuo banyue kan*, 23/24 (1934): 14.

66. Luo Dunwei, "Zhongguo tongzhi jingji de mubiao yu quyu" (The purpose and scope of economic control in China), *Yinhang zhoubao* 17, no. 50 (1933): 3.

67. SHAC, 679/1/26909, IG Circular No. 3873 (March 14, 1929).

68. C. Y. W. Meng, "Tariff Autonomy Must Come," *CW*, September 17, 1927, 68–69.

69. Chen Shiqi, *Zhongguo jindai haiguan shi* (A history of modern China's Maritime Customs) (Beijing: Renmin chubanshe, 2002).

70. Miles Lampson to John Simon (November 7, 1933), FO 371/17064.

71. Chang Fu-yun [Zhang Fuyun], *Reformer of the Chinese Maritime Customs* (Berkeley: Regional Oral History Office, University of California, 1987), 143.

72. Wu Zhaoshen, *Zhongguo shuizhi shi* (History of China's tax system) (Shanghai: Shangwu yin shu guan, 1937), 172.

73. Charles Tilly, "War Making and State Making as Organized Crime," in *Bringing the State Back In*, ed. P. B. Evans, D. Rueschemeyer, and Theda Skocpol (Cambridge: Cambridge University Press, 1985), 169–91; Van de Ven, *Breaking with the Past*, 220.

3. STATE INTERVENTIONS AND LEGAL TRANSFORMATIONS

1. *XFH*, 33, 83–84.

2. Stanley F. Wright, *China's Struggle for Tariff Autonomy, 1843–1938* (Shanghai: Kelly and Walsh, 1938), 657.

3. SHAC, 679/1/930, Inspector General to Kuan-wu Shu (June 24, 1929), in Semi-official Circular No. 61 (October 25, 1929).

4. GDPA, 95/1/235, Kowloon Dispatch No. 9813 (December 13, 1930).

5. SHAC, 679/1/28169, Lappa Dispatch No. 6730 (December 12, 1931).

6. SHAC, 679/1/27750, Antung Dispatch No. 3011 (May 20, 1929).

7. SHAC, 679/1/930, Inspector General to Kuan-wu Shu (June 24, 1929), in Semi-official Circular No. 61 (October 25, 1929).

8. SHAC, 679/1/26912, IG Circular No. 4510 (October 18, 1932). The investigation was headed by two customs commissioners, first F. H. Bell and later A. H. Forbes.

9. SHAC, 679/1/26910, IG Circular No. 4172 (February 4, 1931).

10. Shortly after the inauguration of the Preventive Service, all commissioners were required to submit monthly smuggling reports. Informants were also encouraged to offer better actionable intelligence in exchange for more lucrative rewards.

11. Hans Van de Ven, *Breaking with the Past: The Maritime Customs Service and the Global Origins of Modernity in China* (New Yorker: Columbia University Press, 2014), 242.

12. *ZFD*, 1:168–69, Chapter 19, Articles 271–77, "Opium offenses" (*yapian zui*).

13. *ZFD*, 1:150, Chapter 20, Articles 256–65, "Opium offences." In 1935, the maximum term and fine for trafficking opium was raised to seven years and 3,000 yuan. The term and fine for trafficking morphine, heroin, and cocaine, was three to ten years and 5,000 yuan. Import of any narcotics was punishable by a minimum of five years in prison and a maximum fine of 10,000 yuan—the highest of any offense in the code.

14. *ZFD*, 1:924, "Regulations for the Restriction of Guns or Cannons Used for Military Purposes" (*junyong qiangpao qudi tiaoli*).

15. *ZFD*, 3:3178.

16. SHAC, 679/1/27750, Memo No. 12 to Inspector General: General Considerations Governing the Control of Smuggling and the Formation of a Preventive Service (1930).

17. Alan Baumler, *The Chinese and Opium Under the Republic: Worse Than Floods and Wild Beasts* (Albany: State University of New York Press, 2007); Edward R. Slack, *Opium, State, and Society: China's Narco-Economy and the Guomindang, 1924–1937* (Honolulu: University of Hawai'i Press, 2001).

18. "Customs Cruisers Make Haul of 500 Bales of Smuggled Rayon," *CW*, July 14, 1934, 281.

19. GDPA, 95/1/1053, Pakhoi SR (June and July 1934), 4.

20. SHAC, 679/1/20362, Inspector General Dispatch No. 135367 (June 15, 1931).

21. "Lifa yuanze" (Rationale for legislation), *Lifa zhuankan* 10 (1934): 1.

22. *ZY*, December 14, 1933, 3.

23. *ZY*, November 3, 1934, 3.

24. *ZFD*, 3:3181–3.

25. Inspector General Semi-official Circular No. 67 (May 5, 1930), SHAC, 679/1/930.

26. For more on legal reforms and their role in state-building, see Turan Kayaoglu, *Legal Imperialism: Sovereignty and Extraterritoriality in Japan, the Ottoman Empire, and China* (Cambridge: Cambridge University Press, 2010), and Xiaoqun Xu, *Trial of Modernity: Judicial Reform in Early Twentieth-Century China, 1901–1937* (Stanford, Calif.: Stanford University Press, 2008).

27. SHAC, 679/1/26915, IG Circular No. 4926 (August 23, 1934).

28. See, for instance, SHAC, 679/1/27720, Canton Dispatch No. 14333 (April 13, 1935), and Chefoo Dispatch No. 7469 (April 4, 1935).

29. GDPA, 95/1/1054, Kiungchow SR (June 1935), 2–4.

30. GDPA, 95/1/243, Kowloon Dispatch No. 10666 (March 30, 1935).

31. SHAC, 679/1/27720, Lungkow Dispatch No. 576 (April 3, 1936).

32. GDPA, 95/1/1053, Pakhoi SR (May 1935), "Appendix No. 1: Smuggling and Preventive Activities in Kwangchowwan," 3–4.

33. SHAC, 679/6/1226, "IG Confidential Correspondence with Kuan-wu Shu, 1936," and "Confidential Report of Trip to Tsinanfu" (June 28, 1936), in Inspector General to Director General (June 30, 1936).

34. For negotiations with other warlords, see Van de Ven, *Breaking with the Past*, 247–51, and Emily M. Hill, *Smokeless Sugar: The Death of a Provincial Bureaucrat and the Construction of China's National Economy* (Vancouver: University of British Columbia Press, 2010).

35. For more on extraterritoriality and nationalism in China, see Pär K. Cassel, *Grounds of Judgment: Extraterritoriality and Imperial Power in Nineteenth-Century China and Japan* (Oxford: Oxford University Press, 2012); Wesley R. Fishel, *The End of Extraterritoriality in China* (Berkeley: University of California Press, 1952); Edmund S. K. Fung, "The Chinese Nationalists and the Unequal Treaties 1924–1931," *Modern Asian Studies* 21, no. 4 (1987): 793–819; and Mary C. Wright, "Introduction: The Rising Tide of Change," in *China in Revolution: The First Phase, 1900–1913*, ed. M. C. Wright (New Haven: Yale University Press, 1968): 1–63.

36. C. C. Wu [Wu Chaoshu], "Foreign Relations of the Chinese Nationalist Government," *Foreign Affairs* 6, no. 4 (1928): 668.

37. See, in particular, Antony Anghie, *Imperialism, Sovereignty and the Making of International Law* (Cambridge: Cambridge University Press, 2005); Lauren Benton, *A Search for Sovereignty: Law and Geography in European Empires, 1400–1900* (Cambridge: Cambridge University Press, 2010); Kayaoglu, *Legal Imperialism*; Stephen D. Krasner, *Sovereignty: Organized Hypocrisy* (Princeton, N.J.: Princeton University Press, 1999); and Teemu Ruskola, *Legal Orientalism: China, the United States, and Modern Law* (Cambridge, Mass.: Harvard University Press, 2013).

38. Erik Esselstrom, *Crossing Empire's Edge: Foreign Ministry Police and Japanese Expansionism in Northeast Asia* (Honolulu: University of Hawai'i Press, 2009), 127–28.

39. Barbara J. Brooks, "Japanese Colonial Citizenship in Treaty Port China: The Location of Koreans and Taiwanese in the Imperial Order," in *New Frontiers: Imperialism's New Communities in East Asia, 1842–1953*, ed. R. Bickers and C. Henriot (Manchester: Manchester University Press, 2000), 111–12.

40. Businesses in Xiamen, for instance, displayed signs on storefronts advertising that they were foreign firms (*yanghang*) owned by Japanese nationals (*Riji*) and registered with the local consulate. Ri ji langren shiliao zhengji xiaozu, "Xiamen Ri ji langren jishu" (A record of Japanese vagrants in Xiamen), *Xiamen wenshi ziliao* 2 (1962): 15.

41. See, for instance, T. V. Soong [Song Ziwen], "The Economic and Financial Reconstruction of China," *CW*, May 5, 1928, 280.

42. Lauren Benton, *Law and Colonial Cultures: Legal Regimes in World History, 1400–1900* (Cambridge: Cambridge University Press, 2002), 211. For other cases of semicolonial polities embarking on legal reforms to reverse extraterritoriality, see Kayaoglu, *Legal Imperialism*.

43. For a critical look at the origins of this discourse, see especially Li Chen, *Chinese Law in Imperial Eyes: Sovereignty, Justice, and Transcultural Politics* (New York: Columbia University Press, 2016).

44. SHAC, 679/1/26910, IG Circular No. 4285 (August 15, 1931).

45. SHAC, 679/1/26911, Kuan-wu Shu Dispatch No. 7753 (July 28, 1932), in IG Circular No. 4468 (August 13, 1932).

46. For text of the treaty, see FRUS, 1928, 2:475–77 and *TAC*, 230–31.

47. Wang Ching-wei [Wang Jingwei] to Nelson T. Johnson (March 7, 1934), FRUS, 1934, 3:583.

48. British concessions in smaller treaty ports (e.g., Hankou, Jiujiang, Weihaiwei) were surrendered to the Nationalists in the late 1920s and early 1930s largely without a fight. See Robert A. Bickers, *Britain in China: Community, Culture and Colonialism 1900–1949* (Manchester: Manchester University Press, 1999), 139–43. For treaties regarding their retrocession, see *TAC*, 203–5, and 213–15.

49. Frederic Wakeman, *Policing Shanghai, 1927–1937* (Berkeley: University of California Press, 1995). Tong Lam convincingly argues that the link between policing and recovering sovereignty in China had its roots in late Qing state-building programs at the turn of the twentieth century. Tong Lam, "Policing the Imperial Nation: Sovereignty, International Law, and the Civilizing Mission in Late Qing China," *Comparative Studies in Society and History* 52, no. 4 (2010): 881–908.

50. This new policy was eventually codified in the Preventive Law and implemented across China in 1934.

51. SHAC, 679/1/27723, Preventive Secretary to Chief Secretary (May 23, 1931).

52. Nelson T. Johnson to Frederick Maze, 1 February 1934, FRUS, 1934, 3:579–81. The U.S. government believed that the treaty "did not accord to the Chinese Government any right to assume jurisdiction over the persons or property of American nationals." See William Phillips to Clarence E. Gauss, 5 November 1934, FRUS, 1934, 3:586. For a history of the U.S. Court for China, see Eileen P. Scully, *Bargaining with the State from Afar: American Citizenship in Treaty Port China, 1844–1942* (New York: Columbia University Press, 2001). For the introduction of American extraterritoriality in China, see Ruskola, *Legal Orientalism*.

53. C. W. Orde to Alexander Cadogan (July 8, 1935), FO 371/19322. The British Foreign Office maintained this position on the Joint Investigation Rules as early as 1927 in a memorandum on anticipated treaty revision with China. See Memorandum on Treaty Revision (January 6, 1927), FO 371/12459.

54. Suma Yakichirō to Hirota Kōki (June 2, 1934), *NGB*, Showa II-1-3, 641.

55. Hirota Kōki to Ariyoshi Akira (August 22, 1934), *NGB*, Showa II-1-3, 647. Interestingly, Japanese officials referred to the Joint Investigation Rules as *Kyōdō kaishin*—literally "mutual joint hearing." The word *kaishin* in Japanese is the same as the word *huishen* in Chinese, which had been traditionally used by Qing officials to denote the practice of sharing jurisdiction when adjudicating mixed cases between Han Chinese and non-Han Chinese. Qing officials later used the same term to describe joint hearings on mixed cases between Chinese and extraterritorialized foreigners. See Cassel, *Grounds of Judgment*, 24–25, 75–77. The term's continued usage by the Japanese is another incidental confirmation of Joint Investigation Rules' legally pluralistic heritage.

56. For a sample of such cases, see SHAC, 679/1/28138, Shanghai SR (August 1932), 2–3, and Shanghai SR (October 1932), 1–5. See also *SB*, August 25, 1932, 15, and August 31, 1932, 15.

57. *SB*, October 21, 1932, 10.

58. *SB*, June 12, 1933, 11. For other responses by Chinese chambers of commerce to Maritime Customs policing, see Felix Boecking, *No Great Wall: Trade, Tariffs, and Nationalism in*

Republican China, 1927–1945 (Cambridge, Mass.: Harvard University Asia Center, 2017), 184–85.

59. SHAC, 679/3/27757, Memorandum for Mr. E. A. Pritchard (April 20, 1936), 17.

60. See, for example, Jia Shiyi, *Guanshui yu guoquan* (Tariff autonomy and national sovereignty) (Shanghai: Caizhengbu zhu Hu diaocha huojiachu, 1927), 634–35.

61. *SB*, June 24, 1933, 12.

62. SHAC, 679/1/27723, Shanghai to Inspector General (November 21, 1934).

63. SHAC, 679/1/4135, PN No. 20 (August 19, 1935), 5–13.

64. SHAC, 679/1/901, Memorandum for Commissioner (July 27, 1943).

65. TJMA, W1/1/2658, Tientsin SR (January 1937), 1–3.

66. Such difficulties centered on the issue of proper jurisdiction of courts to hear smuggling cases. Two cases attracted particular attention from officials. On the Pinzhen case, SHAC, 679/1/28139, Shanghai SR (August 1935), 4–6, see *SB*, August 21, 1935, 12, and September 6, 1935, 15. On the Yisheng case, SHAC, 679/1/28139, Shanghai SR (November 1935), Appendix No. 2, and Shanghai SR (December 1935), Appendix No. 3, see *SB*, November 26, 1935, 10, and November 27, 1935, 11.

67. "Annual Resume of Preventive Work for 1936," in SHAC, 679/1/28140, Shanghai SR (December 1936), Appendix, 7.

68. Li Chen, "Law, Empire, and Historiography of Modern Sino-Western Relations: A Case Study of the Lady Hughes Controversy in 1784," *Law and History Review* 27, no. 1 (2009): 2.

69. Zhang Lai, foreword (*bianyan*) to *HFH*.

70. R. G. Howe to Alexander Cadogan (June 7, 1935), FO 371/19323.

71. For an overview of how nineteenth-century Western jurisprudence of sovereignty was linked to legal positivism, see Anghie, *Imperialism*, and Kayaoglu, *Legal Imperialism*.

72. Like other semicolonial and native regimes, China also "actively sought to remake [itself] by appropriating the logic and language of colonialism." Lam, "Policing the Imperial Nation," 885n14.

73. Benton, *Search for Sovereignty*.

74. In 1907, for instance, British ships from Hong Kong forced their way into the West River in Guangdong Province to search Chinese merchant ships in the name of combatting piracy and smuggling. See Lam, "Policing the Imperial Nation," 895.

75. Wright, *China's Struggle for Tariff Autonomy*, 662; SHAC, 679/1/26914, IG Circular No. 4742 (November 11, 1933).

76. Micah. S. Muscolino, *Fishing Wars and Environmental Change in Late Imperial and Modern China* (Cambridge, Mass.: Harvard University Asia Center, 2009), 108–9. For a brief overview of international discussions over the breadth of the territorial sea, see R. R. Churchill and A. V. Lowe, *The Law of the Sea*, 3rd ed. (Manchester: Manchester University Press, 1999), 77–79.

77. Muscolino, *Fishing Wars*, 116.

78. SHAC, 679/1/26910, IG Circular No. 4241 (June 5, 1931).

79. See Articles 10, 11, and 12 of the Preventive Law.

80. IMHA, 11-10-04-03-028, "Haiguan jisi jie cheng an" (Record of anti-smuggling zone limit for Maritime Customs) (March 6, 1935).

81. Rebecca Karl, *Staging the World: Chinese Nationalism at the Turn of the Twentieth Century* (Durham, N.C.: Duke University Press, 2002).

82. Until the late 1960s, the United Kingdom often issued protests affirming the three-mile limit. A. V. Lowe, "The Development of the Concept of the Contiguous Zone," *British Yearbook of International Law* 51, no. 109 (1981): 149 (quoted in Churchill and Lowe, *Law of the Sea*, 78).

83. Shidehara Kijūrō to Shigemitsu Mamoru (July 2, 1931), *NGB* Showa I-1-5, 991. To justify the three-mile limit, the Japanese Foreign Ministry cited the recently ratified Convention Between United States and Japan Respecting the Regulation of the Liquor Traffic of 1930 (*Shurei yusō torishimari ni kan suru jōyaku*). Japan first learned of Chinese plans to extend its claim to the twelve-mile mark from press reports. See Nanjing Consul Uemura to Shidehara Kijūrō (February 5, 1930), *NGB* Showa I-1-4, 817. In 1936, the Customs ordered preventive vessels to stay within the three-mile limit as a precaution in the face of Japanese naval harassment. SHAC, 679/26917, IG Circular No. 5307 (July 7, 1936).

84. FRUS, 1931, 3:971. The State Department cited Section 2760 of the Revised Statutes and Sections 581 and 586 of the Tariff Act of 1930. The United States's original designation of its twelve-mile contiguous zone under the Tariff Act of 1922 also sparked international controversy since it was done unilaterally. For an overview of the concept of the contiguous zone, see Churchill and Lowe, *Law of the Sea*, 132–40.

85. James C. Scott, *Seeing Like a State: How Certain Schemes to Improve the Human Condition Have Failed* (New Haven: Yale University Press, 1998).

86. SHAC, 679/1/26910, IG Circular No. 4161 (January 15, 1931). Native Customs stations (*changguan*) were the old Qing customs tollhouses that continued collecting duties on domestic trade while remaining independent of the Maritime Customs. Control of Native Customs stations within fifty *li* of treaty ports were turned over to the Maritime Customs in 1901 to help fund the disastrous Boxer indemnity. Duties collected from Native Customs stations officially belonged to the central government—the Qing court and later its Republican successor—but had long been expropriated by local governments. See SHAC, 679/1/26910, IG Circular No. 4240 (May 29, 1931).

87. *ZFD*, 4:4846–50, 5:656–60.

88. This figure might understate the level of compliance since re-registrations were not included. Data tabulated from SHAC, 679/1/4135, PN (various).

89. *HFH*, I, 29.

90. *HFH*, I, 31–33.

91. For other cases, see *HFH*, II, 12.

92. Emily Sohmer Tai, "Marking Water: Piracy and Property in the Premodern West," in *Seascapes: Maritime Histories, Littoral Cultures, and Transoceanic Exchanges*, ed. J. H. Bentley, R. Bridenthal, and K. Wigen (Honolulu: University of Hawai'i Press, 2007), 205–20.

93. Janice E. Thomson, *Mercenaries, Pirates, and Sovereigns* (Princeton, N.J.: Princeton University Press, 1996), 13.

94. SHAC, 679/1/20385, Chefoo Commissioner's Comments on Tientsin Commissioner's Dispatch No. 9414 (undated).

95. Data tabulated from SHAC, 679/1/4135, PN (various). For 1930 and 1931 figures, see SHAC, 679/1/27761, Letter from Inspector General to Kuan-wu Shu (October 3, 1935).

96. From 1932 to 1936, annual fines and confiscations at Shanghai, Tianjin, and Guangzhou averaged CN$1.3 million, CN$454,000, and CN$350,000, respectively. Average annual fines and confiscations during the same period at smaller ports were CN$687,000 for Xiamen and CN$424,000 for Shantou in the south, and CN$683,000 for Zhifu and CN$348,000 for Longkou in the north.

97. SHAC, 679/1/4135, PN 10 (August 30, 1933).

98. SHAC, 679/1/26912, IG Circular No. 4626 (May 13, 1933) and No. 4693 (August 17, 1933).

99. The Umezu-Ho and Doihara-Chin agreements of June 1935 created a "demilitarized zone" in North China that formally expelled Nationalist military and political influence from the region. Customs stations that remained in the region had to disarm their staff and patrol teams. East Hebei and Chahar declared their autonomy from Nanjing in late 1935 and sought to import Japanese goods duty free. For more details, see Akira Iriye, "Japanese Aggression and China's International Position, 1931–1949," in *The Cambridge History of China*, vol. 13: *Republican China, 1912–1949, Part 2*, ed. J. K. Fairbank and A. Feuerwerker (Cambridge: Cambridge University Press, 1986), 492–546; Son Jun Sik, *Zhanqian Riben zai Huabei de zousi huodong, 1933–1937* (Japan's prewar smuggling activities in North China, 1933–1937) (Taipei: Guoshi guan, 1997); and Emily M. Hill, "Japanese-Backed Smuggling in North China: Chinese Popular and Official Resistance, 1935–1937," in *Resisting Japan: Mobilizing for War in China, 1935–1945*, ed. D. Pong (Norwalk, Conn.: EastBridge, 2008).

100. Zhongguo wenti yanjiu hui, *Zousi wenti* (The smuggling problem) (Shanghai: Zhongguo wenti yanjiu hui, 1936), 11–12.

101. At the suggestion of the Ministry of Finance and Maritime Customs officials, the Executive Yuan in June 1936 made transacting smuggled goods punishable under Chapter 34, Article 349 of the Criminal Code—"Offenses of Receiving Stolen Property" (*zangwu zui*) (*ZFD*, 1:154). Goods for which import duties had not been paid were now classified as "stolen property." Recipients of such goods could be imprisoned for up to three years and fined up to CN$500. Others who transported, accepted in deposit, purchased, or otherwise aided in the disposal of illicit goods could be imprisoned for up to five years and fined up to CN$1,000. See SHAC, 679/1/26916, Ministry of Finance Dispatch No. 25983 (June 8, 1936), in IG Circular No. 5286 (June 1, 1936).

102. *ZFD*, 5:479–80. Offenders could be sentenced to terms ranging anywhere from three years to life. The new law also specified that attempts to conceal, transport, or sell smuggled goods—successful or otherwise—were to be punished as actual infringements. As its name suggests, the law was enacted provisionally for one year from June 1936, although the Ministry of Finance extended it at least twice for one-year periods in July 1937 and 1938. See SHAC, 679/1/26917, IG Circular No. 5532 (July 12, 1937), and SHAC, 679/1/26918, IG Circular No. 5703 (July 26, 1938). The law was repealed by the Ministry

of Finance under the Wang Jingwei regime in 1942. See SHAC, 679/9/5379, IG Circular No. 5814 (Bogus Customs) (October 23, 1942).

103. For an overview and critique of this literature, see Stuart P. Green, "Why It's a Crime to Tear the Tag off a Mattress: Overcriminalization and the Moral Content of Regulatory Offences," *Emory Law Journal* 46, no. 4 (1997): 1533–1615.

104. See, for instance, SHAC, 679/1/27750, Memo No. 12 to Inspector General: General Considerations Governing the Control of Smuggling and the Formation of a Preventive Service (1930).

105. While financially harmful, such cases, as one commissioner happily noted, were still relatively "rare." SHAC, 679/1/28140, Shanghai SR (March 1936), 4–5.

106. SHAC, 679/1/27720, Chinwangtao Dispatch No. 1241 (April 3, 1935).

107. GDPA, 95/1/1055, Amoy SR (July 1936), 2.

108. SHAC, 679/1/27723, Chefoo Commissioner to Preventive Secretary (October 4, 1934).

109. Hong Shen, *Zousi* (Smuggling) (Shanghai: Yi ban shudian, 1937), 54.

110. For cases in western Shandong, see SHAC, 679/1/28305, "Weekly Report" (May 5, 1937; May 12, 1937; and May 26, 1937). For the case of a coastal villager convicted under the Revised Punishment Code for concealing smuggled goods (thirty bags of sugar and twenty tins of matches) in his home, see GDPA, 95/1/1055, Amoy SR (August 1936), 16–17, and Amoy SR (October 1936), 10. For cases of sailors trafficking in sugar, silver, and rayon who were sentenced to prison from one to more than three years, see GDPA, 95/1/1056, Swatow SR (May 1937), 10–11. For a case of traffickers from two smuggling rings in Qingdao sentenced to prison sentences of various lengths (from a few months to life), see *SB*, February 3, 1937, 10.

111. GDPA, 95/1/1055, Swatow SR (September 1936), 6.

112. Xu, *Trial of Modernity*, 107–11, 172–73.

113. SHAC, 679/1/27720, Amoy Dispatch No. 9094 (August 19, 1935).

114. GDPA, 95/1/1054, Kowloon SR (March 1935), 5.

115. ZFD, 1:151.

116. *XFH*, 33, 83–84.

117. *XFH*, 33, 85–87.

4. SHADOW ECONOMIES AND POPULAR ANXIETIES

1. SHAC, 679/1/20403, Memorandum to Shanghai Commissioner (May 1, 1935), in Shanghai Dispatch No. 27344 (June 12, 1935).

2. Arthur N. Young, *China's Nation-Building Effort, 1927–1937: The Financial and Economic Record* (Stanford, Calif.: Hoover Institution Press, 1971), 74.

3. Toru Kubo, "The Tariff Policy of the Nationalist Government, 1929–36: A Historical Assessment," in *Japan, China, and the Growth of the Asian International Economy, 1850–1949*, ed. K. Sugihara (Oxford: Oxford University Press, 2005), 150.

4. Viscose Company, *The Story of Rayon* (New York: Viscose Company, 1937), 88.

5. Liang-lin Hsiao, *China's Foreign Trade Statistics, 1864–1949* (Cambridge, Mass.: Harvard University Press, 1974), 30.

6. Viscose Company, *Story of Rayon*, 90.

7. Paul K. Whang, "Real Silk vs. Artificial Silk," *CW*, November 25, 1933, 528.

8. The decline of Chinese silk exports not coincidentally occurred at the same time as the rise of the rayon industry. See H. D. Fong (Fang Xianting), *Rayon and Cotton Weaving in Tientsin* (Tianjin: Chihli Press, 1930), 9–10.

9. Inspectorate General of Customs, *Customs Import Tariff of the Republic of China* (Shanghai: Statistical Department of the Inspectorate General of Customs), 1928: 10, 1930: 16, and 1934: 12. Revisions identified by year of promulgation rather than year implemented.

10. Costs do not include transportation or insurance, which would raise costs further still.

11. Quanguo jingji weiyuanhui, *Renzaosi gongye baogaoshu* (Report on the rayon industry) (Nanjing: Quanguo jingji weiyuanhui, 1936), 84–85.

12. Kubo, "Tariff Policy," 163–64.

13. *ZH*, 8, no. 6 (1934): 138; 11, no. 3 (1934): 121.

14. In a series of letters to the *North China Herald*, a writer by the pen name "Merchant" described how rayon was landed in Hong Kong, smuggled into China, repackaged in Guangzhou, and forwarded to Shanghai, thereby bypassing the Customs which at the time did not have the authority to examine parcels. *NH*, August 22, 1934, 286, and September 5, 1934, 361.

15. *GN*, 4:1 (1935), 62.

16. *SF*, 199 (1937): 30–33. The rayon in question was the Heavenly Bridge brand.

17. Paul K. Whang, "China Is to Produce Her Own Artificial Silk," *CW*, November 24, 1934, 442.

18. Quanguo jingji weiyuanhui, *Renzaosi gongye baogaoshu*, 14. Kubo also arrives at the same conclusion. Kubo, "Tariff Policy," 164.

19. Frank Dikötter, *Exotic Commodities: Modern Objects and Everyday Life in China* (New York: Columbia University Press, 2006), 180.

20. Hsiao, *China's Foreign Trade Statistics*, 44.

21. Chu-yuan Cheng, "The United States Petroleum Trade with China," in *America's China Trade in Historical Perspective: The Chinese and American Performance*, ed. E. R. May and J. K. Fairbank (Cambridge, Mass.: Harvard University Press, 1986), 213–14. In 1911, Standard Oil yielded 50 percent of the East Asian market to Asiatic Petroleum Company (APC), a subsidiary of Royal Dutch Shell. In early 1934, it reserved 25 percent of the China market for itself while ceding 30 percent for APC, 25 percent for Soviet Oil Trust Soyuzneft, and 20 percent for Texaco. APC, in particular, proved a formidable competitor by matching Standard Oil's supply and retail network. See Sherman Cochran, *Encountering Chinese Networks: Western, Japanese, and Chinese Corporations in China, 1880–1937* (Berkeley: University of California Press, 2000), 29–31.

22. Cheng, "United States Petroleum Trade," 215–20; Dikötter, *Exotic Commodities*, 178–80.

23. Inspectorate General of Customs, *Customs Import Tariff*, 1928: 30, 1930: 44, and 1934: 31. Tariffs assessed per unit converted to ad valorem. For more details on the impact of

tariffs on the Chinese kerosene market nationwide, see Felix Boecking, *No Great Wall: Trade, Tariffs, and Nationalism in Republican China, 1927–1945* (Cambridge, Mass.: Harvard University Asia Center, 2017), 133–41.

24. *CP*, August 27, 1935, 9.

25. GDPA, 95/1/1053, Amoy SR (March 1934), Appendix No. 1.

26. Dikötter, *Exotic Commodities*, 222–24.

27. Inspectorate General of Customs, *Customs Import Tariff*, 1928: 24; 1930: 36, and 1934: 24–25. Tariffs assessed per unit converted to ad valorem.

28. Felix Boecking, "The Bitterness of Fiscal Realism: Guomindang Tariff Policy, China's Trade in Imported Sugar, and Smuggling 1928–1937," *Harvard Asia Quarterly* 13, no. 2 (2011): 17.

29. Quanguo jingji weiyuanhui, *Zhitang gongye baogaoshu* (Report on the sugar refining industry) (Nanjing: Quanguo jingji weiyuanhui, 1936), 1, 90.

30. Hsiao, *China's Foreign Trade Statistics*, 68. Boecking also agrees that successive increases in tariffs "caused a significant decline in both the quantity and value of legally imported sugar." See Boecking, *No Great Wall*, 133.

31. Quanguo jingji weiyuanhui, *Zhitang gongye baogaoshu* (Report on the sugar refining industry) (Nanjing: Quanguo jingji weiyuanhui, 1936), 55–61.

32. GDPA, 101/1/95, Swatow Dispatch No. 5152 (October 6, 1917).

33. See, for instance, the plaint from the Qinlian Sugar Merchants Guild representative Long Songhui to the Beihai Customs and the Guan-wu Shu in *GN*, 3:8 (1934), 153–54.

34. GDPA, 101/1/689, Letter from Shanghai Customs copied to Swatow Customs (December 5, 1936).

35. GDPA, 101/1/695, Memorandum from Appraising Department to Swatow Commissioner (December 17, 1937).

36. For the most comprehensive study on "official smuggling" by the Guangdong separatist regime, see Emily M. Hill, *Smokeless Sugar: The Death of a Provincial Bureaucrat and the Construction of China's National Economy* (Vancouver: University of British Columbia Press, 2010).

37. An American-educated engineer working at one of the province-owned factories during the 1930s had a slightly different estimate for the "smokeless sugar" sold during 1934. The engineer's estimate differed from the Customs' estimate, but the scale of profits remained substantial. See Xian Zi'en, "Ban tangchang jingguo ji qi zhenxiang" (Managing the sugar factory and other real facts), in *Nantian suiyue: Chen Jitang zhu Yue shiqi jianwen shilu* (Era of the southern empire: eyewitness historical accounts of the period of Chen Jitang's rule in Guangdong), ed. Guangzhou shi weiyuanhui wenshi ziliao yanjiu weiyuanhui (Guangzhou: Guangdong renmin chubanshe, 1987), 260–61.

38. GDPA, 101/1/47, Memorandum from Canton Customs to Swatow Customs (August 3, 1936).

39. SHAC, 679/1/27750, Memo No. 12 to IG (1930).

40. GDPA, 95/1/635, Letter from Guangzhou Sugar Guild to Kowloon Customs (April 22, 1932); "Tianjin zahuo tangye gonghui qing shanghui zhuanhan haiguan deng bumen

xiangcha zousi toushui shefa jinzhi wen" (Tianjin sundry goods and sugar guild requesting chamber of commerce to forward letter to Maritime Customs and other agencies
investigating ways to prohibit smuggling and tax evasion) (January 7, 1932), in *Tianjin
shanghui dang'an huibian, 1928–1937* (Compilation of archives of the Tianjin Chamber of
Commerce, 1928–1937), ed. Tianjin shi dang'an guan (Tianjin: Tianjin renmin chubanshe, 1996), 2:1739–40.

41. Inspectorate General of Customs, *Customs Import Tariff*, 1930: 34.

42. SHAC, 679/1/20419, IG Dispatch to Canton No. 139466 (February 16, 1932).

43. Kai Yiu Chan, *Business Expansion and Structural Change in Pre-war China: Liu Hongsheng and His Enterprises, 1920–1937* (Hong Kong: Hong Kong University Press, 2006),
116–23; Cochran, *Encountering Chinese Networks*, 156–76. For a detailed report on the
influx of smuggled matches from Taiwan into Fujian, see Wang Xuenian, "Huochai
jiashui suo yinqi de loushui huochai wenti" (Problems of smuggled matches arising
from tax increases on matches), in *Liu Hongsheng qiye shiliao* (Historical materials on
Liu Hongsheng's enterprises), ed. Shanghai shehui kexue yuan jingji yanjiusuo (Shanghai: Shanghai renmin chubanshe, 1981), 2: 167–68.

44. Young, *China's Nation-Building Effort*, 23.

45. *SB*, July 20, 1936, 10.

46. *ZY*, March 16, 1936, 2.

47. *NH*, December 9, 1936, 397. For more on the ambivalent attitudes expressed by Japanese
businesses toward smuggling in North China, see Boecking, *No Great Wall*, 174–76.

48. *GZ*, December 3, 1936, 2:3.

49. *GZ*, December 3, 1936, 2:3; December 4, 1936, 2:3.

50. "Resume Relating to the Smuggling Condition During the Year 1936," in TJMA,
W1/2658, Tientsin SR (December 1936), Appendix No. 1, 13.

51. *HZ*, May 10, 1936, 2:2.

52. *GN*, 4:1 (1935), 62.

53. SHAC, 679/1/28159, Canton SR (November 1933), 2–3.

54. GDPA, 95/1/1052, Pakhoi SR (December 1933), Appendix, 2–3.

55. GDPA, 95/1/1055, Swatow SR (December 1936), 6–7.

56. GDPA, 94/283, Tariff Secretary's Printed Memorandum No. 51 (June 5, 1936).

57. SHAC, 679/1/20403, Memorandum to Shanghai Commissioner (May 1, 1935), in
Shanghai Dispatch No. 27344 (June 12, 1935).

58. Xu noted that his family restored its fortunes shortly after this episode. In 1936, his family pooled its resources to secure a smaller bank loan. One of his uncles, blessed with a
"glib tongue" (*neng yan shan bian*), persuaded a supplier in Ji'nan to sell him on credit
120,000 yuan worth of products. The new store, selling hats, shoes, and other assorted
goods, proved to be a success. Xu did not specify whether the goods for the new store
were also smuggled. Xu Xueliang, "Fudong xie mao yang Guang huodian" (The Fudong
shoes, hat, foreign, and Cantonese goods store), in *Zhoucun shangbu* (The port of Zhoucun), ed. Shandong sheng zhengxie wenshi ziliao weiyuanhui (Ji'nan: Shandong renmin chubanshe, 1990), 231–32.

59. *SB*, March 6, 1936, 7; March 16, 1936, 10.

60. *SB*, January 25, 1937, 4.

61. *SB*, June 14, 1936, 9.

62. SHAC, 679/1/31865, Semi-official Dispatch No. 96 (August 13, 1936). The depositors were able to produce proof of duty payment for only 10 percent of the sugar.

63. *SB*, June 16, 1936, 10; May 11, 1936, 4.

64. *NH*, November 6, 1935, 254.

65. *SB*, February 3, 1937, 10. Nie, the Osaka-based supplier, escaped punishment.

66. *XFH*, 31:77–80.

67. While not focused on smuggling specifically, Man-houng Lin examines similar strategies by overseas Chinese merchants. See Man-houng Lin, "Overseas Chinese Merchants and Multiple Nationality: A Means for Reducing Commercial Risk (1895–1935)," *Modern Asian Studies* 35, no. 4 (2001): 985–1009.

68. Eric Tagliacozzo, *Secret Trades, Porous Borders: Smuggling and States Along a Southeast Asian Frontier, 1865–1915* (New Haven: Yale University Press, 2005), 373.

69. SHAC, 679/1/28161, Kowloon SR (April 1932), 3. For similar accounts reported elsewhere, see "Smuggling and Preventive Activities in Kwangchowwan," in GDPA, 95/1/1052, Pakhoi SR (April 1934).

70. *SB*, March 18, 1936, 5; March 20, 1936, 3.

71. GDPA, 95/1/1052, Swatow SR (July 1933), 7.

72. GDPA, 95/1/637, Letter from Superintendent to Kowloon Commissioner (August 9, 1937).

73. GDPA, 95/1/1052, Swatow SR (March 1933), 1.

74. GDPA, 95/1/74, Confidential Semi-official Memo from Kowloon Customs to Amoy Customs (January 16, 1934).

75. *SB*, September 17, 1936, 10.

76. GDPA, 95/1/1056, Swatow SR (December 1937), 10.

77. *SB*, April 14, 1936, 7.

78. Deng Quansheng, "Jiefang qian de Hua'nan haiguan jisi" (Maritime Customs anti-smuggling in South China before Liberation), *Guangdong wenshi ziliao* 9 (1963): 80.

79. GDPA, 95/1/74, Confidential Semi-official Memo from Kowloon Customs to Amoy Customs, May 13, 1933.

80. GDPA, 101/1/671, Canton Semi-official Dispatch No. 651, August 9, 1937.

81. GDPA, 95/1/1054, Amoy SR (March 1935), 7–8.

82. "Match Smuggling Activities Injure Legitimate Business," *CW*, September 1, 1934, 24. For Liu's petition, see *SB*, August 24, 1934, 13. According to the industry, the Customs was the only central-government agency that auctioned rather than destroyed contraband matches. Quanguo jingji weiyuanhui, *Huochai gongye baogaoshu* (Report on the matches industry) (Nanjing: Quanguo jingji weiyuanhui, 1935), 66–67. For another complaint regarding the auction of contraband matches, see letter from Hua Futang, China Match Company Xiamen branch director, to Shao Nantang, Ministry of Finance assistant director, June 7, 1935, in *Liu Hongsheng qiye shiliao*, 2:169.

83. *HFH*, 9, 231–35.
84. Dikötter, *Exotic Commodities*, 43.
85. Karl Gerth, *China Made: Consumer Culture and the Creation of the Nation* (Cambridge, Mass.: Harvard University Asia Center, 2003).
86. Carlton Benson, "Consumers Are Also Soldiers: Subversive Songs from Nanjing Road During the New Life Movement," in *Inventing Nanjing Road: Commercial Culture in Shanghai, 1900–1945*, ed. S. Cochran (Ithaca, N.Y.: East Asia Program, Cornell University, 1999): 91–132; Gerth, *China Made*.
87. See, for example, *Liangyou* 128 (1937): 4–6.
88. Gerth, *China Made*, 40–43.
89. Gerth, 162.
90. GDPA, 95/1/1053, Amoy SR (December 1934), 8–9.
91. *SB*, August 29, 1936, 10. The incident was reported in a report from the Xiamen Customs in far less detail, perhaps reflecting the routine nature of the incident. See GDPA, 95/1/1055, Amoy SR (August 1936), 3–4.
92. SHAC, 679/1/26911, Letter from shipping companies to Shanghai General Chamber of Commerce forwarded to Inspectorate General of Customs, September 25, 1931, in IG Circular No. 4343 (October 23, 1931). The shipping companies included the China Navigation Co. (Butterfield and Swire) and Indo-China Steam Navigation Co. (Jardine Matheson); the Japanese Dairen Kisen Kaisha and Nisshin Kisen Kaisha; and the China Merchants Steam Navigation Co.
93. GDPA, 95/1/239, Kowloon Dispatch No. 10256 (June 3, 1933); SHAC, 679/1/28159, Canton SR (May 1932), 1. The ordinance in question is the Hong Kong Importation and Exportation Amendment Ordinance of 1932.
94. SHAC, 679/1/28138, Letter from Indo-China Steam Navigation Co. to Shanghai Commissioner (May 12, 1933), in Shanghai SR (May 1933).
95. See, for instance, SHAC, 679/1/28162, Letter from Indo-China Steam Navigation Co. to Kowloon Commissioner (August 7, 1933), in Kowloon SR (July 1933).
96. JSSIII, 2/18, 96.1, 40, Shanghai Office to London Office, 1 September 1930. Smuggling proved to be a contentious issue between management and labor. The former, under pressure from the Customs, introduced various disciplinary measures to discourage smuggling. The latter, seeking to unionize, resented the monthly wage deductions for the smuggling deposit.
97. GDPA, 101/1/667, IG to Swatow Commissioner (April 30, 1934).
98. An editorial in the Kuala Lumpur newspaper *Yiqun Ribao* reported on the complaints of returning emigrants from the Straits Settlements regarding customs entry procedures. The *Lingdong Republican News* (*Lingdong Minguo Ribao*) reported on two government officials traveling to Siam and Singapore who received numerous complaints from local Overseas Chinese communities on being "relentlessly fined" by the Shantou Customs when returning to China. See GDPA, 101/1/107, Swatow Dispatch No. 7092 (January 9, 1933).
99. SHAC, 679/1/4135, PN No. 12 (November 22, 1933).

100. GDPA, 101/1/95, Swatow Dispatch No. 7124 (March 30, 1933).

101. "A Discourse on Runners Prepared for the Smuggling Report of July 1936 but not embodied in the Report," in GDPA, 95/1/1055, Swatow SR (July 1936).

102. Article from *Shanghai Times*, January 17, 1934, in SHAC, 679/1/32371, Swatow Semiofficial Dispatch No. 620 (January 30, 1934).

103. GDPA, 101/1/154, IG Dispatch to Swatow No. 158299 (September 2, 1935).

104. SHAC, 679/1/4135, PN No. 27 (July 7, 1936).

105. SHAC, 679/1/4135, PN No. 17 (October 22, 1934).

106. GDPA, 101/1/630, Swatow SR (February 1937), 1–2

107. *GN*, 3:8 (1934), 302–3.

108. See, for instance, complaints from villagers along the Hong Kong–Shenzhen border in GDPA, 95/1/2127, Memo from Chief Tidesurveyor to Commissioner, July 15, 1935.

109. Article 2: "Search of females shall be made by Customs female searchers."

110. One report from 1916, for instance, mentions that a woman searcher was employed among the staff at the Kowloon Railway Station. See GDPA, 95/1/216, Kowloon Dispatch No. 7890, February 1, 1916.

111. GDPA, 95/1/1054, Amoy SR (August 1935), 7.

112. GDPA, 101/1/108, Swatow Dispatch No. 7699 (October 13, 1937).

113. Literally "like wolf and like tiger." This was a common epithet levied at the behavior of customs officials.

114. *XR*, August 10, 1935, 7. This incident was also alluded to in GDPA, 95/1/1056, Swatow SR (February 1937), 2–3.

115. *XR*, June 6, 1937, 4.

116. Gail Hershatter, *Women in China's Long Twentieth Century* (Berkeley: University of California Press, 2007), 53.

117. Xing Sheng, "Zousi huo ren de dong" (The smuggler's cave), *Ertong shijie* 27, no. 24 (1931): 10–14.

118. Xing, "Zousi huo ren de dong," 12.

119. Xiaomei Chen, "Mapping a 'New' Dramatic Canon: Rewriting the Legacy of Hong Shen," in *Modern China and the West: Translation and Cultural Mediation*, ed. H. Y. Peng and I. Rabut (Leiden: Brill, 2014), 229.

120. Hong Shen, *Zousi* (Smuggling) (Shanghai: Yi ban shudian, 1937).

121. David Der-wei Wang, "Chinese Literature from 1841 to 1937," in *The Cambridge History of Chinese Literature*, 2 vols., ed. K. S. Chang and S. Owen (Cambridge: Cambridge University Press), 2:486.

122. Original quotation from Hong, *Zousi*, 1. Translation from Liang Luo, "Reading Hong Shen Intermedially," *Modern Chinese Literature and Culture* 27, no. 2 (2015): 237.

123. Walter J. Meserve and Ruth I. Meserve, "Hung Shen: Chinese Dramatist Trained in America," *Theatre Journal* 31, no. 3 (1979): 32.

124. Hong, *Zousi*, 228.

125. Hong, 236.

126. Hong, 229.

5. ECONOMIC BLOCKADES AND WARTIME TRAFFICKING

1. Office of Strategic Services (OSS), "Trade Between Occupied China and Free China" (Washington, D.C.: Office of Strategic Services, Research and Analysis Branch, Far Eastern Section, 1942).

2. Eastman argues that the wartime Sino-Japanese trade was "a pernicious practice" that corrupted officers that should have been engaged in fighting the enemy and "weakened the already frail moral fiber of the Chinese army." Lloyd E. Eastman, "Facets of an Ambivalent Relationship: Smuggling, Puppets, and Atrocities During the War, 1937–1945," in *The Chinese and the Japanese: Essays in Political and Cultural Interactions*, ed. Akira Iriye (Princeton, N.J.: Princeton University Press, 1980), 283.

3. Brett Sheehan, *Industrial Eden: A Chinese Capitalist Vision* (Cambridge, Mass.: Harvard University Press, 2015), 97.

4. For more details, see Mark Peattie, Edward Drea, and Hans Van de Ven, eds., *The Battle for China: Essays on the Military History of the Sino-Japanese War of 1937–1945* (Stanford, Calif.: Stanford University Press, 2011).

5. SHAC, 679/1/26919, IG Circular No. 5545 (July 26, 1937). The six ports were Tianjin, Qinhuangdao, Qingdao, Zhifu, Weihaiwei, and Longkou.

6. *KJF*, 1:185. The regulation was directed at large-scale export at 100,000 *jin* or more.

7. SHAC, 679/1/26919, IG Circular No. 5582 (September 13, 1937).

8. Resin: SHAC, 679/1/26919, IG Circular No. 5567 (August 24, 1937); mercury: SHAC, 679/1/26919, IG Circular No. 5593 (October 2, 1937); bamboo, hemp, ramie, and seaweed: SHAC, 679/1/26919, IG Circular No. 5597 (October 7, 1937). This list is by no means exhaustive.

9. SHAC, 679/1/26919, IG Circular No. 5609 (October 22, 1937).

10. For examples of Chinese businessmen crossing enemy lines, see the case of New Asia Pharmaceutical Company "fixer" Xu Guanqun in Sherman Cochran, *Chinese Medicine Men: Consumer Culture in China and Southeast Asia* (Cambridge, Mass.: Harvard University Press, 2006), 89–117. See also the case of other Shanghai capitalists in Parks M. Coble, *Chinese Capitalists in Japan's New Order: The Occupied Lower Yangzi, 1937–1945* (Berkeley: University of California Press, 2003).

11. SHAC, 679/1/26919, IG Circular No. 5650 (February 24, 1938).

12. SHAC 679/6/1232, Letter from IG to Kuan-wu Shu (November 8, 1937).

13. SHAC 679/6/232, Letters from IG to Kuan-wu Shu (November 16, 1937; November 17, 1937; November 18, 1937). The incident was also reported in SB, November 17, 1937, 7.

14. "Resume of Smuggling Conditions in Tientsin 1937," in TJMA, W1/2658, Tientsin SR (December 1937), Appendix No. 2, 10.

15. "Annual Resume of Preventive Work at Shanghai for 1937," in SHAC 679/1/28140, Shanghai SR (December 1937), 5.

16. So successful was the Shantou Customs in its efforts, in fact, that it racked up almost CN$325,000 in fines and confiscations during 1938. This amount was lower than the average of CN$424,000 from 1932 to 1936 but ranked second-highest among all ports in 1938.

17. SHAC 679/1/27757, "Memorandum to Mr. A. H. Forbes, Preventive Secretary" (October 23, 1939), 7.

18. For the Regulations Governing the Prohibition of Enemy Goods, see *JJ*, 1938, 1:19, 850–51. For the Regulations Governing the Prohibition on the Transport of Goods to Aid the Enemy, see *JJ*, 1938, 1:19, 851–52.

19. Sifayuan yuanzi no. 2053 (August 22, 1940) and no. 2113 (January 15, 1941), in *Sifayuan jieshi huibian* (Collection of interpretations by Judicial Yuan), ed. Sifayuan (Taipei: Sifayuan mishuchu, 1989), 4:1755, 4:1802. Both interpretations cited Article 6 of the Regulations Governing the Prohibition on the Transport of Goods to Aid the Enemy.

20. "Caizhengbu guanyu zhanshi maoyi zhengce ji sheshi gaikuang de baogao" (Report by the Ministry of Finance on wartime trade policies and measures) (1945), in *MDZ*, 5.2: Caizheng jingji, 9, 414–21.

21. William C. Kirby, "Technocratic Organization and Technological Development in China, 1928–1953," in *Science and Technology in Post-Mao China*, ed. D. F. Simon and M. Goldman (Cambridge, Mass.: Harvard University Press, 1989), 23–43; Kirby, "The Chinese War Economy: Mobilization, Control, and Planning in Nationalist China," in *China's Bitter Victory: The War with Japan, 1937–1945*, ed. J. C. Hsiung and S. I. Levine (Armonk, N.Y.: M. E. Sharpe, 1992), 185–212. The MOEA replaced the Ministry of Industry (Shiye bu) and the National Economic Council (Jingji weiyuanhui).

22. Two companies were the North China Development Company (Hoku Shi kaihatsu kaisha) and the Central China Development Company (Kachū shinkō kaisha). Both were holding companies that organized and financed subsidiary firms. For more details, see John H. Boyle, *China and Japan at War, 1937–1945: The Politics of Collaboration* (Stanford, Calif.: Stanford University Press, 1972) 102–3, 116–19.

23. See, for instance, GMDR, 3 107-950, Enclosure in letter from Weng Wenhao to the National Defense Supreme Commission Secretariat (July 13, 1940).

24. R. Keith Schoppa, *In a Sea of Bitterness: Refugees During the Sino-Japanese War* (Cambridge, Mass.: Harvard University Press, 2011), 281.

25. Yu-kwei Cheng, *Foreign Trade and Industrial Development of China: An Historical and Integrated Analysis Through 1948* (Washington, D.C.: University Press of Washington, D.C., 1956), 128.

26. SHAC, 679/1/4145, CIS No. 16 (February 16, 1942).

27. SHAC, 679/1/4145, CIS No. 61 (March 10, 1942).

28. For overview of some exemptions, see "Caizhengbu guanyu zhanshi maoyi zhengce ji sheshi gaikuang de baogao," in *MDZ*, 5.2: Caizheng jingji, 9, 418–20.

29. See, for instance, *SB*, February 4, 1939, 14. Appeals by Zhejiang cotton merchants pointed to the fact that the city's foreign concession remained unoccupied and stressed how the blockade adversely affected the livelihood of merchants and farmers alike.

30. *JJ*, 1939, 2:7, 164–65. The law effectively ratified the new policy that had been adopted the month before. See *SB*, February 28, 1939, 9.

31. SHAC, 679/1/4145, CIS No. 82 (March 26, 1942).

32. SHAC, 679/8/143, CIS No. 102 (April 14, 1942).

33. See, for instance, the government's announcement in *SB*, July 11, 1939, 10.

34. *JJ*, 1939, 2:20–21, 541. For Liu Hongsheng's wartime activities, see Coble, *Chinese Capitalists in Japan's New Order*, 182–94.

35. *JJ*, 1939, 2:20–21, 542.

36. *JJ*, 1939, 2:20–21, 539–40. Mills #1, #5, #6, #7, and #8 were transferred from the Japanese military to Japanese companies as compensation for property losses elsewhere in China. Mills #2 and #9 were registered as American and British, respectively. For Shenxin textile mills' wartime ownership, see Coble, *Chinese Capitalists*, 115–24.

37. Coble, *Chinese Capitalists*, 19–29.

38. IMHA, 18-26-01-003-02, Telegram from Huang Shaohong to Chiang Kai-shek (July 15, 1940).

39. Duidi jingji fengsuo weiyuanhui, *Gesheng huoyun diaocha baogao* (Investigative report on transport in the provinces) (Chongqing: Guofang zuigao weiyuanhui, 1941), 56, 63.

40. *ZD*, 4, 1940, 25–42.

41. Cheng, *Foreign Trade*, 128.

42. IMHA, 18-26-01-003-02, Executive Yuan Meeting Notes (March 3, 1940).

43. *JJ*, 1942, 5:13–14, 352–63.

44. Zhongyang diaocha tongji ju, *Di wu nian zhi wokou jingji qinlüe* (The fifth year of the Japanese pirates' economic invasion) (Chongqing: Zhongyang diaocha tongji ju, 1943), 77–78.

45. IMHA, 18-26-01-003-02, Proposal from the Transport Control Bureau (June 22, 1940).

46. For more details on Dai Li's wartime smuggling networks, see Frederic Wakeman, *Spymaster: Dai Li and the Chinese Secret Service* (Berkeley: University of California Press, 2003), 320–29, and "Shanghai Smuggling," in *In the Shadow of the Rising Sun: Shanghai Under Japanese Occupation*, ed. C. Henriot and W. H. Yeh (Cambridge: Cambridge University Press, 2004), 116–49.

47. Felix Boecking, *No Great Wall: Trade, Tariffs, and Nationalism in Republican China, 1927–1945* (Cambridge, Mass.: Harvard University Asia Center, 2017), 216. For more on the Customs' breakup, see Robert A. Bickers, "The Chinese Maritime Customs at War, 1941–45," *Journal of Imperial and Commonwealth History* 36, no. 2 (2008): 295–311.

48. *ZD*, 27, 1941, 21–23.

49. "Guomin canzhenghui canzhengyuan Liu Mingyang deng jianyi gaijin maoyi tongzhi banfa de ti'an" (Draft [report] of suggestions on ways to improve commercial controls by National Political Council members Liu Mingyang and others) (December 1943), in *MDZ*, 5.2: Caizheng jingji, 9, 528.

50. For various reports on such incidents, see FO 371/27653.

51. Graham Peck, *Two Kinds of Time* (1950; reprint, Seattle: University of Washington Press, 2008), 573. Qi offers profit figures for wartime trafficking, which varied greatly by time, place, and commodity. Qi Chunfeng, *Zhong Ri jingji zhan zhong de zousi huodong, 1937–1945* (Smuggling activities in Sino-Japanese economic war, 1937–1945) (Beijing: Renmin chubanshe, 2002), 249–52. For the regularity of travel between free and occupied

China during the stalemate from October 1938 on, see Eastman, "Facets of an Ambivalent Relationship," and Parks Coble, *China's War Reporters: The Legacy of Resistance Against Japan* (Cambridge, Mass.: Harvard University Press, 2015), 80–103.

52. *DJH*, 56 (March 1944), Qingbao, 11.

53. Nationalist war zone commanders, for instance, managed their own smuggling pipelines to and from Japanese-occupied areas to supply their own troops. Chiang Kai-shek, for example, criticized General Tang Enbo, hero of the Battle of Taierzhuang, for failing to hold the city of Luoyang during the 1944 Ichigō Campaign because Tang was purportedly "preoccupied with smuggling" rather than with military preparedness. See Hans Van de Ven, *China at War: Triumph and Tragedy in the Emergence of the New China 1937–1952* (London: Profile Books, 2017), 182–85.

54. GMDR, 3 107-942.6: "Opinion on the blockade against the smuggling of enemy goods" (*Chajin dihuo zousi yijian*) from Gu Zhutong to Weng Wenhao (undated), in enclosure to letter from Weng Wenhao to Chiang Kai-shek, Chairman of Committee on Military Affairs (March 30, 1940).

55. On Hong Kong as wartime smuggling entrepôt, see Minami Manshū Tetsudō Kabushiki Kaisha sangyōbu, *Honkon o chūshin to suru tokushu bōeki narabini kaiun jijō* (Concerning the special trade and maritime shipping situation centered in Hong Kong) (Dalian: Minami Manshū Tetsudō Kabushiki Kaisha, 1938), and Minami Manshū Tetsudō Kabushiki Kaisha Shanhai iimusho chōsashitsu, *Bōeki jō no kanten yori mitaru Honkon no enshōsei* (Examination of Hong Kong's support for Jiang from a commercial perspective) (Shanghai: Minami Manshū Tetsudō Kabushiki Kaisha, 1941).

56. Hong Kong's share of imports into Free China increased from 4.7 percent in 1938 to 13.8 percent in 1939, 40.2 percent in 1940, and 58.3 percent in 1941. This increase, of course, was overdetermined by the fall of many coastal ports to the Japanese as well as disruptions from the hostilities. Cheng, *Foreign Trade*, 71.

57. *SB*, March 18, 1939, 5. "National products" (*guohuo*) were classified on a sliding scale depending on the national identity, source, or ownership of capital, management, raw materials, and labor. For more details, see Karl Gerth, *China Made: Consumer Culture and the Creation of the Nation* (Cambridge, Mass.: Harvard University Asia Center, 2003), 196–97.

58. GMDR, 3 107-950, Enclosure in letter from Weng Wenhao to the National Defense Supreme Commission Secretariat (April 19, 1940). For more on trafficking along the Yangzi, see Tobari Keisuke, "NitChū Sensō shita no Chōkō ryūiki ni okeru 'mitsuyu' (1937–1941)" ("Smuggling" around the Yangzi River area during the Second Sino-Japanese War), *Hōgaku kenkyū* 87, no. 7 (2014): 37–99; no. 8 (2014): 39–87; no. 9 (2014): 27–84.

59. *DJQ*, 3 (July 1, 1939), 1:195; 4 (September 1, 1939), 1:348–49. "Jardine, Matheson & Co." was stamped in the company's Chinese name, Yingshang Yihe yanghang. An investigation team would report a few years later that the Henan-Anhui border was "full of repackaged enemy goods." See GMDR, 3 107-950, Enclosure in letter from Weng Wenhao to the National Defense Supreme Commission Secretariat (July 13, 1940).

60. *SB*, January 27, 1940, 8. The "fish market" is also referred to in *SB*, January 20, 1940, 10. For the island's role as "main maritime entrepôt in the coastal smuggling trade," see also Schoppa, *In a Sea of Bitterness*, 270–71.

61. SHAC, 679/1/4145, CIS No. 48 (February 28, 1942).

62. Gerth, *China Made*, 179–80.

63. Stories of merchants or travelers being attacked by pirates or other bandits were not uncommon. See, for example, *HZ*, December 18, 1940, 2:1.

64. See, for instance, *SB*, June 6, 1939, 6; June 24, 1939; and August 22, 1939.

65. *HZ*, July 25, 1940, 2:1.

66. *DJQ*, 5 (December 1, 1939), 2:64–65.

67. Chen Jiadong, "Kang Ri shiqi Li Hanhun chuli Nanlu sixiao neimu" (The inside story on Li Hanhun disposing of Nanlu's smugglers during the War of Resistance), *Guangzhou wenshi ziliao xuanji* 19 (1980): 234–46.

68. See the laws creating the 1938 blockade in table 5.1.

69. GMDR, 3 107-950, Enclosure in letter from Weng Wenhao to the National Defense Supreme Commission Secretariat (July 13, 1940).

70. Peck, *Two Kinds of Time*, 573.

71. Wu employs the example of the southern Guangdong village of Meilü to illustrate his point. The village obtained permission and domestic sales passes from the Ministry of Finance to export its timber, and nearby localities quickly sent their timber to Meilü for export. Wu Yuxuan, "Zhanqu zousi wenti" (The smuggling problem in war zones) *Caizheng pinglun* 5, no. 2 (1941): 30.

72. GMDR, 3 107-950, Enclosure in letter from Weng Wenhao to the National Defense Supreme Commission Secretariat (July 29, 1940).

73. Lu Guoxiang, "Xian jieduan zousi wenti" (The smuggling problem's current phase), *Caizheng pinglun* 3, no. 6 (1940): 40–41.

74. Duidi jingji fengsuo weiyuanhui, *Gesheng huoyun diaocha baogao*, 48.

75. SHAC, 679/1/32566, "Luichow Semi-official, 1943–1945," Luichow Semi-official Dispatch No. 242 (April 23, 1943).

76. See Article 15 of the Regulations Governing the Prohibition of Enemy Goods and Article 7 of Regulations Governing the Prohibition on the Transport of Goods to Aid the Enemy. It should be noted that "harboring" (*baobi*) was a broad category that was sometimes used to refer to protecting.

77. SHAC, 679/1/4145, Ministry of Finance telegram, No. 60163 (March 6, 1942), in CIS No. 70 (March 16, 1942).

78. For policies by North China puppet government, see Zhongyang diaocha tongji ju, *Di wu nian zhi wokou jingji qinlüe*, 54–62. For policies by the Central China puppet government, see Zhongyang diaocha tongji ju, *Di wu nian zhi wokou jingji qinlüe*, 62–65.

79. Schoppa, *In a Sea of Bitterness*, 261–62. Such protection, of course, became more difficult to secure after the outbreak of the Pacific War in 1941.

80. *SB*, April 26, 1940, 10.

81. *SB*, March 18, 1938, 5.

82. *SB*, July 13, 1939, 10.

83. *DJH*, 58 (May 1944), Qingbao, 3.

84. *DJH*, 63 (October 1944), Qingbao, 7.

85. *SB*, December 24, 1938, 11. Such shipments, of course, paid no duties. In one instance, a convoy of more than twenty ships each unloaded a thousand bags of sugar at Ningbo. Losses to the Nationalist government were estimated to be in the hundreds of thousands of yuan.

86. *DJH*, 54 (January 1944), Qingbao, 2–3.

87. Weiting Guo, "From Female Bandit to Legendary Heroine: Life of Huang Bamei in Wartime China, 1937–1955," paper presented at the annual meeting of the Association for Asian Studies, Toronto, 2017.

88. Fuzhou Consul K. W. Tribe to British Ambassador Humphrey Prideaux-Brune (December 30, 1943), FO 371/41648.

89. John C. Caldwell, "General Report on Fukien Province," in Dispatch No. 2234 (February 26, 1944) from American Embassy, Chungking, China to Department of State, U.S. Department of State Document 893.00/15300, 5–7.

90. Lai, for instance, shows how the CCP in Shandong during the war traded with the Japanese army and navy under favorable terms through exchange rate manipulation. So important was this trade that it came to constitute the primary source of the CCP's income and laid the fiscal foundations for the CCP's postwar victory. Sherman Xiaogang Lai, *A Springboard to Victory: Shandong Province and Chinese Communist Military and Financial Strength, 1937–1945* (Leiden: Brill, 2011).

91. From 1905 to 1948, China (28 percent) ranked first in global tungsten production, followed by the United States (13 percent). See K. C. Li and Chongyou Wang, *Tungsten: Its History, Geology, Ore-Dressing, Metallurgy, Chemistry, Analysis, Applications, and Economics*, 3rd ed. (New York: Reinhold, 1955), 424.

92. Reflecting tungsten's importance during World War I, the British government commandeered all tungsten from the empire at a fixed price of 60s. per unit. Market prices in the United States, however, soared to 90s. per unit. See Robert Slessor, "Tungsten Mining in China," *Engineering and Mining Journal* 109, no. 5 (1920): 344.

93. For more information on the value of tungsten in such agreements, see Arthur N. Young, *China and the Helping Hand, 1937–1945* (Cambridge, Mass.: Harvard University Press, 1963), 132–35, and *China's Wartime Finance and Inflation, 1937–1945* (Cambridge, Mass.: Harvard University Press, 1965), 97–108.

94. Xu Weixiao, "Zousi wu" (Tungsten smuggling), *Dafeng xunkan* 14 (1939): 433.

95. Lin Lanfang, *Ziyuan weiyuanhui de tezhong kuangchan tongzhi (1936–1949)* (Control of special minerals by the National Resources Commission [1936–1949]) (Taipei: Guoli zhengzhi daxue lishi xuexi, 1998), 135.

96. Cai Qian, *Yue sheng duiwai maoyi diaocha baogao* (An investigative report on the foreign trade in the Guangdong province) (Shanghai: Shangwu yinshu guan, 1939), 23.

97. *JJ*, 1938, 1:18, 790–93.

98. For description of the central government controls, see William C. Kirby, *Germany and Republican China* (Stanford, Calif.: Stanford University Press, 1984), 211. For an overview of Jiangxi miners' techniques and organization, see Cheng Yifa, "Jiangxi zhi wu ye" (The tungsten industry of Jiangxi), *Ziyuan weiyuanhui jikan* 1, no. 2 (1941): 1–19. For a description of Jiangxi mines during the post–World War I lull, see Robert Slessor, "Tungsten Mining in China" and "Chinese Non-Ferrous Metals," *Proceedings of the Australasian Institute of Mining and Metallurgy*, no. 65 (1927): 51–116.

99. According to estimates, each miner could conceal up to 15 *jin* (roughly 16 pounds) in his clothes. Cai, *Yue sheng duiwai maoyi diaocha baogao*, 24. For description of tungsten smuggling in Guangdong, see "Zhong Jienian zhuan Guangdong wusha dujue zousi zhi liang da genben wenti gao" (Draft [report] of two fundamental problems with stopping tungsten smuggling in Guangdong composed by Zhong Jienian) (February 1938), in *MDZ*, 5.5: Caizheng jingji, 694–97. For particular routes, see Lin, *Ziyuan weiyuanhui de tezhong kuangchan tongzhi*, 172–73.

100. HKPR, HKMS175/1/717, "Xianggang si wu qingxing diaocha baogao" (Investigative report on the situation of smuggled tungsten in Hong Kong) (March 1937).

101. Cai, *Yue sheng duiwai maoyi diaocha baogao*, 24–25. During the same period from 1934 through 1937, Chinese tungsten production made up 30.5 percent, 35.6 percent, and 30.7 percent, respectively, of global tungsten production. Data calculated from Li and Wang, *Tungsten*, 422–23.

102. HKPR, HKMS175/1/717, "Xianggang si wu qingxing diaocha baogao" (March 1937).

103. D. F. Landale to W. J. Keswick (November 23, 1939), FO 371/23495. The junks employed the time-honored tactic of using false bottoms.

104. Minami Manshū Tetsudō Kabushiki Kaisha Shanhai iimusho, *Bōeki jō no kanten yori mitaru Honkon no enshōsei*, 30–33.

105. Xu, "Zousi wu," 433.

106. Hong Shen, *Zousi* (Smuggling) (Shanghai: Yi ban shudian, 1937), 15–56.

107. Xiao Zili, "Zhanshi Riben dui Zhongguo wusha de juelue yu Minguo zhengfu de yingdui" (Wartime plunder of China's tungsten ore by Japan and the Republican government's response), *Kang Ri zhanzheng yanjiu* 1 (2007): 150.

108. Lin, *Ziyuan weiyuanhui de tezhong kuangchan tongzhi*, 197–98. Similar figures were reported elsewhere. In a 1941 report from Dianbai County in Guangdong, for instance, officials reported that smuggled tungsten was sold for CN$16 to CN$20 per kilogram, or four to five times the official price of CN$3.75 per kilogram. AH, 003-010303-0102, Committee on Economic Blockade Against the Enemy to National Resources Commission (December 19, 1941).

109. AH, 003-010303-0102, Qingbao (October 27, 1942), in Ministry of Finance telegram, No. 9052 (November 15, 1942).

110. HKPR, HKMS175/1/708, R. Grimshaw to Wang Wenhao (September 13, 1939); Lu Man, "Guangzhou lunxian hou Wang wei qun chou zhi zheng" (The struggle among

Wang Jingwei puppet regime's mean persons after the fall of Guangzhou), in "Guang-zhou Kangzhan ji shi" (Record of Guangzhou during the War of Resistance), ed. Guangzhou shi zhengxie wenshi ziliao weiyuanhui, special issue, *Guangzhou wenshi* 48, 1995: 74–82; Xiao Zili, "Zhanshi Riben dui Zhongguo wusha de juelue yu Minguo zhengfu de yingdui," 140, 143–44. Jincheng was one of a handful of companies in Macao dealing in smuggled tungsten. See *DJH*, 57 (April 1944), Qingbao, 17–18.

111. "Tongji Hanjian renfan biao" (List of traitor suspects), *Taiwan sheng zhengfu gongbao*, 36/37 (1947), 576.

112. Eastman, "Facets of an Ambivalent Relationship," 283–84.

113. Xiao,"Zhanshi Riben dui Zhongguo wusha de juelue yu Minguo zhengfu de yingdui," 138. In 1944, the market prices for one piece of cotton cloth and one picul of tungsten were CN$750,000 and CN$30,000, respectively.

114. National Resources Commission to Pekin Syndicate (November 26, 1938), FO 371/23495.

115. Lin Meili, "Kangzhan shiqi de zousi huodong yu zousi shizhen" (Smuggling activities and smuggling markets during the War of Resistance period), in *Jinian qiqi Kangzhan liushi zhounian xueshu yantaohui lunwen ji* (Collection of essays from academic confer-ence to commemorate the sixtieth anniversary of the July 7 War of Resistance), ed. Jin-ian qiqi Kangzhan liushi zhounian xueshu yantaohui choubei weiyuanhui (Taipei: Guoshi guan, 1998), 215.

116. Huang Bowen, "Guangdong wuye wenti" (The problem of the tungsten industry in Guangdong), *Ziyuan weiyuanhui jikan* 1, no. 2 (1941): 75–78.

117. Lin, "Kangzhan shiqi de zousi huodong yu zousi shizhen," 216.

118. AH, 003-010303-0102, Tungsten Mining Administration (Guangdong office) to National Resources Commission (April 20, 1942).

119. Ministry of Economic Warfare to British Consulate-General in Chongqing (January 19, 1943), FO 371/35835.

120. AH, 003-010303-0109, Guangdong Yunfu Local Court procurator indictment (March 24, 1944), in Tungsten Mining Administration (Guangdong office) to National Resources Commission (May 26, 1944).

121. The three would have been sentenced to a year in prison and fined CN$1,000 if con-victed. See Article 32.2 of the law in *JJ*, 1938, 1:18, 793.

122. Jack S. Levy and Katherine Barbieri, "Trading with the Enemy During Wartime," *Security Studies* 13, no. 3 (2004): 1–47.

6. STATE REBUILDING AND NEW SMUGGLING GEOGRAPHIES

1. SHMA, Q186/2/28241. For description of the incident, see Shanghai Customs Letter No. 3670 (May 8, 1948). For prosecutor's decision, see Shanghai Municipal Court Pros-ecutor Non-Prosecution and Disciplinary Citation No. 3015 (May 25, 1948).

2. Eastman traces Nationalist defeat back to the party's inability to modernize political, social, and economic institutions during the Nanjing Decade. Johnson and Selden, despite differing interpretations, agree that Communist victory relied on rural support. Others pinpoint the postwar years as the turning point for the Nationalists, focusing on the party's eroding political legitimacy (Pepper) or battlefield contingencies (Levine and Westad). Lloyd E. Eastman, *The Abortive Revolution: China under Nationalist Rule, 1927–1937* (Cambridge, Mass.: Harvard University Press, 1974) and *Seeds of Destruction: Nationalist China in War and Revolution, 1937–1949* (Stanford, Calif.: Stanford University Press, 1984); Chalmers Johnson, *Peasant Nationalism and Communist Power: The Emergence of Revolutionary China* (Stanford, Calif.: Stanford University Press, 1962); Steven I. Levine, *Anvil of Victory: The Communist Revolution in Manchuria, 1945–1948* (New York: Columbia University Press, 1987); Suzanne Pepper, *Civil War in China: The Political Struggle, 1945–1949* (Berkeley: University of California Press, 1978); Mark Selden, *The Yenan Way in Revolutionary China* (Cambridge, Mass.: Harvard University Press, 1971); Odd Arne Westad, *Decisive Encounters: The Chinese Civil War, 1946–1950* (Stanford, Calif.: Stanford University Press, 2003).

3. Kia-ngau Chang, *The Inflationary Spiral: The Experience in China, 1939–1950* (Cambridge, Mass.: Technology Press of Massachusetts Institute of Technology, 1958), 303.

4. Data calculated using wholesale price indices from Wu Gang, *Jiu Zhongguo tonghuo pengzhang shiliao* (Historical materials on inflation in old China) (Shanghai: Renmin chubanshe, 1958), 160–61.

5. Chang, *Inflationary Spiral*, 65–66.

6. Eastman, *Seeds of Destruction*, 173.

7. For full text of the November 1946 regulations, see SHAC, 679/1/28024, IG Circular No. 7095 (July 25, 1947). For full text of the August 1947 regulations, see China Handbook Editorial Board, *China Handbook* (New York: Rockport Press, 1950), 516–23. For summary of the regulations, see China Handbook Editorial Board, *China Handbook*, 513–14.

8. Chang, *Inflationary Spiral*, 333.

9. *SB*, November 29, 1946, 2.

10. China Handbook Editorial Board, *China Handbook*, 515–16. The 1934 tariff was the last prewar revision.

11. GDPA, 95/1/1065, Kowloon SR (1947 Annual), 1.

12. *DB*, July 20, 1948, 5.

13. SHAC, 679/1/28210, Canton SR (September 1947), 4; (March 1948), 1.

14. Chang Yeh, *Recollections of a Chinese Customs Veteran* (Hong Kong: Ye zhen bang, 1987), 59–60.

15. John W. Powell, "Canton Solves Import-Export Trade Problems—with Profit," *CW*, August 23, 1947, 344.

16. SHAC, 679/1/28209, Canton SR (August 1946), 6; (February 1947), 2.

17. *SB*, December 29, 1947, 5.

18. For more on the tepid foreign diplomatic support the postwar Maritime Customs enjoyed, see Robert A. Bickers, "The Chinese Maritime Customs at War, 1941–45," *Journal of Imperial and Commonwealth History* 36, no. 2 (2008): 295–311; and Hans Van de Ven, *Breaking with the Past: The Maritime Customs Service and the Global Origins of Modernity in China* (New Yorker: Columbia University Press, 2014).

19. Shun-hsin Chou, *The Chinese Inflation, 1937–1949* (New York: Columbia University Press, 1963), 64.

20. SHAC, 679/1/31732, Deputy Inspector General Letter Semi-official No. 2 to Inspector General (September 15, 1945).

21. GDPA, 101/1/114, Memorandum from Luk Wing-kue to Huang Chih-chien (September 25, 1945), in Swatow Dispatch No. 7983 (September 25, 1945).

22. SHAC, 679/4/6, Chan I-Kan, Chinwangtao Semi-official Dispatch No. 8 to Deputy Inspector General (November 3, 1945), in Deputy Inspector General Letter No. 180 to Inspector General (November 19, 1945).

23. SHAC, 679/1/31732, Chan I-Kan, Chinwangtao Semi-official Dispatch No. 5 to Deputy Inspector General (October 6, 1945), in Deputy Inspector General Letter No. 105 to Inspector General (October 19, 1945).

24. SHAC, 679/4/6, Deputy Inspector General Letter No. 195 to Inspector General (November 20, 1945).

25. SHAC, 679/25573, Coast Inspector's Office to Tso Chang Chin (January 22, 1944).

26. SHAC, 679/9/5, Wang Hua Min to Ting Kuei-t'ang, "Memorandum on the Sea-borne Facilities and Capacity of Transportation and Shipping in the Port of Tientsin" (September 8, 1945), in Deputy Inspector General Letter No. 105 to Inspector General (October 27, 1945).

27. Inspectorate General of Chinese Customs, *The Trade of China* (Shanghai: Statistical Department of the Inspectorate General of Customs, 1946), 1:55.

28. SHAC, 679/1/31788, Amoy Commissioner's Comments on Preventive Department Semi-official Dispatch No. 14 (November 14, 1947), in "Semi-official, Preventive Department, 1948" (October 21, 1947).

29. SHAC, 679/1/31788, Foochow Commissioner's Comments on Preventive Department Semi-official Dispatch No. 14 (October 30, 1947), in "Semi-official, Preventive Department, 1948" (October 21, 1947).

30. SHAC, 679/1/28209, Canton SR (1946 Annual), 12.

31. SHAC, 679/4/6, Deputy Inspector General Letter No. 257 to Inspector General (December 15, 1945).

32. SHAC, 679/1/32240, Shanghai Semi-official Dispatch No. 1966 (April 11, 1947).

33. For survey of corruption and anti-smuggling in world history, see Alan L. Karras, *Smuggling: Contraband and Corruption in World History* (Lanham, Md.: Rowman and Littlefield, 2010), 118–20.

34. A 1933 customs raid on a firm in the Shanghai International Settlement, for instance, uncovered an elaborate scheme whereby low-level clerks produced forged official

documents certifying that goods paid the required duties. See SHAC, 679/1/28138, Shanghai SR (July 1933), Appendix No. 1; (August 1933), 1; and (September 1933), 1–2. For popular press reports, see especially *SB*, July 22, 1933, 15; September 29, 1933, 11; and January 9, 1934, 11, for court verdict.

35. For details of the incident, see Yu Zhongluo, "1948 nian Jiang Haiguan guanyuan wubi an" (The 1948 Shanghai Customs corruption case), in *Shanghai wenshi ziliao cungao huibian*, ed. Shanghai shi zhengxie wenshi ziliao weiyuanhui (Shanghai: Shanghai guji chubanshe, 2001), 4:113–26. For letters the four agents left for their families and a description of their execution, see *SB*, October 26, 1948, 4.

36. In one case, senior customs officials took care to recognize a low-level assistant examiner who turned down a relatively paltry bribe offered by an importer who had his paperwork in order but wanted speedier clearance for his cargo. See SHAC, 679/1/32242, Shanghai Semi-official Dispatch No. 2147 (February 13, 1947).

37. See chapter 3.

38. SHAC, 679/1/28024, IG Circular No. 6711 (August 23, 1945).

39. SHAC, 679/1/28024, IG Circular No. 6937 (November 5, 1946).

40. Calculations made dividing the fine by the Shanghai general wholesale price index of that month as the deflator. Prices indexed at 1 from the first half of 1937. For data, see Wu, *Jiu Zhongguo tonghuo pengzhang shiliao*, 154–61.

41. SHAC, 679/1/32240, Shanghai Semi-official Dispatch No. 1945 (March 12, 1947).

42. SHAC, 679/1/27723, Shantou Commissioner Telegram to Preventive Secretary (February 26, 1947).

43. SHAC, 679/1/28024, IG Circular No. 7352 (August 10, 1948).

44. SHAC, 679/1/27723, Shanghai Semi-official Dispatch No. 1970 (April 15, 1947).

45. SHAC, 679/1/27723, IG Semi-official Dispatch to Shanghai No. 476 (April 22, 1947).

46. SHAC, 679/1/27723, Canton Semi-official Dispatch No. 889 (May 1, 1947). Article 21 of the Preventive Law permits fines of "a sum not less than the value and not exceeding three times the value of the goods concerned."

47. SHAC, 679/1/27723, Memorandum from Preventive Secretary to IG (December 9, 1946).

48. *ZFD*, 5:479–80.

49. SHAC, 679/1/32243, IG Semi-official Dispatch to Shanghai No. 692 (March 16, 1948). The 1948 law dispensed with tying the degree of punishment to the value of the smuggled goods and duties evaded, a reflection of how hyperinflation rendered meaningless money as a measure of value. The 1936 law, by contrast, explicitly tied the severity of punishment to the value of duties evaded.

50. SHAC, 679/1/32244, IG Semi-official Dispatch to Shanghai No. 712 (April 9, 1948).

51. SHMA, Q185/2/27226. For description of the raid, see Shanghai Customs Letter No. 3774 (May 19, 1948) and No. 3819 (May 25, 1948). For press coverage of the incident, see *SB*, May 21, 1948, 4.

52. SHMA, Q185/2/27226, Shanghai Customs Letter No. 4109 (July 7, 1948).

53. SHMA, Q185/2/27226, Shanghai Municipal Court Judgment No. 1416 (August 4, 1948).

54. For brief background and full text of treaty, see China Handbook Editorial Board, *China Handbook*, 285–301.

55. SHMA, Q186/2/42898. For a description of the incident and Joyce's confession, see Shanghai Customs Letter No. 4798 (October 9, 1948). For the court's decision, see Shanghai Municipal Court Judgment No. 3024 (November 8, 1948). For press coverage of the incident, see *SB*, October 10, 1948, 2.

56. My general impression, in fact, is that foreigners such as Panaitescu and Joyce both retained more effective counsels because of the higher quality of their plaints.

57. Ministry of Finance to Kuan-wu Shu Telegram No. 3773, in SHAC, 679/1/20364, IG Dispatch No. 195257 (November 15, 1947).

58. *SB*, January 20, 1947, 7; March 19, 1947, 6.

59. *SB*, April 1, 1948, 5.

60. *GS*, January 23, 1948, 3.

61. SHAC, 679/1/32243, Ningpo Commissioner's Comment (February 19, 1948), in Shanghai Semi-official Dispatch No. 2136 (January 27, 1948).

62. The Wusong harbor lay at the mouth of the Huangpu River in Shanghai, where ships entered before reaching the city's wharves.

63. *DB*, April 2, 1947, 2.

64. See chapter 3.

65. SHAC, 679/1/32240, Ping Kung Law Offices to Inspector General (March 3, 1947), in IG Semi-official Dispatch to Shanghai Customs No. 450 (March 21, 1947). SHAC, 679/1/32240, Petition from Owners of the *Nee Cheng Hsing* (April 9, 1947), in IG Semi-official to Shanghai Customs No. 473 (April 16, 1947).

66. SHAC, 679/1/26923, IG Circular No. 7113; and No. 7197. Dates not provided in sources.

67. SHAC, 679/1/26925, IG Circular No. 7310 (May 21, 1948).

68. Kuan-wu Shu Telegram No. 6629 (June 29, 1948), in SHAC, 679/1/26925, IG Circular No. 7356 (August 17, 1948). In 1939, Taiwan exported 50 percent of its sugar to Korea while it imported 70 percent of fertilizer from Korea.

69. *SB*, July 21, 1947, 2.

70. "Ri huo zousi, rijian changjue!" (The smuggling of Japanese goods increasingly rampant!), *Gongshang yuekan* 4, no. 9 (1947), 6.

71. *SB*, July 17, 1947, 2.

72. *SB*, August 17, 1947, 1.

73. Both postwar and prewar figures might have been understated. After the war, the proportion of Japanese imports was low due to large-scale imports of relief items from the United States. Before the war, the Japanese takeover of Manchuria in 1931 removed from Chinese control ports that traditionally absorbed considerable amounts of Japanese imports.

74. "Ri huo zousi" (The smuggling of Japanese goods), *Jingji zhoubao* 5, no. 8 (1947): 3.

75. For overview of trafficking between Japan, Hong Kong, and China, see Ministry of Finance to Kuan-wu Shu Telegram No. 3773, in SHAC, 679/1/20364, IG Dispatch No. 195257 (November 15, 1947). See also *SB*, August 17, 1947, 1; August 19, 1947, 5; and March 26, 1948, 7.

76. Using exchange rate and price data for May 1948, HK$245 translated to just under CN$15 million, enough to purchase a basket of goods in Shanghai, including flour (CN$1.9 million for 49 lb.), salt (CN$1.6 million for 110 lb.), and white sugar (CN$9.3 million for 110 lb.). Calculated from market exchange rate of HK$1 = CN$60,497 during the week of May 10–16, 1948. See YZ, 31:26, 27. For market price of commodities in Shanghai during May 1948, see YZ, 32:34, 31–34.

77. GDPA, 94/1/659, Kuan-wu Shu Judgment (May 25, 1948). For the decision regarding the March incident, see GDPA, 94/1/655, Kuan-wu Shu Judgment (July 25, 1947). For the decision regarding the August incident, see GDPA, 94/1/657, Kuan-wu Shu Judgment (January 29, 1948).

78. The *Fatshan* (*Foshan*) was another vessel plying the Hong Kong–Guangzhou route notorious for repeated incidents of smuggling uncovered on board. In one case on July 1947, for example, customs agents uncovered more than 206 packages of medicines, ginseng, dyes, piece goods, film, etc. with a value of CN$631 million hidden on board. The agency fined the owner, also the China Navigation Company, more than CN$5.3 billion. The company subsequently appealed the decision to the Board, which again upheld the penalties. For a report of the incident, see SHAC, 679/1/28210, Canton SR (July 1947), 5–6. For the board's judgment, see GDPA, 94/1/657, Kuan-wu Shu Judgment (January 29, 1948). For the owner's protest, see Hong Kong Office to Canton Customs (August 16, 1947), in JSSIII, 1/22, 2510, 173, Hong Kong Office to London Office (August 22, 1947).

79. Because the incident was uncovered in Guangzhou, I used the Guangzhou wholesale price index to adjust for inflation. The index figures for March, August, and October 1947 were 11,032, 35,013, and 48,634, respectively. Prices indexed at 1 from the first half of 1937. See Wu, *Jiu Zhongguo tonghuo pengzhang shiliao*, 189.

80. JSSIII, 2/24, 2696, 92, Shanghai Office to London Office (November 14, 1947).

81. *GS*, May 17, 1948, 6.

82. SHAC, 679/1/28210, Canton SR (August 1947), 1.

83. Liu Zuoren, "Zousi yu Hua'nan jinrong" (Smuggling and finance in South China), *Jingji zhoubao* 6, no. 5 (1948): 103–4.

84. Chen Zumo, "Zousi wenti de shehui guan" (The social perspective on the smuggling problem), *Zhengfeng* 1, no. 3 (1948): 11.

85. SHAC, 679/1/28209, Canton SR (July 1946), 4; Canton SR (August 1946), 4–5.

86. SHAC, 679/1/28209, Canton SR (July 1946), 1.

87. SHMA, Q185/2/33717. For the court's judgment, see Shanghai Local Court Criminal Judgment No. 4252 (August 13, 1948). For a brief description by the press regarding the seizure in Hangzhou, see *SB*, June 4, 1948, 2.

88. *FR* 3, no. 8 (July 2, 1947): 130. All subsequent mentions of "ounces" refer to troy ounces. 1 troy ounce equals 0.06857 pounds.

89. FR 2, no. 2 (January 8, 1947): 18.

90. Between 1945 and 1971, IMF members agreed to keep their currencies pegged to the US dollar, which in turn was expressed in terms of gold. Maintaining exchange rate

stability sometimes led to significant divergence in gold prices. In August 1947, for example, the price of gold was fixed at US$33 per oz. by IMF regulations but sold for US$51 per oz., a 54 percent premium, in Macao. See *SB*, August 3, 1947, 1.

91. Both planes originated from Manila and belonged to Philippine Airlines. Reports from China alleged that gold was being smuggled out of the Philippines using export permits intended for sugar. See *SB*, August 10, 1947, 1.

92. Catherine R. Schenk, "The Hong Kong Gold Market and the Southeast Asian Gold Trade in the 1950s," *Modern Asian Studies* 29, no. 2 (1995): 387–402. One beneficiary of this trafficking was the airline Cathay Pacific. Founded in 1946, the fledgling company did a healthy business shuttling gold in South China with its fleet of Catalinas. See Gavin Young, *Beyond Lion Rock: The Story of Cathay Pacific Airways* (London: Hutchinson, 1988).

93. *FR* 2, no. 5 (January 29, 1947): 52–53; 2, no. 17 (April 30, 1947): 202–3; 3, no. 32 (December 17, 1947): 681–82. The article "Gold Business with China" in *FR* 4, no. 8 (February 25, 1948): 169–71, was translated in a Chinese financial journal. See *Yinhang Tongxun* 55 (1948): 15–16.

94. "Gold Dealings at Macao," *Economist*, April 17, 1948, 639.

95. "Macau: The Territory and Population," Research Department (Foreign Office) (August 23, 1948), in "General and Economic Report on Macao," FO 371/69633B.

96. China Handbook Editorial Board, *China Handbook*, 322.

7. OLD MENACE IN NEW CHINA

1. *RM*, January 3, 1951, 2.

2. Mo Kaiqin, Yao Maokun, and Sun Xiaohui, Zousi fanzui (The criminal offense of smuggling) (Beijing: Zhongguo renmin gong'an daxue chubanshe, 1999).

3. Paulina Bren and Mary Neuburger, eds., *Communism Unwrapped: Consumption in Cold War Eastern Europe* (Oxford: Oxford University Press, 2012), 253. For a similar point on the many types of markets coexisting in Maoist China, see Feng Xiaocai, "Yi jiu wu ba nian zhi yi jiu liu san nian zhonggong ziyou shichang zhengce yanjiu" (Research on the Chinese Communist Party's free market policy from 1958 to 1963), *Zhonggong dangshi yanjiu* 2 (2015): 38–52.

4. For more on the "second economy" and bottom-up evasion of top-down state controls in Maoist China, see John P. Burns, "Rural Guangdong's 'Second Economy,' 1962–74," *China Quarterly* 88 (1981): 629–44; Anita Chan and Jonathan Unger, "Grey and Black: The Hidden Economy of Rural China," *Pacific Affairs* 55, no. 3 (1982): 452–71; Thomas B. Gold, "Urban Private Business in China," *Studies in Comparative Communism* 23, no. 2/3 (1989): 187–201; Jean C. Oi, *State and Peasant in Contemporary China: The Political Economy of Village Government* (Berkeley: University of California Press, 1989); and Lynn T. White, "Low Power: Small Enterprises in Shanghai, 1949–67," *China Quarterly* 73 (1978): 45–76. For more recent historical research on the black market in Maoist China, see Feng, "Yi jiu wu ba nian." For overviews of the "second economy" in other socialist countries, see

Gregory Grossman, "The 'Second Economy' of the USSR," *Problems of Communism*, September–October 1977, 25–40; Maria Łoś, ed., *The Second Economy in Marxist States* (New York: St. Martin's, 1990); and Bren and Neuburger, *Communism Unwrapped*.

5. An understanding of "how individuals coped with enormous changes set in train by the revolutionary regime" remains elusive in historical scholarship on post-1949 China, according to Julia Strauss, "Introduction: In Search of PRC History," *China Quarterly* 188 (2006): 855–69. For recent research that follows Strauss's agenda, see Jeremy Brown and Paul Pickowicz, eds., *The Dilemmas of Victory: The Early Years of the People's Republic of China* (Cambridge, Mass.: Harvard University Press, 2007), and Jeremy Brown and Matthew D. Johnson, *Maoism at the Grassroots: Everyday Life in China's Era of High Socialism* (Cambridge, Mass.: Harvard University Press, 2015).

6. William C. Kirby, "China's Internationalization in the Early People's Republic: Dreams of a Socialist World Economy," *China Quarterly* 188 (2006): 872. For critical insights into transnational connections in the early People's Republic, see also Karl Gerth, "Compromising with Consumerism in Socialist China: Transnational Flows and Internal Tensions in 'Socialist Advertising,'" *Past and Present* 218, supplement 8 (2013): 203–32.

7. Mao Tse-tung (Mao Zedong), *Selected Works of Mao Tse-tung* (Beijing: Foreign Languages Press, 1961), 4:369.

8. For a comprehensive overview of the embargos and efforts by Communist China to circumvent them, see Shu Guang Zhang, *Economic Cold War: America's Embargo Against China and the Sino-Soviet Alliance, 1949–1963* (Stanford, Calif.: Stanford University Press, 2001).

9. The People's Republic set its first tariffs in 1951. For the full schedule, see Haiguan guanliju, ed., *Zhonghua Renmin Gongheguo haiguan jinchukou shuize* (Import and export tariffs of the customs of the People's Republic of China) (Beijing: Zhongyang renmin zhengfu haiguan zongshu, 1951).

10. For Communist China's foreign trade system, see Xin Yang, *Zhonggong de duiwai maoyi* (The foreign trade of China) (Hong Kong: Youlian chubanshe, 1954); Gene T. Hsiao, "Communist China's Foreign Trade Organization," *Vanderbilt Law Review* 20, no. 2 (1967): 303–19; and Kenneth Wang, "Foreign Trade Policy and Apparatus of the People's Republic of China," *Law and Contemporary Problems* 38, no. 2 (1973): 182–200.

11. Su Shifang, ed., *Dangdai Zhongguo haiguan* (Contemporary China: Customs) (1992; reprint, Beijing: Dangdai Zhongguo chubanshe, 2009), 449.

12. See, for instance, NBCK, 2765 (May 5, 1959), 19. Some officials, however, viewed smuggling as a more innocuous "contradiction among the people" (*renmin neibu maodun*).

13. Internal reports of repeated coastal incursions by American and Nationalist "secret agents" (*tewu*) only fed official paranoia. See, for instance, Ministry of Foreign Trade to State Council (January 27, 1958), in *JJD*, 599; and NBCK, 101 (May 7, 1954), 75–80; and 129 (June 10, 1954), 139–41.

14. Su, *Dangdai Zhongguo haiguan*, 15–16; Song Yuanzhi and Hu Xianglei, "Xin Zhongguo di yi ge renmin haiguan—Yantai haiguan" (New China's first People's Customs—Yantai Customs), *Zhongguo Haiguan* (*China Customs*) 6 (2001): 52–53.

15. See Hans Van de Ven, *Breaking with the Past: The Maritime Customs Service and the Global Origins of Modernity in China* (New York: Columbia University Press, 2014).

16. Mao, *Selected Works*, 4:370.

17. A Jiangxi native, Kong (1906–1990) joined the Communist Youth League in 1924 and cut his teeth as a political operative during the party's dark days of late 1920s and 1930s. He slowly ascended the party hierarchy in a career that took him from Moscow to Yan'an to Chongqing and to Manchuria. Zhongguo haiguan baike quanshu bianzuan weiyuanhu, ed. *Zhongguo haiguan baike quanshu* (Comprehensive encyclopedia of the Chinese Customs Administration) (Beijing: Zhongguo da baike quanshu chubanshe, 2004), 327.

18. For a description of one reeducation session at a South China customs station shortly after takeover, see Yuan Chang Yeh, *Recollections of a Chinese Customs Veteran* (Hong Kong: Ye zhen bang, 1987), 70.

19. *RM*, January 3, 1951, 2; Van de Ven, *Breaking with the Past*, 300–301.

20. *RM*, May 17, 1956, 4.

21. "Zhongguo renmin zhengzhi xieshang huiyi gongtong gangling" (The Common Program of the Chinese People's Political Consultative Conference), Article 17, *FLH*, 1949/50:21.

22. For minor and major smuggling violations, see Haiguan zongshu, ed., *Zhonghua Renmin Gongheguo zanxing haiguan fa* (The Provisional Customs Law of the People's Republic of China) (Beijing: Renmin chubanshe, 1951), 17.175 and 17.176.

23. Haiguan zongshu, 17.178.

24. SHMA, B6/2/330, "Guanyu fan zousi yundong de xingdong jihua" (On plans regarding the operation of the anti-smuggling campaign) (November 23, 1957), in Guangdong Provincial People's Committee to various provincial organs.

25. For the power of interpretive latitude conferred by PRC laws, see Klaus Mühlhahn, *Criminal Justice in China: A History* (Cambridge, Mass.: Harvard University Press, 2009), 188–89.

26. Haiguan zongshu, *Zhonghua Renmin Gongheguo zanxing haiguan fa*, 17.187, 17.188, 17.189.

27. Kong Yuan, "Haiguan zhidu de lishi biange yu Zhonghua Renmin Gongheguo zanxing haiguan fa" (The historical transformation of the Customs system and the Provisional Customs Law of the People's Republic of China), in *Xin Zhongguo haiguan* (New China Customs), ed. Haiguan guanliju (Shanghai: Xinhua shudian, 1951), 25–33.

28. See, for instance, *DG*, February 29, 1952, 2.

29. *NF*, December 23, 1957, 3; *DG*, December 24, 1957, 3.

30. *JF*, March 27, 1958, 27.

31. *DG*, November 3, 1957, 3.

32. Guangzhou haiguan bianzhi bangongshi, ed., *Guangzhou haiguan zhi* (Guangzhou Customs gazetteer) (Guangzhou: Guangdong renmin chubanshe, 1997), 286. For typologies of campaigns, see Julia Strauss, "Morality, Coercion and State Building by Campaign in the Early PRC: Regime Consolidation and After, 1949–1956," *China Quarterly* 188 (2006): 891–912.

33. *RM*, January 18, 1952, 2.

34. *NF*, August 19, 1957, 2; *GS*, August 22, 1957, 3; *SC*, August 21, 1957, 8.

35. "Shanghai haiguan zhi" bianzuan weiyuanhui, ed., *Shanghai haiguan zhi* (Shanghai Customs gazetteer) (Shanghai: Shanghai shehui kexueyuan chubanshe, 1997), 375.

36. Ministry of Foreign Trade to State Council (January 27, 1958), in *JJD*, 600.

37. *DG*, October 26, 1957, 3.

38. Su, *Dangdai Zhongguo haiguan*, 53; "Shanghai haiguan zhi" bianzuan weiyuanhui, *Shanghai haiguan zhi*, 373; *JF*, March 22, 1958, 5; March 27, 1958, 2. For a description of the Beijing exhibition, see *SC*, July 30, 1958, 20.

39. GDPA, 235/1/241, "Guanyu jianjue zhizhi he dujue zousi huodong de zhishi" (Directive on firmly preventing and stopping smuggling activities) (November 1, 1957), in Guangdong Provincial People's Committee to various provincial organs.

40. Kenneth Lieberthal, *Governing China: From Revolution Through Reform*, 2nd ed. (New York: Norton, 2003), 65–68. For more on the "educative function" of mass trials and "paternalistic jurisprudence," see Mühlhahn, *Criminal Justice in China*, 180–86.

41. See, for instance, Yin Zhiyue, "Diguo zhuyi ji canyu feibang de zousi pohuai huodong zuo douzheng" (The struggle against imperialism and smashing smuggling activities by residual bandit gangs), in *Xin Zhongguo haiguan* (New China Customs), ed. Haiguan guanliju (Shanghai: Xinhua shudian, 1951), 47–53.

42. Ministry of Foreign Trade to State Council (January 27, 1958), in *JJD*, 599.

43. *GS*, December 14, 1957, 3.

44. *DG*, March 11, 1952, 2; *HQ*, March 26, 1952, 4.

45. White, "Low Power," 58.

46. SHMA, B170/1/711, Shanghai Customs to General Customs Administration (November 23, 1960). One of the partners, however, had already been incarcerated on unrelated charges.

47. For historiographical debates on the term "Overseas Chinese," see Philip A. Kuhn, *Chinese Among Others: Emigration in Modern Times* (Lanham, Md.: Rowman and Littlefield, 2008); Adam McKeown, "Conceptualizing Chinese Diasporas, 1842 to 1949," *Journal of Asian Studies* 58, no. 2 (1999): 306–37; and Glen Peterson, *Overseas Chinese in the People's Republic of China* (London: Routledge, 2012).

48. Peterson, *Overseas Chinese*, 111.

49. "Haiguan dui laiwang Xianggang huo Aomen lüke xingli wupin jian'guan banfa" (Customs regulations on inspecting luggage and goods of Hong Kong and Macau travelers) (February 20, 1956), *FGH*, January–June 1956, 257–61. For the regulations for other Overseas Chinese, see "Haiguan dui guiguo Huaqiao xiedai xingli wupin youdai banfa" (Customs regulations on the preferential treatment of luggage and goods carried by returning Overseas Chinese) (February 20, 1956), *FGH*, January–June 1956, 254–56.

50. GDPA, 222/2/42, "Guanyu laiwang Gang Ao lüke xinglipin jiancha gongzuo baogao" (Report on the inspection work of Hong Kong and Macao travelers' luggage) (January 29, 1957), in Guangzhou Customs to Guangdong Provincial People's Committee. See also NBCK, 2127 (February 13, 1957), 168.

51. "Haiguan dui guiguo huaqiao xiedai xingli wupin youdai banfa," *FGH*, January–June 1956, 254–56.
52. SHMA, B182/1/1163, "Youguan waihuo shichang de yixie qingkuang" (Concerning some conditions on the market for foreign goods) (November 7, 1962), in Shanghai Municipal Industrial and Commercial Administration Bureau to Municipal People's Committee Office and Municipal Finance and Trade Office.
53. NBCK, 2328 (October 20, 1957), 14–15.
54. Instructions to Ministry of Foreign Trade, Ministry of Commerce, Ministry of Finance, and State Administration for Industry and Commerce (June 22, 1962), in *JJD*, 610.
55. For the Hong Kong–China currency traffic in the immediate years preceding and following 1949, see Catherine R. Schenk, "Another Asian Financial Crisis: Monetary Links Between Hong Kong and China, 1945–50," *Modern Asian Studies* 34, no. 3 (2000): 739–64; and Tomoko Shiroyama, "The Hong Kong–South China Financial Nexus: Ma Xuchao and His Remittance Agency," in *The Capitalist Dilemma in China's Communist Revolution*, ed. S. Cochran (Ithaca, N.Y.: Cornell East Asia Series, 2014). Although Shenk does not explicitly say so, China was also a source of gold flowing between Hong Kong and Southeast Asia during the 1950s. See Catherine R. Schenk, "The Hong Kong Gold Market and the Southeast Asian Gold Trade in the 1950s," *Modern Asian Studies* 29, no. 2 (1995): 387–402.
56. Instructions to Ministry of Foreign Trade, Ministry of Commerce, Ministry of Finance, and State Administration for Industry and Commerce (June 22, 1962), in *JJD*, 610.
57. Aomen xi'nan chubanshe, ed., *Huanxiang fan Gang xuzhi* (Things to know when returning to native village and returning to Hong Kong) (Macao: Aomen xi'nan chubanshe, 1956), 30–32.
58. *RM*, January 10, 1958, 4. The accusation had some merit: the guide was certainly pro-Nationalist in its sympathies and makes candid, disparaging remarks about life under communist rule.
59. For example, *NF*, August 16, 1957, 7; and GDPA, 222/2/42, "Guanyu laiwang Gang Ao lüke xinglipin jiancha gongzuo baogao" (January 29, 1957).
60. "Shanghai haiguan zhi" bianzuan weiyuanhui, *Shanghai haiguan zhi*, 352.
61. Kuo-chün Chao, *Economic Planning and Organization in Mainland China: A Documentary Study (1949–1957)* (Cambridge, Mass.: Center for East Asian Studies, Harvard University, 1960), 2:51–54.
62. For more on the PRC's policies toward minorities during the 1950s and Han chauvinism, see Henry G. Schwarz, "Ethnic Minorities and Ethnic Policies in China," *International Journal of Comparative Sociology* 20 (1979): 137–50. For treatment of minorities regarding criminal matters including smuggling, see Zhao Bingzhi, "Lun shaoshu minzu gongmin de xingshi zeren wenti" (On the problem of criminal responsibility of ethnic minority citizens), *Zhongguo faxue* 5 (1998): 65–72.
63. Ministry of Foreign Trade to State Council (January 27, 1958), in *JJD*, 598–602.

64. SHMA, B6/2/330, "Guanyu fan zousi yundong de xingdong jihua" (November 23, 1957).

65. SHMA, B6/2/286, "Shaoshu minzu danbang fanyun sihuo de gaikuang" (Survey of ethnic minorities peddlers trading smuggled goods) (June 11, 1957), in Shanghai Customs to Shanghai Municipal People's Committee. SHMA, A65/2/37, "Guanyu zousi jinkou de yang zahuo neiyun xiaoshou de qingkuang baogao" (Report on the sale of domestic transport and sale of smuggled assorted foreign goods) (April 22, 1957), in Shanghai Customs to Shanghai Municipal Party Committee, Finance and Trade Work Department.

66. NBCK, 52 (March 8, 1952), 61–65.

67. *SC*, July 10, 1951, 10. For an anti-communist exposé of smuggling and corruption in Guangdong, see Ba Dun, *Yue gong zousi zhenxiang* (The true situation of smuggling by communists in Guangdong) (Hong Kong: Ziyou chubanshe, 1951).

68. Julia Kwong, *The Political Economy of Corruption in China* (Armonk, N.Y.: M. E. Sharpe, 1997), 16.

69. See, in particular, Bren and Neuburger, *Communism Unwrapped*; Julie Hessler, *A Social History of Soviet Trade: Trade Policy, Retail Practices, and Consumption, 1917–1953* (Princeton, N.J.: Princeton University Press, 2004); János Kornai, *Economics of Shortage* (Amsterdam: North Holland, 1980) and *The Socialist System: The Political Economy of Communism* (Princeton, N.J.: Princeton University Press, 1992); and Łoś, *Second Economy in Marxist States*.

70. Nicholas Lardy, "Economic Recovery and the 1st Five-Year Plan," in *The Cambridge History of China*, vol. 14: *The People's Republic, Part 1: The Emergence of Revolutionary China 1949–1965*, ed. R. MacFarquhar and J. K. Fairbank (Cambridge: Cambridge University Press, 1987), 175; Barry Naughton, *The Chinese Economy: Transitions and Growth* (Cambridge, Mass.: MIT Press, 2007), 66. Guangzhou, in particular, was excluded from industrialization under the Five-Year Plan and had to focus on developing its agricultural and commercial sectors instead. See Ezra. F. Vogel, *Canton Under Communism: Programs and Politics in a Provincial Capital, 1949–1968* (Cambridge, Mass.: Harvard University Press, 1969), 128–32.

71. Naughton, *Chinese Economy*, 61.

72. Kirby, "China's Internationalization," 883.

73. See, especially, Dorothy J. Solinger, *Chinese Business Under Socialism: The Politics of Domestic Commerce, 1949–1980* (Berkeley, Calif.: University of California Press, 1984), and Andrew G. Walder, *China Under Mao: A Revolution Derailed* (Cambridge, Mass.: Harvard University Press, 2015).

74. SHMA, B6/2/286, "Zhongyang shangchang yang baihuo diaocha cailiao" (Investigative materials on general foreign merchandise at the Central Market" (June 11, 1957), in Shanghai Customs to Shanghai Municipal People's Committee.

75. See, for instance, NBCK, 2373 (December 3, 1957), 15–19; and 3263 (September 1, 1961), 7–9.

76. *SC*, January 5, 1954, 13.

77. For pre-1949 status of watches, see Frank Dikötter, *Exotic Commodities: Modern Objects and Everyday Life in China* (New York: Columbia University Press, 2006), 214. The other two of the 'big three' were radios and bicycles. Sewing machines was often added to the mix as the 'big four.' *SC*, September 28, 1960, 14.

78. Aomen xi'nan chubanshe *Huanxiang fan Gang xuzhi*, 30–31.

79. SHMA, B6/2/286, "Diaocha shoubiao zousi de chubu cailiao" (Preliminary materials on the investigation of wristwatch smuggling) (June 11, 1957), in Shanghai Customs to Shanghai Municipal People's Committee.

80. The Swiss Watchmakers' Guild accused Hong Kong of being "the world's center for the nefarious business of applying false trade marks on watches." See *SC*, April 15, 1955, 16.

81. NBCK, 4 (January 12, 1956), 65–66.

82. For Shanghai, see NBCK, 62 (March 24, 1956), 562–3. For Tianjin, see NBCK 92 (April 24, 1956), 476–77.

83. SHMA, B6/2/286, "Diaocha tanhua wugang daotou zousi de chubu cailiao" (Preliminary materials on the investigation of carbonized tungsten steel cutter smuggling) (June 11, 1957), in Shanghai Customs to Shanghai Municipal People's Committee.

84. SHMA, B6/2/286, "Diaocha tanhua wugang daotou zousi de chubu cailiao."

85. SHMA, B6/2/286, "Guanyu yang shenhuo liuxiang Shanghai shichang de qingkuang baogao" (Report on the flow of assorted foreign goods into the Shanghai market) (January 25, 1957), in Shanghai Customs to Shanghai Municipal People's Committee.

86. SHMA, B6/2/286, "Diaocha nilongmao zousi de chubu cailiao" (Preliminary materials on the investigation of nylon smuggling) and "Diaocha kekefen zousi de chubu cailiao" (Preliminary materials on the investigation of cocoa powder smuggling) (June 11, 1957), in Shanghai Customs to Shanghai Municipal People's Committee.

87. White, "Low Power," 69.

88. Ministry of Foreign Trade to State Council (January 27, 1958), in *JJD*, 599.

89. SHMA, B6/2/286, "Guanyu yang shenhuo liuxiang Shanghai shichang de qingkuang baogao" (January 25, 1957).

90. SHMA, B6/2/286, "Guanyu guanli shichang sihuo wenti de baogao" (Report on the problem on the management of smuggled goods in markets) (June 11, 1957), in Shanghai Customs to Shanghai Municipal People's Committee.

91. See, for instance, Jeremy Brown, *City Versus Countryside in Mao's China: Negotiating the Divide* (Cambridge: Cambridge University Press, 2012), 40–43, 73–75.

92. See, for instance, Guangdong sheng difang shi zhi bianzuan weiyuanhui, *Guangdong sheng zhi: haiguan zhi*, 260.

93. SHMA, B182/1/1163, "1962 nian san jidu zousi qingkuang cailiao" (Materials on smuggling during the third quarter of 1962) (October 16, 1962), in Shanghai Customs Anti-Smuggling Department. Similar data were reported elsewhere. See, for instance, *Guangdong sheng zhi: haiguan zhi*, 265.

94. For Chen Yun's "high-price policy," see Solinger, *Chinese Business Under Socialism*, 107–12; and Nicholas Lardy "The Chinese Economy Under Stress, 1958–1965," in *The Cambridge History of China*, vol. 14: *The People's Republic, Part 1: The Emergence of*

Revolutionary China, 1949–1965, ed. R. MacFarquhar and J. K. Fairbank (Cambridge: Cambridge University Press, 1987), 394.

95. NBCK, 3263 (September 1, 1961), 9.

96. The increase of returnees in the early 1960s—who left Indonesia and Malaysia in response to anti-Chinese policies—also led to a corresponding increase in smuggling. See Jiulong haiguan bianzhi bangongshi, ed. *Jiulong haiguan zhi* (Kowloon Customs gazetteer) (Guangzhou: Guangdong renmin chubanshe, 1993), 288.

97. Su, *Dangdai Zhongguo haiguan*, 225.

98. Ministry of Foreign Trade to State Council (January 27, 1958), in *JJD*, 599; NBCK, 2328 (October 9, 1957), 3–14.

99. NBCK, 2266 (July 25, 1957), 4–5; 2468 (April 29, 1958), 14–15.

100. GDPA, 235/1/241, "Pizhuan Guangzhou haiguan "guanyu Bao'an xian Fuyong xiang qianjin renmin gongshe sheyuan toudu zousi wenti baogao" (Transmitting Guangzhou Customs "Report on the problem of border crossing smuggling by commune members of the Bao'an County Fuyong Village commune") (June 18, 1959), in Guangzhou Customs to Guangdong Provincial People's Committee.

101. See especially Burns, "Rural Guangdong's 'Second Economy'"; Chan and Unger, "Grey and Black"; and Oi, *State and Peasant*.

102. Ministry of Foreign Trade to State Council (January 27, 1958), in *JJD*, 599.

103. See, in particular, Micah. S. Muscolino, *Fishing Wars and Environmental Change in Late Imperial and Modern China* (Cambridge, Mass.: Harvard University Asia Center, 2009), and Dian H. Murray, *Pirates of the South China Coast, 1790–1810* (Stanford, Calif.: Stanford University Press, 1987).

104. NBCK, 139 (June 19, 1953), 313–15.

105. NBCK, 2035 (October 26, 1956), 1246–48.

106. NBCK, 2468 (April 29, 1958), 14–15. For early PRC fishery reforms, see Muscolino, *Fishing Wars*, 181–86.

107. NBCK, 2855 (August 26, 1959), 17–18. Other reports recounted cases of fishermen sailing to Hong Kong to take advantage of foreign-sponsored relief programs. See, for instance, NBCK, 118, May 29, 1956, 505–6.

108. James C. Scott, *The Art of Not Being Governed: An Anarchist History of Upland Southeast Asia* (New Haven: Yale University Press, 2009).

109. Austin Coates, "Cheung Chau" (1955), in *Southern District Officer Reports: Islands and Villages in Rural Hong Kong, 1910–60*, ed. J. Strickland (Hong Kong: Hong Kong University Press, 2010), 193.

110. NBCK, 90 (April 20, 1955), 317–18.

111. Michael Szonyi, *Cold War Island: Quemoy on the Front Line* (Cambridge: Cambridge University Press, 2008), 94.

112. Fishermen were active participants of cross-strait smuggling when hostilities with Taiwan were relaxed during the 1970s and 1980s. See Lin Meiling, "Jieyan shiqi daluhuo zousi Taiwan diqu wenti (1949–1987)" (The problem of smuggling of mainland goods in the Taiwan area during the period of marital law [1949–1987]) (MA thesis, National

Taiwan Normal University, 1998); Muscolino, *Fishing Wars*; Szonyi, *Cold War Island*; and Wang Shengze, "Gaige kaifang chuqi Fujian fan zousi shulun" (A discussion of anti-smuggling in Fujian in the early days of Reform and Opening), *Zhonggong dangshi yanjiu*, no. 5 (2006): 96–104.

113. Łos, *Second Economy in Marxist States*, 5.

114. Peterson, *Overseas Chinese*, 7.

115. Joseph W. Esherick, "Ten Theses on the Chinese Revolution," *Modern China* 21, no. 1 (1995): 48.

CONCLUSION

1. For England, see John Brewer, *The Sinews of Power: War, Money and the English State, 1688–1783* (Cambridge, Mass.: Harvard University Press, 1990), and Cal Winslow, "Sussex Smugglers," in *Albion's Fatal Tree: Crime and Society in Eighteenth-Century England*, ed. D. Hay et al. (New York: Pantheon, 1975). For France, see Michael Kwass, *Contraband: Louis Mandrin and the Making of a Global Underground* (Cambridge, Mass.: Harvard University Press, 2014). For the United States, see Peter Andreas, *Smuggler Nation: How Illicit Trade Made America* (Oxford: Oxford University Press, 2013); Andrew W. Cohen, *Contraband: Smuggling and the Birth of the American Century* (New York: Norton, 2015); and Gautham Rao, *National Duties: Custom Houses and the Making of the American State* (Chicago: University of Chicago Press, 2016).

2. Su Shifang, ed., *Dangdai Zhongguo haiguan* (Contemporary China: Customs) (1992; reprint, Beijing: Dangdai Zhongguo chubanshe, 2009), 226–27. For smuggling across the Taiwan Straits during the 1970s, see Lin Meiling, "Jieyan shiqi daluhuo zousi Taiwan diqu wenti (1949–1987)" (The problem of smuggling of mainland goods in the Taiwan area during the period of marital law [1949–1987]) (MA thesis, National Taiwan Normal University, 1998); Micah S. Muscolino, "Underground at Sea: Fishing and Smuggling Across the Taiwan Strait, 1970s–1990s," in *Mobile Horizons: Dynamics Across the Taiwan Strait*, ed. W. H. Yeh (Berkeley: Institute of East Asian Studies, University of California, Center for Chinese Studies, 2013), 99–123; and Wang Shengze, "Gaige kaifang chuqi Fujian fan zousi shulun" (A discussion of anti-smuggling in Fujian in the early days of Reform and Opening), *Zhonggong dangshi yanjiu* 5 (2006): 96–104.

3. During the first decade of the reform era, from 1978 through 1988, cases from the Pearl River Delta made up nearly half of all smuggling cases nationwide, while cases from the rest of Guangdong and all of Fujian made up 6.8 and 7.8 percent of total cases, respectively. Data calculated from Su, *Dangdai Zhongguo haiguan*, 449; Guangdong sheng difang shi zhi bianzuan weiyuanhui, ed., *Guangdong sheng zhi: haiguan zhi* (Guangdong provincial gazetteer: customs gazetteer) (Guangzhou: Guangdong renmin chubanshe, 2002), 270–71; and Fujian sheng difang zhi bianzuan weiyuanhui, ed., *Fujian sheng zhi: haiguan zhi* (Fujian provincial gazetteer: customs gazetteer) (Beijing: Fangzhi chubanshe, 1995), 179–80.

4. *RM*, March, 7 1982, 1.
5. Thomas B. Gold, " 'Just in Time!': China Battles Spiritual Pollution on the Eve of 1984," *Asian Survey* 24, no. 9 (1984): 950.
6. In 1985, tariffs ranging from 90 to 130 percent were levied on imported clothing, electronics, and cars. Guowuyuan, *Zhonghua Renmin Gongheguo jinchukou guanshui tiaoli, fu Zhonghua Renmin Gongheguo haiguan jinchukou shuize* (Regulations on import and export tariffs of the People's Republic of China, including the import and export tariffs of the People's Republic of China Customs) (Beijing: Zhongguo duiwai fanyi chubanshe gongsi, 1985), 213, 222, 246.
7. The "dual-track system" (*shuangguizhi*) carved out a market economy coexisting alongside—but remaining separate from—the command economy. Whereas the former was initially confined to the southeast coast, the latter still dominated the rest of China, with strategic industries and state-owned enterprises guided by central planning.
8. Chen Yun, *Chen Yun wenxuan* (The selected works of Chen Yun) (Beijing: Renmin chubanshe, 1995), 2:287.
9. Dong Shantao. "Gaige kaifang chuqi nan Yue fan zousi neimu" (The inside story of anti-smuggling in southern Guangdong during the early days of reform and opening), *Jiancha fengyun* 21 (2009): 67. For details on conservative pushback during late 1981 and early 1982, see Ezra F. Vogel, *Deng Xiaoping and the Transformation of China* (Cambridge, Mass.: Belknap Press of Harvard University Press, 2011), 414–18.
10. For more on the early 1980s anti-crime campaigns, see Keith Forster, "The 1982 Campaign Against Economic Crime in China," *Australian Journal of Chinese Affairs* 14 (1985): 1–19, and Harold M. Tanner, *Strike Hard! Anti-Crime Campaigns and Chinese Criminal Justice, 1979–1985* (Ithaca, N.Y.: Cornell East Asia Series, 1999).
11. Especially notorious was the case of Lai Changxing, head of the Yuanhua Group (Yuanhua jituan youxian gongsi), who purportedly smuggled billions of yuan worth of cars, cigarettes, and oil in Xiamen during the late 1990s with the connivance of local officials. "Legal persons" (*faren*)—businesses connected to local governments, the Customs Administration, and even the People's Liberation Army—were also notorious for abusing their semiofficial status to engage in trafficking.
12. For comments by Jiang and Zhu on the urgency of the fight against smuggling, see, respectively, RM, July 14, 1998, 1; and July 16, 1998, 1.
13. Dali L. Yang, *Remaking the Chinese Leviathan: Market Transition and the Politics of Governance in China* (Stanford, Calif.: Stanford University Press, 2004), 125.
14. John Kamm, "Reforming Foreign Trade," in *One Step Ahead in China: Guangdong Under Reform*, by Ezra Vogel (Cambridge, Mass.: Harvard University Press, 1989), 365.
15. The Customs Administration was accorded the authority to review contracts between local governments and foreign firms, essentially exercising veto power over what the former could import from the latter. Kamm, "Reforming Foreign Trade," 365. From 1981 through 1986, the agency also held five nationwide conferences focused on anti-smuggling work in Shanghai as well as the three southeast coastal provinces of Guangdong, Fujian, and Zhejiang. *Dangdai Zhongguo haiguan*, 209–11.

16. The 1979 Criminal Law—the first criminal law of the People's Republic—included a section on "crimes undermining the socialist economic order" (*pohuai shehuizhuyi jingji zhixu zui*) that explicitly singled out smuggling. "Zhonghua Renmin Gongheguo xingfa" (Criminal Law of the People's Republic of China), Article 116, *FGH*, 1979: 73. The 1987 Customs Law (Haiguan fa)—which formally replaced the 1951 Provisional Customs Law—expanded the definition of smuggling. "Zhonghua Renmin Gong-heguo haiguan fa xingzheng chufa shishi xize" (Detailed regulations on implementing administration punishments of the Customs Law of the People's Republic of China), Articles 3 and 4, *FGH*, 1987: 561–62; Su, *Dangdai Zhongguo haiguan*, 197–99.

17. Beijing increased the agency's budget, issued new disciplinary regulations, and placed a dedicated Smuggling Investigation Bureau (Zousi fanzui zhencha ju) under the direct leadership of central authorities. The bureau was later renamed the Anti-Smuggling Bureau (Jisi ju). Yang, *Remaking the Chinese* Leviathan, 122–24, 204.

18. "China's Customs Crack Down on Secret Smuggling Method," *China Daily*, December 3, 2010, http://usa.chinadaily.com.cn/2010-12/03/content_11648521.htm (accessed November 20, 2017).

19. Xin Ren, "The Second Economy in Socialist China," in *The Second Economy in Marxist States*, ed. M. Łoś (New York: St. Martin's, 1990), 140–56. Scholarship in this vein typically overemphasizes the radical departure of the reform era and overlooks the enduring continuities from pre-1978 and pre-1949 China.

20. Wojtek Zafanolli, "A Brief Outline of China's Second Economy," *Asian Survey* 25, no. 7 (1985): 736.

BIBLIOGRAPHY

Adshead, Samuel A. M. *The Modernization of the Chinese Salt Administration, 1900–1920.* Cambridge, Mass.: Harvard University Press, 1970.

Andreas, Peter. "Illicit Globalization: Myths, Misconceptions, and Historical Lessons." *Political Science Quarterly* 126, no. 3 (2011): 1–23.

———. *Smuggler Nation: How Illicit Trade Made America.* Oxford: Oxford University Press, 2013.

Anghie, Antony. *Imperialism, Sovereignty and the Making of International Law.* Cambridge: Cambridge University Press, 2005.

Antony, Robert J. *Like Froth Floating on the Sea: The World of Pirates and Seafarers in Late Imperial South China.* Berkeley: Institute of East Asian Studies, 2003.

Aomen xi'nan chubanshe. *Huanxiang fan Gang xuzhi* (Things to know when returning to native village and returning to Hong Kong). Macao: Aomen xi'nan chubanshe, 1956.

Ba Dun. *Yue gong zousi zhenxiang* (The true situation of smuggling by communists in Guangdong). Hong Kong: Ziyou chubanshe, 1951.

Bailyn, Bernard. *Atlantic History: Concept and Contours.* Cambridge, Mass.: Harvard University Press, 2005.

Baumler, Alan. *The Chinese and Opium Under the Republic: Worse Than Floods and Wild Beasts.* Albany: State University of New York Press, 2007.

Bayly, Christopher A. *The Birth of the Modern World, 1780–1914: Global Connections and Comparisons.* Oxford: Blackwell, 2004.

Benton, Lauren. *Law and Colonial Cultures: Legal Regimes in World History, 1400–1900.* Cambridge: Cambridge University Press, 2002.

———. *A Search for Sovereignty: Law and Geography in European Empires, 1400–1900.* Cambridge: Cambridge University Press, 2010.

Beijing tushuguan, ed. *Minguo shiqi zong shumu (jingji lei)* (Complete catalog of the Republican era [economics category]). 2 vols. Beijing: Shumu wenxian chubanshe, 1986.

Benson, Carlton. "Consumers Are Also Soldiers: Subversive Songs from Nanjing Road During the New Life Movement." In *Inventing Nanjing Road: Commercial Culture in Shanghai, 1900–1945*, edited by Sherman Cochran, 91–132. Ithaca, N.Y.: East Asia Program, Cornell University, 1999.

Bergère, Marie-Claire. *The Golden Age of the Chinese Bourgeoisie, 1911–1937*. Cambridge: Cambridge University Press, 1989.

———. *Sun Yat-sen*. Stanford, Calif.: Stanford University Press, 1998.

Bian, Morris L. *The Making of the State Enterprise System in Modern China: The Dynamics of Institutional Change*. Cambridge, Mass.: Harvard University Press, 2005.

Bickers, Robert A. *Britain in China: Community, Culture and Colonialism, 1900–1949*. Manchester: Manchester University Press, 1999.

———. "The Chinese Maritime Customs at War, 1941–45." *Journal of Imperial and Commonwealth History* 36, no. 2 (2008): 295–311.

Blue, A. D. "The China Coasters." *Journal of the Hong Kong Branch of the Royal Asiatic Society* 7 (1967): 80–90.

Boecking, Felix. "The Bitterness of Fiscal Realism: Guomindang Tariff Policy, China's Trade in Imported Sugar, and Smuggling 1928–1937." *Harvard Asia Quarterly* 13, no. 2 (2011): 13–20.

———. *No Great Wall: Trade, Tariffs, and Nationalism in Republican China, 1927–1945*. Cambridge, Mass.: Harvard University Asia Center, 2017.

Boyle, John H. *China and Japan at War, 1937–1945: The Politics of Collaboration*. Stanford, Calif.: Stanford University Press, 1972.

Bren, Paulina, and Mary Neuburger, eds. *Communism Unwrapped: Consumption in Cold War Eastern Europe*. Oxford: Oxford University Press, 2012.

Brewer, John. *The Sinews of Power: War, Money and the English State, 1688–1783*. Cambridge, Mass.: Harvard University Press, 1990.

Brokaw, Cynthia. *Commerce in Culture: The Sibao Book Trade in the Qing and Republican Periods*. Cambridge, Mass.: Harvard University Asia Center, 2007.

Brook, Timothy, and Bob Tadashi Wakabayashi, eds. *Opium Regimes: China, Britain, and Japan, 1839–1952*. Berkeley: University of California Press, 2000.

Brooks, Barbara J. "Japanese Colonial Citizenship in Treaty Port China: The Location of Koreans and Taiwanese in the Imperial Order." In *New Frontiers: Imperialism's New Communities in East Asia, 1842–1953*, edited by Robert Bickers and Christian Henriot, 109–24. Manchester: Manchester University Press, 2000.

Brown, Jeremy. *City Versus Countryside in Mao's China: Negotiating the Divide*. Cambridge: Cambridge University Press, 2012.

Brown, Jeremy, and Matthew D. Johnson, eds. *Maoism at the Grassroots: Everyday Life in China's Era of High Socialism*. Cambridge, Mass.: Harvard University Press, 2015.

Brown, Jeremy, and Paul Pickowicz, eds. *The Dilemmas of Victory: The Early Years of the People's Republic of China*. Cambridge, Mass.: Harvard University Press, 2007.

Burns, John P. "Rural Guangdong's 'Second Economy,' 1962–74." *China Quarterly* 88 (1981): 629–44.

Cai Qian. *Yue sheng duiwai maoyi diaocha baogao* (An investigative report on the foreign trade in Guangdong province). Shanghai: Shangwu yinshu guan, 1939.

Cai Zhitong. "Wo guo zousi wenti zhi jiantao" (A thorough discussion of our nation's smuggling problem). *Zhonghang yuebao* 12, no. 5 (1936): 1–7.

Cassel, Pär K. *Grounds of Judgment: Extraterritoriality and Imperial Power in Nineteenth-Century China and Japan.* Oxford: Oxford University Press, 2012.

Chan, Anita, and Jonathan Unger. "Grey and Black: The Hidden Economy of Rural China." *Pacific Affairs* 55, no. 3 (1982): 452–71.

Chan, Anthony B. *Arming the Chinese: The Western Armaments Trade in Warlord China, 1920–1928.* Vancouver: University of British Columbia Press, 1982.

Chan, Kai Yiu. *Business Expansion and Structural Change in Pre-War China: Liu Hongsheng and His Enterprises, 1920–1937.* Hong Kong: Hong Kong University Press, 2006.

Chang Fu-yun [Zhang Fuyun]. *Reformer of the Chinese Maritime Customs.* Berkeley: Regional Oral History Office, University of California, 1987.

Chang, Kia-ngau. *The Inflationary Spiral: The Experience in China, 1939–1950.* Cambridge, Mass.: Technology Press of Massachusetts Institute of Technology, 1958.

Chang, Kornel. *Pacific Connections: The Making of the U.S.-Canadian Borderlands.* Berkeley: University of California Press, 2012.

Chao, Kuo-chun. *Economic Planning and Organization in Mainland China: A Documentary Study (1949–1957).* 2 vols. Cambridge, Mass.: Center for East Asian Studies, Harvard University, 1960.

Chen Cungong. "Minchu lujun junhuo zhi shuru" (The import of arms by the army in the early Republic). *Jindaishi yanjiusuo jikan* 6 (1977): 237–309.

Chen Jiadong. "Kang Ri shiqi Li Hanhun chuli Nanlu sixiao neimu" (The inside story on Li Hanhun disposing of Nanlu's smugglers during the War of Resistance). *Guangzhou wenshi ziliao xuanji* 19 (1980): 234–46.

Chen, Li. *Chinese Law in Imperial Eyes: Sovereignty, Justice, and Transcultural Politics.* New York: Columbia University Press, 2016.

——. "Law, Empire, and Historiography of Modern Sino-Western Relations: A Case Study of the Lady Hughes Controversy in 1784." *Law and History Review* 27, no. 1 (2009): 1–54.

Chen Shiqi. *Zhongguo jindai haiguan shi* (A history of modern China's Maritime Customs). Beijing: Renmin chubanshe, 2002.

Chen, Xiaomei. "Mapping a 'New' Dramatic Canon: Rewriting the Legacy of Hong Shen." In *Modern China and the West: Translation and Cultural Mediation*, edited by Peng Hsiao-yen and Isabelle Rabut, 224–47. Leiden: Brill, 2014.

Chen Yun. *Chen Yun wenxuan* (The selected works of Chen Yun). 3 vols. Beijing: Renmin chubanshe, 1995.

Chen Zumo. "Zousi wenti de shehui guan" (The social perspective on the smuggling problem). *Zhengfeng* 1, no. 3 (1948): 10–12.

Cheng, Chu-yuan. "The United States Petroleum Trade with China." In *America's China Trade in Historical Perspective: The Chinese and American Performance*, edited by Ernest R. May and John K. Fairbank, 205–33. Cambridge, Mass.: Harvard University Press, 1986.

Cheng Yifa. "Jiangxi zhi wu ye" (The tungsten industry of Jiangxi). *Ziyuan weiyuanhui jikan* 1, no. 2 (1941): 1–19.

Cheng, Yu-kwei. *Foreign Trade and Industrial Development of China: An Historical and Integrated Analysis Through 1948.* Washington, D.C.: University Press of Washington, D.C., 1956.

Chiang Kai-shek [Jiang Jieshi]. *China's Destiny and Chinese Economic Theory.* Translated by Philip J. Jaffe. 1947. Reprint, Leiden: Global Oriental, 2013.

China Handbook Editorial Board. *China Handbook.* New York: Rockport Press, 1950.

China Weekly Review, ed. *Who's Who in China: Biographies of Chinese Leaders.* 5th ed. Shanghai: China Weekly Review, 1936.

——. *Who's Who in China: Containing the Pictures and Biographies of Some of China's Political, Financial, Business and Professional Leaders.* 3rd ed. Shanghai: China Weekly Review, 1925.

Chou, Shun-hsin. *The Chinese Inflation, 1937–1949.* New York: Columbia University Press, 1963.

Chu, Chin [Zhu Jin]. *The Tariff Problem in China.* New York: Columbia University Press, 1916.

Churchill, R. R., and A. V. Lowe. *The Law of the Sea.* 3rd ed. Manchester: Manchester University Press, 1999.

Clemens, Michael A., and Jeffrey G. Williamson. "Why Did the Tariff-Growth Correlation Change After 1950?" *Journal of Economic Growth* 9, no. 1 (2004): 5–46.

Coates, Austin. "Cheung Chau" (1955). In *Southern District Officer Reports: Islands and Villages in Rural Hong Kong, 1910–60*, edited by John Strickland, 183–95. Hong Kong: Hong Kong University Press, 2010.

Coble, Parks M. *China's War Reporters: The Legacy of Resistance Against Japan.* Cambridge, Mass.: Harvard University Press, 2015.

——. *Chinese Capitalists in Japan's New Order: The Occupied Lower Yangzi, 1937–1945.* Berkeley: University of California Press, 2003.

——. *The Shanghai Capitalists and the Nationalist government, 1927–1937.* Cambridge, Mass.: Harvard University Press, 1980.

Cochran, Sherman. *Chinese Medicine Men: Consumer Culture in China and Southeast Asia.* Cambridge, Mass.: Harvard University Press, 2006.

——. *Encountering Chinese Networks: Western, Japanese, and Chinese Corporations in China, 1880–1937.* Berkeley: University of California Press, 2000.

Cohen, Andrew W. *Contraband: Smuggling and the Birth of the American Century.* New York: Norton, 2015.

Dai Dongyang. "Riben xiugai tiaoyue jiaoshe yu He Ruzhang de tiaoyue renshi" (Japan's treaty revision negotiations and understanding of treaties by He Ruzhang). *Jindaishi yanjiu*, no. 6 (2004): 161–97.

Dalian haiguan zhi bianzuan weiyuanhui, ed. *Dalian haiguan zhi* (Dalian Customs gazetteer). Beijing: Zhongguo haiguan chubanshe, 2005.

Deng Quansheng. "Jiefang qian de Hua'nan haiguan jisi" (Maritime Customs anti-smuggling in South China before Liberation). *Guangdong wenshi ziliao* 9 (1963): 73–80.

Dikötter, Frank. *Exotic Commodities: Modern Objects and Everyday Life in China*. New York: Columbia University Press, 2006.

———. *The Tragedy of Liberation: A History of the Chinese Revolution, 1945–1957*. New York: Bloomsbury, 2013.

Dong Shantao. "Gaige kaifang chuqi nan Yue fan zousi neimu" (The inside story of anti-smuggling in southern Guangdong during the early days of reform and opening). *Jiancha fengyun* 21 (2009): 66–68.

Duara, Prasenjit. *Culture, Power, and the State: Rural North China, 1900–1942*. Stanford, Calif.: Stanford University Press, 1988.

Duidi jingji fengsuo weiyuanhui. *Gesheng huoyun diaocha baogao* (Investigative report on transport in the provinces). Chongqing: Guofang zuigao weiyuanhui, 1941.

Eastman, Lloyd E. *The Abortive Revolution: China Under Nationalist Rule, 1927–1937*. Cambridge, Mass.: Harvard University Press, 1974.

———. "Facets of an Ambivalent Relationship: Smuggling, Puppets, and Atrocities During the War, 1937–1945." In *The Chinese and the Japanese: Essays in Political and Cultural Interactions*, edited by Akira Iriye, 275–303. Princeton, N.J.: Princeton University Press, 1980.

———. *Seeds of Destruction: Nationalist China in War and Revolution, 1937–1949*. Stanford, Calif.: Stanford University Press, 1984.

Edwards, R. Randle. "Ch'ing Legal Jurisdiction Over Foreigners." In *Essays on China's Legal Tradition*, edited by Jerome Cohen, R. Randle Edwards, and Fu-Mei Chang Chen, 222–69. Princeton, N.J.: Princeton University Press, 1980.

Eichengreen, Barry J. *Golden Fetters: The Gold Standard and the Great Depression, 1919–1939*. Oxford: Oxford University Press, 1992.

Esherick, Joseph. "Ten Theses on the Chinese Revolution." *Modern China* 21, no. 1 (1995): 45–76.

Esselstrom, Erik. *Crossing Empire's Edge: Foreign Ministry Police and Japanese Expansionism in Northeast Asia*. Honolulu: University of Hawai'i Press, 2009.

Fairbank, John K. "Maritime and Continental in China's History." In *The Cambridge History of China*, vol. 12: *Republican China, 1912–49, Part 1*, edited by John K. Fairbank, 1–27. Cambridge: Cambridge University Press, 1983.

———. *Trade and Diplomacy on the China Coast: The Opening of the Treaty Ports, 1842–1854*. Cambridge, Mass.: Harvard University Press, 1953.

Feng Sheng. "Chuangkan ci ji qita" (Words for the inaugural issue and other matters). *Guanshui wenti* 1, no. 1 (1928): 1–5.

Feng Xiaocai. "Yi jiu wu ba nian zhi yi jiu liu san nian zhonggong ziyou shichang zhengce yanjiu" (Research on the Chinese Communist Party's free market policy from 1958 to 1963). *Zhonggong dangshi yanjiu* 2 (2015): 38–52.

Feuerwerker, Albert. "Economic Trends, 1912–49." In *The Cambridge History of China*, vol. 12: *Republican China, 1912–1949, Part 1*, edited by John K. Fairbank, 28–127. Cambridge: Cambridge University Press, 1983.

———. "The Foreign Presence in China." In *The Cambridge History of China*, vol. 12: *Republican China, 1912–1949, Part 1*, edited by John K. Fairbank, 128–207. Cambridge: Cambridge University Press, 1983.

Fishel, Wesley R. *The End of Extraterritoriality in China*. Berkeley: University of California Press, 1952.

Fong, H. D. (Fang Xianting). *Rayon and Cotton Weaving in Tientsin*. Tianjin: Chihli Press, 1930.

———. *Toward Economic Control in China*. Shanghai: China Institute of Pacific Relations, 1936.

Forster, Keith. "The 1982 Campaign Against Economic Crime in China." *Australian Journal of Chinese Affairs* 14 (1985): 1–19.

Fu Huiqing. "Shantou haiguan gailüe (1910–1942)" (Summary of the Shantou Customs), *Guangdong wenshi ziliao* 14 (1964): 141–48.

Fujian sheng difang zhi bianzuan weiyuanhui, ed. *Fujian sheng zhi: haiguan zhi* (Fujian provincial gazetteer: customs gazetteer). Beijing: Fangzhi chubanshe, 1995.

Fung, Edmund S. K. "The Chinese Nationalists and the Unequal Treaties, 1924–1931." *Modern Asian Studies* 21, no. 4 (1987): 793–819.

Gerschenkron, Alexander. *Economic Backwardness in Historical Perspective: A Book of Essays*. Cambridge, Mass.: Belknap Press of Harvard University Press, 1962.

Gerth, Karl. *China Made: Consumer Culture and the Creation of the Nation*. Cambridge, Mass.: Harvard University Asia Center, 2003.

———. "Compromising with Consumerism in Socialist China: Transnational Flows and Internal Tensions in 'Socialist Advertising.'" *Past and Present* 218, supplement 8 (2013): 203–32.

Godley, Michael R. "Socialism with Chinese Characteristics: Sun Yatsen and the International Development of China." *Australian Journal of Chinese Affairs* 18 (1987): 109–25.

Gold, Thomas B. "'Just in Time!': China Battles Spiritual Pollution on the Eve of 1984." *Asian Survey* 24, no. 9 (1984): 947–74.

———. "Urban Private Business in China." *Studies in Comparative Communism* 23, no. 2/3 (1989): 187–201.

Grant, Jonathan A. *Rulers, Guns, and Money: The Global Arms Trade in the Age of Imperialism*. Cambridge, Mass.: Harvard University Press, 2007.

Green, Stuart P. "Why It's a Crime to Tear the Tag off a Mattress: Overcriminalization and the Moral Content of Regulatory Offences." *Emory Law Journal* 46, no. 4 (1997): 1533–1615.

Grossman, Gregory. "The 'Second Economy' of the USSR." *Problems of Communism*, September–October 1977, 25–40.

Guangdong sheng difang shi zhi bianzuan weiyuanhui, ed. *Guangdong sheng zhi: haiguan zhi* (Guangdong provincial gazetteer: customs gazetteer). Guangzhou: Guangdong renmin chubanshe, 2002.

Guangzhou haiguan bianzhi bangongshi, ed. *Guangzhou haiguan zhi* (Guangzhou Customs gazetteer). Guangzhou: Guangdong renmin chubanshe, 1997.

Guo, Weiting. "From Female Bandit to Legendary Heroine: Life of Huang Bamei in Wartime China, 1937–1955." Paper presented at the annual meeting of the Association for Asian Studies, Toronto, 2017.

Guowuyuan. *Zhonghua Renmin Gongheguo jinchukou guanshui tiaoli, fu Zhonghua Renmin Gongheguo haiguan jinchukou shuize* (Regulations on import and export tariffs of the

People's Republic of China, including the import and export tariffs of the People's Republic of China Customs). Beijing: Zhongguo duiwai fanyi chuban gongsi, 1985.

Haiguan guanliju, ed. *Zhonghua Renmin Gongheguo haiguan jinchukou shuize* (Import and export tariffs of the customs of the People's Republic of China). Beijing: Zhongyang renmin zhengfu haiguan zongshu, 1951.

Haiguan zongshu, ed. *Zhonghua Renmin Gongheguo zanxing haiguan fa* (The Provisional Customs Law of the People's Republic of China). Beijing: Renmin chubanshe, 1951. Citation by chapter and article.

Halsey, Stephen R. *Quest for Power: European Imperialism and the Making of Chinese Statecraft.* Cambridge, Mass.: Harvard University Press, 2015.

Hamashita Takeshi. *Chūgoku kindai keizaishi kenkyū: Shinmatsu kaikan zaisei to kaikōjō shijōken* (Research on the Modern Chinese economy: The Late Qing Maritime Customs finance and open port market). Tokyo: Tōkyō daigaku Tōyō Bunka kenkyūjo, 1989.

Hao, Yen-p'ing. "Cheng Kuan-ying: The Comprador as Reformer." *Journal of Asian Studies* 29, no. 1 (1969): 15–22.

———. *The Commercial Revolution in Nineteenth-Century China: The Rise of Sino-Western Mercantile Capitalism.* Berkeley: University of California Press, 1986.

Hershatter, Gail. *Dangerous Pleasures: Prostitution and Modernity in Twentieth-Century Shanghai.* Berkeley: University of California Press, 1997.

———. *Women in China's Long Twentieth Century.* Berkeley: University of California Press, 2007.

———. *The Workers of Tianjin, 1900–1949.* Stanford, Calif.: Stanford University Press, 1986.

Hessler, Julie. *A Social History of Soviet Trade: Trade Policy, Retail Practices, and Consumption, 1917–1953.* Princeton, N.J.: Princeton University Press, 2004.

Hill, Emily M. "Japanese-Backed Smuggling in North China: Chinese Popular and Official Resistance, 1935–1937." In *Resisting Japan: Mobilizing for War in China, 1935–1945,* edited by David Pong. Norwalk, Conn.: EastBridge, 2008.

———. *Smokeless Sugar: The Death of a Provincial Bureaucrat and the Construction of China's National Economy.* Vancouver: University of British Columbia Press, 2010.

Hong Shen. *Zousi* (Smuggling). Shanghai: Yi ban shudian, 1937.

Hsiao, Gene T. "Communist China's Foreign Trade Organization," *Vanderbilt Law Review* 20, no. 2 (1967): 303–19.

Hsiao, Liang-lin. *China's Foreign Trade Statistics, 1864–1949.* Cambridge, Mass.: Harvard University Press, 1974.

Hsieh, Winston. "Triads, Salt Smugglers, and Local Uprisings: Observations on the Social and Economic Background of the Waichow Revolution of 1911." In *Popular Movements and Secret Societies in China, 1840–1950,* edited by Jean Chesneaux. Stanford, Calif.: Stanford University Press, 1972.

Hu, Jichuang. *A Concise History of Chinese Economic Thought.* Beijing: Foreign Languages Press, 1998.

Huang Bowen. "Guangdoong wuye wenti" (The problem of the tungsten industry in Guangdong). *Ziyuan weiyuanhui jikan* 1, no. 2 (1941): 67–86.

Huang Guosheng. *Yapian zhanzheng qian de dongnan si sheng haiguan* (The customs of the four southeast provinces before the Opium War). Fuzhou: Fujian renmin chubanshe, 2000.

Huang, Philip C. C. *Code, Custom, and Legal Practice in China: The Qing and the Republic Compared*. Stanford, Calif.: Stanford University Press, 2001.

Inspectorate General of Chinese Customs. *Decennial Reports on the Trade Navigation Industries, etc., of the Ports Open to Foreign Commerce in China and Corea, and on the Conditions and Development of the Treaty Port Provinces, 1882–1891*. 1st issue. Shanghai: Statistical Department of the Inspectorate General of Customs, 1893.

———. *Foochow: "Taiwan" False Manifest Case*. Shanghai: Statistical Department of the Inspectorate General, 1878.

———. *Returns of Trade*. Published annually for 1882–1919. Shanghai: Statistical Department of the Inspectorate General of Customs, 1882–1919.

———. *The Trade of China*. Published annually for 1932–1940, 1946. Shanghai: Statistical Department of the Inspectorate General of Customs, 1933–1947.

Iriye, Akira. "Japanese Aggression and China's International Position, 1931–1949." In *The Cambridge History of China*, vol. 13: *Republican China, 1912–1949, Part 2*, edited by John K. Fairbank and Albert Feuerwerker, 492–546. Cambridge: Cambridge University Press, 1986.

Jia Shiyi. *Guanshui yu guoquan* (Tariff autonomy and national sovereignty). Shanghai: Caizhengbu zhu Hu diaocha huojiachu, 1927.

Jiulong haiguan bianzhi bangongshi, ed. *Jiulong haiguan zhi* (Kowloon customs gazetteer). Guangzhou: Guangdong renmin chubanshe, 1993.

Johnson, Chalmers. *Peasant Nationalism and Communist Power: The Emergence of Revolutionary China*. Stanford, Calif.: Stanford University Press, 1962.

Jones, William C., trans. *The Great Qing Code*. New York: Oxford University Press, 1994.

Kamm, John. "Reforming Foreign Trade." In *One Step Ahead in China: Guangdong Under Reform*, by Ezra Vogel, 338–92. Cambridge, Mass.: Harvard University Press, 1989.

Karl, Rebecca. *Staging the World: Chinese Nationalism at the Turn of the Twentieth Century*. Durham, N.C.: Duke University Press, 2002.

Karras, Alan L. *Smuggling: Contraband and Corruption in World History*. Lanham, Md.: Rowman and Littlefield, 2010.

Kayaoglu, Turan. *Legal Imperialism: Sovereignty and Extraterritoriality in Japan, the Ottoman Empire, and China*. Cambridge: Cambridge University Press, 2010.

King, Wunsz. *China at the Paris Peace Conference in 1919*. New York: St. John's University Press, 1961.

———. *China at the Washington Conference, 1921–1922*. New York: St. John's University Press, 1963.

Kirby, William C. "China's Internationalization in the Early People's Republic: Dreams of a Socialist World Economy." *China Quarterly* 188 (2006): 870–90.

———. "The Chinese War Economy: Mobilization, Control, and Planning in Nationalist China." In *China's Bitter Victory: The War with Japan, 1937–1945*, edited by James C. Hsiung and Steven I. Levine, 185–212. Armonk, N.Y.: M. E. Sharpe, 1992.

———. "Engineering China: Birth of the Developmental State, 1928–1937." In *Becoming Chinese: Passages to Modernity and Beyond*, edited by W. H. Yeh, 137–60. Berkeley: University of California Press, 2000.

———. *Germany and Republican China*. Stanford, Calif.: Stanford University Press, 1984.

———. "Technocratic Organization and Technological Development in China, 1928–1953." In *Science and Technology in Post-Mao China*, edited Denis Fred Simon and Merle Goldman, 23–43. Cambridge, Mass.: Harvard University Press, 1989.

Kindleberger, Charles P. *The World in Depression, 1929–1939*. 1973. Reprint, Berkeley: University of California Press, 1986.

Köll, Elisabeth. *From Cotton Mill to Business Empire: The Emergence of Regional Enterprises in Modern China*. Cambridge, Mass.: Harvard University Asia Center, 2004.

Kong Yuan. "Haiguan zhidu de lishi biange yu Zhonghua Renmin Gongheguo zanxing haiguan fa" (Historical transformation of the customs system and the Provisional Customs Law of the People's Republic of China). In *Xin Zhongguo haiguan* (New China Customs), edited by Haiguan guanliju, 25–33. Shanghai: Xinhua shudian, 1951.

Kornai, János. *Economics of Shortage*. Amsterdam: North Holland, 1980.

———. *The Socialist System: The Political Economy of Communism*. Princeton, N.J.: Princeton University Press, 1992.

Krasner, Stephen D. *Sovereignty: Organized Hypocrisy*. Princeton, N.J.: Princeton University Press, 1999.

Kwong, Julia. *The Political Economy of Corruption in China*. Armonk, N.Y.: M. E. Sharpe, 1997.

Kubo, Toru. "The Tariff Policy of the Nationalist Government, 1929–36: A Historical Assessment." In *Japan, China, and the Growth of the Asian International Economy, 1850–1949*, edited by Kaoru Sugihara, 145–76. Oxford: Oxford University Press, 2005.

Kuhn, Philip A. *Origins of the Modern Chinese State*. Stanford, Calif.: Stanford University Press, 2002.

Kwass, Michael. *Contraband: Louis Mandrin and the Making of a Global Underground*. Cambridge, Mass.: Harvard University Press, 2014.

Lai, Chi-Kong. "Chinese Business History: Its Development, Present Situation, and Future Direction." In *Business History Around the World*, edited by F. Amatori and G. Jones, 298–316. Cambridge: Cambridge University Press, 2003.

Lai Jiancheng. *Liang Qichao de jingji mianxiang* (Liang Qichao's economic orientation). Taipei: Lianjing, 2006.

Lai, Sherman Xiaogang. *A Springboard to Victory: Shandong Province and Chinese Communist Military and Financial Strength, 1937–1945*. Leiden: Brill, 2011.

Lam, Tong. "Policing the Imperial Nation: Sovereignty, International Law, and the Civilizing Mission in Late Qing China." *Comparative Studies in Society and History* 52, no. 4 (2010): 881–908.

Lardy, Nicholas. "The Chinese Economy Under Stress, 1958–1965." In *The Cambridge History of China*, vol. 14: *The People's Republic, Part 1: The Emergence of Revolutionary China, 1949–1965*, edited by Roderick MacFarquhar and John K. Fairbank, 360–97. Cambridge: Cambridge University Press, 1987.

————. "Economic Recovery and the 1st Five-Year Plan." In *The Cambridge History of China*, vol. 14: *The People's Republic, Part 1: The Emergence of Revolutionary China, 1949–1965*, edited by Roderick MacFarquhar and John K. Fairbank, 144–84. Cambridge: Cambridge University Press, 1987.

Lee, Seung-joon. *Gourmets in the Land of Famine: The Culture and Politics of Rice in Modern Canton*. Stanford, Calif.: Stanford University Press, 2011.

Lee Yu-ping [Li Yuping]. "Yi jiu san ling niandai Zhongguo de jiujing jingji konghuang shuo (1931–1935)" (Discussions in China on relieving the economic crisis during the 1930s). *Zhongyang yanjiuyuan jindaishi yanjiusuo ji* 27 (1997): 232–72.

Levine, Steven I. *Anvil of Victory: The Communist Revolution in Manchuria, 1945–1948*. New York: Columbia University Press, 1987.

Levy, Jack S., and Katherine Barbieri. "Trading with the Enemy During Wartime." *Security Studies* 13, no. 3 (2004): 1–47.

Li, Chuan-shih [Li Quanshi]. *A Plea for Tariff Autonomy in China*. New York: Chinese Students' Committee on Washington Conference, 1921.

Li, Huaiyin. *Village Governance in North China: Huailu County, 1875–1936*. Stanford, Calif.: Stanford University Press, 2005.

Li, K. C., and Chongyou Wang. *Tungsten: Its History, Geology, Ore-Dressing, Metallurgy, Chemistry, Analysis, Applications, and Economics*. 3rd ed. New York: Reinhold, 1955.

Li Lixia. "Maoyi tongzhi lun yu Zhongguo maoyi tongzhi wenti" (On economic control and China's economic control problem) *Zhongshan wenhua jiaoyu guan jikan* 4, no. 2 (1937): 479–94.

Li Pei'en. "Guanshui zizhu" (Tariff autonomy). *DZ* 22, no. 20 (1925): 34–48.

Li Quanshi. *Zhongguo guanshui wenti* (The tariff problem in China). Shanghai: Shangwu yin-shu guan, 1936.

Lian Xinhao. *Jindai Zhongguo de zousi yu haiguan jisi* (Smuggling and customs anti-smuggling in modern China). Xiamen: Xiamen daxue chubanshe, 2011.

Liang Qichao. "Guanshui quan wenti" (The problem of tariff autonomy, 1906). In *Yin bing shi he ji* (Collected works from the ice-drinker's studio), 12 vols., 2:68–76. Beijing: Zhonghua shu ju, 1989.

————. "Lun jiashui" (On increasing taxes, 1896). In *Yin bing shi he ji*, 1:103–4. Beijing: Zhonghua shu ju, 1989.

Lieberthal, Kenneth. *Governing China: From Revolution Through Reform*. 2nd ed. New York: Norton, 2005.

Lin Lanfang. *Ziyuan weiyuanhui de tezhong kuangchan tongzhi (1936–1949)* (Control of special minerals by the National Resources Commission [1936–1949]). Taipei: Guoli zhengzhi daxue lishi xuexi, 1998.

Lin, Man-Houng. "Overseas Chinese Merchants and Multiple Nationality: A Means for Reducing Commercial Risk (1895–1935)." *Modern Asian Studies* 35, no. 4 (2001): 985–1009.

Lin Meili. "Kangzhan shiqi de zousi huodong yu zousi shizhen" (Smuggling activities and smuggling markets during the War of Resistance period). In *Jinian qiqi Kangzhan liushi zhounian xueshu yantaohui lunwen ji* (Collection of essays from academic conference to commemorate the 60th anniversary of the July 7 War of Resistance), edited by Jinian qiqi

Kangzhan liushi zhounian xueshu yantaohui choubei weiyuanhui, 2 vols., 2:1–52. Taipei: Guoshi guan, 1998.

Lin Meiling. "Jieyan shiqi daluhuo zousi Taiwan diqu wenti (1949–1987)" (The problem of smuggling of mainland goods in the Taiwan area during the period of marital law [1949–1987]). MA thesis, National Taiwan Normal University, 1998.

Liu Cuirong. "Guanshui yu Qing ji ziqiang xinzheng" (Tariffs and late Qing self-strengthening new policies). In *Qingji ziqiang yundong yantaohui lunwen ji* (Collection of essays from academic conference on late Qing self-strengthening movement), edited by Zhongyang yanjiuyuan jindaishi yanjiusuo, 2:1005–32. Taipei: Zhongyang yanjiuyuan jindaishi yanjiusuo, 1988.

Liu, Ting Mien. *Modern Tariff Policies with Special Reference to China*. New York: Alliance, 1924.

Liu Zuoren. "Zousi yu Hua'nan jinrong" (Smuggling and finance in South China). *Jingji zhoubao* 6, no. 5 (1948): 103–4.

Łoś, Maria, ed. *The Second Economy in Marxist States*. New York: St. Martin's, 1990.

Lu Guoxiang. "Xian jieduan zousi wenti" (The smuggling problem's current phase). *Caizheng pinglun* 3, no. 6 (1940): 29–46.

Lu, Hanchao. *Beyond the Neon Lights: Everyday Shanghai in the Early Twentieth Century*. Berkeley: University of California Press, 1999.

Lu Man. "Guangzhou lunxian hou Wang wei qun chou zhi zheng" (The struggle among Wang Jingwei puppet regime's mean persons after the fall of Guangzhou). In "Guangzhou Kangzhan ji shi" (Record of Guangzhou during the War of Resistance), edited by Guangzhou shi zhengxie wenshi ziliao weiyuanhui. Special issue, *Guangzhou wenshi* 48 (1995): 74–82.

Luo Dunwei. "Zhongguo tongzhi jingji de mubiao yu quyu" (The purpose and scope of economic control in China). *Yinhang zhoubao* 17, no. 50 (1933): 3–6.

Luo, Liang. "Reading Hong Shen Intermedially." *Modern Chinese Literature and Culture* 27, no. 2 (2015): 208–48.

Ma Yinchu. *Zhongguo guanshui wenti* (The tariff problem in China). 1923. Reprint, Shanghai: Shangwu yinshu guan, 1925.

Macauley, Melissa. "Entangled States: The Translocal Repercussions of Rural Pacification in China, 1869–1873. *American Historical Review* 121, no. 3 (2016): 755–79.

——. "Small Time Crooks: Opium, Migrants, and the War on Drugs in China, 1819–1860." *Late Imperial China* 30, no. 1 (2009): 1–47.

Maier, Charles S. *Leviathan 2.0: Inventing Modern Statehood*. Cambridge, Mass.: Belknap Press of Harvard University Press, 2012.

Mann, Michael. "The Autonomous Power of the State: Its Origins, Mechanisms and Results." *Archives européenes de sociologie* 25 (1984): 185–213.

Mann, Susan. *Local Merchants and the Chinese Bureaucracy, 1750–1950*. Stanford, Calif.: Stanford University Press, 1987.

Mao Tse-tung [Mao Zedong]. *Selected Works of Mao Tse-tung*. 5 vols. Beijing: Foreign Languages Press, 1961.

Martin, Isaac William, Ajay K. Mehrotra, and Monica Prasad, eds. *The New Fiscal Sociology: Taxation in Comparative and Historical Perspective*. Cambridge: Cambridge University Press, 2009.

Marx, Karl. *Grundrisse*. Translated by Martin Nicolaus. 1939. Reprint, London: Penguin Books, 1993.

Mathew, Johan. *Margins of the Market: Trafficking and Capitalism Across the Arabian Sea*. Berkeley: University of California Press, 2016.

McKeown, Adam. "Conceptualizing Chinese Diasporas, 1842 to 1949." *Journal of Asian Studies* 58, no. 2 (1999): 306–37.

Meijer, Marinus J. *The Introduction of Modern Criminal Law in China*. Batavia: De Unie, 1950.

Meserve, Walter J., and Ruth I. Meserve. "Hung Shen: Chinese Dramatist Trained in America." *Theatre Journal* 31, no. 3 (1979): 25–34.

Minami Manshū Tetsudō Kabushiki Kaisha sangyōbu. *Honkon o chūshin to suru tokushu bōeki narabini kaiun jijō* (Concerning the special trade and maritime shipping situation centered in Hong Kong). Dairen: Minami Manshū Tetsudō Kabushiki Kaisha, 1938.

Minami Manshū Tetsudō Kabushiki Kaisha Shanhai iimusho chōsashitsu. *Bōeki jō no kanten yori mitaru Honkon no enshōsei* (Examination of Hong Kong's support for Jiang from a commercial perspective). Dairen: Minami Manshū Tetsudō Kabushiki Kaisha, 1941.

Mo Kaiqin, Yao Maokun, and Sun Xiaohui. *Zousi fanzui* (The criminal offense of smuggling). Beijing: Zhongguo renmin gong'an daxue chubanshe, 1999.

Mühlhahn, Klaus. *Criminal Justice in China: A History*. Cambridge, Mass.: Harvard University Press, 2009.

Muir, Edward, and Guido Ruggiero. "Afterword: Crime and the Writing of History." In *History from Crime*, edited by E. Muir and G. Ruggiero, 226–36. Baltimore: Johns Hopkins University Press, 1994.

Murphey, Rhoads. "The Treaty Ports and China's Modernization." In *The Chinese City Between Two Worlds*, edited by Mark Elvin and G. William Skinner, 17–71. Stanford, Calif.: Stanford University Press, 1974.

Murray, Dian H. *Pirates of the South China Coast, 1790–1810*. Stanford, Calif.: Stanford University Press, 1987.

Muscolino, Micah S. *Fishing Wars and Environmental Change in Late Imperial and Modern China*. Cambridge, Mass.: Harvard University Asia Center, 2009.

——. "Underground at Sea: Fishing and Smuggling across the Taiwan Strait, 1970s–1990s." In *Mobile Horizons: Dynamics Across the Taiwan Strait*, edited by Wen-hsin Yeh, 99–123. Berkeley: Institute of East Asian Studies, University of California, Center for Chinese Studies, 2013.

Naughton, Barry. *The Chinese Economy: Transitions and Growth*. Cambridge, Mass.: MIT Press, 2007.

North, Douglass C. *Institutions, Institutional Change, and Economic Performance*. Cambridge: Cambridge University Press, 1990.

——. *Structure and Change in Economic History*. New York: Norton, 1981.

Office of Strategic Services (OSS). "Trade Between Occupied China and Free China." Washington, D.C.: Office of Strategic Services, Research and Analysis Branch, Far Eastern Section, 1942.

Oi, Jean C. *State and Peasant in Contemporary China: The Political Economy of Village Government*. Berkeley: University of California Press, 1989.

Olson, Mancur. *The Logic of Collective Action: Public Goods and the Theory of Groups*. Cambridge, Mass.: Harvard University Press, 1965.

Parillo, Nicholas R. *Against the Profit Motive: The Salary Revolution in American Government, 1780–1940*. New Haven: Yale University Press, 2013.

Peattie, Mark, Edward Drea, and Hans Van de Ven, eds. *The Battle for China: Essays on the Military History of the Sino-Japanese War of 1937–1945*. Stanford, Calif.: Stanford University Press, 2011.

Peck, Graham. *Two Kinds of Time*. 1950. Reprint, Seattle: University of Washington Press, 2008.

Pepper, Suzanne. *Civil War in China: The Political Struggle, 1945–1949*. Berkeley: University of California Press, 1978.

Perry, Elizabeth J. *Rebels and Revolutionaries in North China, 1845–1945*. Stanford, Calif.: Stanford University Press, 1980.

Peterson, Glen. *Overseas Chinese in the People's Republic of China*. London: Routledge, 2012.

Phipps, Catherine L. *Empires on the Waterfront: Japan's Ports and Power, 1858–1899*. Cambridge, Mass.: Harvard University Asia Center, 2015.

Pomeranz, Kenneth. *The Making of a Hinterland: State, Society, and Economy in Inland North China, 1853–1937*. Berkeley: University of California Press, 1993.

Qi Chunfeng. "Ping jindai Riben dui Hua junhuo zousi huodong" (Review of modern Japan's arms smuggling activities in China). *Anhui shixue*, no. 3 (2002): 58–63.

——. *Zhong Ri jingji zhan zhong de zousi huodong, 1937–1945* (Smuggling activities in Sino-Japanese economic war, 1937–1945). Beijing: Renmin chubanshe, 2002.

Quanguo jingji weiyuanhui. *Huochai gongye baogaoshu* (Report on the matches industry). Nanjing: Quanguo jingji weiyuanhui, 1935.

——. *Renzaosi gongye baogaoshu* (Report on the rayon industry). Nanjing: Quanguo jingji weiyuanhui, 1936.

——. *Zhitang gongye baogaoshu* (Report on the sugar refining industry). Nanjing: Quanguo jingji weiyuanhui, 1936.

Ransmeier, Johanna S. *Sold People: Traffickers and Family Life in North China*. Cambridge, Mass.: Harvard University Press, 2017.

Rao, Gautham. *National Duties: Custom Houses and the Making of the American State*. Chicago: University of Chicago Press, 2016.

Rawski, Thomas G., et al. *Economics and the Historian*. Berkeley: University of California Press, 1991.

Rawski, Thomas G., and Lillian M. Li. *Chinese History in Economic Perspective*. Berkeley: University of California Press, 1992.

Ren, Xin. "The Second Economy in Socialist China." In *The Second Economy in Marxist States*, edited by Maria Łoś, 140–56. New York: St. Martin's, 1990.

Ri ji langren shiliao zhengji xiaozu. "Xiamen Ri ji langren jishu" (A record of Japanese vagrants in Xiamen). *Xiamen wenshi ziliao* 2 (1962): 1–49.

Rogaski, Ruth. *Hygienic Modernity: Meanings of Health and Disease in Treaty-Port China*. Berkeley: University of California Press, 2004.

Rowe, William T. *Saving the World: Chen Hongmou and Elite Consciousness in Eighteenth-Century China*. Stanford, Calif.: Stanford University Press, 2001.

Rupert, Linda M. *Creolization and Contraband: Curaçao in the Early Modern Atlantic World*. Athens: University of Georgia Press, 2012.

Ruskola, Teemu. *Legal Orientalism: China, the United States, and Modern Law*. Cambridge, Mass.: Harvard University Press, 2013.

Schayegh, Cyrus. "The Many Worlds of 'Abud Yasin; or, What Narcotics Trafficking in the Interwar Middle East Can Tell Us About Territorialization." *American Historical Review* 116, no. 2 (2011): 273–306.

Schendel, Willem van, and Itty Abraham, eds. *Illicit Flows and Criminal Things: States, Borders, and the Other Side of Globalization*. Bloomington: Indiana University Press, 2005.

Schoenhals, Michael. "Elite Information in China." *Problems of Communism*, September–October 1985, 65–71.

Schoppa, R. Keith. *In a Sea of Bitterness: Refugees During the Sino-Japanese War*. Cambridge, Mass.: Harvard University Press, 2011.

Schwartz, Benjamin I. *In Search of Wealth and Power: Yen Fu and the West*. Cambridge, Mass.: Belknap Press of Harvard University Press, 1964.

Schwartz, Henry G. "Ethnic Minorities and Ethnic Policies in China." *International Journal of Comparative Sociology* 20 (1979): 137–50.

Scott, James C. *The Art of Not Being Governed: An Anarchist History of Upland Southeast Asia*. New Haven: Yale University Press, 2009.

——. *Seeing Like a State: How Certain Schemes to Improve the Human Condition Have Failed*. New Haven: Yale University Press, 1998.

Scully, Eileen P. *Bargaining with the State from Afar: American Citizenship in Treaty Port China, 1844–1942*. New York: Columbia University Press, 2001.

Selden, Mark. *The Yenan Way in Revolutionary China*. Cambridge, Mass.: Harvard University Press, 1971.

Sewell, William H., Jr. *The Logics of History: Social Theory and Social Transformation*. Chicago: University of Chicago Press, 2005.

——. "A Strange Career: The Historical Study of Economic Life." *History and Theory*, no. 49 (2010): 146–66.

Shandong sheng difang shi zhi bianzuan weiyuanhui, ed. *Shandong sheng zhi: haiguan zhi* (Shangdong provincial gazetteer: customs gazetteer). Ji'nan: Shandong renmin chubanshe, 1997.

"Shanghai haiguan zhi" bianzuan weiyuanhui, ed. *Shanghai haiguan zhi* (Shanghai customs gazetteer). Shanghai: Shanghai shehui kexueyuan chubanshe, 1997.

Shanghai shehui kexue yuan jingji yanjiusuo, ed. *Liu Hongsheng qiye shiliao* (Historical materials on Liu Hongsheng's enterprises). 3 vols. Shanghai: Shanghai renmin chubanshe, 1981.

Sharpe, J. A. *Crime in Early Modern England, 1550–1750*. London: Longman, 1998.

Sheehan, Brett. *Industrial Eden: A Chinese Capitalist Vision*. Cambridge, Mass.: Harvard University Press, 2015.

———. *Trust in Troubled Times: Money, Banks, and State-Society Relations in Republican Tianjin*. Cambridge, Mass.: Harvard University Press, 2003.

Sheehan, James J. "The Problem of Sovereignty in European History." *American Historical Review* 111, no. 1 (2006): 1–15.

Shenk, Catherine R. "Another Asian Financial Crisis: Monetary Links Between Hong Kong and China, 1945–50." *Modern Asian Studies* 34, no. 3 (2000): 739–64.

———. "The Hong Kong Gold Market and the Southeast Asian Gold Trade in the 1950s." *Modern Asian Studies* 29, no. 2 (1995): 387–402.

Shiroyama, Tomoko. "The Hong Kong–South China Financial Nexus: Ma Xuchao and His Remittance Agency." In *The Capitalist Dilemma in China's Communist Revolution*, edited by Sherman Cochran. Ithaca, N.Y.: Cornell East Asia Series, 2014.

Sifayuan, ed. *Sifayuan jieshi huibian* (Collection of interpretations by Judicial Yuan). 5 vols. Taipei: Sifayuan mishuchu, 1989.

Skinner, G. William. "Regional Urbanization in Nineteenth-Century China." In *The City in Late Imperial China*, edited by G. William Skinner, 211–49. Stanford, Calif.: Stanford University Press, 1977.

Skocpol, Theda. "Bringing the State Back In: Strategies of Analysis in Current Research." In *Bringing the State Back In*, edited by P. B. Evans, D. Rueschemeyer, and Theda Skocpol, 3–37. Cambridge: Cambridge University Press, 1985.

Slack, Edward R. *Opium, State, and Society: China's Narco-Economy and the Guomindang, 1924–1937*. Honolulu: University of Hawai'i Press, 2001.

Slessor, Robert. "Chinese Non-ferrous Metals." *Proceedings of the Australasian Institute of Mining and Metallurgy* 65 (1927): 51–116.

———. "Tungsten Mining in China." *Engineering and Mining Journal* 109, no. 5 (1920): 344–55.

So, Billy K. L. "Modern China's Treaty Port Economy in Institutional Perspective: An Introductory Essay." In *The Treaty Port Economy in Modern China: Empirical Studies of Institutional Change and Economic Performance*, edited by B. K. L. So and R. H. Myers, 1–27. Berkeley: Institute of East Asian Studies, 2011.

Solinger, Dorothy J. *Chinese Business Under Socialism: The Politics of Domestic Commerce, 1949–1980*. Berkeley: University of California Press, 1984.

Sommer, Matthew H. *Polyandry and Wife-Selling in Qing Dynasty China: Survival Strategies and Judicial Interventions*. Berkeley: University of California Press, 2015.

———. *Sex, Law, and Society in Late Imperial China*. Stanford, Calif.: Stanford University Press, 2000.

Son Jun Sik. *Zhanqian Riben zai Huabei de zousi huodong, 1933–1937* (Japan's prewar smuggling activities in North China, 1933–1937). Taipei: Guoshi guan, 1997.

Song Yuanzhi and Hu Xianglei. "Xin Zhongguo di yi ge renmin haiguan—Yantai haiguan" (New China's first People's Customs—the Yantai customs). *Zhongguo Haiguan* 6 (2001): 52–53.

Spruyt, Hendrik. "War, Trade, and State Formation." In *The Oxford Handbook of Comparative Politics*, edited by C. Boix and S. Stokes, 211–35. Oxford: Oxford University Press, 2007.

Strauss, Julia C. "Introduction: In Search of PRC History." *China Quarterly* 188 (2006): 855–69.

———. "Morality, Coercion and State Building by Campaign in the Early PRC: Regime Consolidation and After, 1949–1956." *China Quarterly* 188 (2006): 891–912.

———. *Strong Institutions in Weak Polities: State Building in Republican China, 1927–1940*. Oxford: Oxford University Press, 1998.

Su Shifang, ed. *Dangdai Zhongguo haiguan* (Contemporary China's customs). 1992. Reprint, Hong Kong: Xianggang zuguo chubanshe, 2009.

Sun Baogen. *Kangzhan shiqi Guomin zhengfu jisi yanjiu* (Research on the Nationalist government's anti-smuggling during the War of Resistance period). Beijing: Zhongguo dang'an chubanshe, 2006.

Sun Yat-sen [Sun Zhongshan]. *San Min Chu I: The Three Principles of the People*. Translated by Frank W. Price. 1924. Reprint, Taipei: China Publishing Co., 1950.

Szonyi, Michael. *The Art of Being Governed: Everyday Politics in Late Imperial China*. Princeton, N.J.: Princeton University Press, 2017.

———. *Cold War Island: Quemoy on the Front Line*. Cambridge: Cambridge University Press, 2008.

Tagliacozzo, Eric. *Secret Trades, Porous Borders: Smuggling and States Along a Southeast Asian Frontier, 1865–1915*. New Haven: Yale University Press, 2005.

Tai, Emily Sohmer. "Marking Water: Piracy and Property in the Premodern West." In *Seascapes: Maritime Histories, Littoral Cultures, and Transoceanic Exchanges*, edited by Jerry H. Bentley, Renate Bridenthal, and Kären Wigen, 205–20. Honolulu: University of Hawai'i Press, 2007.

Tanner, Harold M. *Strike Hard! Anti-Crime Campaigns and Chinese Criminal Justice, 1979–1985*. Ithaca, N.Y.: Cornell East Asia Series, 1999.

Thaxton, Ralph. *Salt of the Earth: The Political Origins of Peasant Protest and Communist Revolution in China*. Berkeley: University of California Press, 1997.

Thilly, Peter. "Treacherous Waters: Drug Smuggling in Coastal Fujian, 1832–1938." PhD thesis, Northwestern University, 2015.

Thompson, E. P. *Whigs and Hunters: The Origin of the Black Act*. New York: Pantheon Books, 1975.

Thomson, Janice E. *Mercenaries, Pirates, and Sovereigns*. Princeton, N.J.: Princeton University Press, 1996.

Tianjin haiguan bianzhi shi, ed. *Tianjin haiguan zhi* (Tianjian Customs gazetteer). Tianjin: Tianjin haiguan bianzhi shi, 1993.

Tianjin shi dang'an guan, ed. *Tianjin shanghui dang'an huibian, 1928–1937* (Compilation of archives of the Tianjin Chamber of Commerce, 1928–1937). 2 vols. Tianjin: Tianjin renmin chubanshe, 1996.

Tilly, Charles. *Coercion, Capital, and European States, AD 900–1992*. Cambridge, Mass.: Blackwell, 1992.

———. "Reflections on the History of European State-Making." In *The Formation of National States in Western Europe*, edited by C. Tilly, 3–83. Princeton, N.J.: Princeton University Press, 1975.

———. "War Making and State Making as Organized Crime." In *Bringing the State Back In*, edited by P. B. Evans, D. Rueschemeyer, and Theda Skocpol, 169–91. Cambridge: Cambridge University Press, 1985.

Tobari Keisuke, "NitChū Sensō shita no Chōkō ryūiki ni okeru 'mitsuyu' (1937–1941)" ("Smuggling" around the Yangzi River area during the Second Sino-Japanese War). *Hōgaku kenkyū* 87, no. 7 (2014): 37–99; no. 8 (2014): 39–87; no. 9 (2014): 27–84.

Truxes, Thomas M. *Defying Empire: Trading with the Enemy in Colonial New York*. New Haven: Yale University Press, 2008.

Tsin, Michael. *Nation, Governance, and Modernity in China: Canton, 1900–1927*. Stanford, Calif.: Stanford University Press, 1999.

Van de Ven, Hans. *Breaking with the Past: The Maritime Customs Service and the Global Origins of Modernity in China*. New York: Columbia University Press, 2014.

———. *China at War: Triumph and Tragedy in the Emergence of the New China, 1937–1952*. London: Profile Books, 2017.

Viraphol, Sarasin. *Tribute and Profit: Sino-Siamese Trade, 1652–1853*. Cambridge, Mass.: Council on East Asian Studies, Harvard University, 1977.

Viscose Company. *The Story of Rayon*. New York: Viscose Company, 1937.

Vogel, Ezra F. *Canton Under Communism: Programs and Politics in a Provincial Capital, 1949–1968*. Cambridge, Mass.: Harvard University Press, 1969.

———. *Deng Xiaoping and the Transformation of China*. Cambridge, Mass.: Belknap Press of Harvard University Press, 2011.

———. *One Step Ahead in China: Guangdong Under Reform*. Cambridge, Mass.: Harvard University Press, 1989.

Wakeman, Frederic. "Models of Historical Change: The Chinese State and Society, 1839–1989." In *Perspectives on Modern China: Four Anniversaries*, edited by Kenneth Lieberthal et al., 68–93. Armonk, N.Y.: M. E. Sharpe, 1991.

———. *Policing Shanghai, 1927–1937*. Berkeley: University of California Press, 1995.

———. "Shanghai Smuggling." In *In the Shadow of the Rising Sun: Shanghai Under Japanese Occupation*, edited by Christian Henriot and Wen-hsin Yeh, 116–49. Cambridge: Cambridge University Press, 2004.

———. *Spymaster: Dai Li and the Chinese Secret Service*. Berkeley: University of California Press, 2003.

Walder, Andrew G. *China Under Mao: A Revolution Derailed*. Cambridge, Mass.: Harvard University Press, 2015.

Wang, David Der-wei. "Chinese Literature from 1841 to 1937." In *The Cambridge History of Chinese Literature*, edited by K. S. Chang and S. Owen, 2:413–564. Cambridge: Cambridge University Press.

Wang, Dong. *China's Unequal Treaties: Narrating National History*. Lanham, Md.: Lexington Books, 2005.

Wang Ermin. "Shangzhan guannian yu zhongshang sixiang" (War of commerce concept and mercantilist thought). *Zhongyang yanjiuyuan jindaishi yanjiusuo ji* 5 (1976): 1–91.

———. *Wan Qing shangyue waijiao* (The diplomacy of the commercial treaties between China and foreign powers during the late Qing period). Hong Kong: Chinese University Press, 1998.

———. "Wan Qing waijiao sixiang de xingcheng" (The formation of late Qing diplomatic thought). *Zhongyang yanjiuyuan jindaishi yanjiusuo ji* 1 (1969): 19–46.

Wang, Kenneth. "Foreign Trade Policy and Apparatus of the People's Republic of China." *Law and Contemporary Problems* 38, no. 2 (1973): 182–200.

Wang Liangxing. "1929 nian Zhongguo guoding shuize xingzhi zhi shuliang fenxi" (Quantitative analysis of the nature of the 1929 Chinese national tariff). *Jindai shi yanjiu* 4 (1995): 209–48.

Wang, Shaoguang. "The Rise of the Regions: Fiscal Reform and the Decline of Central State Capacity in China." In *The Waning of the Communist State: Economic Origins of Political Decline in China and Hungary*, edited by Andrew G. Walder, 88–114. Berkeley: University of California Press, 1995.

Wang Shengze. "Gaige kaifang chuqi Fujian fan zousi shulun" (A discussion of anti-smuggling in Fujian in the early days of reform and opening). *Zhonggong dangshi yanjiu* 5 (2006): 96–104.

Wang, Wensheng. *White Lotus Rebels and South China Pirates: Crisis and Reform in the Qing Empire*. Cambridge, Mass.: Harvard University Press, 2014.

Weber, Max. *Economy and Society: An Outline of Interpretative Sociology*. Edited by G. Roth and C. Wittich. 2 vols. 1956. Reprint, Berkeley: University of California Press, 1978.

Westad, Odd Arne. *Decisive Encounters: The Chinese Civil War, 1946–1950*. Stanford, Calif.: Stanford University Press, 2003.

White, Lynn T. "Low Power: Small Enterprises in Shanghai, 1949–67." *China Quarterly* 73 (1978): 45–76.

Wilbur, C. Martin. *The Nationalist Revolution in China, 1923–1928*. Cambridge: Cambridge University Press, 1983.

Willoughby, Westel Woodbury. *China at the Conference: A Report*. Baltimore: Johns Hopkins University Press, 1922.

Winslow, Cal. "Sussex Smugglers." In *Albion's Fatal Tree: Crime and Society in Eighteenth-Century England*, edited by Douglas Hay et al., 119–66. New York: Pantheon, 1975.

"Wo guo ying shixing tongzhi maoyi." *Guohuo ban yue kan* 23/24 (1934): 13–14.

Wong, R. Bin. *China Transformed: Historical Change and the Limits of European Experience*. Ithaca, N.Y.: Cornell University Press, 1997.

Wright, Mary C. "Introduction: The Rising Tide of Change." In *China in Revolution: The First Phase, 1900–1913*, edited by Mary C. Wright, 1–63. New Haven: Yale University Press, 1968.

———. *The Last Stand of Chinese Conservatism: The T'ung-chih Restoration, 1862–1874*. Stanford, Calif.: Stanford University Press, 1957.

Wright, Stanley F. *China's Struggle for Tariff Autonomy, 1843–1938*. Shanghai: Kelly and Walsh, 1938.

Wu, C. C. [Wu Chaoshu] "Foreign Relations of the Chinese Nationalist Government." *Foreign Affairs* 6, no. 4 (1928): 668–70.

Wu Gang. *Jiu Zhongguo tonghuo pengzhang shiliao* (Historical materials on inflation in old China). Shanghai: Renmin chubanshe, 1958.

Wu Yugan. *Zhongguo guanshui wenti* (The tariff problem in China). Shanghai: Shangwu yinshu guan, 1930.

Wu Yuxuan. "Zhanqu zousi wenti" (The smuggling problem in warzones). *Caizheng pinglun* 5, no. 2 (1941): 25–35.

Wu Zhaoshen. *Zhongguo shuizhi shi* (History of China's tax system). Shanghai: Shangwu yin shu guan, 1937.

Xian Zi'en. "Ban tangchang jingguo ji qi zhenxiang" (Managing the sugar factory and other real facts). In *Nantian suiyue: Chen Jitang zhu Yue shiqi jianwen shilu* (Era of the southern empire: eyewitness historical accounts of the period of Chen Jitang's rule in Guangdong), edited by Guangzhou shi weiyuanhui wenshi ziliao yanjiu weiyuanhui, 245–61. Guangzhou: Guangdong renmin chubanshe, 1987.

Xiao Zili. "Zhanshi Riben dui Zhongguo wusha de juelue yu Minguo zhengfu de yingdui" (Wartime plunder of China's tungsten ore by Japan and the Republican government's response). *Kang Ri zhanzheng yanjiu* 1 (2007): 133–56.

Xin Ying. *Zhonggong de duiwai maoyi* (The foreign trade of China). Hong Kong: Youlian chubanshe, 1954.

Xing Sheng. "Zousi huo ren de dong" (The smuggler's cave). *Ertong shijie* 27, no. 24 (1931): 10–14.

Xu Weixiao. "Zousi wu" (Tungsten smuggling). *Dafeng xunkan*, no. 14 (1939): 432–33.

Xu, Xiaoqun. *Trial of Modernity: Judicial Reform in Early Twentieth-Century China, 1901–1937*. Stanford, Calif.: Stanford University Press, 2008.

Xu Xueliang. "Fudong xiemao yang Guang huodian" (The Fudong shoes, hat, foreign, and Cantonese goods store). In *Zhoucun shangbu* (The port of Zhoucun), edited by Shandong sheng zhengxie wenshi ziliao weiyuanhui, 231–35. Ji'nan: Shandong renmin chubanshe, 1990.

Yang, Dali L. *Remaking the Chinese Leviathan: Market Transition and the Politics of Governance in China*. Stanford, Calif.: Stanford University Press, 2004.

Yeh, Wen-hsin. *Shanghai Splendor: Economic Sentiments and the Making of Modern China, 1843–1949*. Berkeley: University of California Press, 2007.

Yeh, Yuan Chang. *Recollections of a Chinese Customs Veteran*. Hong Kong: Ye zhen bang, 1987.

Yin Zhiyue. "Diguo zhuyi ji canyu feibang de zousi pohuai huodong zuo douzheng" (The struggle against imperialism and smashing smuggling activities by residual bandit gangs). In *Xin Zhongguo haiguan* (New China Customs), edited by Haiguan guanliju, 47–53. Shanghai: Xinhua shudian, 1951.

Young, Arthur N. *China and the Helping Hand, 1937–1945*. Cambridge, Mass.: Harvard University Press, 1963.

———. *China's Nation-Building Effort, 1927–1937: The Financial and Economic Record*. Stanford, Calif.: Hoover Institution Press, 1971.

———. *China's Wartime Finance and Inflation, 1937–1945*. Cambridge, Mass.: Harvard University Press, 1965.

Young, Gavin. *Beyond Lion Rock: The Story of Cathay Pacific Airways*. London: Hutchinson, 1988.

Yu Zhongluo. "1948 nian Jiang Haiguan guanyuan wubi an" (The 1948 Shanghai Customs corruption case). In *Shanghai wenshi ziliao cungao huibian*, edited by Shanghai shi zhengxie wenshi ziliao weiyuanhui, 4:113–26. Shanghai: Shanghai guji chubanshe, 2001.

Zafanolli, Wojtek. "A Brief Outline of China's Second Economy." *Asian Survey* 25, no. 7 (1985): 715–36.

Zanasi, Margherita. *Saving the Nation: Economic Modernity in Republican China*. Chicago: University of Chicago Press, 2006.

Zelin, Madeleine. *The Merchants of Zigong: Industrial Entrepreneurship in Early Modern China*. New York: Columbia University Press, 2005.

Zhang, Sheldon. *Chinese Human Smuggling Organizations: Families, Social Networks, and Cultural Imperatives*. Stanford, Calif.: Stanford University Press, 2008.

Zhang, Shu Guang. *Economic Cold War: America's Embargo Against China and the Sino-Soviet Alliance, 1949–1963*. Stanford, Calif.: Stanford University Press, 2001.

Zhang Xiaoye. *Qing dai siyan wenti yanjiu* (Research on the salt smuggling problem during the Qing dynasty). Beijing: Shehui kexue wenxian chubanshe, 2001.

Zhao Bingzhi. "Lun shaoshu minzu gongmin de xingshi zeren wenti" (On the problem of criminal responsibility of ethnic minority citizens). *Zhongguo faxue* 5 (1998): 65–72.

Zhao, Gang. *The Qing Opening to the Ocean: Chinese Maritime Policies, 1684–1757*. Honolulu: University of Hawai'i Press, 2013.

Zheng Guanying. *Zheng Guanying Ji* (Collected writings of Zheng Guanying), edited by Xia Dongyuan. Beijing: Zhonghua shu ju, [Qing] 2014.

Zhongguo haiguan baike quanshu bianzuan weiyuanhui, ed. *Zhongguo haiguan baike quanshu* (Comprehensive encyclopedia of the Chinese Customs Administration). Beijing: Zhongguo da baike quanshu chubanshe, 2004.

Zhongguo wenti yanjiu hui. *Zousi wenti* (The smuggling problem). Shanghai: Zhongguo wenti yanjiu hui, 1936.

Zhongyang diaocha tongji ju. *Di wu nian zhi wokou jingji qinlüe* (The fifth year of the Japanese pirates' economic invasion). Chongqing: Zhongyang diaocha tongji ju, 1943.

Zhu Jin. "Changguan yu lijin ka zhi butong" (Dissimilarities between Native Customs stations and *lijin* barriers). In *Zhongguo guanshui shiliao*, edited by Jiang Hengyuan, changguan 1–5. Shanghai: Renwen bianji suo, 1931.

———. *Zhongguo guan shui wen ti* (The tariff problem of China). N.p.: Zhuzhang guoji shuifa pingdeng hui, 1919.

INDEX

Page numbers in italics indicate figures, maps, or tables.

STUDIES OF THE WEATHERHEAD
EAST ASIAN INSTITUTE

Columbia University

Selected Titles (Complete list at: http://weai.columbia.edu/publications/studies-weai/)

Making Time: Astronomical Time Measurement in Tokugawa Japan, by Yulia Frumer. University of Chicago Press, 2018.

Resurrecting Nagasaki: Reconstruction and the Formation of Atomic Narratives, by Chad Diehl. Cornell University Press, 2018.

Promiscuous Media: Film and Visual Culture in Imperial Japan, 1926–1945, by Hikari Hori. Cornell University Press, 2018.

Aesthetic Life: Beauty and Art in Modern Japan, by Miya Mizuta Lippit. Harvard University Asia Center, 2018.

The End of Japanese Cinema: Industrial Genres, National Times, and Media Ecologies, by Alexander Zahlten. Duke University Press, 2017.

The Chinese Typewriter: A History, by Thomas S. Mullaney. The MIT Press, 2017.

Mobilizing Without the Masses: Control and Contention in China, by Diana Fu. Cambridge University Press, 2017.

Forgotten Disease: Illnesses Transformed in Chinese Medicine, by Hilary A. Smith. Stanford University Press, 2017.

Food of Sinful Demons: Meat, Vegetarianism, and the Limits of Buddhism in Tibet, by Geoffrey Barstow. Columbia University Press, 2017

Youth For Nation: Culture and Protest in Cold War South Korea, by Charles R. Kim. University of Hawaii Press, 2017.

Socialist Cosmopolitanism: The Chinese Literary Universe, 1945–1965, by Nicolai Volland. Columbia University Press, 2017.

Yokohama and the Silk Trade: How Eastern Japan Became the Primary Economic Region of Japan, 1843–1893, by Yasuhiro Makimura. Lexington Books, 2017.

The Social Life of Inkstones: Artisans and Scholars in Early Qing China, by Dorothy Ko. University of Washington Press, 2017.

Darwin, Dharma, and the Divine: Evolutionary Theory and Religion in Modern Japan, by G. Clinton Godart. University of Hawaii Press, 2017.

Dictators and Their Secret Police: Coercive Institutions and State Violence, by Sheena Chestnut Greitens. Cambridge University Press, 2016.

The Cultural Revolution on Trial: Mao and the Gang of Four, by Alexander C. Cook. Cambridge University Press, 2016.

Inheritance of Loss: China, Japan, and the Political Economy of Redemption After Empire, by Yukiko Koga. University of Chicago Press, 2016.

Homecomings: The Belated Return of Japan's Lost Soldiers, by Yoshikuni Igarashi. Columbia University Press, 2016.

Samurai to Soldier: Remaking Military Service in Nineteenth-Century Japan, by D. Colin Jaundrill. Cornell University Press, 2016.

The Red Guard Generation and Political Activism in China, by Guobin Yang. Columbia University Press, 2016.

Accidental Activists: Victim Movements and Government Accountability in Japan and South Korea, by Celeste L. Arrington. Cornell University Press, 2016.

Ming China and Vietnam: Negotiating Borders in Early Modern Asia, by Kathlene Baldanza. Cambridge University Press, 2016.

Ethnic Conflict and Protest in Tibet and Xinjiang: Unrest in China's West, coedited by Ben Hillman and Gray Tuttle. Columbia University Press, 2016.

One Hundred Million Philosophers: Science of Thought and the Culture of Democracy in Postwar Japan, by Adam Bronson. University of Hawaii Press, 2016.

Conflict and Commerce in Maritime East Asia: The Zheng Family and the Shaping of the Modern World, c. 1620–1720, by Xing Hang. Cambridge University Press, 2016.

Chinese Law in Imperial Eyes: Sovereignty, Justice, and Transcultural Politics, by Li Chen. Columbia University Press, 2016.

Imperial Genus: The Formation and Limits of the Human in Modern Korea and Japan, by Travis Workman. University of California Press, 2015.

Yasukuni Shrine: History, Memory, and Japan's Unending Postwar, by Akiko Takenaka. University of Hawaii Press, 2015.

The Age of Irreverence: A New History of Laughter in China, by Christopher Rea. University of California Press, 2015.

The Knowledge of Nature and the Nature of Knowledge in Early Modern Japan, by Federico Marcon. University of Chicago Press, 2015.

The Fascist Effect: Japan and Italy, 1915–1952, by Reto Hofmann. Cornell University Press, 2015.

The International Minimum: Creativity and Contradiction in Japan's Global Engagement, 1933–1964, by Jessamyn R. Abel. University of Hawai'i Press, 2015.

Empires of Coal: Fueling China's Entry into the Modern World Order, 1860–1920, by Shellen Xiao Wu. Stanford University Press, 2015.